ANCIENT BRITAIN

From the First Farmers to the Early Celts

An Introduction and Survey

Paul Ashbee

David & Charles
Newton Abbot   London   Vancouver

0 7153 6568 1

© Paul Ashbee 1974

All rights reserved. No part of this publication may be reproduced, stored in a retrieval system, or transmitted, in any form or by any means, electronic, mechanical, photocopying, recording or otherwise, without the prior permission of David & Charles (Holdings) Limited

Set in 11 on 13 pt Imprint
and printed in Great Britain
by Ebenezer Baylis & Son Ltd
The Trinity Press Worcester and London
for David & Charles (Holdings) Limited
South Devon House Newton Abbot Devon

Published in Canada by
Douglas David & Charles Limited
3645 McKechnie Drive West Vancouver BC

Ancient Scilly

From the First Farmers to the Early Christians

Contents

		page
	Preface and Acknowledgements	13
1	Antiquaries, Archaeologists and the Isles of Scilly	17
2	Geology, Topography and Environment	37
3	Submergence and Scillonian Archaeology	52
4	Chamber Tombs and Barrows	70
5	Stone Cists and Cist-grave Cemeteries	120
6	Standing Stones	148
7	Houses and Settlements	156
8	Forts and Enclosures	209
9	Cult Sites and Early Christians	216
10	Material Culture and Equipment	231
11	Subsistence Economy and Trade	264
12	Scillonian Communities: Origins and Affinities	279

Appendices

1	Chamber Tombs and Barrows	295
2	Cists and Cist-grave Cemeteries	311
3	Standing Stones	313
4	Houses and Settlements	315
5	Forts and Enclosures	321
6	Flint Industries	323
7	Early Bronze Artifacts	325
	Bibliography	327
	Index	341

List of Illustrations

PLATES

		page
1 a	Dr William Borlase. Portrait by Allen Ramsey at Truro Museum (*photo Charles Woolf*)	
b	B. H. StJ. O'Neil (*portrait by Elliot & Fry, London*)	49
2 a	Natural granite basins on Porth Hellick Down, St Mary's	
b	Wall on Samson Flats at low tide	50
3 a	Cist exposed on the shore in Higher Town Bay, St Martin's	
b	Wall of a hut in the cliff of Halangy Porth, St Mary's	67
4 a	Passage grave on Porth Hellick Down, St Mary's (*photo Alexander Gibson*)	
b	Bant's Carn, St Mary's	68
5 a	Innisidgen chamber tomb, St Mary's	
b	Ruined chamber on the North Hill of Samson	85
6 a	Cist found beneath a cairn on the North Hill of Samson	
b	Cist on Content Farm, St Mary's	
c	Cist in Klondyke Field, Telegraph Hill, St Mary's (*photo Alexander Gibson*)	86
7 a	Cist cemetery at Porth Cressa, Hugh Town, St Mary's (*photo James Gibson*)	
b	A Porth Cressa cist	103
8 a	The Day Mark, Porth Mellon, St Mary's (*photo Alexander Gibson*)	
b	The Long Rock, McFarland's Down, St Mary's	
c	Post-base or mortar from Samson	104

LIST OF ILLUSTRATIONS

9 a Lower slope complex at Halangy Down, St Mary's
  b Circular chamber at Halangy Down, St Mary's 121
10 a Nornour: detail of hearth in main chamber
   b Nornour: detail of walling in antechamber 122
11 a Roman altar, now at Tresco Abbey (*photo Alexander Gibson*)
   b Column base opposite Atlantic Hotel, Hugh Town 139
12 a The Oratory, St Helen's (*photo H. E. O'Neil*)
   b Saddle quern from Halangy Down, St Mary's
   c Bowl quern from Halangy Porth, St Mary's 140
13 a Urn from Knackyboy Cairn, St Martin's (*photo B. H. St J. O'Neil*)
   b Urn from Obadiah's Barrow, Gugh (*photo Alexander Gibson*) 157
14 Roman figurines from Nornour (*photo Charles Woolf*) 158
15 Sherd from Halangy Porth, St Mary's 175
16 a Limpet-shell midden at Halangy Down, St Mary's
   b Faience and glass beads from Knackyboy Cairn, St Martin's (*photo B. H. St J. O'Neil*) 176

Note: Unless otherwise indicated, the photographs listed above were taken by the author.

IN TEXT

page

1 Title-page of William Borlase's *Observations of the Islands of Scilly*, 1756   18
2 William Borlase's plans of chamber tombs on Buzza Hill, St Mary's   20
3 The Isles of Scilly, by William Borlase, 1756   38

LIST OF ILLUSTRATIONS

4	Marine contour map showing submerged and cliff-exposed sites	54
5	Relative diameters of Scillonian chamber tombs	71
6	Relative diameters of Scillonian chamber tombs in terms of cemeteries	72
7	Orientation of Scillonian chamber tombs	73
8	Distribution of Scillonian chamber tombs	75
9	Plan and section of passage grave, Porth Hellick Down, St Mary's	80
10	Plans of Bant's Carn, St Mary's and Innisidgen, St Mary's	81
11	Longitudinal and transverse sections, Bant's Carn, St Mary's	82
12	Plans of lesser chamber tombs, Porth Hellick Down, St Mary's	83
13	Plan and section of chamber tomb on the North Hill of Samson	91
14	Plan and section of Obadiah's Barrow, Gugh	93
15	Plan of chamber tomb on Middle Arthur	95
16	Longitudinal and transverse sections, Innisidgen, St Mary's	98
17	Plan of burial deposits, Obadiah's Barrow, Gugh	109
18	Plan of burial deposits, Knackyboy Cairn, St Martin's	114
19	Cists on the Isles of Scilly	124
20	Plan of cist on the North Hill of Samson	126
21	Plan and section of cist on Content Farm, St Mary's	130
22	Plans of cists on Par Beach, Higher Town Bay, St Martin's	132
23	Plan of cist on Old Man	133
24	Excavation at Porth Cressa, Hugh Town, St Mary's, cist-grave cemetery	136
25	Porth Cressa cists before removal of cover-stones	137
26	Porth Cressa cists, sections	138

LIST OF ILLUSTRATIONS

27	Porth Cressa cists, after removal of cover-stones	142
28	Standing stones on the Isles of Scilly	150
29	Scillonian house and settlement sites	160
30	George Bonsor's section of Halangy Porth midden, showing layers observed	161
31	Storage pot from Halangy Porth, St Mary's	163
32	Plan of remains of building near Halangy Porth, St Mary's	163
33	Structure at English Island Carn, St Martin's	165
34	Structures at May's Hill, St Martin's	167
35	Oval hut on Par Beach, Higher Town Bay, St Martin's	168
36	Modified hut with corn-drying ovens at Perpitch, St Martin's	169
37	Remains of structures in Little Bay, St Martin's	171
38	Plan of large chamber of courtyard house on Halangy Down, St Mary's	178
39	Hut, with intrusive grave, on Par Beach, Higher Town Bay, St Martin's	180
40	Remains of hut on Little Arthur	181
41	Structures below high-water mark on Par Beach, Higher Town Bay, St Martin's	182
42	Courtyard house on Halangy Down, St Mary's	188
43	Lower slope foundations, Halangy Down, St Mary's	190
44	Nornour: the western buildings	198
45	Nornour: the eastern buildings	201
46	Scillonian promontory forts	210
47	Plan of hermitage on St Helen's	226
48	Surface flint industries on the Isles of Scilly	232
49	Bone points and bronze awl from Obadiah's Barrow, Gugh	240
50	Torque from Peninnis Head, St Mary's	241

LIST OF ILLUSTRATIONS

51 Bronze brooches from Porth Cressa, Hugh Town, St Mary's, cist-grave cemetery — 242
52 Enamelled penannular brooch from St Martin's — 245
53 Urns from Knackyboy Cairn, St Martin's — 248
54 Urns from Knackyboy Cairn, St Martin's — 250
55 Pottery from Obadiah's Barrow, Gugh — 251
56 Pottery from Bant's Carn, St Mary's — 253
57 Romano-British pots from Porth Cressa, Hugh Town, St Mary's, cist-grave cemetery — 260

Preface and Acknowledgements

The Isles of Scilly, twenty-five miles beyond Land's End, have long been considered as an exceptional locality supporting a distinctive community. Such considerations applied in earlier times, and the many Scillonian chamber tombs, dwelling sites and other surviving field antiquities as well as the material equipment embody the technological, economic and social behaviour and traditions of the ancient inhabitants. Much of the evidence is fragmentary and even ambiguous but, notwithstanding, a general if incomplete narrative emerges. Indeed, as William Borlase, the Cornish antiquary, so aptly remarked 'GREAT perfection cannot be expected, where the Subject is so obscure, the Age so remote, and the Materials so dispersed, few, and rude ...' (Borlase, 1769, viii).

In the following work, as in my other synthetic narratives, the traditional technological 'Three Age' arrangement of pre- and protohistory has been avoided and the presentation is continuous and chronological when possible, within an economic and social framework. Such an approach to prehistory may be unfamiliar to many readers but it should be remembered that human society is normally uninterruptedly multi-dimensional, particularly when, as in early Scilly, a steady-state economy has emerged, and therefore archaeologists should endeavour to evaluate all elements simultaneously.

I first saw the Isles of Scilly twenty-five years ago, in October 1949, sun-lit and foam-licked, from the cabin of an ancient aircraft. That autumn and the following summer saw, besides the conduct of excavations, the initial explorations and fieldwork which have led to this book. Some excursions were undertaken with the late B. H. StJ. O'Neil, then

PREFACE AND ACKNOWLEDGEMENTS

Chief Inspector of Ancient Monuments. Since 1947, O'Neil had been reconnoitring and, annually, carrying out a series of critical excavations on Scilly, besides writing the Ministry's handbook to the islands (O'Neil, 1949), and it is with pleasure and gratitude that I recall the constant personal encouragement that he gave to me. His untimely death in 1954 prevented the extended study of Scilly that he had planned. Thus, this book, although perhaps not couched in the idiom that he intended, owes much to him. When, during the 1960s, I began to assemble the material for *Ancient Scilly*, Mrs Helen O'Neil most kindly made the manuscript accounts and the plans of their excavations available, and allowed me to draw freely upon them in advance of her own publication. I can but record my sincere appreciation of this privilege, for such subsequent work as the present writer and others have done in Scilly stands upon the sure foundation of Bryan O'Neil's realistic appraisals of the problems involved.

I am especially beholden to Professor Charles Thomas for unreservedly placing at my disposal his narrative of the 1956 excavations on Teän, together with his work on the problems of Scillonian submergence, as well as for discussion and aid with fieldwork and a range of problems down the years. He has done more during the past twenty years to advance the study of Cornwall and the Isles of Scilly than anyone else and my personal indebtedness to him in terms of friendship and scholarship is considerable.

In 1965 I had the good fortune to meet the son of Mr Alec Gray who, thirty years before, had set down an account of his fieldwork on Scilly. This has now been edited and published in *Cornish Archaeology* (1972) and, as I write, Alec Gray's letter to Charles Thomas upon seeing his journal in print lies beside me. Personal fieldwork, particularly upon St Mary's, was greatly helped by the friendship and guidance of the late J. H. (Joe) Treneary of Telegraph Hill who had assisted Alec Gray, and who had an unequalled knowledge of the Scillonian archaeological scene.

For four generations now, the Gibson family have photographed Scilly and Scillonian life. Many of Alexander Gibson's pictures must be

PREFACE AND ACKNOWLEDGEMENTS

among the earliest archaeological photographs taken in Britain and, as such, constitute a unique record deserving of especial study. Thus I am especially indebted to Frank Gibson of Hugh Town for copies of early pictures and permission to reproduce them, for anecdotes of his forbear's activities and an ever friendly welcome whenever I visit Scilly.

Voyages to remember were captained by Miss Dorothy Dudley who in successive years picked up the present writer and his entire excavation staff at Pendrathen Quay and piloted them to Nornour to land upon the beach and see the nuances of that complex and spectacular site. Thanks are tendered for these unforgettable passages enlivened by much detailed discussion pertaining to Scilly and the South West.

A further good friend whose kindness has eased and expedited aspects of this book is Andrew Saunders (Chief Inspector of Ancient Monuments and President of the Cornwall Archaeological Society) who, as Inspector of Ancient Monuments, brought about the resumption of excavations on Halangy Down and who has, since 1964, visited the site annually. His continuing more-than-ordinary interest, unfailing support, ready help and sound advice has made so much possible.

Works of synthesis invariably owe much to many, as is shown by the bibliography. Thus to those whose books and papers I have read and with whom I have conversed and corresponded, my obligation is considerable.

Individuals and Institutions have most kindly allowed me to make use of their photographs and line drawings, as well as giving me permission to publish. It is with pleasure that I acknowledge their generosity: Miss S. Butcher; Mr H. L. Douch and the Museum of the Royal Institution of Cornwall, Truro; Miss D. Dudley; Dr G. C. Dunning; Messrs Elliot & Fry, London; Mr Alec Gray; Mr Frank Gibson; Professor H. O'Neill Hencken; Mrs H. E. O'Neil; Mr C. F. Tebbutt; Professor Charles Thomas; Mr Charles Woolf.

I am particularly grateful to Mr P. Z. Mackenzie who gave me access to the collections and library of the Isles of Scilly Museum in Hugh Town, and to all those who have laboured long and through turbulent weather on Halangy Down. In London, library usage has been eased

PREFACE AND ACKNOWLEDGEMENTS

and expedited by the unflagging energy and unfailing patience of Mr John Hopkins, Librarian of the Society of Antiquaries of London.

William Borlase, whose eighteenth-century work looms large in my writing, refers to his studies being aided by 'his happy connection with one who took more than her part of domestick cares'. Likewise, whether excavating, writing or drawing, my work has been enhanced by my wife's constant encouragement and help.

PAUL ASHBEE

University of East Anglia

CHAPTER 1

Antiquaries, Archaeologists and the Isles of Scilly

No account of Scillonian archaeology can be presented without, as a necessary preliminary, describing the studies and investigations through which our present knowledge has been assembled. The interpretation of archaeological evidence obviously changes, but that evidence as preserved in print, whether a straightforward description of visible remains, a discussion of the possible identification of an artifact, or a painstaking account of an excavation, remains the sole authority for what existed. The passage of time and the improvement of techniques may yield increased knowledge of sites, but they also destroy the physical evidence of the landscape. For this reason, although too easily looked down upon by this scientifically knowledgeable age, many of the archaeologists' firmest allies remain the early antiquaries whose pens set down honestly what they beheld, even if their subsequent inferences require correction in the light of more recent study. As this book will show in its reliance upon their records, no apology is required for these chronicles and their ambitions.

Systematic Scillonian archaeology was begun by William Borlase (Plate 1a). He was the first to classify what he termed 'ancient Sepulchres' into 'Caves' (apparently chambered tombs from which most, or all of the covering cairn or barrow had been removed) and 'Barrows' (chambered tombs with cairn and surrounding kerb). He saw and recorded on 'the Guêw, a part of Agnes ... a large stone erect nine feet

OBSERVATIONS
ON THE
Ancient and Preſent State
OF THE
ISLANDS OF SCILLY,
And their Importance to the
TRADE of *GREAT-BRITAIN*.

In a LETTER to the Reverend

CHARLES LYTTELTON, LL.D.
Dean of EXETER, and F. R. S.

By WILLIAM BORLASE, *M. A. F. R. S.*

O X F O R D:
PRINTED BY W. JACKSON.

Sold by W. SANDBY, in *Fleetſtreet*, and R. BALDWIN, in *Pater-noſter Row, London*; Meſſ. FLETCHER, CLEMENTS, and PARKER, in *Oxford*; Meſſ. LEAKE and FREDERICK at *Bath*; Meſſ. SCORE and THORN at *Exeter*; and Meſſ. JEWELL and MICHELL in *Cornwall.*

M.DCC.LVI.

Fig 1 Title-page of William Borlase's Observations on the Ancient and Present State of the Islands of Scilly, *1756*

high by two feet six inches wide'. Other standing stones that he recorded and called 'Rude Stone Pillars' were on St Mary's: '... there are two still standing in this island; one on the summit of a round hill, on a little tumulus near Harry's Battery, ten feet above the ground, by two feet nine inches wide; another, near Bant's-Karn, nine feet three inches high, by two feet six inches square at a medium'. On the 'Guêw' he did not miss 'signs of Stone hedges and Inclosures, plain evidences of its having been once cultivated and inhabited'. These comments were set down in *Observations on the Ancient and Present State of the Islands of Scilly, And their Importance to the Trade of Great Britain. In a letter to the Reverend Charles Lyttelton, LL.D. Dean of Exeter and F.R.S.* published at Oxford in 1756 (Fig 1).

The remarkable quality and breadth, by the standards of the eighteenth century, of William Borlase's field archaeology emerges from his account of his visit to Samson:

> ... The Sand ... has been blown up by the Northern winds, and covered great part of that which is called the Brehar Hill of Samson: it is blown off again in some little breaks and channels of the Hill, where I saw Hedges of Stone (The Fences of Fields made of Rude Stones laid edgeways, and not in Mortar, we call, in Cornwall, Hedges) six feet under the common run of the Sand-banks: here are also many remains of Hedges descending from the Hill, and running many feet under the level of the sea towards Trescaw, and I must observe to you that the flats here abouts betwixt Trescaw, Brehar and Samson, are quite dry at the low water of a Spring-Tide, and men easily pass dry-shod from one Island to another over Sand-banks, where Hedges and Ruins are frequently discovered upon the shifting of the Sands, and upon which at full sea there are ten and twelve feet of water.
>
> These are certain evidences that the Islands last mentioned were once one continued tract of Land, divided into Fields, and cultivated even in those low parts which are now over-run with the Sea and Sand.

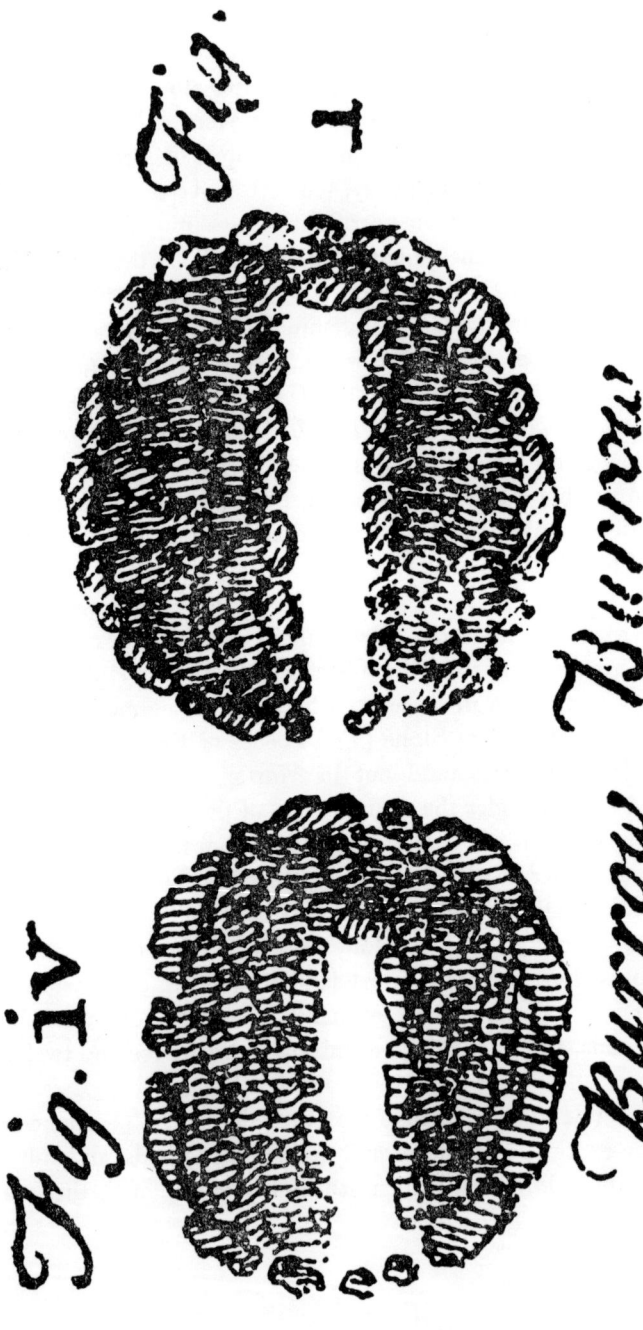

Fig 2 William Borlase's plans of chamber tombs on Buzza Hill, St Mary's

ANTIQUARIES, ARCHAEOLOGISTS AND THE ISLES OF SCILLY

Borlase's description of submerged walls and his conclusions, contained in this 'Letter' to Lyttelton, had but a short time before been the subject of a paper in the *Philosophical Transactions of the Royal Society* (XLVIII, 1753) entitled 'Of the Great Alterations Which the Islands of Scilly Have Undergone since the Time of the Ancients'. To further his knowledge of the 'Burrows', Borlase had undertaken in June 1752, excavations (Fig 2). These operations are among the earliest of their kind in the British Isles and, in spite of obscurities, the account of them, and the deductions based upon them, reach a standard scarcely equalled until this century. The two barrows excavated were, so John Troutbeck (Troutbeck, 1794, 54) chaplain on the Scillies from 1780 to 1796 alleges, both on Buzza Hill, St Mary's. In Borlase's own inimitable words:

> We pitch'd upon a hill, where there are many of these *Barrows* and, as the common story goes, *Giants* were buried, with a design to search them, and on *Wednesday, June* the third, having hired some soldiers, proceed to open them.
>
> In the first we found no bones, nor urns, but some strong unctuous earth which smelt cadaverous. In the middle of this *Barrow* was a large cavity full of earth: there was a passage into it at the Eastern end one foot eight inches wide, betwixt two stones set on end; the cavity was four feet eight inches wide in the middle, the length of it twenty two feet, it was walled on each side with masonry and mortar, the walls or sides four feet ten inches high; at the Western end it had a large flat stone on its edge which terminated the cavity; its length bore East and by North, and it was covered from end to end with large flat stones several of which we removed, and others had been carried off before for building the new *Pier*.
>
> Forty two feet distant to the North, we opened another Barrow of the same kind, the Cave [chamber] was less in all respects, the length fourteen feet, bearing North-east by East, the walled sides two feet high; where narrowest, one foot eight inches, in the middle, four feet wide; in the floor was a small round cell dug deeper than the rest. In this we found some earths of different colours from the natural

one, but nothing decisive. It was covered with stones like the former.

Digging out the chambers of the two barrows took Borlase a day. The work was attended, like many present-day Scillonian archaeological enterprises, by inclement weather.

> In the afternoon it rained excessively hard, so that we could not proceed in our enquiries; the wind blew, and about midnight it was the most violent storm while it lasted, I ever knew.
>
> You that are curious will think very innocently of our searching these repositories of the dead for the satisfaction of the living, but will you not be surprised if I tell you that it appeared in a very different light to the poor people of Scilly? ... I met a person who soon began to talk about the weather, and to complain of the bitterness of the last night's hurricane, that it had almost ruined him and many of his neighbours ... this courteous landlady ... she told me ... that the last night's storm was very outrageous; then asked me whether we had not been digging up the Giant's graves the day before ... she ... asked, whether I did not think that we had disturbed the Giants; and said that many good people of the Islands were of opinion that the Giants were offended, and had really raised that storm ...

Borlase listened to his landlady and reflected on belief in Giants. This led him to consider the function of the large chambers in the barrows:

> All I shall say of the *Burrows* is, that in our searches we discovered nothing but the structure of them, neither could I find, upon the strictest enquiry, that ever any Urn was found in *Scilly*; and the reason why the cavities of Masonry are so much beyond the dimensions of the human body seems to me that they might contain more bodies than one. However it is not easy to convince these Islanders but that the graves were made according to the size of the body there interr'd.

ANTIQUARIES, ARCHAEOLOGISTS AND THE ISLES OF SCILLY

It was the results of this visit to Scilly which were published a year later in the *Philosophical Transactions of the Royal Society*.

In the years following Borlase made frequent visits to Oxford, his university, to facilitate the publications of his many books. While *Observations on the Ancient and Present State of the Islands of Scilly* was not published until 1756, this was preceded by the monumental *Observations on the Antiquities of Cornwall* (Oxford, 1754) and succeeded by the searching *The Natural History of Cornwall* (Oxford, 1758). *Antiquities Historical and Monumental of the County of Cornwall*, published in London, did not appear until 1769.

William Borlase must be considered as one who has made a unique contribution to British prehistoric studies. His archaeological fieldwork follows the standards set by John Aubrey (A. Powell, 1948) in his *Monumenta* and runs parallel to that of the celebrated William Stukeley (Piggott, 1950). Indeed, in their devotion to Druids and development of idiosyncratic religious notions, in later life, they have much in common. His natural history has much about it that stems from Aubrey, Plot and Dugdale (Fox, ed, 1956). Colt Hoare (Colt Hoare, 1810, 9) sets store by his views, Evans (Evans, 1864, 6) notes his accuracy in regard to the depiction of 'Ancient British Coins' while *The Archaeology of Cornwall and Scilly* (Hencken, 1932), in this century, shows by constant references to his work the magnitude of his contribution.

William Borlase, born in February 1695, was the second son of John Borlase, Member of Parliament for St Ives in Cornwall, and Lydia Harris, his wife, from Hayne in Devonshire. He began his education at a school in Penzance, moved on to another school in Plymouth in 1709, finishing his schooldays at Tiverton. As a West Countryman he joined Exeter College, Oxford, in about 1712, taking in due course his degrees. In 1719 he was ordained deacon and in 1720 priest, in the Church of England. In 1722 he returned to live in his native Cornwall, having been presented to the living of Ludgvan, near Penzance.

In Cornwall opportunities of classical study and the captivations of the 'Grand Tour' eluded him. He wrote at one point (*Antiquities of Cornwall*, 1769, v); 'My situation in life (whatever my inclinations might be) confined me to a different track: I saw myself placed in the midst of Monuments, the Works of the Ancient Britans, where there were few Grecian or Roman Remains to be met with; my curiosity, therefore, could only be gratified by what was within its reach, and was confined to the study of our own Antiquities.' 'Our own Antiquities' and natural history were to be his great achievement. He considers the work of an antiquary directly and deliberately: 'Now, the study of Antiquity is the study of Ancient History; and the proper business of an Antiquary is, to collect what is dispersed, more fully to unfold what is already discovered, to examine controverted points, to settle what is doubtful, and, by the authority of Monuments and Histories, to throw light upon the Manners, Arts, Languages, Policy, and Religion, of past Ages.'

If William Stukeley (Piggott, 1950) restored Stonehenge and Avebury to the Druids, William Borlase, a self-confessed admirer of Stukeley (Pool, 1966), accredited them with the use of 'Rock-Basons' and 'Logan Stones'. Later ages and geological knowledge see these as products of the natural weathering of rocks, as, indeed, did Stukeley (Palmer, 1964, 285n). To Borlase, as to Aubrey and Stukeley, stone circles, in Scilly perhaps the remnants of chambered tombs but in Cornwall stone circles in their own right (Atkinson, 1951, 92), had to be the work of Druids. As we read them today, Borlase's chapters on the Druids and the origins and uses of rock-basins, quoting Euripides, Pliny, Theocritus, Strabo, Job etc, with historical references to the Athenians, Jews, Syrians, Egyptians, Persians and others, containing descriptions of aspect, shape, measurements and distribution of rock-basins, logan stones and the like, seem but fantasia fermenting in his mind as he ordered his notes and drawings in the quiet of Ludgvan rectory. However, as Piggott (Piggott, 1950, 120) has emphasised with regard to Stukeley, a cleric in later life, such notions are not original nor are they the aberrations that, over the years, they have appeared to be. For it must be remembered that any consideration of antiquity had to be fitted into a Biblical framework. Chronology had to conform to Archbishop Ussher's accepted scheme (Daniel, 1962, 11) whereby the date of the Creation was set at 4004 BC. There was also the consideration of a cataclysmic deluge, the repeopling of the world after this event, not to mention the Tower of Babel and other Biblical circumstances. All these influenced the minds of Borlase and his contemporaries.

Besides antiquities, Borlase was preoccupied with pure geology and he was elected to the Fellowship of the Royal Society following the communication of a paper on 'Spar and Sparry Productions, Called Cornish Diamonds'. In all, he made nineteen contributions to the *Philosophical Transactions*. Shortly after 1758, he presented the whole of his collections to the Ashmolean Museum in Oxford. For this and for his scholarship his university conferred upon him, by diploma, the degree of Doctor of Laws in 1766. For all his antiquarian and scientific labours, Borlase did not neglect his parish which he tended with 'the most rigid punctuality and exemplary duty'.

In later life, at the age of seventy, he laboured at a *Parochial History of Cornwall*, which he never finished and, curiously, repeating the career patterns of Newton and Stukeley (Piggott, 1950, 130–1), he turned his attention to theology; he paraphrased Ecclesiastes, the Canticles and the Lamentations and wrote some speculations on the Creation and Deluge which, again, were never published.

On 31 August 1772, William Borlase died at Ludgvan at the age of seventy-seven, having been rector of that parish for fifty-two years. Rock-basins and logan stones still find a place in the modern topographical literature of the Isles of Scilly as do, indeed, occasional offshoots of the 'arkite ogdoad'. However, it is with Borlase, who was of the decided view that '... though these Islands are so near us, they are very little known, and much less valued than in all reason they ought to be' that Scillonian archaeology begins.

The wide interests and abilities of autocratic Augustus Smith (Inglis-Jones, 1969) who leased the Isles of Scilly from William IV and whose benevolent despotism brought prosperity to the islanders, extended like those of Sir John Lubbock (Duff, 1934), with whom he had much in common, to geology and archaeology. Indeed, he had pursued the study of geological science at Oxford under Dr Buckland. We hear of him taking the chair at a meeting of the Royal Cornish

Geological Society at Truro in 1858 and expressing a hope that the forthcoming work by Mr Charles Darwin would be worthy and would assert the eternal providence of the Creator and justify his ways and works. In 1863, having apparently perused, in the meantime, the *Origin of Species* we find him declaring to the same society that he finds himself unable to agree with Mr Darwin on the antiquity of man.

It was at a meeting of the Royal Institution of Cornwall on 29 May 1863 that Augustus Smith read a paper on the opening of a barrow, the previous September, on the northern hill of Samson. This barrow opening was for the benefit of a 'select party of Cambrian archaeologists' and the remarkable features which it contained are discussed in detail on page 125. Today, the great capstone still lies beside this cist in the crown of the gutted barrow and would seem to be, but for grass and flowers, much as it was left by the Lord Proprietor and his Cambrian company in 1862.

Nineteenth-century Scillonian archaeological activity was not, however, the exclusive prerogative of its reforming Lord Proprietor. The Rev S. M. Mayhew wrote *Notes in the Scilly Isles together with some Cornish Antiquities* (Mayhew, 1877) in which he makes observations on topography, flora, the Maypole on 1 May, a tin lamp and Phoenician influence, besides describing how he set up the cross at Salakee (the 'High Cross' in Highcross Lane) on St Mary's. Chamber tombs are referred to in a paper entitled *Typical Specimens of Cornish Barrows* read to the Society of Antiquaries of London on 3 February 1881, by William Copeland Borlase (1886) the second antiquary in that family. This writer, in his *Naenia Cornubiae* (W. C. Borlase, 1872), had considered 'Chambered Tumuli', as he termed them, in Scilly and those in the parish of Zennor, in Cornwall. He called attention to a comparison with an Irish monument—'especially with one specimen figured in the Kilkenny Archaeological Society's publication for 1868'. In the same work (W. C. Borlase, 1872, 162), under the general heading of 'Explorations and Discoveries in the Tumuli', he quotes from Augustus Smith's paper to the Royal Institution of Cornwall and features a woodcut of one of the 'bronze armlets' found 'about fifty years ago in a barrow on the Peninnis Head, in the island of St Mary's, Scilly'. This discovery is mentioned in Smith's paper but, until recently (Douch, 1962, 97) the precise circumstances were not known. These massive torques have for long been preserved in Truro museum.

During the years 1899, 1900 and 1901 Mr George Bonsor, a retired Cornish engineer and antiquary, residing in Spain, visited the Isles of Scilly seeking proof for his hypothesis that they were the Cassiterides, the fabled tin islands of the Atlantic. As far as the early tin trade was concerned his work proved entirely negative but, during his visits, he excavated and planned chamber tombs, namely entrance graves on the islands of St Mary's and Gugh, besides drawing a detailed section of a midden exposed in the cliff at Halangy Porth, St Mary's. This last was a feature of the earlier phase of the Halangy Down 'Ancient Village'.

Bonsor unfortunately never published an account of his meticulous work, but kept the notes and excavated material in his castle at Mairena del Alcor, near Seville. There he was visited during 1926 by Mr T. D. Kendrick (now Sir Thomas Kendrick), then an Assistant Keeper of British and Mediaeval Antiquities in the British Museum. As a result of this visit, pottery and other objects as well as the plans and excavation notes passed to the British Museum. Much of this was described and featured by H. O'Neill Hencken in *The Archaeology of Cornwall and Scilly* (Hencken, 1932). Reginald Smith, then Keeper of British and Mediaeval Antiquities, had for a long time urged Bonsor to communicate the results of his Scillonian work to the Society of Antiquaries of London, but he died without having done so. Subsequently Smith obtained further plans and manuscripts (written in French) and these were published by Hencken (Hencken, 1933), to supplement his earlier work.

On St Mary's, Bonsor excavated the largest of the chamber tombs, now designated entrance graves, on Porth Hellick Down and surveyed another close by. He dug into the Bant's Carn entrance grave, which is on the crest of the Down above the 'Ancient Village', finding pottery which Hencken notes he was subsequently unable to trace, as well as observing and drawing a detailed section of the midden at that time visible in the cliff of Halangy Par (or Porth) at the foot of the hill. A plan and section were made of what is now termed the Upper Innisidgen entrance grave at the same time. The linear cemetery of chamber tombs on Kittern Hill, Gugh, initially attracted Bonsor's attention. He turned from these to the standing stone to the south-east of Kittern Hill, which he dug around without result. After this he dug, in 1901, into what was an apparently undisturbed chamber also on Kittern Hill, some sixty yards north-west of what the Ordnance Survey had called Carn Valla. This he called 'Obadiah's Barrow' after Obadiah Hicks, with whom he lodged on St Agnes.

During March 1926, O. G. S. Crawford, who had in 1920 been appointed Archaeology Officer to the Ordnance Survey (Crawford, 1955) visited the Isles of Scilly. He had read Borlase's paper in the 1753 *Philosophical Transactions* and, accompanied by Mr Alexander Gibson and his camera, he chartered a boat and crossed to Samson. It was on 16 March of that year, the day of the lowest spring tides, and they photographed on Samson Flats, first from the high ground on Samson and then at closer quarters, the lines of stones which are still visible and now are considered to be submerged boulder-hedges. Afterwards they planned to walk to Tresco and thence to Bryher. While Gibson took photographs, Crawford picked up flint flakes on the sands. Crawford compared the submerged Samson stone-hedges with modern examples on St Mary's near Watermill and was, subsequently, able to procure air-photographs of Samson Flats. As the result of this visit, the first paper in Volume I, No 1, of the journal *Antiquity*, founded by Crawford and edited by him until his death in 1957, was entitled 'Lyonesse' and was from the pen of its distinguished editor. This classic paper remains, after forty years, the most comprehensive account of the problems of recent marine transgression in the islands.

While he was in the Isles of Scilly, Crawford would seem to have visited many of the chamber tombs and to have discussed the problems of the locality with Alexander Gibson: for *Antiquity* for December 1928 had in it a paper (Crawford, 1928) entitled 'Stone Cists'. In this he described the cist on the North Hill of Samson, which had been opened

ANTIQUARIES, ARCHAEOLOGISTS AND THE ISLES OF SCILLY

by Augustus Smith in 1862, reproduced an early photograph by Alexander Gibson showing his son James, holding his father's walking stick, and standing by a cist which was for long visible in the surface of Town Lane, St Mary's, and another photograph of a cist on the shore of St Martin's. In the same paper illustrations of the Harlyn Bay, Cornwall, cists were featured: this site had been studied by Crawford who had cycled over when convalescing after a wound received when flying as an observer in the Royal Flying Corps. He established that these west-country cists were plainly quite different from the chamber tombs on Normandy and Porth Hellick Downs, St Mary's.

The Archaeology of Cornwall and Scilly (Hencken, 1932) was in great measure compiled between 1926 and 1929 beginning as a dissertation on the Bronze and Iron Ages in Devon and Cornwall which led to the degree of Doctor of Philosophy at the University of Cambridge. H. O'Neill Hencken, now Professor of European Archaeology in the University of Harvard, records in his preface that it was O. G. S. Crawford who first suggested this subject to him and who, when the work had begun, contributed a vast amount of helpful advice and information. Indeed, during his visit to the Islands in 1926, Crawford made plans of chamber tombs and these were added to material which Hencken had obtained from Bonsor.

Hencken visited the Isles of Scilly and viewed his material at first-hand, meeting Alexander Gibson and Major A. Dorrien Smith, and received help from them. He also made contact with Bonsor who allowed him to publish the results of his 1899–1901 excavations and fieldwork. He visited the chamber tombs, and set them into order, island by island, by devising a system of numeration, followed by subsequent workers, besides tabulating their dimensions (Hencken, 1932, 317–18). These Scillonian chamber tombs were described in an especial sub-section of his book to which an archaeological map of the islands was attached (Hencken, 1932, 18–19). There was also an exhaustive list of Scillonian antiquities, extant and published, besides a list of museums and collections in which Scillonian material was preserved.

In August 1930, Hencken undertook the excavation of a chambered barrow on the summit of the North Hill of Samson (Samson 1, Hencken, 1932, 18–19, Fig 7). An account of this excavation was published in the *Antiquaries Journal* for 1933 (Hencken, 1933) together with a much more detailed account of Bonsor's 1899–1901 excavations, plans, sections and records.

During June 1933, C. F. Tebbutt discovered and excavated a stone cist in a surface revealed by the sea erosion of Old Man, a small island by Teän (Tebbutt, 1934). The discovery was of considerable importance because the good photographs and plan made by Tebbutt, together with his admirable note, gave for the first time adequate details of a Scillonian cist, a number of which had previously been identified. The value of this record and its prompt publication was manifest when in 1949 the present writer was confronted with a cemetery of such cists at Porth Cressa, on St Mary's (Ashbee, 1954).

From the outset, archaeological activity in the Isles of Scilly, with the notable exception of the activities and observations of Augustus Smith during the nineteenth century, has been mostly by visitors from the mainland. Since the beginning of this century, however, Scillonians have paid increasing attention to their antiquities. It is regrettable that owing to difficulties of isolation and communication so little of this work has received detailed notice or publication. All, from the outset, have taken great pains to aid and guide those who have worked upon the archaeological problems of the Isles.

Of special note is the series of photographs taken of chamber tombs and other island antiquities by Alexander Gibson (1857–1944) of Hugh Town, St Mary's, many of which record the appearance of the monuments and the landscape of the islands at the beginning of this century. Many things down the years have been coming to light as the result of cliff erosion and Alexander Gibson, and his son Mr James Gibson, have photographed and so preserved in their collection, much that would otherwise have been lost (Hencken, 1932, 315–16).

Between 1923 and 1927, and from 1930 to 1936, Mr Alec Gray, now living in Cornwall, was in residence at the flower farm by Halangy

Point, on St Mary's. Over the years, during the reclamation of land below Halangy Down for flower growing, he excavated parts of the structures visible in the cliffs of Halangy Porth. At the same time he defined the hut on Halangy Down subsequently excavated by the present writer in 1950 (Ashbee, 1955). Records of this work, and descriptions of numerous other traces of habitations, in the form of the remains of stone-built huts and middens on St Mary's, St Agnes, Samson, Bryher, Tresco, St Martin's, Teän and Arthur were written out by Alec Gray during 1936 (Ashbee, 1972).

What might be termed the World War II period in Scillonian archaeology is neatly bracketed by Glyn Daniel's visits in 1936 and 1946. The fieldwork that he carried out during the time that he was in the Isles of Scilly was incorporated in his general account of the prehistoric chamber tombs of England and Wales (Daniel, 1950). Like Hencken before him, he emphasised the great number of tombs extant, for there are 'between a fifth and a quarter of all the chamber tombs in southern Britain on the islands'. In ordering their distribution he introduced a new numeration, giving in his inventory the Hencken equivalent, making additions, and providing a map to illustrate this. The problems of marine transgression were surveyed as were all the possible aspects of the tomb concentration, in the light of knowledge available at that time. In a later general work, *The Megalith Builders of Western Europe* (Daniel, 1958), Glyn Daniel included further matter on the Scillonian tombs, again emphasising their number and pointing to their European affinities. This distinguished writer has also reconsidered 'Lyonesse and The Lost Lands of England' (Daniel, 1955).

In the post-war period, Stuart Piggott included, under the heading of 'Miscellaneous Chambered Tombs' a succinct and definitive survey of the Scillonian examples in his *The Neolithic Cultures of the British Isles* (Piggott, 1954). He envisaged them as the major component of what he termed 'The Scilly-Tramore Group' calling particular attention to an analagous group of tombs of identical type studied by Powell (1941) in the Tramore region of Ireland, near Waterford. At the same time he noted, following Daniel (1950), that only four tombs in West

Cornwall could justifiably be included in the group. Piggott incorporated post-war work but as these treatments of the Scillonian tombs are relevant one to another it is necessary that they be considered together.

Early in World War II a German incendiary bomb set alight the vegetation on the uninhabited island of St Helen's. The burning revealed the remains of the hermitage, the church walls of which were standing to roof-level when seen by Borlase in 1752. Mr H. C. Cotton, at the instigation of Major A. Dorrien Smith, visited the island and made a plan of what he was able to see and trace. The results of this visit, and a plan, were communicated to the *Antiquaries Journal* by Mr C. A. Ralegh Radford (1941).

Stuart Piggott had visited the Isles of Scilly during 1937 and had made a plan, and taken photographs of details of the method of construction of the cist opened by Augustus Smith in 1862 on the North Hill of Samson. In a note (Piggott, 1941), entitled 'Grooved Stone Cists, Scotland and the Scillies' he contended, citing Bronze Age plank-coffin burials, that the Samson cist and a number of similar ones in Scotland, were stone versions of wooden coffins.

A war-time extension to the St Mary's airfield on Salakee Down made necessary the excavation of a chamber tomb. This was undertaken during 1942 by Mr (now Professor) W. F. Grimes for a number of chamber tombs and barrows had been destroyed without record during the making and enlarging of this airfield. It was due to the zeal of the war-time Office of Works that Grimes was able to examine this tomb in detail. A full report of this excavation was published in 1960, in the Ministry of Work's *Excavations on Defence Sites, 1939–1945*, I: *Mainly Neolithic–Bronze Age* (Grimes, 1960).

Post World War II Scillonian archaeology began when the Rev H. A. Lewis became Chaplain of St Martin's. He was fascinated with the environment in which he found himself and began detailed archaeological fieldwork. One of his first discoveries was a cist in the cliff-face, between Knackyboy Cairn and Yellow Rock Carn. He also started to dig into Knackyboy Cairn and was able to establish the character of the burials in its chamber besides beginning to examine the foundations of a stone-built hut on the beach below the high-water mark. His booklet, devoted to St Martin's and close-by islands (Lewis, 1948) is a mine of information and inference for an intending fieldworker.

It was owing to the discoveries of the Rev H. A. Lewis that B. H. StJ. O'Neil (Plate 1b) first visited the Isles of Scilly in 1947. Accompanied by his wife he came to the islands annually until his untimely death in 1954, studying their prehistory and later history as well as undertaking a series of excavations. He was particularly devoted to the island of St Martin's and much of his work was connected with its abundant problems.

Notably, he excavated Knackyboy Cairn in 1948 (O'Neil, 1952). When he began his scheme of excavation on the Isles of Scilly he was, to quote his own words, 'bent upon the details of the houses of the living rather than of the dead. For already in 1947 there was evidence of at least one habitation site which yielded pottery similar to that already found in some of the chambered tombs of Scilly'. In that year it had seemed to both Lewis and O'Neil that the Knackyboy Cairn had in it yet another rifled tomb chamber, the excavation of which would have been pointless in the face of more informative tasks. To quote O'Neil's words again, 'Mr. Lewis, however, persisted in his prospecting. He had found flints outside a large rock, which proved to be the back end of the chamber. He transferred his attention to the other side of the rock. At once he began to find pottery, but stopped when he had recovered one hundredweight.' When he returned to St Martin's in 1948, O'Neil continued the excavation for 'he saw before him in section across the chamber a stratigraphic sequence of squashed urns such as must have fallen to the lot of few archaeologists in this century'.

Among other excavations carried out by O'Neil were a continuation of work on the native Romano-British hut on Par Beach, begun by Lewis; of a rectilinear stone-built hut with pottery, similar to that from the chamber tombs, at English Island Carn; of a stone-built hut at May's Hill; and of another hut, similar to that at English Island Carn, at Lawrence's Brow, all on St Martin's. He excavated and planned a small chamber tomb on Arthur, and shortly before his death he had begun an investigation of the hermitage on St Helen's. This last work was completed by Mrs O'Neil in the summers of 1956 and 1957 (H. E. O'Neil, 1964).

It was during 1956 that Professor Charles Thomas worked on the island of Teän, excavating a small oratory and other structures, besides surveying the island and carrying out extensive work which has led to an assessment of marine features about the islands.

Besides his report on Knackyboy Cairn (O'Neil, 1952); notes on an enamelled penannular brooch from St Martin's of c AD 650 of Irish affinity (O'Neil, 1953), the Arthur chamber tomb (O'Neil, 1954) and brief accounts of the above-mentioned excavations, O'Neil, who had, since 1945, been Chief Inspector of Ancient Monuments for the then Ministry of Works, wrote the Ministry's guide to the ancient monuments of the Isles of Scilly (O'Neil, 1949). This, a model of its kind and, indeed, the only work which deals exclusively with the full range of Scillonian archaeology, summarises all aspects of the prehistory and later history of the islands. When O'Neil wrote, seven ancient monuments in the Isles of Scilly, namely the chamber tombs at Innisidgen, Bant's Carn with the adjacent 'Ancient Village', the largest tomb on Porth Hellick Down, together with Harry's Walls all on St Mary's, and King Charles' Castle, Cromwell's Castle and the Old Blockhouse on Tresco, had been placed in the guardianship of the Ministry, those on St Mary's by the Duchy of Cornwall, those on Tresco with the agreement of Major A. Dorrien Smith. In order that these monuments should be understood in their true relationship one to another and to the other numerous monuments on the islands, the guidebook was written in connected form as an archaeological and historical study of the Islands.

It was due to O'Neil that the present writer first came to the Isles of Scilly in October 1949 and was enabled to excavate the Porth Cressa cist-grave cemetery (Ashbee, 1954) and, during the summer of 1950, to examine a component of what is at present termed the 'Bant's Carn Ancient Village' (Ashbee, 1955).

Fieldwork by O'Neil and the present writer at the end of 1949, carried out in the depths of the jungle of fern and furze that enshrouded the hillside of Halangy Down suggested that the 'village' there consisted of about eleven apparently associated huts, together with a system of paths and plots. It was emphasised that much clearance and excavation was necessary before a complete plan could be made. The component selected for excavation in 1950 was the oval 'hut' which, perhaps on account of its size and prominence, had been partially uncovered by Mr Gray almost twenty years before. A trench had exposed the internal wall-face and the entire length of a stone drain was uncovered. A further small trench scarcely went below the humus in the interior. The 1950 excavation disclosed the full details of the hut's interior, the external character of the downhill wall and a small chamber built partially into the thickness of the wall on the northern side. The entrance had seemingly been elaborated by the addition of a rectangular annexe. Beginning again in 1964 and continuing to the present, further clearance and excavation has begun to disclose the full character of this remarkable site. The remains of structures visible in the cliff of Halangy Porth and those disclosed by Mr Gray's excavations were the earliest phase, those on the hillside, later. Not all buildings were in use at the same time.

During 1950 further fieldwork was undertaken and it was possible to make sketch plans of a number of chamber tombs and cists on St Mary's (Ashbee, 1953, 1963). In concluding the report on the Porth Cressa cist-grave cemetery, regret was expressed that the limited objective, together with existing buildings and gardens did not permit further investigation (Ashbee, 1954, 16). However, further building work during 1960 brought to light more such cist-graves in Poynter's Garden, the land adjacent to and west of the Porth Cressa cemetery site. Excavations carried out by Miss D. M. Dudley during 1960 (Dudley, 1961), showed that they had also contained contracted burials and that they had been furnished in the same manner.

A great storm during March 1962, eroded further the low sandy cliffs on the south side of Nornour, which is one of the Eastern Islands. The stone walls of a building were exposed and brooches and coins were picked up. In view of the seemingly spectacular character of this site an excavation was arranged by the Ministry of Public Buildings and Works, following upon overtures made by the Duchy of Cornwall's Scillonian Land Steward, Major R. Maclaren. This operation was undertaken later in 1962 by Miss D. M. Dudley (Dudley, 1967), who has worked on it annually to the present. In 1962, two sub-rectangular chambers were uncovered, the larger one having a central hearth. Quantities of bronze brooches, rings, bracelets, coins (AD 69–371), beads, glass fragments, and 'pipe-clay' female figurines were found, also much pottery. In the following year the main chamber was further explored and its internal fitments disclosed. Work on this important site is continuing at the present time (Butcher, 1970).

Since 1963 archaeological activity by those living on the Isles of Scilly has moved from an individual to a corporate basis. The Isles of Scilly Museum Association has been formed while a proper and permanent museum is now open in Hugh Town. Members of the association have taken part in excavations and an archaeological field survey, based upon the 25in Ordnance Survey Maps, has been embarked upon.

CHAPTER 2

Geology, Topography and Environment

The Isles of Scilly (Fig 3), which on a clear day can be seen from Land's End, are composed almost entirely of granite, the products of granite weathering and blown sand. They are the westernmost of the Cornish granite masses or bosses. These are, from east to west, the Bodmin, St Austell, Carn Menellis, and St Just (or Land's End) masses. Each forms an area of higher ground rising above the country formed by the slaty rocks. The granite islets, the Isles of Scilly, are apparently a granite cupola which has been cut up by erosion and isolated by submergence. Of the one-time-encompassing slaty rocks, only a minute quantity remains to be observed on White Island. Only five of these islets are now inhabited. The largest, St Mary's, is about 2 miles long and 160ft in height. From this dimension there is every gradation to a mere speck of rock visible only at low water.

Deposits formed by the denudation of the granite are important components of some of the islands. Such deposits take two forms: 'head' and blown sand. When an island is more than a mere rock it consists of granite 'carns' standing solidly above the weathering and denudation deposits which are about them. These granite exposures have often weathered into grotesque forms, as for example on Peninnis or in Porth Hellick. A feature of this weathering process is the formation of rock basins (Plate 2a), so beloved by Borlase (Borlase, 1756, 13), which can be seen in such numbers on Porth Hellick Down.

The Scillonian carns and rocks convey an infinite spectrum of colour, varying with sky and season. No words can properly portray the subtle

GEOLOGY, TOPOGRAPHY AND ENVIRONMENT

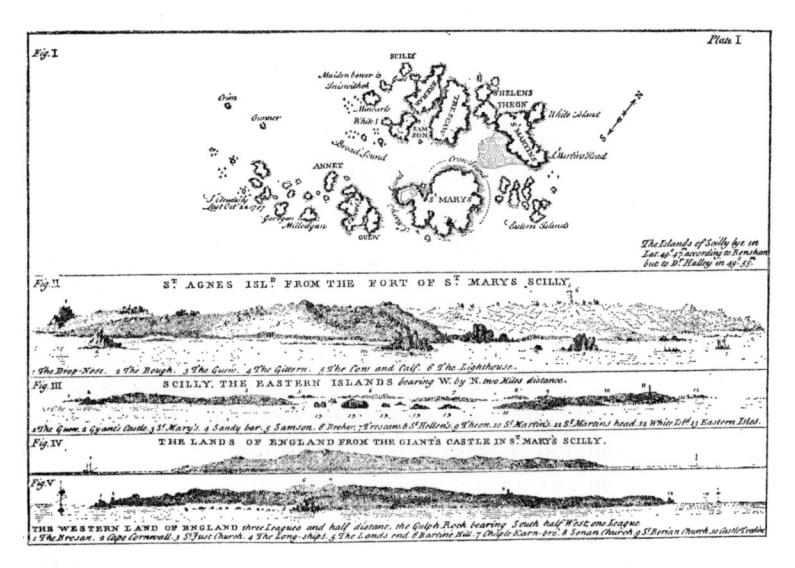

Fig 3 The Isles of Scilly as depicted by William Borlase, 1756

shifts of texture and tint, or the myriad varieties of substance. In grey winter, with a dull leaden sky lowering with the promise of more rain, they seem nearly black. In spring and summer, when struck by sunlight, they glow as if activated by inner phosphorescence. When closely examined, each stone has its individual grain in which there is quartz varying in appearance from coarse marble to fine white lump sugar, while innumerable micas sparkle like diamonds. Luxuriant growths of grey-green lichen mantle all but the most exposed surfaces, which are sometimes stressed by vivid patches of scaly yellow. Plants such as sea-pink, hawkweed, ling and stonecrop, often thrive in their fissures. Other stones have only their furring and bearding of lichen, the tufts of which whisper and rustle in the wind. These ever-present rocks give to the Scillonian landscape a quality of timeless permanence, but everywhere they are being etched and ground by the relentless agencies of wind and weather, tide and time.

Nowhere in the Isles of Scilly can one forget the sea. For the sea both unites and divides the islands. From the air one views their broken irregular contours coalesced by the shallow waters between. At low tide, when each island, rock or reef is ringed about with an irregular base of weed-blackened rock, this impression is heightened. And each island, reef or rock, has an individuality of silhouette which shifts, changes and blends one into the other as the vantage point of an observer alters. At high tide and in a calm sea, each island, seen from the other, seems separated and half submerged. In a gale with wind and great waves hammering at every cliff, cove and porth, and everywhere the boom of the angry surf, there is a sense of siege. On the headlands the tumultuous waves are held back by the great granite buttresses, but on the softer mantle of deposits the sea exerts its insidious forces. As a result the total land area is being perceptibly reduced, a process particularly noticeable among the smaller islands, until one day even the larger islands will be split by the waves. When the grass and flowers go and the waves win, all will be as bare as the rocks of Mincarlo.

The deposit termed 'head', which accounts for so much of the land mass of the islands, is an accumulation of angular or sub-angular blocks of granite, many in an advanced state of decomposition, compounded into a solid mass found, more than anywhere else, at the foot of the inner cliffs and slopes. In general, it has the character of a scree in that the coarsest material always lies close to the bottoms of the steepest slopes. There are smaller quantities at the foot of some of the outer cliffs and in receding hollows and small bays. Individual boulders tend to be rather flat on one face and rounded on the other. It is claimed (Barrow, 1906, 18) that an upper and a lower head can be seen in some localities, notably in the cliffs at Porthloo, on St Mary's and to the east of Hugh Town, which is rubble resulting from Pleistocene periglacial weathering and solifluxion (Zeuner, 1964, 27; Wright, 1937, 113–21).

Apparently cloaking this angular debris, but also a part of it, is the material termed 'rabb' or 'ram'. It is impervious, and water tends to accumulate on its surface. It is sometimes called clay, but when removed and redeposited it dries hard, setting like cement. Heath (1750, 67) recounts how it was used in buildings in place of mortar. This surface would seem to have been the foundation surface for stone-built tombs and houses, while being also used, as Heath described, as a mortar or luting agent. This rabb would seem to be an end-product of the weathering of granite head, containing quartz, orthoclase, felspar and mica, cemented, originally, by soluble silicates and iron. This process would be intensified by rainfall which is, owing to a prevailing south-westerly wind and a hilly topography, more generous than in many parts of Britain.

Accumulations of blown sand have formed considerable dunes along the south facing and south-westerly inner shores of the islands. These result in the first place from what must have been the relatively rapid destruction by the sea of considerable easily-eroded areas and in the second from their subsequent life as sandy flats and thus collecting areas for the wind. Earlier phases of this sand accumulation are now mantled by soil and covered by vegetation. A good example is the sand which filled the shallow valley and made the earlier lower part of the Halangy 'village' uninhabitable. More recent would seem to be the dunes on the south side of St Martin's and their continuum, now cut by Crow Sound, on the northern extremity of St Mary's at Bar Point. Tresco's southern extremity, Crow Point, has its sand dunes, presumably derived from Samson Flats, as has the neck of Samson.

A superficial deposit that has exercised considerable influence on the destiny of man in the Isles of Scilly is the sub-angular flint and greensand chert gravel to be found in certain places along the northern edges of the northern islands and particularly at 100–160ft Ordnance Datum on Chapel Down, St Martin's. Pieces of flint range from hazel nut to potato in size, but in cliff sections and on beaches lumps as large as Rugby footballs can be found. That this source of good raw material was attractive to early man is shown by the large numbers of flint implements and waste flakes, patently from pebble flint, that are found either as surface scatters or associated with early habitation sites and tombs.

This flint and gravel deposit has in the past been thought of as having been laid down by the sea in the Tertiary period many millennia before the appearance of men. There is also the view that it derives from the Antrim glacial tills, having been transported by sea-ice and dropped offshore during the Pleistocene period, as in Cornwall (Barton, 1964, 142). Storm waves would then, down the years, bring pebbles inshore on to beaches. Yet again, Thomas (1957–8, 11) suggests that southern shore flint could come from the south-eastern English chalk or from some submerged bed in the Channel. Mitchell (1960) has bracketed these St Martin's deposits with the St Erth Beds and Hele Gravels as evidence of a Lower Pleistocene 200ft high sea-level. However, recent research, discussed below, has shown that these gravels on St Martin's derive from an actual ice-sheet which covered the north-western part of the islands.

The evidence of Pleistocene high sea-levels on the Isles of Scilly has been observed and documented by Dollar (1957–8). He has found indications of raised beaches on St Mary's at 25ft, 44ft, and 64ft above Ordnance Datum. There is also a summit erosion surface at about 100ft. Large water-worn boulders dug up in about 1880 close by the Old Guard Room at the entrance to the Garrison above Hugh Town (A. Gibson and H. Gibson, 1932, 15), and placed on the walls bordering the road, might be from the 64ft series. At Old Town Bay, Carn Leh is a fossil stack of the 25ft shore-line. It is notched at 44ft and has a summit at 66ft. On Tresco, at New Grimsby, there is a fossil promontory, Vane Hill, with wave-cut notches, the bases of erstwhile sea-cliffs, at 44ft and 64ft. Head, capped by chalk flints, greensand chert and killas, was observed at Cromwell's Castle and on the 100ft summit-surface which is Castle Down. This is part of, or derived from, the deposits on Chapel Down, St Martin's. At Piper's Hole, the north-eastern extremity of Tresco, a raised beach at 25ft is well marked by the beach conglomerate which also forms part of the roof of the well-known cave of that name. That this beach formed part of the roof of the cave has long been known although its significance was not recognised. On St Martin's, Chapel Down provides a number of gulley sections through the 25ft beach. There are also several promontories and stacks of the 44ft and 64ft shores. In the flanks of White Island's north-easterly direction-facing

Chad Girt the whole series are visible, thus providing the type-succession for Pleistocene deposits in the Isles of Scilly.

Recently (Mitchell and Orme, 1967) evidence has been adduced for an actual Pleistocene ice invasion of the Isles of Scilly from the Irish Sea. Certain of the so-called logan stones, that is perched blocks, must result from proximity to glaciation, while the frost-shattering of the south hill of Samson is clear and unambiguous. Indeed, the tangled blocks which surround the more prominent Scillonian carns also originated in the same manner. Peninnis Head, St Mary's, is an excellent example as are the rocks scattered across the north end of Tresco (a veritable *mer des roches*). On the northern headlands of St Martin's can be seen the moranic material denoting the proximity of the ice-sheet. Melt-water run-off, at a time of low sea-level, could account for such features as the deep channel between Bryher and Tresco and its linear continuum, the low land between Porth Mellon and Old Town Bay, St Mary's. Indeed, the general north-west to south-east run of declivities, such as that separating St Agnes and Gugh, or cirque-like Holy Vale, on St Mary's, may reflect erstwhile periglacial run-off and erosion.

Appreciation of the submergence of a considerable area of the Isles of Scilly, the archaeological implications of which are discussed in the next chapter, giving us the archipelago of the present time begins with Borlase (1753, 1756). He adduced the already quoted 'certain evidences that the Islands last mentioned [Tresco, Bryher and Samson] were once one continued tract of land'. Reference to this Neothermal transgression was made by Barrow (1906), Reid (1913, 100, 106) and Ward (1922, 49–51). The last writer also refers to the (earlier) raised beaches 'particularly well preserved on the Cornish side of the Scilly Isles'. Crawford's (1927) classic paper is still the most comprehensive account of the problems of recent marine transgression in Scilly. However, Hencken (1932, 31–3) outlined matters while later, following upon his work in Ireland, Movius (1942, 290) referred to Scilly as did Daniel (1950, 24–6) when he studied the chamber tombs. But much detailed work remains to be done upon the sequential mechanics of the fission into islands and the complex shifts and chronology involved.

GEOLOGY, TOPOGRAPHY AND ENVIRONMENT

A sight of the Isles of Scilly from a vantage point such as the coastguard tower on Telegraph Hill, St Mary's, shows that at low tide the extent of the islands is vastly greater than at high tide and that very little depression of the sea-level, or elevation of the land, would convert them into one large island. Extensive sand flats are exposed all about the inner shores of the main islands and some, such as White Island and St Martin's, Gugh and St Agnes, Old Man and Teän, which are separate at high tide, are joined together. There is shallow water from Pednathise Head in the Western Rocks to Round Island and White Island, and from Maiden Bower to Menawethen. Picturesque and detailed stories abound of how, at low spring-tides, people have walked from St Mary's to St Martin's, from there to the Eastern Islands or to Tresco, and from Tresco to Bryher and Samson (Mothersole, 1919, 169; Gibson, 1932, 44, 89). Crawford (1927, 11) designed a map which suggested the present 10 fathom line as the ancient shore of Scilly. On this the present islands became eminences on one larger island about 7 miles long and less than 6 miles wide, with a long narrow peninsula projecting some 3 miles to the south-west. This would involve a reduction of sea-level by some 60ft which is by no means excessive if the estimates of low sea-level for the Last Glaciation are accepted (Zeuner, 1964, 306).

Not only in the Isles of Scilly, but all about southern Britain the coastline has differed from that of today. The evidence for this is in the submerged forests, peat beds and other ancient surfaces, covered by clays and muds, many being some 50ft below present-day high-water level. They were first studied in detail by Clement Reid (1913) and have been subsequently summarised by Movius (1942, 288-93) and Godwin (1956, 23-7). What must be appreciated, however, is that the submerged forests, submerged peats and submerged soils are no more than evidence of submergence in general terms, for they have formed at all times during Neothermal times, and it is misleading in the extreme to conceive of the 'Submerged Forest' period.

With a coastline standing some 5 to 10 fathoms farther out than at present, Britain would differ only slightly since the separation from the continent by the breaching of the English Channel chalk and the submergence of the greater part of the North Sea floor took place quite early (Clark, 1936; Oakley, 1943; Godwin, 1956, 23). However, low-lying land would have stretched out into most of what are now bays and estuaries: into Mount's Bay, Falmouth and St Austell bays, into the Solent, around the Thames estuary and the coast as far as the Humber among other places.

Besides eustatic rise of sea-level there has been isostatic movement of land in Britain. Thus in the north and in Scotland there has been land emergence. There seems good reason to locate the hinge of Neothermal tilting in the British Isles somewhere near an east-west line from the Humber to Anglesey. South of this, downward tilting of the coast has prevailed and this has accentuated the effects of submergence due to the general eustatic rise in sea-level. With this in mind the implications for Cornwall and the Isles of Scilly in the extreme south-west are clear. For the interplay of isostatic land movement and the eustatic rise of the sea-level, leading to transgression, were not constant. The melting of the ice brought about rapid rise in ocean level by about 6000 BC. Thereafter, during the dry climatic optimum of Atlantic times (Godwin, 1956, 62, Fig 29) it rose only slightly and there would appear to have been relative stability for some two millennia. At about 500 BC, which broadly corresponds with the beginning of the Iron Age in Britain, there is considerable evidence, principally from palaeobotanical sources, of rapid climatic deterioration. Thereupon, in Roman times, there was a minor eustatic rise of sea-level. This is evident in the uppermost clays and silts of such regions as the Wash and the Somerset Levels, and is also abundantly documented in archaeological terms, particularly about the coasts at the western end of the English Channel. There are, for example, the well-known half-submerged stone circles and cremation cemetery at Er Lannic, in Brittany (Le Rouzic, 1930). At Yelland, in Devon (Rogers, 1946), a stone row and a Late Neolithic flint industry have been recorded from a submerged surface, while at Brean Down in Somerset (Dobson, 1931, 35; ApSimon, Donovan and Taylor, 1960-1), where the Mendips meet the Bristol Channel, sherds of bell and pot-beaker were found below present tide level. The upper limits, in time, of this submergence are evident in the Isles of Scilly (Ashbee, 1954, 25), for cist-graves of Roman times have been found cut in cliffs and on foreshores below present-day high-water mark.

Scillonian submergence appears to be local and unrelated to the mainland sequences so far as they are known. For the sea is eating into glacial deposits which stand some 30ft higher in nearby Cornwall. Clearly there is no question of local marine transgression, therefore there has been some subsidence of the basic granite boss. This boss lies on the limits of the 40 fathom isobath and, indeed, at no great distance from the edge of the continental shelf as delineated by the 50 fathom isobath. In these circumstances the Isles of Scilly, as in so many things, are subject to their own laws and usages. The cutting-up and fragmentation of the erstwhile granite cupola took place in the distant geological past. All the rocks and islands that remain are the more resistant or higher parts of the one-time land-mass of which the lower parts have been submerged and etched away by the sea. An appreciation of the processes by which the sea reduced Scilly to its present form can be made from scrutiny of coastal topography about the inner shores of the islands. Everywhere today, even about these inner shores, where the huge Atlantic rollers never exert their full force, wave-erosion reduces inexorably and annually more of the blanket of soft solifluxion deposits. Bays have been eaten out, and islands even broken right through by the sea in recent times, like Old Man where a surface was exposed, 3ft below the present height of the modern turf, in which was a cist-grave (Tebbutt, 1934). Such exposures add to the sum total of shore-sand area and in this way collecting grounds are formed for sand duning. Sand-bars block some bays, bringing about the formation of lagoons. The great sand dunes on St Martin's, at Crow Bar, on the neck of Samson, and the remains of dunes at the foot of Halangy Down, could all derive from the areas exposed when this considerable area of low-lying land was submerged by the sea.

Barrow (1906) in his Geological Survey memoir, appreciated the wind-borne character of the dunes when he observed both how the granite masses were united by granite waste products and that sand dunes of disparate ages abounded. Indeed, the sand's granite origin is often dramatically seen when a glimpse is caught of its dazzling whiteness, this distinction being a quality of quartz and white feldspar composition. Barrow was of the view that the spectacular dunes which extend across St Martin's, and cloak much of the southern end of Tresco and the northern extremity of St Mary's, derived from an ancient bar of blown sand and head now submerged beneath the interior sea about which the islands lie.

There are extensive areas of blown sands which have developed in relatively recent times on the coasts of both sides of the Bristol Channel. They ultimately result from the interplay of marine transgression and the marked land subsidence of the south-west and thus are a wider aspect of those processes which have produced the present state of the Isles of Scilly. These blown sand areas, known in Cornwall as towans (Barton, 1964, 164) can be seen chiefly on its exposed north-western coasts where at the present time cliffs are low or absent. Here ample areas are exposed at low water for sand to be borne inland by the prevailing winds. Indeed, such sand is a constant threat to agricultural land, though arrested in some measure by the planting of marram grass. Dunes along the Hayle River are some 200ft wide, while near Perranporth they have reached a height of 270ft.

Sand dunes overwhelmed the church of St Piran near Perranporth at an early date, and have buried other churches and villages. The Iron Age cemetery at Harlyn Bay (Bullen, 1912, 12, Pl 2) was beneath 12 to 15ft of sand, while dunes put an end to the Dark Age hamlet at Mawgan Porth (Bruce-Mitford, 1956, 196). Between Newquay and Perranporth (Harding, 1950) several yards of green turf flanking the dunes have been seen to become completely covered in the course of a few hours, and collections made of Mesolithic, Iron Age and Medieval materials have provided evidence of the progressive sanding of this coast.

The problems of the sand-dune areas of the South Wales coast have been discussed in detail by Higgins (1933). Here local traditions exist of besanding from storms during the thirteenth to fifteenth centuries, while archaeology has shown that sand was already present on certain sites at least during the later prehistoric periods. During the Middle Ages, despite the fact that erosion on this coast was taking place, nothing is known as to the condition of the sand deposits. While erosion was still active in the nineteenth century, the dunes were stabilised by plant-cover. On the extreme west of the Pembrokeshire coast the blown sand was, it is thought, post-Neolithic in date, but it had reached its present position, in the low areas, by the Bronze Age. However, it had probably not reached the higher parts occupied by it today. Further up the Bristol Channel, sand movement, even from apparently grassed dunes, appears to have continued almost into this century. Along the South Wales coast the basic causes of dune formation were the same as those which obtained in Cornwall and the Isles of Scilly (Reid, 1913). Erosion, marine transgression together with land subsidence, the formation of bars across bays and the separation of smaller land areas, as for example Caldey Island, are familiar patterns.

Such sand-duning as has been discussed above is an integral part of the progresses of submergence still to be seen taking place in Scilly. So clear is the abounding evidence, and so opaque and varied are the attendant 'Lyonesse' legends, that attention was focused upon it more than two-and-a-half centuries ago. Borlase (1756, 63) was stimulated by the sight of the stone hedges descending from a hill and disappearing beneath the water and equated these, and other observations, with what he thought was preserved by tradition, though he tartly remarked that it was 'greatly enlarg'd and obscured by fable'. Numerous early essays, often leaning largely upon Borlase, inevitably followed. De La Beche in his 1839 Report gave a lucid account of the appearance of the submergence problem at that time. This, and much of the miscellaneous early literature, was summarised by Barrow (1906) in his Geological Survey memoir.

Archaeological visitors to the islands have found themselves inescapably involved in 'Lyonesse' problems. Crawford (1927) strips this legend of Lyonesse to its essentials and his essay, discussed in a subsequent chapter, is the basic work. Hencken (1932) and Daniel (1950) found that their treatments of the numbers of chambered tombs drew them into it, as did also O'Neil (1949). Basically it is the problem of how large a land-mass was Scilly between about 2000 BC and AD 500, the period of time which encompasses so much of the evidence of early occupation. So varied is the evidence, both direct and indirect, and so wide is the range of estimates that have been put forward, that the matter has been treated separately in Chapter 3.

The climate of the Isles of Scilly, in common with that of western Scotland with its numerous islands, of western Ireland, of Cornwall, and to a lesser degree of the whole of south-west England and western Wales, can be termed extremely oceanic. This means that there is an equable temperature and a lack of variation between day and night temperatures especially in winter. Rainfall is fairly evenly spread throughout the seasons and frost and snow are entirely absent in normal years. The prevailing wind is from the south-west and the air it brings comes from the sub-tropics around the Azores. It is this equable temperature which accounts for the success of the basic industry of the islands, the growing of early daffodils and narcissi in open fields protected from winter's gales by high fences (hedges) of escallonia, pittosporum and veronica.

From the sea, from the air, and from any point of vantage, the long narrow fields with their evergreen fences, stand apart from the fern and heather 'downlands' about them and denote the measure of man's success against the exigencies of the environment. Yet the 'unbroken' downs, despite their appearance, such as Porth Hellick on St Mary's, or Chapel Down on St Martin's, are just as much the end-products of man's activities as are the chequer-board, green-surrounded bulb gardens. Like the landscape of the mainland of England and Ireland today, they show almost nothing of their original character.

Scilly's present-day weather conditions, like those of the rest of the British Isles, are ultimately the product of the Post-Pleistocene 'Neothermal' climatic amelioration. The European forest belts, at one point, moved northwards to latitudes higher than they now occupy and ascended the mountains, to descend again during climatic degeneration.

Page 49   1a Dr William Borlase. Portrait by Allen Ramsey at Truro Museum

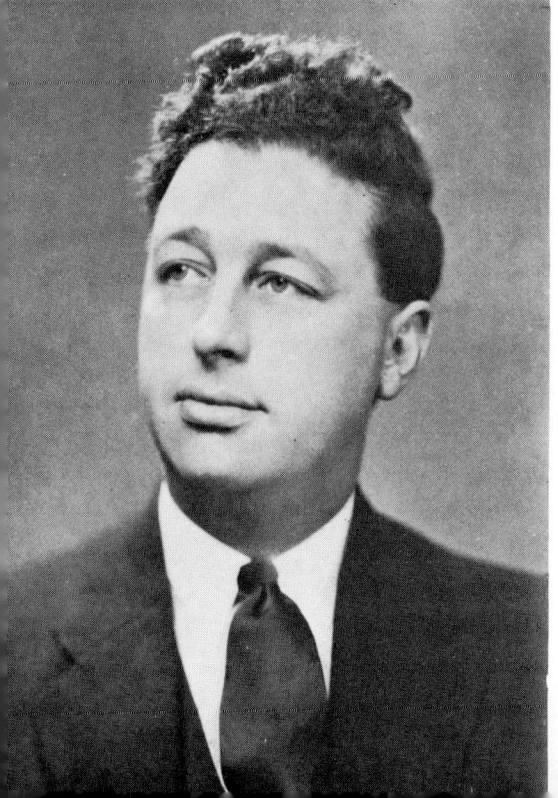

1b B. H. St J. O'Neil, Chief Inspector of Ancient Monuments, 1945–54

Page 50 2a Natural granite basins on Porth Hellick Down, St Mary's
2b A submerged wall on Samson Flats at low tide

However, such fluctuations would not have affected the extreme south-west more than marginally. Thus, by about 3000 BC the island and islets that are now the Isles of Scilly, were like Cornwall, Wales and Ireland, forest clad to their very shores. Only such factors as soil, incidental climatic extremes, streams, lakes and salt water inhibited its growth. Oak, ash and elm were the dominant species with, perhaps, some pine.

The foregoing is assumed from what is known of the general environmental history of the British Isles. It must be noted that there are on the islands specific localities which would repay investigation with a view to establishing the particular Scillonian pattern. Heather clad downlands, such as Porth Hellick, have acid soils of podsol character, which might well preserve pollen grains (Dimbleby; 1955; 1967); and on St Mary's, there are the marshes, initially observed by Borlase (1756, 70). These, the Lower Moors between Downderry and Old Town Lane, and the Higher Moors, inland from Porth Hellick, and their extension to the bottom of Holy Vale, would appear to be peat-choked one-time lakes, of which the Porth Hellick fishpond is the only remaining sheet of open water. A programme of boring into the silts and peats of these areas could yield significant information.

CHAPTER 3

Submergence and Scillonian Archaeology

Any account of marine transgression in terms of Scillonian archaeology must begin with reference to the submerged walls on Samson Flats. These were Borlase's 'Hedges descending from the Hill, and running many feet under the level of the sea towards Trescaw' (1756, 63). It was these walls on Samson Flats in fact which stimulated him to write his pioneer and prescient paper (Borlase, 1753). O. G. S. Crawford on his visit sought out Borlase's vantage points for the purposes of photography (Crawford, 1927, 6) and then availing himself of the spring tides he walked, with Alexander Gibson, out on to the sands. He wrote of the walls:

> We found ... that the line of stones was undoubtedly a wall of human construction. It consisted of a number of boulders and stones of about the size and shape of a milestone, some of them still standing upright. All round on either side of the wall were scattered the smaller stones which once filled the spaces between the larger uprights. Elsewhere the sands were almost bare. The fact that some of these stones still remained standing proved conclusively that the thing was artificial, but indeed its general appearance left no doubt in our minds with regard to this.
>
> The wall was about 250 yards long, and ended at a bare, rocky eminence called Black Ledge. On the further (north-eastern) side of this rock, a line of stones was visible, half covered by the sea even at this exceptionally low tide. I waded out to it in the hope of being

able to discover whether it was another of these walls; but the water was over my knees and the tide was on the point of turning, so I could not satisfy myself on this point.

Crawford and Gibson waded from Samson to Tresco, 'though neither of us dry-shod', but were too late to wade on to Bryher. For on Bryher, as he had seen from his 25in Ordnance Survey Map, were marked some good examples of seemingly prehistoric stone walls. He later found these and observed that such walls are to be seen on all the larger islands and some of the smaller uninhabited ones. His view was that they were field walls as on Samson Flats (Plate 2b) and he saw many modern walls built in the same way besides a wall in the course of construction. The technique that he saw involved the setting up of large upright stones some few yards apart, and their filling in with smaller stones, whenever possible obtained from the area to be enclosed.

Crawford argued that the boulder-hedge on Samson Flats could not have possibly been built when the land stood at its present level on account of the fact that it is completely submerged except at ordinary low tide. He then had to face the question of how it had resisted destruction by the sea waves. It was observed that the Samson Flats are within the inland sea of Scilly and are thus protected from the huge Atlantic rollers. Erosion too, he suggested, would be less violent than around the outer shores. To account for the sand he quoted Barrow's memoir (Barrow, 1906) and suggested that before being submerged the low land, which is now the flats, was sand blanketed. The flats as they are today would be this submerged sand-blanketing secure from tidal scour. Indeed, something of this sanding of the erstwhile flats can be seen on the neck of Samson at the present time, the more ancient sand dunes being a remnant.

Many years after his visit to the Isles of Scilly a paper was published in *Antiquity*, the journal which Crawford founded and edited for three decades, on 'Prehistoric Fishing Methods in South Africa' (Goodwin, 1946). These methods involved the use of dry-stone walls built out on sandy, gently shelving shores and in river mouths. An enclosure was

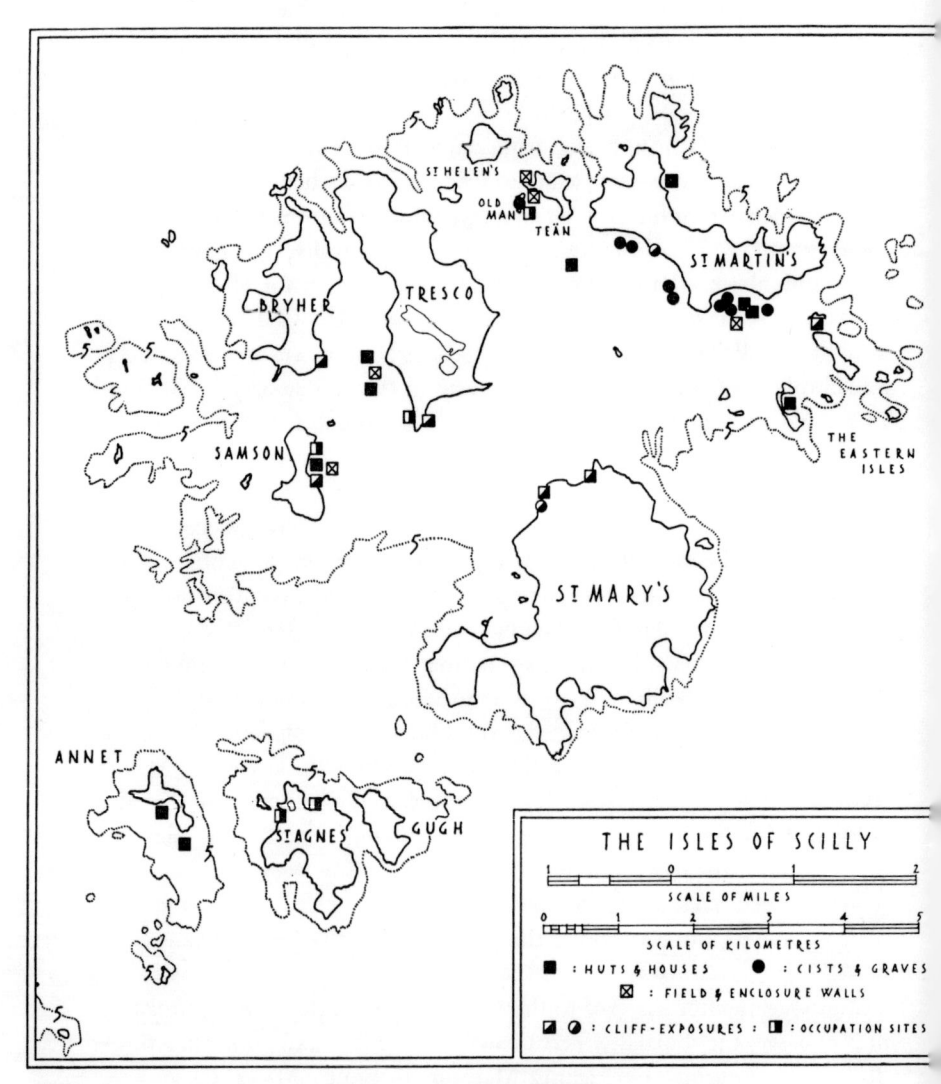

Fig 4 Marine contour map showing submerged and cliff-exposed sites

built with dry-stone to such a height that normal high tides would cover it and allow fish to swim freely over the enclosed area. As the tide fell, the water ran out through the interstices between the stones. The fish were thus trapped and could be caught and clubbed by hand. Indeed, it was but a permanent application of seine netting methods. In a short editorial comment Crawford called attention to medieval fish-weirs on the English coasts (notably three on Southampton Water, two of which belonged to the town and one to Queen's College, Oxford) and also observed that remains of stone walls are to be seen on the shore near Minehead and in the Isles of Scilly. Of the last, he commented that it now seems possible that these too, namely the stone walls on Samson Flats, were fish-traps. At the same time he remarked that were this the case the conclusions reached in his article (Crawford, 1927) would not hold good. This point was subsequently taken up by Piggott (1954, 264), quoting Goodwin (1946), who remarked that the alleged submerged field-walls often quoted as a point in favour of comparatively recent subsidence seem in fact more likely to be those of medieval fish-weirs.

This ingenious alternative suggestion regarding the function of the submerged walls on Samson Flats does not mean that they should be disregarded in future. For they neither face the open sea nor do the boulders of which they were built seem appropriate to prevent fish from escaping, although they might retain and discourage them. Again, were they fish-traps one might legitimately expect repetition and outlines appropriate to marine topography and this is clearly not the case.

While the walls on Samson Flats, and the literature that they have attracted, are by far the best known of the alleged evidence of submergence in Scilly, there is much more that can be observed (Fig 4) either submerged, on foreshores, or else in the process of erosion. At the same time there are further features, not all entirely reliable but all, in a general sense, substantiating the first category.

Since the present writer's visit to Samson Flats in 1950, and preceding his subsequent visits to the Isles of Scilly from 1964 onwards, a comprehensive survey of the archaeological evidence pertaining to submergence had been undertaken by Professor Charles Thomas. This was work supplementary to his excavations on the island of Teän in 1956 and was impelled by his observations made on the shore of that island. Visits were made by boat, during the extreme low waters of early September in that year, to Samson Flats and other places where submerged phenomena might be seen. Submerged walls were the prime objective of the operation and in connection with these an extensive collection of flint artifacts was assembled. It will be remembered that Crawford (1927, 6, Fig 1) had collected a number from Samson Flats, while the present writer found a few more heavily water-worn examples during his visits in 1950 and 1969. In 1956 nearly a thousand were amassed from the shores of Samson and Teän. From them it would seem that the flint industry was for the most part, like other flint industries recorded in Scilly (Ashbee, 1954), devoted to the production of scrapers.

Reference was made in the preceding chapter to the numerous observations, made since the earlier part of the eighteenth century, of evidence for submergence in Scilly. Some of these are quasi-geological and often of doubtful quality. On the other hand many factors are of an archaeological character although associated with natural processes. Almost all are relative to specific islands and thus reflect observations made from these. Thus, before embarking upon a general discussion of the implications involved, a summary of these marine and cliff-exposed features is desirable. Fuller details of incidental discoveries, and such excavation work as has been undertaken, are in relevant chapters throughout the book.

Marine features, that is for the most part walls, hut foundations and burial cists observed below or at about high-water mark are as follows:

Annet. Borlase (1756, 40) describes how 'the sand being washed away a few years since by some high tides, discovered the walls of a house; but what is more remarkable, there are some *Rock-basons* on several large stones, which, lying at present under full sea-mark, are covered by the Sea when the Tide is in ...' This house is presumably the ruins of houses on the beach recorded by Troutbeck (1794, 157).

Great Arthur. An 'archaeological diving group' (Kingsford-Curram, 1966) located, in about 4 fathoms of water, at a point east of and adjacent to Arthur Head, what they described as a 'quay'. This was a natural promontory, 30yd long and not connected to the island. It had, allegedly, been levelled on the top, and the sides cut so that they dropped vertically 15ft to the sea bed. The Rev H. J. Whitfield (1852, 114) records the submerged remains of a harbour near Arthur and an aged Scillonian told him that it is known as 'Arthur's Quay'. An alternative explanation is that it is the submerged extension of a carn levelled by marine plantation at a period of low sea-level.

Little Arthur. O'Neil (1961, 9) noted a piece of walling on the shore which 'showed from pottery and other evidence that it belonged to the Early Iron Age'. Excavation in 1951 disclosed the remains of a substantial hut. During 1935, Mr Alec Gray dug into the sandy neck, below high-water mark, which joins Little and Middle Arthur. He found bones, one pointed, limpet shells, patches of black clay and one fragment of coarse pottery associated with a large flat stone (Ashbee, 1972, 42).

It is not impossible that these two separate observations are of aspects of the same site.

Bryher. A wall on Bryher Flats opposite Tresco (Troutbeck, 1794, 144; Borlase, 1753, 63). The 'Hedges on this Ridge, which is now mostly laid bare by the violent spray of the Sea' (Borlase, 1756, 56) are clearly on land. No trace of this wall could be found in 1956.

St Martin's. A cist (Plate 3a) on the shore between Crethus (Cruthers) Hill and English Island Carn, at about high-water mark, allegedly contained a contracted inhumation burial. Nearby, to the west, were two or three other cists of the same type, and many years before yet others were seen, both round this bay and 'at Lawrence's to the west of Crethus Hill' (Crawford, 1928, 420, Pl II). During 1949 B. H. StJ. O'Neil excavated a small barrow-covered cist on Par Beach. A sherd of Bronze Age pottery was close by, but unstratified (Ashbee, 1954, 25). Lower down the beach from the cist two lines of stone hedges have become visible in recent years. An oval house foundation of Early Iron Age affinities has been excavated on the same beach (O'Neil, 1950, 9). Half of a round Romano-British hut was found and examined there by the Rev H. A. Lewis in 1948 (O'Neil, 1949, 163). A few yards to the west, other structures have been investigated which seem to have been parts of actual dwellings. The barrow-covered cist referred to above, 15ft down the beach from the hut and dwellings, which may be one of those noted by Crawford, and another cist 300ft to the east, are mentioned in this passage. O'Neil excavated another oval hut on this beach during 1951.

Troutbeck (1794, 112) tells of 'cist' graves found shortly before his time on the sanded low lands at high tides, near Middle Town at a point designated 'Neck of the Pool'. These may be the cists that Crawford (1928, 420) described as 'at Lawrence's to the west of Crethus Hill'. Lewis (1948, 8) lists under Higher Town Bay that within living memory heavy gales and low spring tides revealed burial cists close to the small upright stone still in place, at about the high-water line of neap tides, where a complete crouched burial was seen from which the skull was said to have been removed. From these confused accounts it would seem that here on the southern side of St Martin's the remains of, perhaps, two separate cist-grave cemeteries have been caught sight of submerged on the sand-flats, that at the eastern end associated with houses.

St Mary's. The remains of a lagoon barrier or duned bar which stretched from Bar Point, St Mary's, to just east of Middle Town, St Martin's, and which is termed Crow Bar, have been looked upon as part of a man-made causeway between the two islands. There is no evidence for this; it is plainly a natural feature (O'Neil, 1950, 4). A supposed 'paved causeway', sometimes alleged to be a Roman road, is said to connect Tobaccoman's Point on Tresco with Bar Point, St Mary's (Gibson, 1932, 89; Leechman, 1946). Photographs of this, taken at an extreme low water during the last century are said to exist. This again is natural and may well be exposures of the Tobaccoman's or

Diamond Ledges as shown on the Admiralty Chart (1906). See also Dunbar (1958, 147-53).

Samson. On Samson Flats there are the walls observed by Crawford (1927) and illustrated from the flats (Crawford, 1927, Pl I, 1; II, 1) and the air (Crawford, 1927, Pl III). These were seen by Borlase (1753; 1756, 63) and Troutbeck (1794, 144). Traces of hut foundations are indicated in Troutbeck's account. Crawford (1927, 7 fn) remarked that Alexander Gibson had reported that he had been told of similar submerged walls between the west coast of Samson and White Island. A square structure 2m across and just below high-water mark was recorded by Mr John Layard, in 1934, in East Par (Porth). It yielded 'thin biscuit coloured pottery' (Ashbee, 1972, 41).

Teän and Old Man. A cist excavated (Tebbutt, 1934, 302) on the shore of the central waist of Old Man, now breached by the sea, yielded atypical Romano-British brooches. On the flats that are Teän's southern shore, Charles Thomas has planned a system of walls, mostly between high- and low-water mark, a few continuing below low-water mark. There are also huts below high-water mark connected with the West Porth wall system. There are also possible foundations in East Porth at about high-water mark (Ashbee, 1955, 198). A hut was noted on the east side of St Helen's Par and was photographed by Mr Alec Gray.

Off Teän, and just north of West Broad Ledge, Professor Charles Thomas and Mr Bernard Wailes saw, in about a fathom at very low water, a group of two or more huts of circular plan. They appeared as rings of large stone blocks, seaweed festooned, which contrasted well against the lighter sandy sea bottom. They had been pointed out by Mr Goddard, the boatman, in September 1956, when the tide, on a still day, was some 7ft below mean sea-level.

Tresco. Submerged walls are alleged to have been observed off the west coast of Tresco (Crawford, 1927, 7 fn). These may be those on Tresco Flats noted as walls, fields and ruined huts. Gibson (1932) speaks of 'six feet below the sand'. They were visited by Professor Charles Thomas in 1956.

Charles Thomas has drawn attention to references regarding a supposed causeway connecting Tresco Abbey and St Helen's (Mothersole, 1919, 62) and comments that since this would cross two deep channels, it is physically improbable and must be dismissed.

Cliff-exposed features are burial cists and the indications of habitation sites. From time to time down the years, storms and resulting cliff erosion have brought about fresh exposures, as for example on Nornour in 1962. Others such as in Halangy Porth, St Mary's, have been known and observed for more than half a century. This latter and the burial cist close by are but indications of extensive sites beneath the bulb gardens to landward. Such cliff-exposed sites are:

Bryher. Mr Alec Gray noted, just below Bonfire Carn, at the extreme south-east point of the island, a hut floor exposed in the cliff-face. Stones bounded it, while flints and pottery were upon it. Some 10cm of sand, mantled by the modern surface, was above it (Ashbee, 1972, 40, Fig 13).

Nornour. The great storm of 1962 exposed indications of a stone building in the low sandy cliffs on the south side of the island. Romano-British brooches and coins were picked out. Subsequent excavation has revealed a wide range of structures to landward (Dudley, 1967).

St Agnes. Mr Alec Gray discovered, immediately below the lifeboat house at Periglis, an exposure of black earth with bones and a good deal of pottery of the 'usual type'. He describes also how, in the south corner of Perkillier (Porth Killier), an ancient surface inclines downwards and is lost beneath sand and shingle. He obtained from this exposure a considerable amount of pottery associated with shells, charcoal and bones (Ashbee, 1972, 42).

St Martin's. A cist was found in the cliff-face between Knackyboy Cairn and Yellow Rock Carn (Lewis, 1949).

St Mary's. Half of a cist of Porth Cressa type can be seen in the cliff at the southern end of Halangy Porth (Ashbee, 1954, 25). In the middle of the same porth are exposed the walls of huts (Plate 3b) and the end of a drain (Ashbee, 1965, 36), an earlier phase of the settlement on the hill-slope above (Ashbee, 1955). These remains are upon an ancient soil covered by about 3ft of sand upon which the modern soil has grown. They were noted by George Bonsor more than sixty years ago (Hencken, 1932, 30; 1933, 16, Fig 4) and at that time a shell midden was exposed.

Samson. Mr Alec Gray found extensive signs of occupation on both sides of East Par (East Porth). On the south side there were traces of stone structures which, in two or three places, ran up beneath the sand dunes. These structures were associated with flints and pottery. Mr Gray remarked that most of the pottery was of the 'usual type' (Ashbee, 1972, 41).

Teän and Old Man. Pottery and worked flints found in the cliff-face (Lewis, 1948, 9).

Tresco. About 50yd north-east of the landing slip at Carn Near, Mr Alec Gray found a layer of soil 30cm in depth which was covered by blown sand. There was much flint and fragments of the 'usual' rough pottery. Close by was walling running up into covering sand. On the west side of Carn Near, in the corner of Apple Tree Bay, he found pottery and flints in the cliff-face (Ashbee, 1972, 38).

These features, both marine and 'cliff-exposed', are located almost exclusively in and around the interior shallow waters of the archipelago. From the evidence from both categories, ie the accounts of marine features disappearing into or buried in the sand and the sand-buried sections still to be seen at certain cliff-exposed sites, it seems clear that fields and dwelling sites were abandoned in the face of blown sand. That is to say, blown sand, and its progressive extinction of plant life in fields and about homesteads, made the occupants move. As observed in the previous chapter, such movement was and still is a constant factor on the coasts of the south-west. Sand dunes on Samson, the southern end of Tresco, the southern shores of St Martin's, the northern end of St Mary's and Crow Bar, all point to prevailing wind from the south-west causing, perhaps, the besanding of a great part of the inland plain. Brooks (1949, 312) considers that there were periods of stormy winds from west or south-west before 200 BC and again from about AD 1300 to

1550, while during the intervening and succeeding periods these winds were less frequent and less strong. An optimum period of sanding before 200 BC would, in general terms, accord well with the Scillonian evidence.

Following upon the sanding would be the processes of progressive submergence. One effect of this would have been the removal of the earlier sand mantle by tidal scour, and the re-exposure of walls and other resistant features. Estimates of the degree of submergence brought about by the rising sea-level of Neothermal times, together with progressive sinking of the land of the South West, are difficult to make and have tended, recently, to become more conservative. Crawford's (1927, 11) generous estimate depicting the coastline of Scilly as it would be if the land were raised 60ft (10 fathoms) above its present level may well have been influenced by Solinus who, when writing in the third century AD, refers in the singular to *Siluram insulam* (Solinus, Polyhistor, XXIV) and by the only other ancient writer who mentions the islands, Sulpicius Severus who in about AD 400 also uses the singular. These early writers may have been relying upon earlier accounts or talking of a large island with smaller islands about it. Hencken (1932, 33), following Crawford, visualised a single large island about 7 miles in length and less than 6 miles in width, with a long narrow peninsula projecting about 3 miles to the south-west. On this island the present islands would have been low hills while the prehistoric inhabitants would have dwelt on and about the central plain, in sight of the chamber tombs all around. Daniel (1950, 25–6) observed also that very little elevation would convert all Scilly into one island and, although he remarked that Crawford's estimate depicted the coastline at one stage in prehistoric times, he thought that, in common with much of southern Britain, the Scillonian coastline had stood even some 5 to 10 fathoms further out than at present. O'Neil (1949, 4) pointed out that if a line were drawn along the 25ft marine contour, and all the land within that limit were to be raised above water, the land area of the islands would be doubled. He added, also, that a greater elevation than this would add but little more land. In a map, illustrating the islands, he showed the marine contour at 2 fathoms (12ft) and from this it can be clearly seen that this elevation would join most of the inhabited islands into a single mass and would also almost double the land area. With such a scheme, St Agnes and Gugh would be a separate island and about twice their present size, while Annet would be substantially greater in area.

The archaeological sites provide little direct evidence as to the date of the sanding or submergence. However, some relevant facts do emerge from a study of them. While the cliff-exposed sites found by Mr Alec Gray which have (Ashbee, 1972, 21) yielded pottery of the 'usual type' (which refers, as far as can be seen, to pottery comparable with that encountered at Halangy Porth and in the chamber tombs) may reflect the progressive sanding from the south-west, they do not in any way, as they are above the present high-water mark, delimit, in archaeological terms, the submergence. Again, the evidence of the submerged features is indirect. The only datable evidence, the cist on Old Man and the houses on St Martin's shores, and perhaps Teän's also, is late—Romano-British or a century or so earlier. Certain of the cists on St Martin's shore might be comparable with the smaller earlier type (Ashbee, 1952) encountered on St Mary's, but this is not conclusive. Moreover, all that have been found were at about the present high-water mark. All these later features could have been on dry land with a sea-level but very little below that of the present when they were constructed. Such a sea-level would still leave numerous other features lower and presumably earlier. Indeed, it seems inescapable that these latter must be associated with the earlier, perhaps the earliest, phases of occupation of the Isles of Scilly.

Leaving to one side the flint industries of the islands (Ashbee, 1954), a quantitive assessment of which has not as yet been made, the earliest human occupation is that of those who built the chamber tombs. With these it must be recognised that they, as we see them today, were not built simultaneously but form a pattern that emerged as the result of construction during a considerable period of time. In the absence of radiocarbon dates, there are but archaeological estimates of age. Such of these as have been made (Daniel, 1950, 164; Stone, 1952; Piggott, 1954, 266; Wailes, 1957–8, 30; Daniel, 1961, 577) broadly concur in alloting a place in the first half of the second millennium BC for the Scillonian chamber tombs. With such factors as the early radiocarbon dates for the Breton passage graves (Daniel, 1961, 580) in mind, the possibility of an earlier date for the first tombs must be envisaged, while a number may be appreciably later. In view of the foregoing, a starting date of 2000 BC for an estimate of the degree of marine transgression in Scilly is convenient.

Crawford (1927, 6) observed in his pioneer paper how the flats between Tresco, Bryher and Samson, are covered by some 10 to 12 feet of water at full sea. Charles Thomas has seen off Teän circular huts at a depth of at least 14ft below present mean sea-level. For the Samson walls to have been on dry land at the time of their construction, some 10 to 15 feet must be added to full-tide mark. This figure is suggested by approximations of the height above mean sea-level suggested by the average height of the low cliffs of remnants of the erstwhile internal Scillonian plain as, for example, at the foot of Halangy Down, St Mary's. From this, one is led to suggest that a difference between levels of the present and of the time of the construction of the Samson Walls is of the order of 30ft. For the submerged huts off Teän, Charles Thomas, taking their depth as an extreme example, has computed a difference of some 34 or 35 feet between past and present levels. In this connection, Charles Thomas has also pointed out that all the submerged structures of Scilly are contained well within a possible coastline based upon the present 2 fathom marine contour (O'Neil, 1949, map). Such a coastline would involve a mean sea-level at least 10ft lower than the average low land at that time. By this consideration a difference of some 34 to 35 feet is once again arrived at.

From the evidence of the progressive sanding, brought about by the wide sand-flats which must have marked the earlier stages of submergence, it would seem that the major processes, in their first stages, were most marked in the wide gap between the Garrison Hill, the western high extremity of St Mary's, and Samson. This is suggested by the marked indentation, into the Road, of the submarine contours, pointing to a great bay or porth eaten into the soft glacial soil of the inland plain. A further relevant fact is that the submerged features of Romano-British times are all about the inner shores of the northern islands, while their counterparts at the southern end are on land (eg the Porth Cressa and Poynter's Garden cist-graves). Yet another indication of the circumstances leading to the fragmentation of Scilly into its present form has emerged from a further assessment, and from excavations, of the settlement at Halangy Porth and Down, on St Mary's. Here, the homesteads of the chamber-tomb period were abandoned to the sand and, probably in pre-Romano-British times, a move made further up the hill. In the event this sand-enveloped, abandoned, settlement below was only partly destroyed by the sea, much of it still remaining as a cliff-exposed site.

Some further support for the foregoing has been forthcoming from examination of the submerged walls on the shores of the island of Teän. Two types of walling have been detected here, unlike those on Samson Flats. There are firstly short stretches built with double faces of medium-sized stones, one of which was seen to have a certain amount of rubble core *in situ*. The second, as shown in a square lay-out in West Porth, is essentially lines of single stones, some of good size. The former, close below the present high-water mark, have a mode of construction comparable to those of the Halangy Down huts (Ashbee, 1955, 1965, 1966) and could have a Romano-British date. Indeed, a sherd of pottery of precisely the same paste and type as the Scillonian coarse native wares was found in close association with one of them. The second type, the lines of single stones, are of the same character as those to be seen at low tides on Samson Flats.

From their degree of submergence, and their position at the southern end of the islands, it would seem likely that the walls on Samson Flats are the earliest of the submerged series. Indeed, Thomas has suggested that they could well represent remaining divisions of the one-time central Scillonian plain. Indeed, any farmer in that area would have had to clear the results of Pleistocene frost-shattering as evidenced by the *mer des roches* girdling the South Hill of Samson. Besides flint artifacts associated with these walls a sherd, of the same character as the chamber tomb wares, has been found close by one of them. Precisely similar boulder walls, now functionless, are still to be seen on many of the smaller islands, and were noted by Borlase (1756, 40 for Gugh, 51 for Northwethel, 65 for Arthur). On Kittern Hill, Gugh, such a wall links certain chamber tombs, as does one on the North Hill of Samson, and a wall is also alleged to connect others on St Mary's, at Inner Blue Carn (Hencken, 1932, 31) a little way east of Old Town. The chamber tomb on Old Man, Teän, also stands within such a wall system.

The use of stone walls for delimiting agricultural areas, contemporaneous with chamber tombs, is attested by the low wall beneath the Late Neolithic cairn containing a long cist at Millin Bay in Ireland (Collins and Waterman, 1955, 8) and perhaps by the stone wall associated with the court cairn at Behy, Co Mayo (de Válera and Ó Nuálláin, 1964, 6). Another relevant early example is the low bank of stones and soil, overlain by two stone alignments, associated with a pair of stone circles at Beaghmore, Co Tyrone (Proudfoot, 1958).

From the foregoing account of the submergence of the Isles of Scilly and the archaeological features connected with it a pattern emerges, although by no means clearly. As regards the degree of submergence, it would seem in general terms that there has been a marine transgression of the order of at least 30ft. If Crawford's original scheme (Crawford, 1927, 11) be considered excessive and one which allows a coastline lying between the 2 and 5 fathom marine contours be adopted, it would seem that the Isles of Scilly at the beginning of their human occupation, were a substantial island, with a low central plain, and smaller off-islands to the south-west. Marine transgression may, by Romano-British times, have made considerable inroads into the large island, and Samson and Bryher may even have become detached from the main mass. In Romano-British times, and for a period following, Tresco, St Martin's, the Eastern Isles and St Mary's were joined; while the northern part of the erstwhile large island still remained. This, at least, is attested by the submerged and cliff-exposed Romano-British features in the northern area and also, indirectly, by the evidence of sand accumulation and prevailing winds, discussed above.

Page 67 3a A cist exposed on the sea shore, Higher Town Bay, St Martin's, 1950

3b The wall of a hut exposed in the cliff of Halangy Porth, St Mary's, 1950

Page 68 4a The passage grave on Porth Hellick Down, St Mary's (H1:D7) showing the character of Bonsor's excavations, photographed *c* 1900

4b Bant's Carn, St Mary's (H2:D3) after replacement of fallen coverstone and jamb-stone in 1970

SUBMERGENCE AND SCILLONIAN ARCHAEOLOGY

With Scilly in this condition in Romano-British times, the use of the singular term *Siluram insulam* by Solinus and the even later reference in the singular by Sulpicius Severus, to describe what was apparently known to them, emerges as literally true. As Crawford (1927, 12) remarked, their account is not in conflict with the evidence from other sources.

The final severance, following upon which the islands assumed much of their present form, took place following upon a post-Romano-British period of marine transgression. Fields, cemeteries and huts in the northern area were submerged, while settlement contracted on to the remaining land-masses. Perhaps when the Irish missionaries found Scilly, its broken character enabled the ready establishment of a microcosm of their tradition. The islands would each facilitate the peculiar Celtic penitential exile, expressed by Adamnan as 'solitude in the pathless sea' (de Paor, 1964, 52).

CHAPTER 4

Chamber Tombs and Barrows

A chamber tomb is normally a cairn or barrow covering and containing a chamber built of large blocks, or walling, of stone and roofed with horizontally laid, large stone slabs or, exceptionally, by the technique of corbelling. Their enduring substance, distinctive architectural convention, and number, have made them one of the better-known antiquities of the western British countryside. The more prominent have attracted attention in all ages and, since the eighteenth century, speculative topographical and antiquarian writers have constantly conjectured upon their origin and character.

The Scillonian chamber tombs are strikingly similar in plan: a circular cairn with a massive kerb having in it a roughly rectangular chamber. The massive and regular kerbs are built of either large slabs and blocks or sizeable stones set in courses from which the chamber opens abruptly without incurving. The chambers, similarly built, which occupy more than half the diameter of the cairns, display subtle variations: they are either parallel-sided, wider at the distal end, or often coffin or boat-shaped in plan while the sides of the chambers are not always vertical; there is partial corbelling.

In size (Figs 5, 6) the circular chamber tombs average 20ft to 40ft in diameter, with extremes of 60ft, 70ft and 75ft in diameter. However, a small cairn of about 10ft in diameter is known, as are a few below 20ft in diameter. For the most part the entrances and long axes of Scillonian tomb chambers and their entrances are oriented (Fig 7) to the east, the north-east or the north-west, but some are aligned to all other points of

CHAMBER TOMBS AND BARROWS

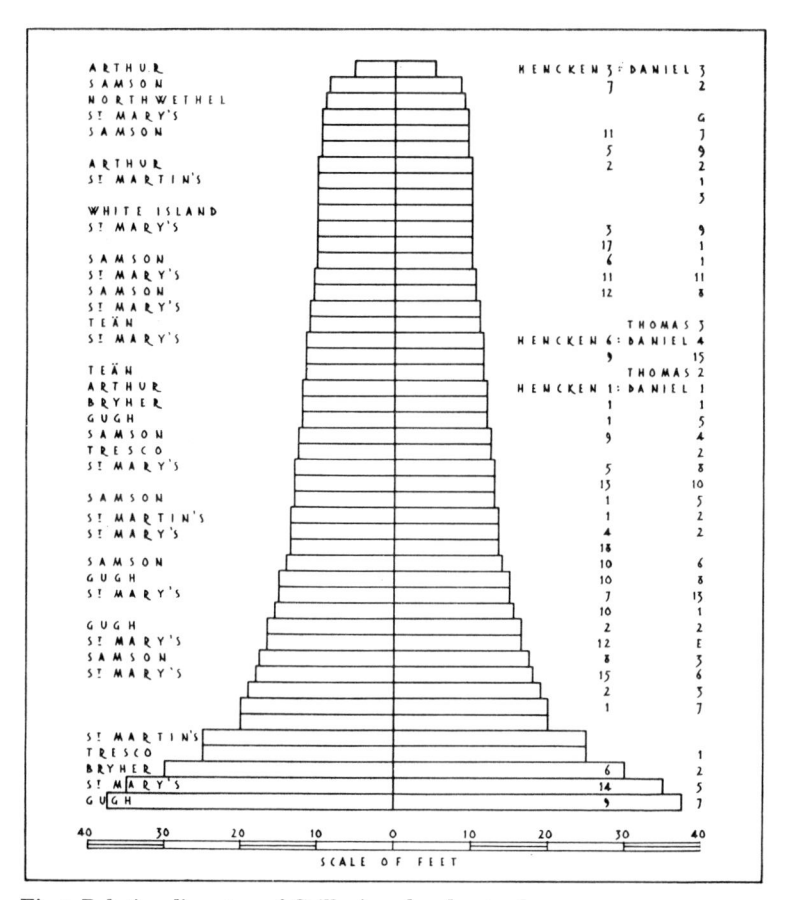

Fig 5 Relative diameters of Scillonian chamber tombs

the compass. This near-random orientation would seem to be a product of siting. Level sites are at a premium and thus the chamber tombs are generally set on slopes, and entrances were seemingly contrived, frequently but not always, to face down the slope and give an optimum view of the structure. From the facts of orientation all that could be said is that the dominant choices of axial and entrance direction might reflect some specific desire of the builders.

71

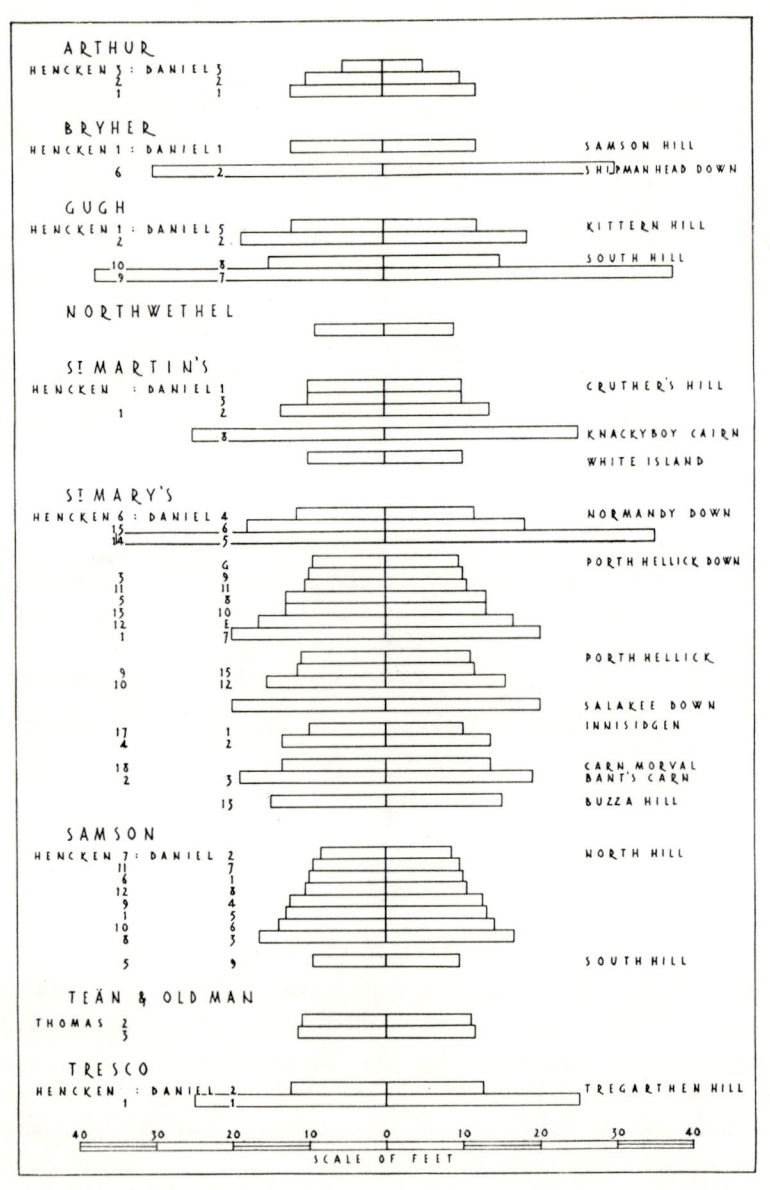

Fig 6 *Relative diameters of Scillonian chamber tombs in terms of cemeteries*

[Figure: compass rose diagram showing orientations from N.W. through N, N.N.W., N.N.E., N.E., E.N.E., E, E.S.E., S.E., S.S.E., S, S.S.E., S.E. with legend]

ORIENTATIONS OF ENTRANCES
AND LONG AXES OF SCILLONIAN
CAIRN CHAMBERS

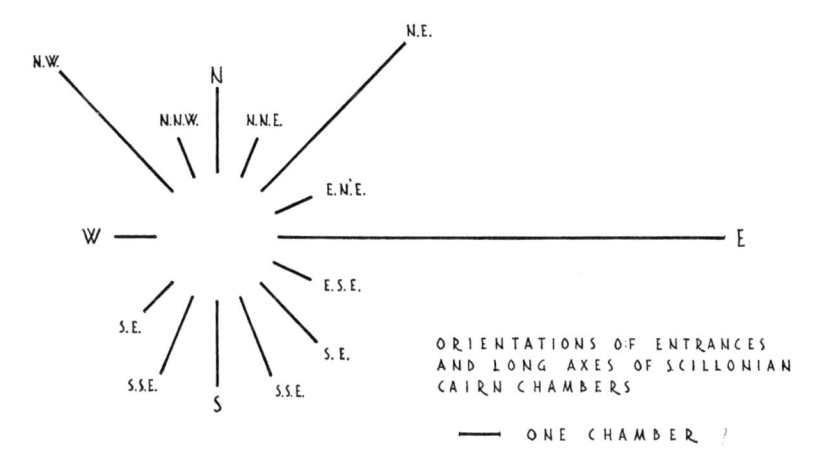

——— ONE CHAMBER

Fig 7 Orientation of Scillonian chamber tombs

Any visitor to the Isles of Scilly is surprised at the number of chamber tombs still standing, as he is by their considerable variety of size. At least fifty identifiable chamber tombs is the oft-quoted number, to which total can be added many barrows and ruined sites. An inventory with details of every tomb in Scilly is a long-felt want and such a survey should not be beyond the powers of active individuals or institutions.

Some mention must be made, at this point, of the varying names by which the Scillonian chamber tombs have found their place in archaeological literature. Borlase (1756) called them 'sepulchral *Burrows*', 'stone *Burrows*', 'Caves' or 'as they are call'd by some authors, *Barrows*'. Bonsor, and Hencken (1932; 1933) after him used the term 'covered gallery', although the largest chamber tomb on Porth Hellick Down and Bant's Carn, St Mary's, were termed passage graves. Childe (1940, 75) comments that 'A small group of collective tombs in Cornwall, the Scilly Isles and south-eastern Ireland are generally classed as entrance graves.' Hawkes (1941, 144) used the term 'entrance graves' while Daniel (1950, 64) calls them 'undifferentiated passage graves or entrance graves'. The present writer in 1954 (Ashbee, 1963) drew attention to 'a few entrance graves' which term had been accepted by O'Neil (1949, 164–5).

As the entrance, that is the way through the kerb into the chamber, is normally the least prominent and distinctive characteristic of the series the term 'entrance graves' seems a misnomer. Furthermore, in view of the variations of chamber form any name based upon this could be equally misleading, as would any strictly typological term. Indeed, in view of the occurrence of chamber tombs approximating to the Scillonian series in Ireland and Scotland, not to mention Cornwall, it would seem desirable to adhere to 'Scillonian chamber tombs' as a term of reference. For the excavation of chamber tombs in Scilly has, with one exception (Grimes, 1960), been restricted to the clearance and examination of chambers and their contents; consequently little, if anything, is known of their structural nuances, and description has to be based upon what is visible. As a result it is quite possible that extension surrounds termed 'platforms' or 'outer settings' may have encircled many more of the Scillonian chamber tombs (Ashbee, 1963, 11), as at the strikingly similar Harristown, Co Waterford (Hawkes, 1941) chamber tomb. Thus those who would see the series as an aspect of the passage-grave principle may not be too wide of the mark.

DISTRIBUTION AND SITING

More than half of the extant chamber tombs (Fig 8) of the Isles of Scilly are concentrated into three linear, and one semi-nuclear, cemeteries (Ashbee, 1960, 34). Some seven chamber tombs, in part connected by a wall of some antiquity, lie evenly along the north-east slope of Kittern Hill, on Gugh; three more on the crest of Kittern Hill make a short line parallel to the main cemetery. Twelve chamber tombs lie on Samson's North Hill around the barrow which covered the famous grooved cist and some four are on the ridge. At least four similarly line the rocky spine of Samson's South Hill, forming the third linear concentration. On St Mary's, six chamber tombs, all of smaller size, stand apart and to the south-east of the large 'passage grave' on Porth Hellick Down. Others lie just to the north at no great distance, and within sight of one another, on Normandy Down, while five more are just to the south-west across and about Porth Hellick and beyond on

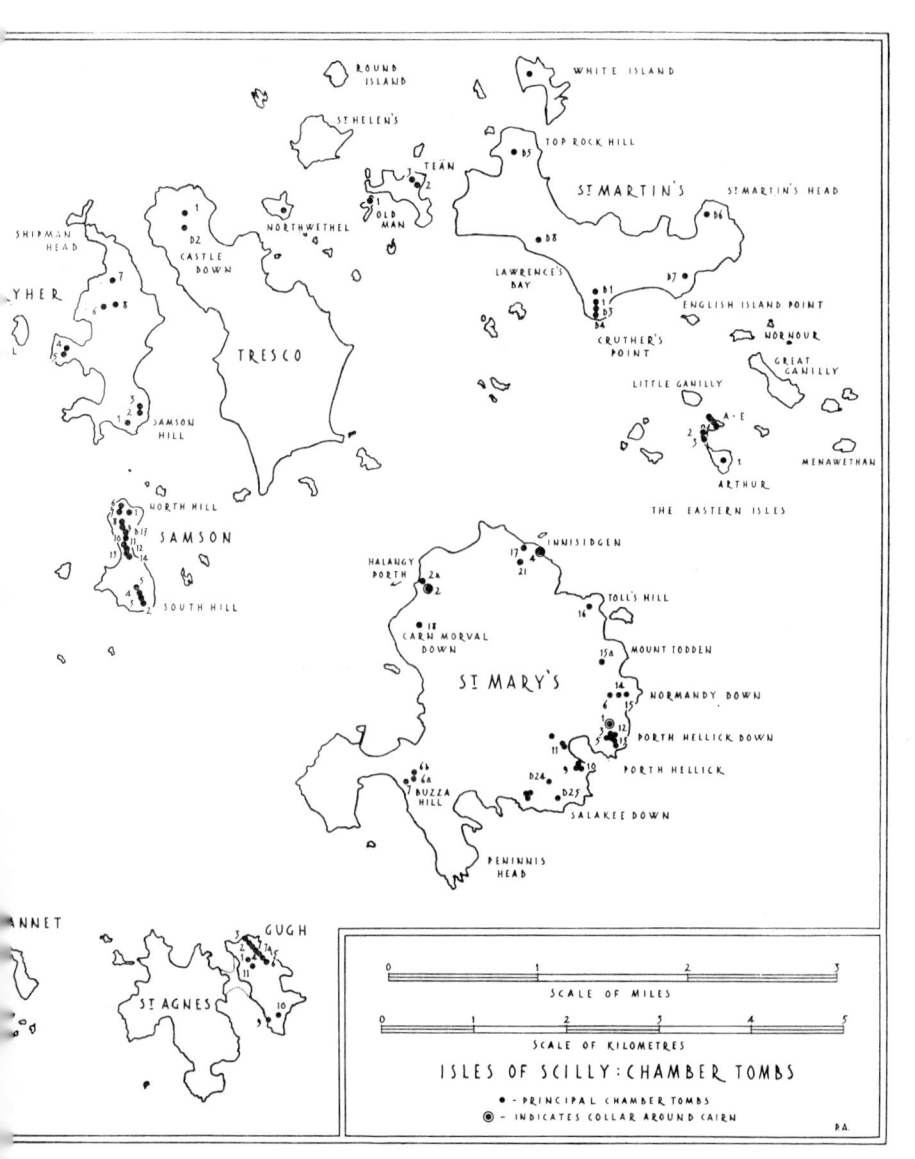

3 *Distribution of Scillonian chamber tombs*

Salakee Down, now the airfield. It is this concentration which has the characteristics of both a nuclear and a dispersed cemetery.

Apart from these greater concentrations, Shipman Head Down, the northern extremity of Bryher, has at least three chamber tombs, with other smaller and apparently unchambered barrows about them. This concentration has characteristics similar to that on Porth Hellick Down, St Mary's. Two chamber tombs crown Gweal Hill, the western summit of this island, while at least three ring Samson Hill, the southern summit. Both chamber tombs and barrows make two modest linear cemeteries extending from Castle Down on to Tregarthen Hill, the northern part of Tresco. Three chamber tombs are on the crest of Cruther's Hill (Troutbeck, 1794, 112), the southern height of St Martin's. Small barrows are alleged to exist on Chapel Down, but little trace can be found, nor is there much remaining of the other small barrows of the high ridges of St Martin's with the exception of the chamber tombs on Top Rock Hill and White Island. Nothing visible remains of the chamber tomb by English Island Point. Little Arthur, the near central island of the Eastern Isles, has five chamber tombs upon it while there are others on Old Man, Teän and Northwethel. Indeed, even on the glacially rounded eminence of Round Island it has been observed that 'on the top of this solitary island standing in deep water, were three immense funeral mounds' (Gibson, 1932, 92).

Apart from the main concentration of chamber tombs about Porth Hellick on St Mary's, others still are to be seen around the perimeter of this island. Three cairns stood on the eminence of Buzza Hill above Hugh Town. One, still to be seen, may have had within it a massive rectangular cist, the second has been destroyed, while the last bears a commemorative tower built as a windmill in 1821. Bant's Carn, which stands above Halangy Porth (Troutbeck, 1794, 102), has another tomb, partially destroyed and obscured, close by it at the foot of the hill, adjacent to contemporary settlement at Halangy Porth. The Innisidgen chamber tomb stands near the prominent natural carn which bears that name (Troutbeck, 1794, 99). Another, smaller tomb lies a few yards to the north, while there is a small barrow still standing in a bulb garden just above. Others may lie under the blown sand which mantles much of this area.

Each of these concentrations of chamber tombs contains a series of all sizes. Those of the greatest diameter are dispersed in the various groups and associated with them are cairns of graduated size. The closely associated Porth Hellick complex contains more larger monuments than the others, those on Gugh are of good size, although those on Arthur and Samson seem more modest in conception.

For the most part the Scillonian chamber tombs are sited either along ridges, such as the linear cemeteries on Samson, on relatively level or gently sloping downs, as on Shipman Head Down or Porth Hellick Down, or set upon summits such as Cruther's Hill, St Martin's. The precise factors that determined the choice of these features for chamber tomb cemeteries evade us but, assuming a first or 'founder's barrow' in each cemetery, one or two principles emerge. A ridge such as Samson's North Hill would only permit linear development if the cairns were to be visible against the skyline. On the other hand a relatively level or slightly sloping plane such as Porth Hellick or Shipman Head Down would allow development in almost any direction and thus a nuclear cemetery could result. The siting of the Innisidgen chamber tomb leads one to suspect that proximity to a distinctive natural feature, here the Innisidgen Carn, was desired. Indeed, such a factor may have determined the sitings on Little Arthur, Teän, Northwethel and by English Island Carn on St Martin's. Again, the distinctive characters of Samson's South Hill and Round Island may have attracted tombs to them. Two chamber tombs are at the bottom of slopes. The second Bant's Carn tomb lies at the bottom of the steep slope of Halangy Down, only some 15ft above modern sea-level. The tomb just to the north of Innisidgen Carn is at the bottom of a similar steep slope while the tomb on Old Man, a low-lying islet detached from Teän, is on a very low-lying surface.

These low-sited chamber tombs lead one to consider how far the distribution of the Scillonian chamber tombs has been affected by the inroads of the sea. For tombs such as that on Old Man or a problematic chamber exposed in the cliff at Porth Mellon, on St Mary's, are within measurable danger of being destroyed by it. Two observations are permissible here. The first is, that in the distribution of sites that can be seen in present-day Scilly, low-lying ones seem the exception rather than the rule. The second is, that, as on the mainland, cairns and barrows are a feature of higher ground which is by and large on the perimeter of the archipelago, therefore vanished sites would, perhaps, have only affected the distribution pattern quantitatively and would, like the additional sites found by fieldwork on St Mary's (Ashbee, 1963), only have intensified the existing pattern.

As observed in the preceding chapter, apparently functionless boulder walls link, or run from, certain chamber tombs. The most notable of such boulder lines or walls is that linking the two prominent chamber tombs (H3:D1 and H7:D3) on Kittern Hill, Gugh. It runs between them in a straight line and in its 440ft length it includes three small cairns which may once have housed chambers. A further stretch joins the southernmost cairn with yet another sizeable example some 170ft distant and deviating a few degrees from the line of the main wall. A similar wall runs up the slope for some 120ft from one of the cairns (H11:D7) on the North Hill of Samson while another such wall, considered dilapidated by Hencken (1932, 31), connected three cairns on St Mary's a little to the east of Old Town at Inner Blue Carn. A wall starting from a chamber tomb on Great Arthur (H1:D1) incorporates what seems to be the remains of small cairns, while Crawford (1927, 7) saw a similar thing on Bryher.

These remains of boulder walls linking many of the numerous small cairns on Shipman Head Down, Bryher, may well denote an early system of enclosures which were set out to utilise land and at the same time respect and preserve the cairns. However, the boulder lines or walls linking cairns on Kittern Hill, Gugh, and elsewhere, do not seem to have been any part of enclosure systems. Although their function is far from clear, they could be compared with, for example, the stone rows which run from and link many of the cairns on Dartmoor (Brailsford, 1938).

FORMS OF CHAMBER TOMBS

Although the Scillonian chamber tombs are strikingly similar in plan, they do, apart from their considerable variation in size, exhibit a degree of uniformity almost unique among British and Irish forms. However, field scrutiny of large numbers does reveal variations not all of which are due to difficulty in, or mode of, building, while within the range of structures there are certain basic principles to which the tomb builders adhered.

For the most part the chamber tombs are regular and circular, but certain of the large and very small monuments are pronouncedly angular. The large tomb on Porth Hellick Down (Plate 4a), St Mary's (H1:D7) has a kerb set out in short straight lengths (Fig 9), each of about 15ft, while another close by (H13:D10) has a part of its otherwise circular kerb set in a straight line. The small cairn, described as 11ft in diameter (O'Neil, 1954) is but a V-form chamber little more than 8ft in length with a kerb built closely about it. This consists of fourteen stones set in lines of threes and fours. The tomb excavated on Samson by Hencken (1933, 24–9; H1:D2) can best be described as of angular oval form. This markedly oval form is also a feature of Bant's Carn on St Mary's (H2:D3).

The renowned Bant's Carn (Plate 4b; Fig 10), possibly the most grandiose of all the Scillonian chamber tombs, shows how height of kerb and headroom within the chamber are related one to another (Fig 11). Here the kerb is of massive coursed stones built up to enclose a cairn which covers neither the top of the chamber walls nor its capstones. The Innisidgen tomb (H4:D2) has a massive high chamber and similarly massive kerbstones.

Bant's Carn stands surrounded by an extension 'collar' or 'platform' some 10ft in width, which can be seen as particularly well built on the downhill side. One side of a passage, through this adjunct, remains. Traces of such a supplementary kerb or platform could be seen about the passage grave on Porth Hellick Down, St Mary's (H1:D7) prior to its restoration by the Ministry of Works, while such a collar can be seen about the Innisidgen Carn. Knackyboy Cairn on St Martin's may

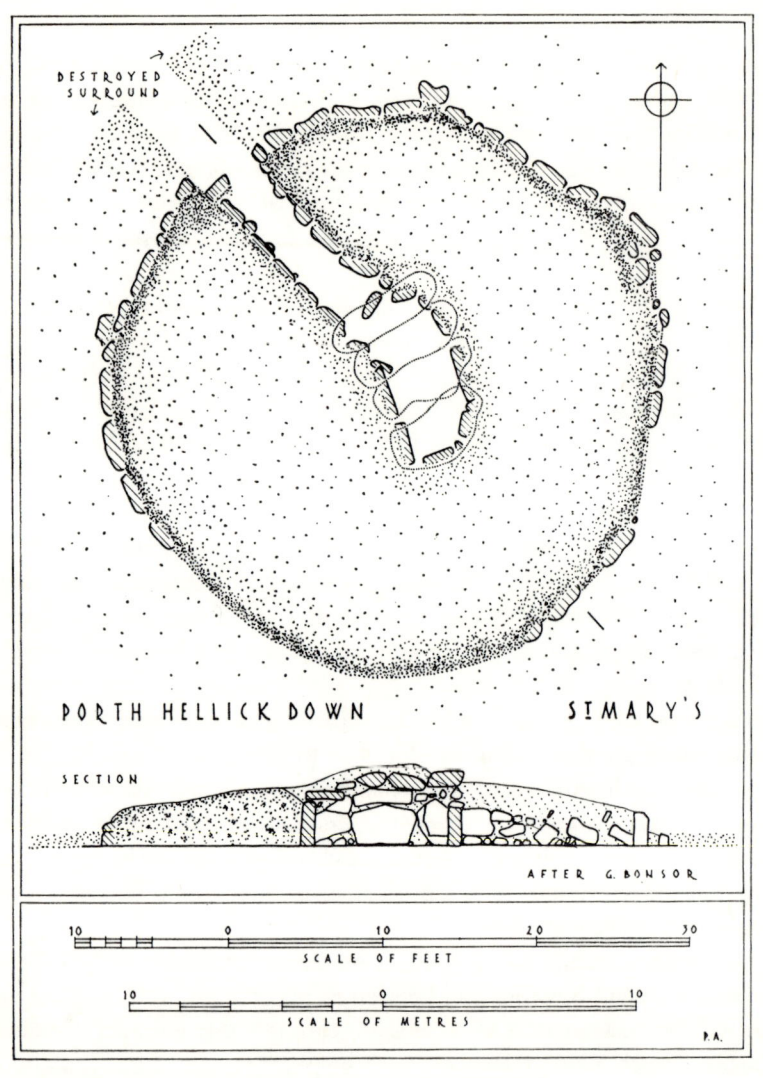

Fig 9 Plan and section of passage grave, Porth Hellick Down, St Mary's

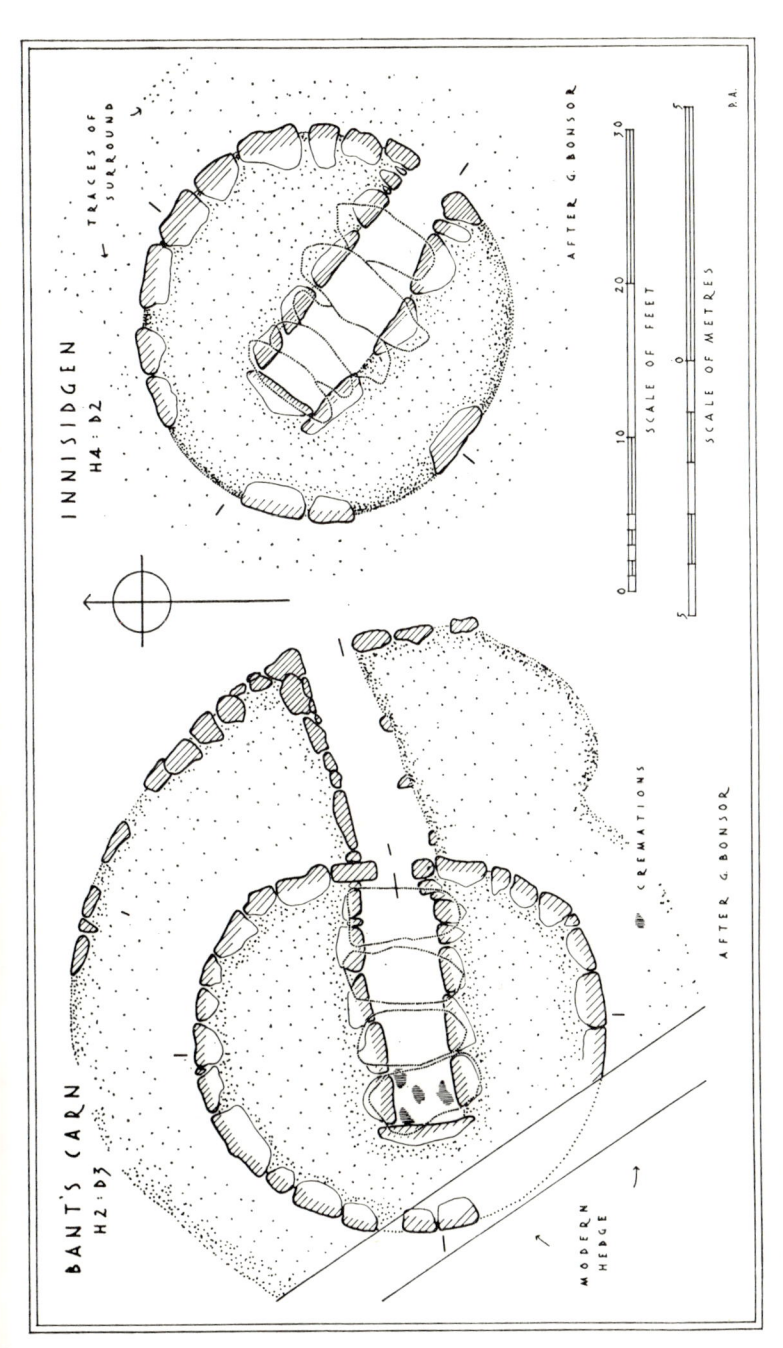

Fig 10 Plans of Bant's Carn, St Mary's and Innisidgen, St Mary's

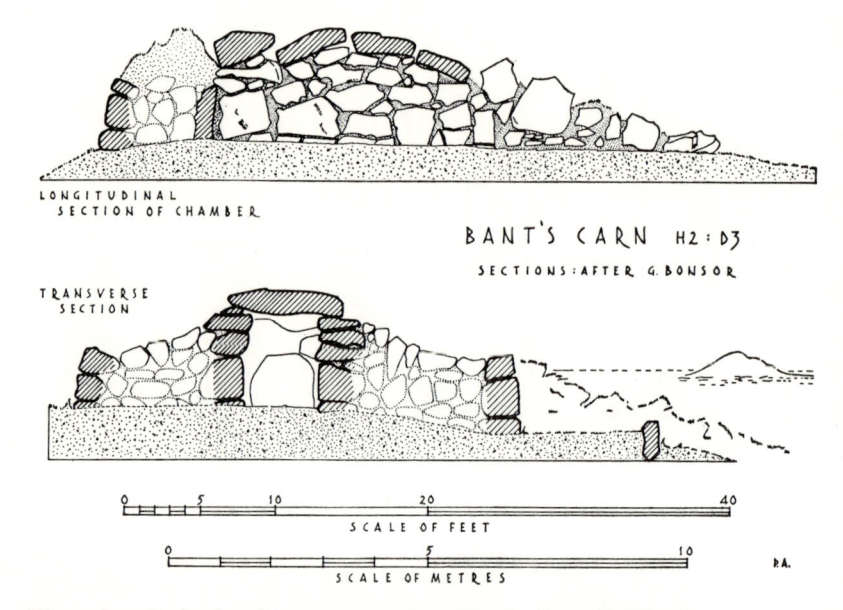

Fig 11 Longitudinal and transverse sections, Bant's Carn, St Mary's

also have had such a collar or platform about it. Arthur 1 (Hencken) also has double concentric walls. A similar arrangement surrounding or carrying three chamber tombs on Samson (H4: D10 with H3: D11 and H2: D12) converts them (Daniel, 1950, 249) into a long barrow 44ft in length, 14ft in width, oriented north-west and south-east. More apposite, perhaps, is comparison with the Wessex earthen double, triple and quadruple barrows surrounded, apparently, by single ditches (Ashbee, 1960, 28). However, a recent visit and inspection of this feature has led to a belief that the extra kerb may well be natural rock. Excavation of the Harristown, Co Waterford (Hawkes, 1941) chamber tomb, so similar to the Scillonian series, showed how slight such an extra-surround or platform could be. Thus it is reasonable to suppose that other such surrounds lie beneath turf and vegetation or that they have been destroyed.

In many instances, natural outcrops of rock have been utilised by

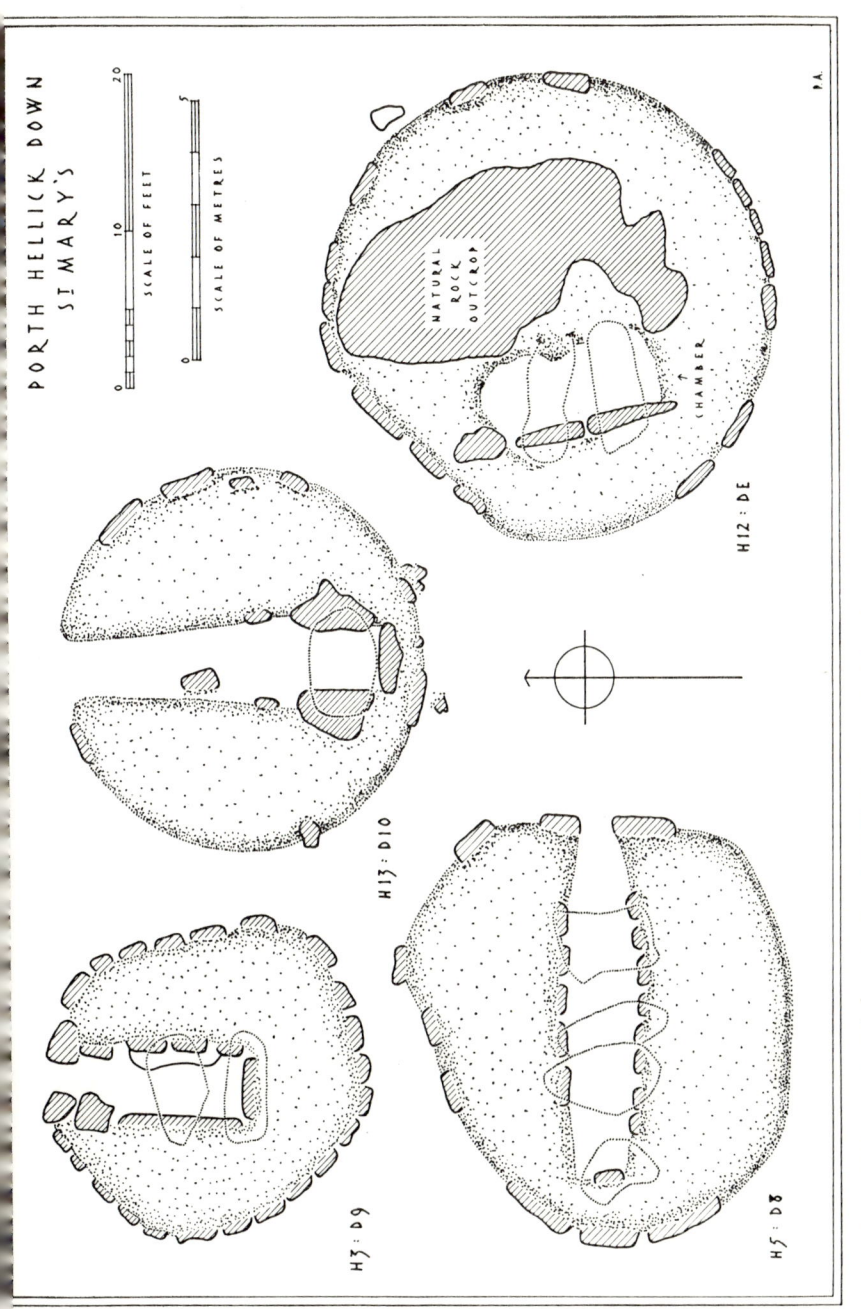

Fig 12 Plans of lesser chamber tombs, Porth Hellick Down, St Mary's

the tomb builders. Two notable examples of this mode of structure are on Porth Hellick Down, St Mary's. One tomb (H12: DE), some 20ft in diameter (Fig 12), is built closely around and against a long irregular outcrop. The chamber is to one side of the axis of the circle, the entrance has a straight façade, while the cover-stones slope from the natural rock to the built-up side of the chamber. The other, smaller, tomb, much ruined, has a mass of natural rock protruding from its kerb (no 31, Ashbee, 1963). Another ruined cairn at Mount Todden uses an elongated outcrop which is about half of the cairn (no 23, Ashbee, 1963). One of the tombs which crown Cruther's Hill on St Martin's (H1:D2) has the natural rock as the floor and wall of the chamber, while there are two more outcrops in the cairn. One of the three seemingly kerb-enclosed tombs on the South Hill of Samson (H2: D12) has its chamber partially cut into the rock. Excavation of the Knackyboy Cairn on St Martin's (O'Neil, 1952) demonstrated that here also the chamber had been built against, and the cairn around, a massive outcrop. The natural rock formed one end and part of the northern side of the chamber. Excavation of a tomb on Teän (Thomas, 1957, 34) suggested that a platform had been built by levelling in against an outcrop, the debris being thrown downhill. Thereupon the kerb and cairn had been set against the outcrop on the prepared platform.

Concerning the character of the Scillonian cairns, the excellent sectional drawings of Bonsor (Hencken, 1933, Figs 2, 5) in which broken lines denote their hypothetical erstwhile form, may well convey the impression that they were originally hemispherical, rocky, faced, versions of ideal bowl-barrow shape. Inspection, however, has failed to reveal a single one approaching to these reconstructions. The untouched cairn on the summit of the Great Hill of Teän (Tomb 3, Thomas, 1957, 34) was in the form 'of a giant bun ... a few feet in height, defined by a number of kerb slabs which form a revetment'. Since it is unlikely that uniform robbing to a relatively uniform form would have taken place ubiquitously, there are grounds, perhaps, for thinking that the original appearance of the Scillonian chamber tombs may have been drum-shaped. Such a design, set upon their supple-

Page 85 5a Innisidgen chamber tomb, St Mary's (H4:D2) from the south-east, 1964

5b Ruined chamber on the North Hill of Samson (H7:D2) from the east

Page 86 6a Rectangular tongued and grooved cist found beneath the cairn on the North Hill of Samson in 1862

6b Cist on Content Farm, St Mary's, found by J. H. Treneary in 1939. Photograph taken in 1950

6c Cist in the Klondyke Field, Telegraph Hill, St Mary's, photographed *c* 1899

mentary kerbed 'platforms' would have given them a striking terraced appearance.

TYPES OF CHAMBER

Although such a large number of chamber tombs still stand on the downs and summits of the Isles of Scilly only a few of them allow any precise notion of their chamber form. These are either the more massive and prominent, which have resisted destruction, the smaller which have escaped notice, or those on uninhabited islands. Other information is available from the few excavations of chamber tombs which have been undertaken down the years, beginning with Borlase.

Following Daniel (1950, 64) and Piggott (1954, 264) it is possible to detect examples of three clearly defined and different types of chamber. There are extant some six or seven examples of each, excluding the so-called 'passage graves' and the abnormal chambers. For the remainder it is impossible, on account of their dilapidation and thus ruined condition, to say much more than to observe that they were most probably chambered. In a number of instances, as on Salakee Down, St Mary's (Grimes, 1960), critical excavation might well reveal something of a chamber's character. These three types comprise first of all, the parallel-sided rectangular chambers. This means that the chamber is more or less of the same width throughout, from entrance to end-stone. Secondly, there are those chambers which are wider at the distal than at the proximal end, that is the breadth at the end-stone, or stones, may be as much as twice the width of the chamber at its portal. These are sometimes referred to as V-formed chambers. Thirdly, there are those chambers which are of about the same width at their proximal and distal ends but in which the side walls are angular or arcuate so that the middle of the chamber is much wider than either end. The effect is frequently a coffin or boat-shaped plan and, in view of the characteristics of numerous ruined tombs, this might be thought of as the most frequently occurring Scillonian type. However, it must be borne in mind that both the second and third types tend to incorporate the characteristics of both forms and thus only extreme examples can define the differences.

A number of good examples of parallel-sided or rectangular chambers are extant upon St Mary's. Perhaps the best and most regularly built is Innisidgen North, sometimes called Innisidgen Lower (H17:D1; Ashbee, 1963, Fig 2). Until a few years ago the site was overgrown and the chamber soil-choked. The chamber was dug out nefariously, early in 1950, and it is not known what, if anything, was found. Recently it has been cleared and the kerb exposed by the Ministry of Works. It is built of regular selected slabs and the side walls have been lined-up and built with considerable care, the lighter masonry at the entrance having been set with regard for the more massive stones within. Only two massive cover-stones remain, while the cairn set closely around the chamber is remarkably small.

A cairn on Porth Hellick Down (H3:D9; Fig 12), some 20ft in diameter, has a markedly rectangular chamber 13ft long, oriented north to south with an entrance at the northern end. The eastern side of the chamber is in part formed by the natural rock outcrop, the western side by one immense slab. This cairn is notable on account of its double portal stones, which are more massive than the surrounding kerb and which restrict the entrance. Indeed, Hencken considered it as a possible passage grave. A partially ruined counterpart to this cairn can be seen on Salakee Down (H9:D15; Ashbee, 1963, Fig 3). Sufficient of the cairn remains to suggest a rectangular chamber, the northern side of which is also a single long slab of stone. A regularly built rectangular chamber may also be seen on Normandy Down (H6:D4). One capstone remains and the end-stone and a side-stone are missing.

In this context of parallel-sided or rectangular chambers on St Mary's, mention must be made of the chamber at Porth Mellon (Ashbee, 1963, 13). This, built of lighter and more regularly selected stones than most chambers and set, apparently without a cairn about it, against what was possibly an early sea-cliff, is much longer than most tomb chambers, although to some extent similar in form and convention. Light walling on the seaward side of its entrance may be modern: this gives the impression of a forecourt. A bulge opposite, on the landward side, may result from earth movement. It was suggested by the late

B. H. StJ. O'Neil that the monument may have been a fougou, an underground storage chamber, similar to the Cornish series (Hencken, 1932, 137–50). On the other hand, it could possibly be a rectangular chamber without a cairn, comparable to the cairned series.

The renowned Knackyboy Cairn on St Martin's (O'Neil, 1952) had a chamber which careful excavation showed to be 12ft in length and 3ft in breadth, although the entrance was narrower by 6in. The inner end and part of the northern side, were, as observed on page 113, formed by a natural rock outcrop. However, almost the whole of the wall of the chamber on this side had disappeared, probably having been destroyed when it was broken into in 1912. The southern side of the chamber was straight and the excavator remarks that the northern side may have been convex. A chamber similar in plan to that of the Knackyboy Cairn and, like that, with one side differing slightly from the other, but basically rectangular, is Obadiah's Barrow on Gugh (H1:D5): on account of its complex entrance and contents, this is discussed on page 92 with the passage-grave series. When one side of a chamber is straight and the other irregular or convex it is difficult to apply morphological criteria. At Knackyboy Cairn the basic desideratum of the tomb builders seems to have been a rectangular chamber. The Innisidgen tomb (H4:D2; Fig 10) has one side only very slightly concave, while the other is markedly so. This characteristic, combined with an entrance narrower than the end-stone, produces a more-or-less coffin-shaped form or plan. While in such a case it is difficult to make a distinction, it seems proper to consider it in the latter category.

Only three clear examples of chambers wider at the distal end than at the proximal entrance end can be identified on St Mary's, and one of these is partially ruined. Perhaps the best on the islands, the chamber called Halangy Down Lower (Ashbee, 1963, Fig 6) lacks, as far as can be seen, a surrounding cairn. This would seem to have fallen victim to the construction of a series of bulb gardens. At the present it appears as set longitudinally to the Halangy Down scarp and forms in part the boundary between track and bulb garden. It was opened in 1929 and pottery was found. The distal end is about twice as wide as the entrance, the sides are straight and built of slabs of diminishing size from the interior to the entrance. From the two capstones that remain it would seem that more massive stones covered the distal end, slighter stones the proximal end. A circular cairn with much of its kerb missing, on Porth Hellick Down (Ashbee, 1963, Fig 4, 30) had a chamber occupying almost its entire diameter. Only the end and adjacent side-stones remain, covered by a single capstone. From the pattern of cairn material left by the removal of the side-stones it is judged that it was a straight-sided but widening chamber comparable with that of Halangy Down Lower. Such a chamber on Cruther's Hill, St Martin's (H1:D2) is also markedly straight-sided but increasing in width. A small chamber in a fairly well-preserved cairn on Normandy Down (H15:D6), like the similar example on Porth Hellick Down, has only its distal end remaining. The proximal end was closed by a slab about half the width of the distal-end slab, set in several feet from the kerb, and is thus comparable with the markedly V-formed chamber set within a small cairn on Arthur (O'Neil, 1954). This latter has been described as triangular or boat-shaped for the sides are not straight but slightly concave. It is 4ft wide at the distal end and nearly 8ft long from end-stone to apex. The wall-stones of this small closed chamber, which its apex-stones and massive kerb-stones effectively close, are all orthostats (standing stones) except at the apex where there is a little walling. None of these orthostats is more than 3ft in height and they are set on smaller stones, so that the height of the chamber would have been just over 3ft. Only a capstone covering the proximal end remains. Between the kerb and this chamber there is room for but a small quantity of filling. Indeed, the excavator commented that there was no trace of cairn material in the vicinity such as could derive from a covering cairn and that it was possible that the monument never had any such covering. A small cairn on Northwethel (Hencken, 1932, Fig 11 B; Daniel, 1950, Fig 10, 3) has a chamber with concave sides, recalling those of the Arthur closed chamber. Here again the distal end-stone is about twice the breadth of the entrance. A markedly boat-shaped chamber recently examined on Teän (Thomas, 1957, Tomb 2) should be compared with the Northwethel chamber.

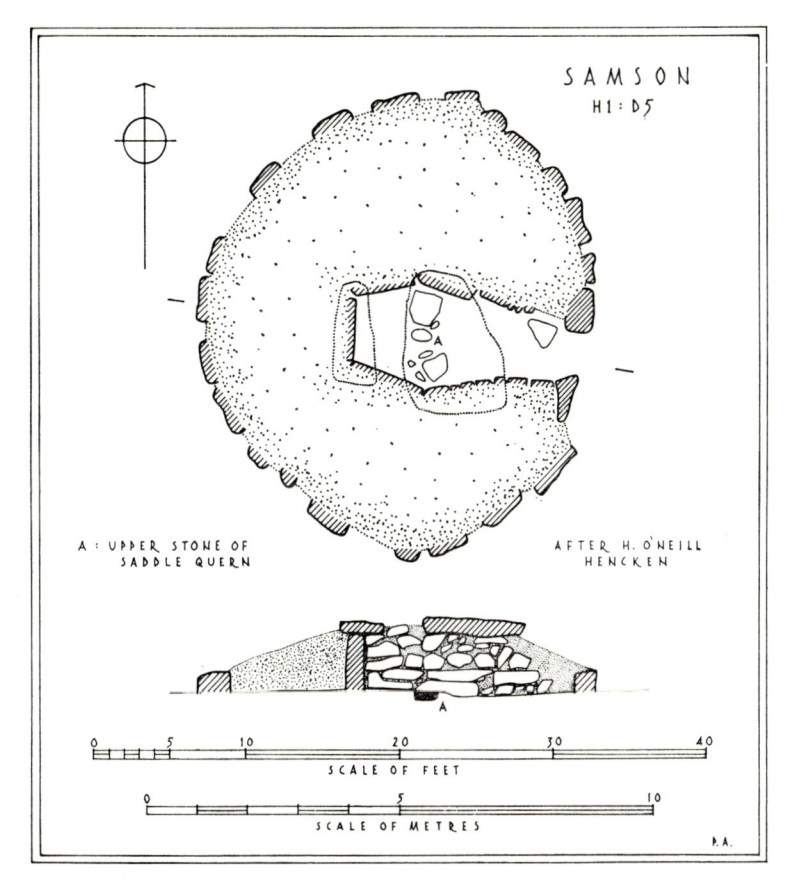

Fig 13 Plan and section of chamber tomb on the North Hill of Samson

An angular oval cairn, excavated by Hencken in 1930 (1933, 24–9), on the North Hill of Samson (H1:D5; Fig 13), is wider at the distal endstone than at the proximal portal stones. For the first two-thirds of its length, from the entrance, the sides diverge, and then they converge, so that the chamber is broader here than at the distal end. Of the two remaining capstones, the larger covers the chamber at this point. The shape is thus an angular coffin or boat form. A chamber on Kittern Hill,

Gugh (Hencken, 1933, Fig 6 [unfinished plan by Bonsor] H2:D2) has one only slightly angular side and one pronouncedly angular one, and is thus coffin or boat-shaped also. Perhaps the best and ideal example of a coffin or boat-shaped chamber is on Porth Hellick Down, St Mary's (H5:D8; Fig 12). Both proximal and distal ends are almost equal in breadth while the sides are arcuate, one rather more than the other.

Three of the Scillonian chamber tombs differ from the examples described above in so much as they have passages leading to their chambers. Two are on St Mary's: the first on Porth Hellick Down (H1:D7) and the second on the crest of Halangy Down—the renowned Bant's Carn (H2:D3). One more is Obadiah's Barrow on Kittern Hill, Gugh (H1:D5).

The angular cairn of the Porth Hellick passage grave is 40ft in diameter. It had, until restored, traces of an extra kerb or platform about it which was in great measure mutilated when Bonsor cleared and exposed the impressive kerb. The passage, 3ft in width and unroofed, curves to the left from the entrance, leading to a chamber, almost 5ft in width, which curves to the right and is covered by four capstones. Entrance from passage to chamber is restricted to 2ft in width by a single upright slab, set at right angles to the left-hand wall. This bend may indicate that at some stage it had been lengthened.

Bant's Carn was of the order of 50ft in diameter if the outer kerb or platform be included, although the main cairn, oval in plan, is only 30ft by about 20ft overall. Like the Porth Hellick passage grave, the passage through the outer platform veers to the left but, unlike it, is straight. Its irregularity of construction, and the irregularity of the outer kerb, has led O'Neil (1949, 7) to suggest that passage and platform may represent enlargement of the initial monument. Entrance to the well-built rectangular chamber from the passage is restricted by two portal stones, each of which projects from the line of the wall of the chamber, thereby restricting the actual entrance to 3ft in width.

Obadiah's Barrow on Kittern Hill, Gugh (Fig 14), was excavated by Bonsor in 1901. From his carefully drawn plan, it seems likely that the chamber, one side of which was straight and the other curved, was

CHAMBER TOMBS AND BARROWS

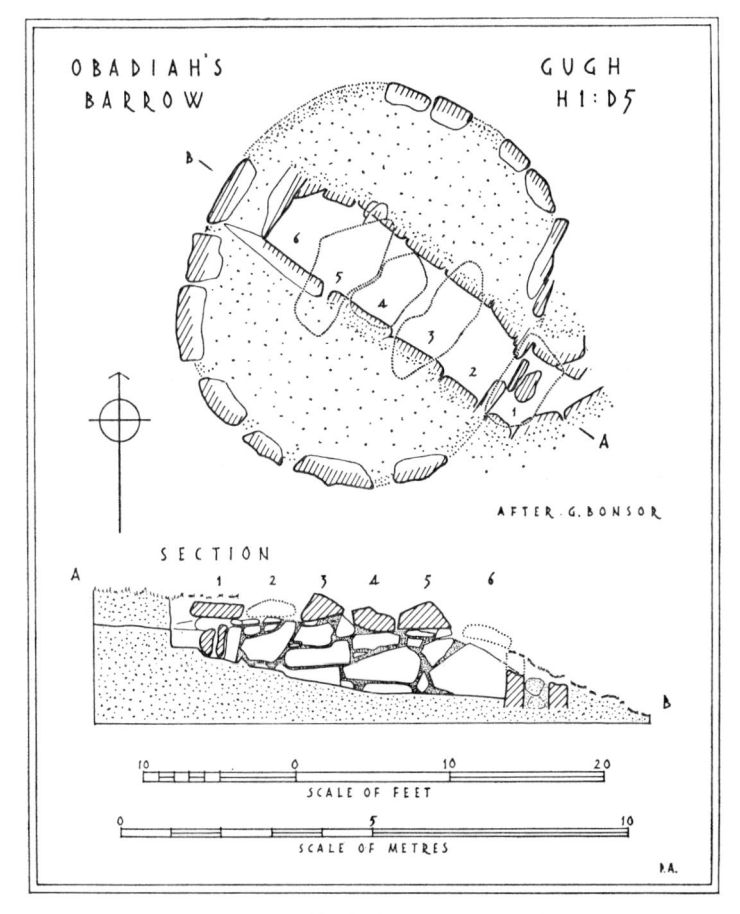

Fig 14 Plan and section of Obadiah's Barrow, Gugh

approached via a passage which veered to the left from its outer entrance, which was not fully bared. As at Bant's Carn, entrance to this chamber was restricted, in this instance by projecting slabs. Bonsor's account was written in French and translated by Hencken (1933, 21) but it best describes this chamber entrance: 'The first roofing stone covered the entrance, which is at the south-eastern end of the chamber, and here everything had remained in place. Originally the interior of the tomb was reached by crawling through this narrow opening which was hardly 50cm. wide by 75cm. high. A small rectangular slab closed the entrance, and a second stone was placed against it to hold it in place.' Three other capstones remained of the six which originally covered this undisturbed chamber.

In this context of Scillonian passage graves, mention must be made of the chamber in the small cairn excavated on Salakee Down, St Mary's, in 1942. It was much ruined and only a few stones remained. Despite this the excavator was able to detect how cairn material preserved its lineament. He expressed the view (Grimes, 1960, 177), held by the present writer, that the concave curve of the remaining part of the north side of the chamber, and the sympathetic setting of the one surviving orthostat on the south, suggested that it might be included in the small group of passage graves described above.

Restricted entrances, however, are not confined to the so-called passage graves. When Borlase (1756, 29) excavated two of the three chamber tombs on Buzza Hill he remarked of the largest (Hencken 6a): 'there was a passage into it at the eastern end one foot eight inches wide, betwixt two stones set on end'. There is also the rectangular chamber on Porth Hellick Down (H3:D9), mentioned on page 88, which has a restricted entrance contrived by double portal stones while the so-called V-formed chambers also display a form of restricted entrance.

A particular characteristic of the Scillonian chamber tombs which marks them off from other such monuments elsewhere is that the length of the chamber, or in the few instances passage and chamber, is hardly ever less than the radius of the cairn and frequently it is almost as long as its diameter. Thus the small cairn on Arthur (Fig 15) (H3:D3; O'Neil, 1954) has a kerb which clings closely around its chamber. The chamber of Obadiah's Barrow on Gugh (H1:D5) occupies almost all its cairn's diameter and the back of the chamber is but a few feet from the kerb. On White Island the cairn is 20ft in diameter and the chamber 16ft in length while on Porth Hellick Down, St Mary's, a cairn (H5:D8) 26ft in diameter houses a chamber 22ft long. The passage and chamber

CHAMBER TOMBS AND BARROWS

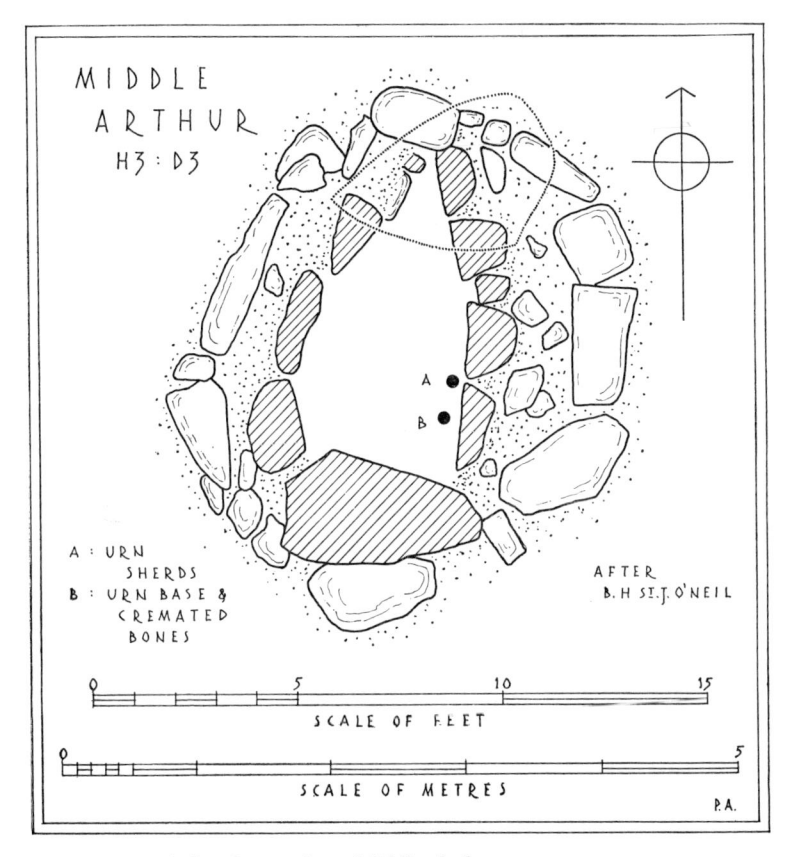

Fig 15 Plan of chamber tomb on Middle Arthur

of the passage grave on Porth Hellick Down (H1:D7) account for three-quarters of the main cairn's diameter.

Apart from closed cists, discussed in Chapter 5, there are one or two other anomalous structures in cairns. The large low cairn on Normandy Down (H14:D5) could conceivably, as far as can be judged from its ruined central structure, have housed an angular chamber approached by a narrow passage. In some measure this cairn recalls the passage grave at Paignton, in Devon (Fox, 1964, 50, Fig 12), excavated by

C. A. Ralegh Radford in 1957. When first seen this passage was taken for an early excavation trench, but it is possible that it became constricted when side-stones were taken away and cairn material fell.

A megalithic structure, built partly of great stones and partly of stone walling, stands within a circular enclosure on Mount Todden, St Mary's. The walling and the signs of splitting on the cover-stones denote a recent, that is later than prehistoric, construction. However, the character of the stones suggests the destruction and partial re-erection of the chamber of a tomb of some size, perhaps to serve as a magazine for the Civil War fortifications of the island.

A large cairn on Bryher (possibly H6:D2, which is about 60ft in diameter) may have had unusual features. Borlase's (1756, 57) account is as follows:

> Passing from this Hill to another (Pl III, No 15b) [ie on to Shipman Head Down] and keeping to the highest ground we came to a very large circular *Burrow* of stones seventy-seven feet in diameter: Within this *Burrow* are many *Kistvaens* (as the *Britans* call Stone-cells) and many of the flat stones which covered them lie here and there, some keeping their first station, and some removed to make Stands for shooting Rabbits, with which this part of the Hill abounds.
> This *Burrow*, you see, was not the Sepulchre of one only, but of many.

It would seem from this that Borlase saw either a cairn with a number of burial chambers, a phenomenon which would not be impossible in the context of Scillonian chamber tombs, for large barrows with more than one passage and chamber are not unknown among passage graves, or a series of closed cists which had been encompassed by a single cairn.

BUILDING METHODS

Borlase (1756, 29) succinctly summarised the construction of the Scillonian chamber tombs, and twentieth-century excavation has shown the precision of his observations: 'The outer ring is composed of large stones pitched on end [the kerb], and the heap within consists of smaller stones, clay, and earth mix'd together: they have generally a cavity of stonework in the middle cover'd with flat stones [the chamber], but the *Barrows* are of various dimensions, and the cavities [chambers], which being low and cover'd with rubble, are scarce apparent in some, consists of such large materials in others, that they make the principal figure in the whole Monument.'

Excavation (Grimes, 1960) during 1942 of a chamber tomb on Salakee Down, St Mary's, was total. The kerb, robbed cairn and the ruined chamber were exposed in their entirety. Of the kerb, Grimes observed that it was built partly of vertical blocks and partly of blocks and slabs laid horizontally and here and there coursed to provide a battering wall-face. As in most Scillonian monuments, these stones were secured into position by 'trig-stones', that is smaller stones to act as wedges and preclude movement. Concerning the cairn, he said that it was composed of numerous granite boulders of varying size, quite tightly packed, but showing no signs of any ordered arrangement. Such soil as there was amongst the stones appeared to have been due to natural causes rather than to deliberate admixture. This cairn composition is Borlase's 'smaller stones, clay, and earth, mix'd together'. Grimes also comments upon how the cairn material has fallen outward and over the kerb, suggesting that this kerb was largely preserved to its original height. From the quantity involved it seems, as observed above, that kerbs were visible and the top was, at the most, bun-shaped and not high and hemispherical.

Cover-stones on Scillonian chambers consist, for the greater part, of roughly parallel-sided slabs selected for the purpose. Sometimes a bolster-like block finds a place with slabs or, exceptionally, such massive blocks are used to cover a tomb completely. Their ends rest on the tops of chamber walls, usually about 1ft 6in of each end of a stone laps on to the wall at either side. Often they have been levelled up with small stones used as wedges, 'trig-stones'. Usually cover-stones are set edge-to-edge but in some chamber covers overlaps can be seen. Now and again the more massive slab or stone was used to cover the chamber end,

CHAMBER TOMBS AND BARROWS

with progressively slighter stones used towards the entrance. For the most part such cover-stones seem to have been selected to cover a required span. Thus, when a chamber's greatest width is at the middle point of its length, the greatest stone would span the gap. Their dimensions and form have made them invaluable to Islanders for thresholds, gateposts and the like, and even as Borlase saw on Bryher, 'to make Stands for shooting Rabbits' and the cover-stones remain on but few. On the substantial tomb at Innisidgen (Plate 5a), St Mary's (H4:D2),

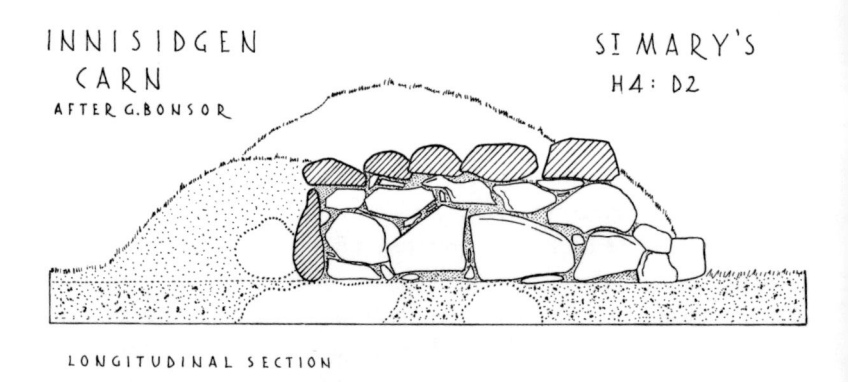

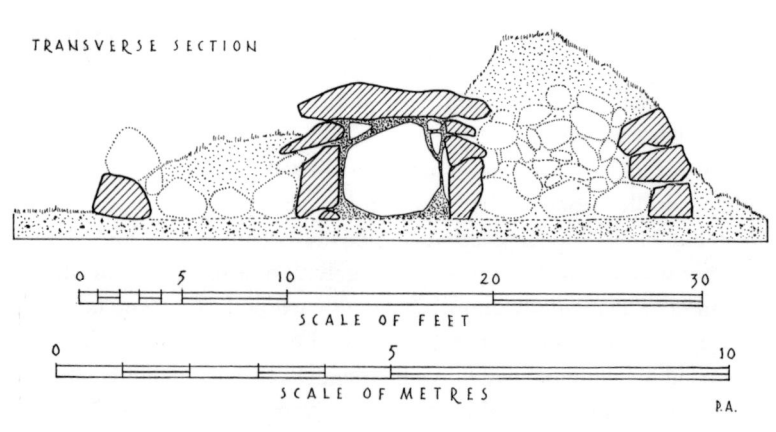

Fig 16 Longitudinal and transverse sections, Innisidgen, St Mary's

the massive bolster-like blocks remain (Fig 16). At Bant's Carn, also St Mary's (H2:D3), three heavy slabs still cover the chamber, while the fourth, which covered the entrance (Hencken, 1933, Fig 1) is out of place; it was being removed by a farmer when an enlightened Lord Proprietor halted the destruction. This displaced stone was set back into position during 1970.

The structure of the Scillonian chambers, as already mentioned, follows regular patterns. Smaller chambers are built of slabs or light walling while larger chambers exhibit combinations of slabs and walling. In their erection great slabs and blocks were set on their sides and then above them walling was built, while the interstices were filled in with smaller stones. A variation of this practice was seen on Samson (H1:D5) where the chamber was built of dry walling; with the bottom course of massive stones while higher up lighter stones were used. The side walls of the chamber of Knackyboy Cairn where the natural rock was not utilised, were of walling built up out of quite small stones.

Normally the side walls of Scillonian chambers are more or less vertical or have a slight inwards batter. One feature of Bant's Carn, St Mary's (H2:D3) is, however, of note. Above the large lower stones are two or three courses of stone-work which have been carried out so that the width of the chamber is narrower at the top than at floor-level. This near-corbelling is unique amongst the Scillonian tombs and is the only deviation from a regular structural pattern; unfortunately no particular significance can be attached to this isolated occurrence. It seems here nothing more than a means of adapting an over-generous ground-plan to the size of the cover-stones so that their ends should have adequate seating.

A feature of the Knackyboy Cairn chamber was that the stone walling was not dry-built; the stones had been set in a granite-clay paste (O'Neil, 1952, 23) which seems (O'Neil, 1949, 6) to have covered most of the face of the walls. Hencken observed, when he excavated the chamber of a tomb on North Hill, Samson (H1:D5; Hencken, 1933, 25) that a coarse yellow sandy mortar could be distinguished between the wall stones. Long before, Borlase (1756, 30) had said of his larger barrow's chamber on Buzza Hill, St Mary's, that 'it was walled on each side with masonry and mortar'. Crawford pointed out to Hencken (1932, 24) that in the chamber of the Innisidgen Cairn (H4:D2) there was a 'rough kind of mortar surviving in places between the stones'. Cists are fully discussed in the next chapter, but it is relevant here that, when writing of stone cists, Crawford (1928, 419) remarks that he observed mortar, mixed with grit, in a chambered barrow on Normandy Down, St Mary's. It is possible that here is a confusion of location, for the Normandy Down tombs are open and exposed to the weather which would rapidly destroy such material. But granite clay-mortar was used to seal the joints and interstices of a grooved and covered cist on Samson (Smith, 1860, 53) while the same medium luted the interstices of the later covered cists at Porth Cressa (Ashbee, 1954, 8) but was absent from the similar cists in Poynter's Garden (Dudley, 1960–1) which had definitely been disturbed, perhaps partially exposed. It can therefore be seen that such mortar survives in optimum conditions such as in a well-covered chamber. Thus it is not surprising that this feature of mortar has not been observed elsewhere between the open and weathered stones of the many Scillonian burial chambers.

O'Neil's (1949, 6) observation to the effect that mortar had covered most of the face of the walls of the Knackyboy chamber cannot be passed without comment. For this, and the mortar remnants between stones, taken with Borlase's (1756, 30) observations to the effect that he found in the smaller chamber on Buzza Hill 'some earths of different colours from the natural one' may well indicate that the interiors of the Scillonian tombs were originally rendered. Some indirect evidence to the effect that such stone walls were finished in this way was recorded by O'Neil (1949, 163) in a later native hut on Par Beach, St Martin's. Again positive traces of such rendering were found in one of the huts recently excavated on Halangy Down (Ashbee, 1966, 26). The exiguous fragments, all burnt, bore curvilinear incisions which, if developed, might prove to be a panel of patterning. The quantities of this yellow clay which covered the burials in the Porth Cressa cists (page 141) make it likely that their interiors were also rendered.

CHAMBER TOMBS AND BARROWS

If the interiors of the Scillonian chamber tombs had been rendered this might account for the absence of mural art in the form of devices cut into the stones (Daniel, 1950, 115). Relevant in the present context is a large holed stone, preserved at Watermill Farm, St Mary's. A similar stone is preserved in a garden at Rocky Hill. The Watermill Farm stone has appeared in literature as a 'good example of a Men-an-tol' (Gibson, 1932, 52) but may well be derived from the watermill. The port-hole principle (Daniel, 1950, 43-6) is closely allied to, and appears as an especial form of the principle of a restricted entrance, already referred to in connection with various tombs. Two isolated slabs with holes through them stand in Cornwall: the Men-an-tol in Madron parish, Penwith, and the Tolven at Constantine (Hencken, 1932, 46) which have, from time to time, been claimed as the surviving entrances of burial chambers. Nothing remains about them to suggest that they were, but it is possible that they, like the Watermill Farm holed stone were brought, for some reason, to their present sites from elsewhere.

FINDS IN CHAMBER TOMBS

The Knackyboy Cairn had been broken into before its excavation in 1948 and one or two urns removed from its well-filled chamber. Other digging into chamber tombs on the islands has taken place from time to time and record of such operations ranges from rumour to allusion. One long-standing rumour related to tiers of pots, and of beads in a cairn on St Martin's. O'Neil's work at Knackyboy Cairn showed that this particular story contained a residue of truth. A huge number of pots apparently without barrows are said to have been destroyed on the north-western side of Samson Hill, on Bryher (Whitfield, 1852, 79), according to Alexander Gibson (Hencken, 1932, 29). This might relate to a cairn from which stone had been progressively removed leaving only the chamber. According to John Troutbeck (1794, 154-5) plunderers found crude pots containing human ashes, which they destroyed, in a chamber on Gugh. Bonsor believed that he had identified the barrow, which he partially planned and sketched in 1901 (Hencken, 1933, 19, Fig 6; 20, Fig 7). In his detailed account of Scillonian fieldwork and digging, Alec Gray alludes to 'the small covered gallery', close by Halangy Porth, St Mary's (H2a:D14) 'which I cleared in 1932'. Part of the jaw of a pig was found and probably, as Mr Treneary recalls, a considerable quantity of pottery. When the present writer first saw the small cairn to the north of Innisidgen Cairn, St Mary's, in 1949 it was overgrown and the chamber was seemingly undisturbed. When he visited it the following year the chamber infill had been dug out and dumped on the cairn. Similar clandestine digging has recently taken place on Porth Hellick Down.

One other account of an early Scillonian barrow 'opening' is of particular note. Two heavy bronze torques, now in Truro Museum, are alleged to have been found 'in a barrow on the Peninnis Head, in the island of St Mary's, Scilly' (W. C. Borlase, 1872, 162; Ashbee, 1960, 114). Recent research amongst early nineteenth-century newspapers (Douch, 1962, 97) has unearthed what may be an account of this discovery. The 'foundation stones of a very ancient building' referred to in the report could well be the remains of a cairn seen by uninformed eyes. The extract, from the *West Briton* of 30 October 1812, under the heading of 'Scilly, St. Mary's' runs:

> On Tuesday the 21st inst., as some workmen, employed in removing the foundation stones of a very ancient building which was on a piece of waste ground, belonging to Mr. Lemon Collector of Customs at these islands, they discovered a heap of human bones of a very large size, which were deposited within the walls. On removing a large stone, five feet high and two feet six inches in breadth, which stood on its end inside the walls of the building, they discovered two pieces of a composition, supposed to be a very fine brass, nearly in the shape of a horseshoe. They weighed three quarters of a pound each, and are exactly alike.

Then follows a series of speculations regarding their use as handles, ornaments and musical instruments. The article concludes by saying that 'The whole of the rubbish not being removed, it is expected that

Page 103 7a The Porth Cressa, St Mary's, cist cemetery, after excavation, 1949
7b A Porth Cressa cist (no 11) after removal of the cover-stones

Page 104 8a Standing stone: the Day Mark, Porth Mellon, St Mary's, photographed *c* 1900

8b Standing stone: the Long Rock, McFarland's Down, St Mary's, 1964

8c Granite post-base or mortar found on the shore of the Neck of Samson in 1969

other discoveries may be made.' The possibility that this barrow might have been built about a standing stone might be envisaged. The stone by Harry's Walls stands on or has a small cairn about it while Borlase saw a stone on a 'Karn' when he landed on St Martin's.

Apart from those that have been subjected to archaeological excavation, the greater number of the Scillonian chamber tombs stand empty and bare (Plate 5b). To account for the wholesale clearance of burial chambers one might invoke the activities of stone-hungry and inquisitive islanders down the years. Yet there is evidence that, at least during a good part of the nineteenth century, which saw improvement in Scilly as never before, the writ of the Lord Proprietor afforded some protection to its monuments. It is not impossible that one of the Commissions which opened barrows to replenish royal coffers from time to time during the Middle Ages and later, was active on the islands. Such Commissions worked in Cornwall and Devon (Grinsell, 1953, 110) although with what results is not known.

It is hard to assess numbers of persons represented by the burial deposits. Bonsor's account (Hencken, 1933, 21-4) allows for the possibility of the remains of fourteen or sixteen people, there being a dozen urns with both burnt and unburnt bones in Obadiah's Barrow. In Bant's Carn there were four piles of cremated bones, while sixteen urns were numbered from Knackyboy Cairn, in addition to the deposit of charcoal and cremated bones that may have represented very many more. Part of, apparently, only one cremation came from the chamber of the small cairn on Arthur. These Scillonian burial urns, which are discussed in Chapter 10 in more detail, are, in their commonest forms, biconical flat-based pots which sometimes have lugs or handles and are not infrequently decorated with cord or coarse hyphenated ornament. A fragment of a round-bottomed bowl from Bant's Carn was allegedly of much finer ware. One lug figured by Bonsor has been considered by Grimes (1960, 177) as suspiciously like a south-western trumpet-lug, a claim that could be made for some of the Knackyboy Cairn lug forms.

Like many burials in chamber tombs, the Scillonian ones were modestly furnished. Bone points, a small fragment of, perhaps, a rectangular sectioned bronze awl and a hammer-stone were in the chamber of Obadiah's Barrow on Gugh. Hencken found the stone rider of a saddle quern built into the floor of the chamber that he excavated on Samson. Eight oblate glass beads and one faience star bead were in the deposits in Knackyboy Cairn on St Martin's, as well as pieces of bronze, perhaps the corroded remains of armlets. Here also was found an unpolished flint axe or adze incorporated in the cairn.

Borlase's excavations of the burial chambers of two of the cairns on Buzza Hill, St Mary's (Borlase, 1756, 30) yielded to him only structural details, and he was unable to establish 'upon the strictest enquiry, that ever any Urn was found in Scilly'. None the less, he came to the conclusion that the chambers had contained collective burials. His negative evidence, is, however, not uninformative. He emptied the earth-filled chamber of the larger of the two cairns, recorded its dimensions and found 'no bones, nor urns, but some strong earth which smelt cadaverous'. Similarly in the smaller chamber, besides a pit, presumably in the rabb, he found 'some earths of different colours from the natural one'. As has been suggested, it is not impossible that this deposit was the remains of rendering washed from the walls and that this chamber, and the other, for both were apparently intact when he began his operations, had, for some reason, never housed human burials. If this is the case, that Borlase happened upon two unused burial chambers, there is the question of the precise character of the deposits that this perceptive pioneer worker encountered. Chemical weathering (Cornwall, 1958, 76), the process that accompanies the percolation of rainwater into the soil, has come to the eyes (and noses) of archaeologists in various guises. Recent examination of such tombs in the high rainfall region of the west, and on acid granite-based soils, indicates that what Borlase encountered was perhaps a podsolisation phenomenon, with some washing and leaching, as found within the confines of many monuments. Indeed, the character of the rendering, washed from the walls, might well promote such conditions.

In four Scillonian burial chambers, one dug into almost a century ago, another more than half a century ago, the third in 1930 and the last as recently as 1942, there has been unequivocal evidence of their having contained pottery but no burials. The first, a cairn on the farm of a Mr W. M. Gluyas 'at Old Town, St Mary's', perhaps one of the Salakee Down concentration, was dug into (Cornish, 1874). Like Borlase before him, Mr Gluyas cleared out the chamber and noted its dimensions. Regarding its contents, he reported 'The urns (there were undoubtedly two, but one was nearly all gone to dust) were deposited at the west end ... The urns were broken when discovered. No bones were found, but at the bottom of one urn there was a small quantity of greasy matter. I had the earth that came out of the cairn carefully examined but found no coins nor bones.' The second burial chamber is the passage grave on Porth Hellick Down, St Mary's (H1:D7) examined by George Bonsor (Hencken, 1932, 20). He considered that it had already been disturbed by treasure seekers and found no human remains, but several pieces of pottery as well as a piece of pumice stone. This last he considered a foreign import and told Hencken that it was often found in Iberian burial chambers. Amongst this pottery were substantial pieces of a biconical zig-zag cord-ornamented urn (Hencken, 1932, 22, Fig 9 A). When Hencken excavated the best preserved of the many chamber tombs on the North Hill of Samson (H1:D5), the third of the tombs in question, he found the chamber choked with some 2ft of rabbit-burrow riddled sandy soil. Indeed, rabbit bones, scraps of a modern iron container, shotgun cartridges and half-decayed vegetable matter were found throughout. Only inside the chamber beneath the remaining capstones (Hencken, 1933, 26, Fig 11) was the chamber deposit less disturbed and it was from here that the rider of a saddle-quern (Hencken, 1933, Fig 13), an end-battered pebble and a number of sherds of pottery came. There was, in Hencken's words 'no trace of human remains, either inhumed or cremated'. In view of the care with which the excavation was conducted, and the resistance to decay of cremated bone, it would seem reasonable to suppose that had burial deposits, on the scale of those met with in other tombs, been inserted in the first place, a few scraps would have survived. Under the larger of the cover-stones of the chamber were flat stones, presumably paving, and it was amongst these that the saddle-quern rider stone had been placed. Just outside the entrance to this chamber, on the south side, was a deposit consisting of eighty-two, mostly very small, sherds representing the remains of two pots. A battered lump of flint was by the northern jamb-stone of the entrance.

The chamber of the fourth cairn, that excavated in 1942 by Grimes (1960), on Salakee Down, St Mary's, appears to have been one of the small number that can be called passage graves. Little remained to define passage and chamber except a course of walling on the north side, an orthostat on the south side and the run of the cairn material (Grimes, 1960, 172, Fig 69). Inside the chamber the granite was mantled with a thin layer of humus and when the chamber area was cleared and defined two clusters of broken pottery were found. The first was at the extreme western end of the chamber, the second close by the walling on the north side. It was emphasised that nothing else was found and here, again, it would seem unlikely that deposits of cremated bone would vanish without trace. From the broken pottery two vessels were reconstructed and the possibility of base fragments representing pieces of a third was commented upon.

Similarly, unquestionable evidence has been recovered from four Scillonian burial chambers, namely Obadiah's Barrow on Gugh, Bant's Carn on St Mary's, Knackyboy Cairn on St Martin's and the small closely-restricted-entranced chamber on Arthur, of burials subsequent to cremation. In the chamber of Obadiah's Barrow a deposit of unburnt bones was with and beneath the cremation burials (Figs 14, 17). To quote in full Hencken's (1933, 21) translation of Bonsor's manuscript in French:

> The chamber lies north-west and south-east and measures 5m. long by 1·50m. to 1·20m. wide. The circular exterior wall, a dozen stones of which still remain in place, is 7·20m. in diameter. This tomb was covered by six large stones, four of which still remain in place, but the other two have been removed, and the part of the chamber which

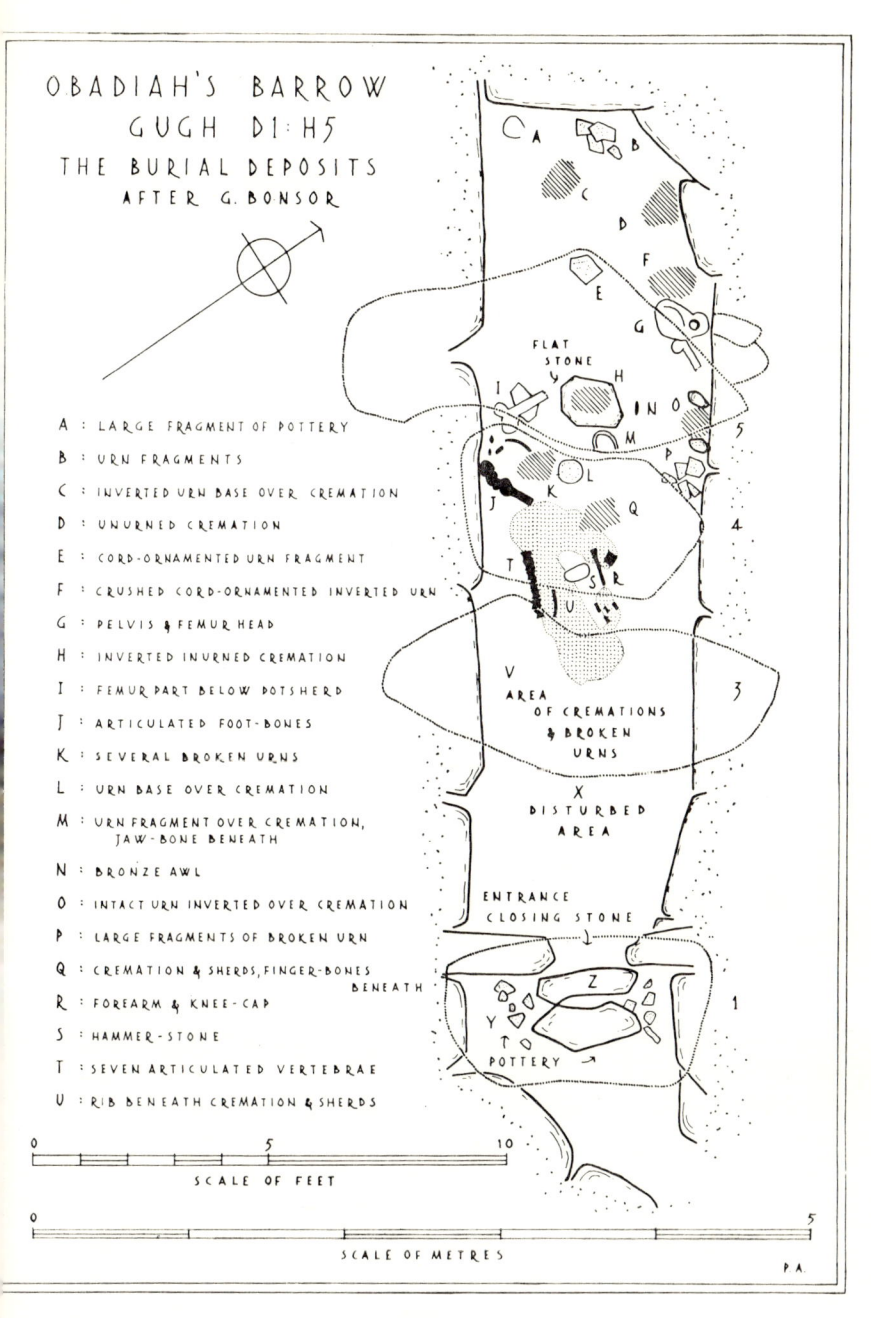

Fig 17 Plan of burial deposits, Obadiah's Barrow, Gugh

they covered had already been disturbed by treasure seekers. Under the sixth stone, however, their excavation had been only superficial. The first roofing stone covered the entrance, which is at the southeastern end of the chamber, and here everything had remained in place. Originally the interior of the tomb was reached by crawling through the narrow opening which was hardly 50cm. wide by 75cm. high. A small rectangular slab closed the entrance, and a second stone was placed against it to hold it in place.

It was only under the second covering stone that the soil in the chamber had been excavated deeply, and the rest of the deposit inside under stones 3, 4, 5, and 6 remained practically intact. Here was found at a depth of 80cm. a layer of hard blackish soil upon which the urns had been placed. In this layer of soil were parts of the contracted skeleton of a man which had been the primary interment in the tomb. The bones in place are indicated on my plan in black, and the others such as the pelvis, the head of a femur and a jaw-bone, were found at a little distance.

Later the dolmen must have received about a dozen cinerary urns, only one of which was intact. They had all been inverted upon the layer of soil according to the custom observed by the people of Brittany at this time. By inverting the urns in this way, sacrilege was prevented, for even though an urn was carried away—and indeed fragments of one were found at the entrance of the tomb—the ashes of the dead remained in place.

From the carefully drawn section (Hencken, 1933, 22, Fig 9a) which accompanies Bonsor's detailed plan, the 'depth of 80cm.' is taken from the underside of the cover-stone (no 5 on the plan) and the 'layer of hard blackish soil' covers the, apparently paved, floor of the chamber to a depth of almost 1ft 4in. Bonsor's 'parts of the contracted skeleton of a man', which in his own words were 'In this layer of soil' appear to be the remains of an assemblage of unburned disarticulate bones. From Bonsor's longitudinal section (Hencken, 1933, 21, Fig 8) which admirably depicts the chamber's structure, it can be seen that its floor slopes quite steeply from entrance to about the middle and then more gradually to the end-stone. The deposit of blackish soil which contained the unburned bones clearly occupied much of the inner end of the chamber but must have tailed off to the slope towards the entrance—indeed, it may have been put in to provide a level floor. It is possible that this circumstance of the inward sloping floor of the chamber promoted a degree of water-logging, which might in some measure have accounted for the blackness, apparent homogeneity and hardness of the dark soil, if Bonsor dug into it when it was dry. Under such conditions the unburned bones would have been well preserved. These comprised seven vertebrae in articulation (T—capital letters refer to Bonsor's plan of the chamber) with, close by, a rib (U), a forearm and knee-cap (R) and the bones of a foot, part of a tibia, the astragalus, an os calcis and some metatarsi (J) together with some finger-bones beneath burnt bones (Q). On the other side of the chamber was a pelvis and head of a femur (G). Bonsor was of the view that the first group of bones (J,R,T,U,Q) were all that remained of a contracted skeleton which had lain there, that they were 'in place' and thus he depicted them in black on his plan. In the absence of a laboratory study of these bones, of the character of that of the bones from the Fussell's Lodge long barrow (Brothwell, 1966), it cannot be certain that these bones were those of a single individual. On the other hand, from his drawings and notes, Bonsor appears, in the light of his time, as a skilled and observant fieldworker and it must be admitted that his view of relationship of the bones in question might be significant. In the circumstances, it is possible that Bonsor may have been correct for such skeletons in burial chambers are not unknown (Keiller and Piggott, 1938, 127). The alternative view is that expressed by Hencken (1933, 22 fn), namely that the deposit is one of skeletal debris. This could imply that, as in earthen long-barrow mortuary houses and certain stone-built chambers (Ashbee, 1966, 37), the bones, and perhaps soil, had been brought from elsewhere and put into the chamber.

The deposit above the dark soil and its unburned bones, Bonsor thought to be the remains of 'about a dozen cinerary urns'. He found only one more or less intact (the rim is missing) and that was stone-protected and against one side of the chamber (O). As far as can be seen pride of place in this deposit was taken by a cremation, with its broken urn, set on a slab of stone (H) about 1ft 6in by 1ft in the middle of the chamber, the remainder being arranged around it (C,D,F,O,Q,K). Such a rite recalls that found in passage graves elsewhere, for example in Ireland (Piggott, 1954, 200), where cremations were placed in stone basins. This arrangement occupied the inner part of the chamber. There was, however, towards the entrance a deposit (V)—'a mass of ashes and pieces of broken urns'. As with the unburned remains two explanations seem possible. Either the whole deposit represents sequential burials, the mass of ashes and broken urns being earlier burials cleared away from the interior to make way for the arrangement about the slab, or the whole deposit represents remains brought from another place, the better preserved and later urns and their cremations being set in position while the broken urns and mixed cremations were tipped in after them.

At the stone-stopped and restricted entrance to the chamber of Obadiah's Barrow, and apparently at each side, were deposits (Y) of 'Fragments of broken urns'. The number is not stated in the account of the excavation, but, on the plan, many appear to be depicted. In all, the amount of pottery recovered from this burial chamber, and presumably from the deposit at the entrance, filled a large basket.

With regard to the egregious furnishings of these burials: the fragment of a bronze awl appears (Hencken, 1933, 22, Fig 9a, N) as close by the large flat stone with the cremation upon it. The hammer-stone, a battered pebble, was in the middle of the chamber towards the entrance. No precise location for the bone points is given.

When Bonsor excavated the chamber of Bant's Carn on St Mary's (H2:D3), he did not, it appears, prepare a detailed plan of the burial deposit. Four piles of cremated human bones, unurned, were found at the inner end of the chamber. In the oblique passage through the platform-collar extension of the cairn were sherds of pottery. All, with the exception of one piece of a round-based bowl which has been thought to be of Earlier Neolithic type, were pieces of biconical Hencken remarks that he had never been able to find the pottery from this tomb.

An account of the relatively undisturbed and well-furnished Knackyboy Cairn chamber on St Martin's (Fig 18) was published by O'Neil (1952) in advance of an ultimate full and more detailed narrative. Although it had been broken into in 1912 and had been the subject of an exploratory excavation by the Rev H. A. Lewis, O'Neil was able to clear it totally and recover full details of the rite. Like that of Obadiah's Barrow, the bedrock below this chamber sloped sharply downwards at its inner end towards the natural outcrop which comprised much of the cairn. Here the floor had been levelled up and paved. Below the filling was dark soil containing small abraded sherds and, as on Gugh, periodic water-logging may have occurred. Towards the entrance, rock outcrops showed through the floor.

As with the burial deposits in the chamber of Obadiah's Barrow, two explanations are possible to account for the character of the chamber's contents: they either represent a sequence of burials carried out over a long period of time (O'Neil suggested about 500 years), or they result from the single act of interment of inurned cremations, intact as well as broken and confused, which had been previously kept in another place. In other words, burial was single and successive or simultaneous from storage. Are we, as Atkinson (1962, 8) has said so succinctly in another similar context, dealing with family vaults or mass graves?

Whatever the view regarding the character of the contents of the Knackyboy Cairn's chamber, four stratified, and thus sequential, compounded deposits were found. A hollow in the floor had been filled with charcoal and granite sand. It will be remembered that Borlase (1756, 30) observed in his smaller chamber on Buzza Hill that 'in the floor was a small round cell dug deeper than the rest'. Over this hole lay a flat stone a few inches higher than the other paving stones and on it, in the prime place, stood an urn (VII—urn numbers follow O'Neil's notation of 1952). At the distal end of the chamber stood, on the floor, close by, six more urns (I,II,III,IV,V,VI), in two rows of three.

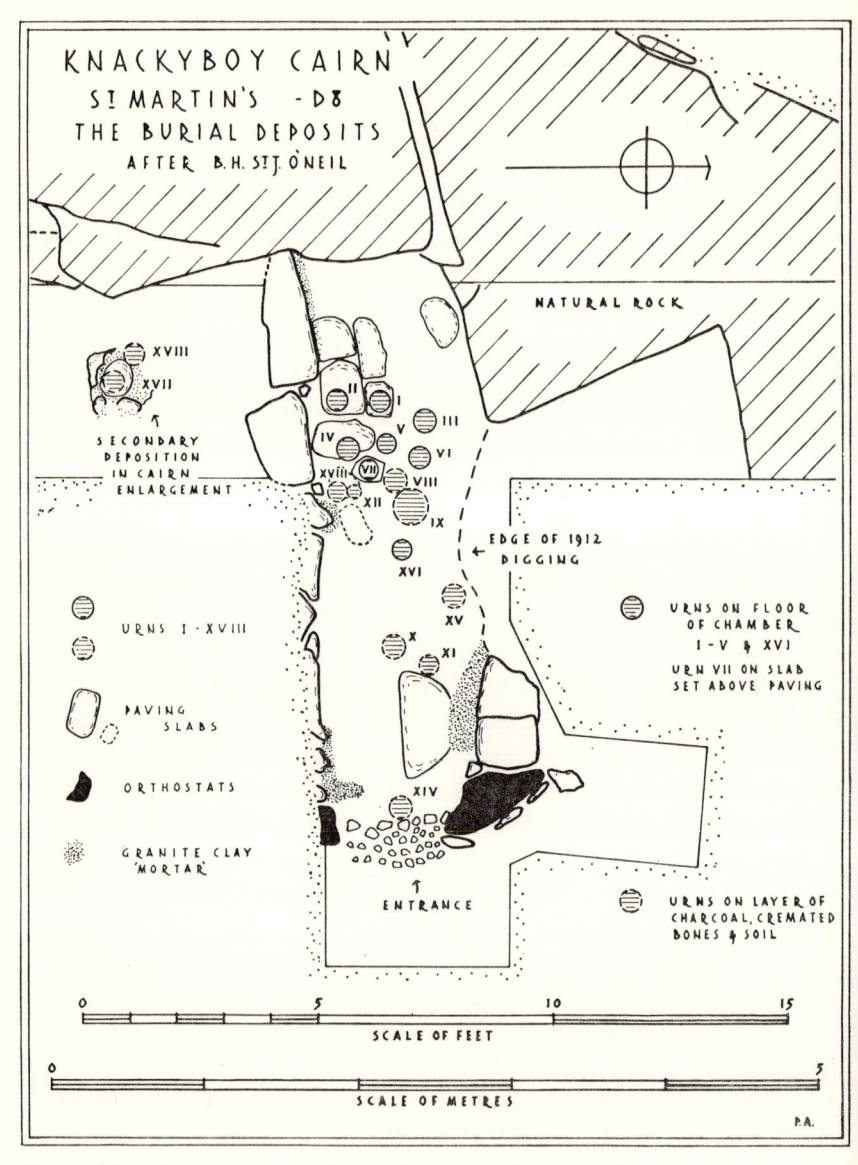

Fig 18 Plan of burial deposits, Knackyboy Cairn, St Martin's

Towards the proximal end, and medially, stood another urn (XVI). Although the contents of specific urns are not mentioned in O'Neil's text, it appears that they all contained cremated bones. Around this initial setting of urns and partly over them was a thick deposit of what was termed 'ashes'. This was comprised of small pieces of charcoal and cremated bones with a little soil. It contained several large sherds of pottery and also in it were most of the beads and the pieces of bronze. On top of this heaped material, which almost filled the full length of the chamber, were more urns, notably three (IX,X,XIV) along its axis. Other urns were also in a similar position but at the sides of the chamber. O'Neil was able to observe the relationship of specific urns one to another. Thus VIII was on IX and XIII higher than XII, while XIV, on the axis at the proximal end, was considered as the last urn placed in position before closure of the chamber.

Besides excavating the chamber, O'Neil cut a section across the cairn to explore relationships. As well as exposing the internal kerb, mentioned earlier in this chapter, and showing that the monument had characteristics more proper to a composite barrow, he came upon two stone-protected urns (XVII,XVIII) contained in it which were either satellite or secondary burials. Close by, at the base of the barrow, was a flint axe or adze.

In this burial deposit, which was contained within the Knackyboy burial chamber, was grave furniture in the form of beads, eight oblate glass ones and one star-form faience, and some corroded scraps of bronze, one perhaps an earring fragment. One glass bead was in Urn XVI, four were in the compound mass of material between the two settings of urns, as were the pieces of bronze. The faience bead was in dark-brown soil close by the base of Urn XVI, while four glass beads were unstratified.

From the foregoing accounts of excavations in two undisturbed Scillonian burial chambers, that of Obadiah's Barrow on Gugh, and the Knackyboy Cairn on St Martin's, certain points of similarity emerge. Both contained initial settings of urns, each with an urn on a flat stone in a prime place. Both had tipped-in deposits; described by Bonsor referring to Obadiah's Barrow this was 'a mass of ashes and pieces of broken urns', while in the Knackyboy Cairn there was, over the first setting of urns and extending to the entrance, a 'thick deposit of ashes, ie. tiny pieces of charcoal, cremated bones, etc., with a little soil' which had in it 'a few large sherds of urns which cannot be restored' while 'a few such sherds were also found flat on the floor of the chamber under the ashes'. Only, however, in the Knackyboy Cairn was there a second setting of urns on top of the tipped-in deposit. Again, scraps of bronze artifacts were found in both chambers although other accompanying articles differed.

Until a laboratory examination is undertaken of the mass of cremated bones from the Knackyboy Cairn burial chamber, only the most approximate estimates can be made of the number of persons represented in its contents. In his interim report, O'Neil (1952, 29) infers twenty-two reconstructable urns and, in all, 4cwt of pottery from the tomb (O'Neil, 1952, 25). The twenty-two urns presumably contained cremations, although this is not specifically said, but O'Neil does conclude that the mass of material over the first setting of urns, and in great measure filling the chamber, was the product of cremations. In the circumstances it would seem likely that the Knackyboy Cairn's chamber contents represent the remains of at least sixty individuals.

During 1953, O'Neil (1954) cleared the vegetation from, and exposed the closed chamber of the small cairn on Arthur (H3:D3). He excavated the chamber, finding the side and part of the base of a single cinerary urn. Adhering to this base were cremated bones. This was the sole occupant of this chamber.

That these burial deposits result in each case from a single act of mass burial is questionable. It is, however, indisputable that the process of cremation must have been carried out, so far as can be seen, elsewhere. Such numbers of cremations as were represented by only two tombs, would have entailed the consumption of considerable quantities of timber and must, in the course of time, have accounted for a large acreage of Scilly's erstwhile forest cover. One early observation might point to the site of a cremation pyre. When, in December 1876, Mr

Gluyas dug into, and presumably about, the cairn on his farm at Old Town, St Mary's (Cornish, 1874), he found that 'A little on one side of the barrow was another circle of small stones, and within that was a quantity of something resembling ashes'.

If the burial deposits in Obadiah's Barrow on Gugh and the Knackyboy Cairn on St Martin's represented burials which had been stored elsewhere and which were brought together at one time and put into these chambers, it would be legitimate to enquire as to the character of such temporary housing. Of course evidence of the deposition of bones and the subsequent infilling of burial chambers has been met with elsewhere in the British Isles (Piggott, 1962, 68–71) and a somewhat similar rite seems to have been carried out in the timber and stone mortuary houses beneath the earthen long barrows (Ashbee, 1966, 37–42). With the evidence of such practices in mind, it must be admitted that the 'tipped-in deposits' in these two Scillonian burial chambers do conform in great measure to an emerging general pattern. A question is posed, therefore, as to the nature of the circumstances in which the cremation-filled urns might have been stored in numbers over a period until the appointed time for burial.

Unlike, for example, the excavators of the renowned West Kennet stone-chambered long barrow (Piggott, 1962) we are not dealing with the problems of burial and subsequent filling, but with the supposed single act of the burial of urns and the debris of urns and cremations. Thus some form of ossuary might be supposed or, alternatively, as has been suggested with reference to the rites of the earthen long barrows (Ashbee, 1966, 38), exhumation and reburial might account for the observed phenomena. From time to time a small series of stone cists, to be discussed in detail in the following chapter, containing either pottery, closely comparable to that from the chamber tombs, or cremations, has come to light. An urn closely resembling those from the Knackyboy Cairn has been found isolated in a natural cleft in the rock on St Martin's. The periodic opening of such cists and the collection and concentration of their contents, an act which could have been followed by mass interment in a chamber tomb, would accord well with the recurring record of partially broken and fragmented urns, masses of sherds, cremated bones, soil and charcoal in burial chambers.

The external relationships of the Scillonian chamber tombs to other monuments are discussed in detail in Chapter 12. At this stage it can be said that there are other not dissimilar chamber tombs, concentrated mainly in the Penwith district of Cornwall (Daniel, 1950, 237-42), while close counterparts can be seen in Ireland. Indeed, these Irish chamber tombs have been bracketed with the Scillonian series and have been perpetuated in archaeological literature as comprising a 'Scilly-Tramore' group (Daniel and Powell, 1949, 178).

SUMMARY

It has been possible in this chapter to consider the Scillonian chamber tombs broadly in terms of their distribution and siting, their variations of size and structure, and the burials that they housed. In conclusion it must be emphasised that, in spite of the numbers and density of these tombs, the Isles of Scilly are minute in size, have been computed as no more than one eight-thousandth part of England and Wales (Daniel, 1950, 29) and are still relatively little known. We have as yet no corpus of accurate plans of these chamber tombs and although efforts at conservation, at one point not entirely happy, have been made, periodic vandalism, particularly on the off-islands, does take place. Excavations of a remarkable standard for the eighteenth and late nineteenth century have been carried out and there have been two exemplary undertakings in this century. Notwithstanding, yet another excavation of a selected monument entered into with sympathetic attention to every aspect and enlisting all the now available nuances of knowledge and technique, could reap a rich harvest.

Any account of the Scillonian chamber tombs must of necessity be based in great measure upon the better preserved and more painstakingly excavated examples. This was well said by William Borlase (1756, 30) concerning the *'Giants-Cave*, near *Tol's Hill'*, St Mary's (H16:D18), now destroyed, when he introduced these monuments to Charles Lyttelton more than two centuries ago: 'the description of this therefore may give you a just notion of the rest, but that they are neither so large, nor so entire. You see the mouth of it, it is four feet six inches wide, thirteen feet eight inches long, and three feet eight high; we that were living were forced to creep into it, but it may admit *Giants* when they are dead. It is covered from end to end with large flat stones, which shelter the sheep, and has a *tumulus* of rubbish on the top of all.'

CHAPTER 5

Stone Cists and Cist-grave Cemeteries

In its simplest form a cist is four slabs of stone set at right angles to one another, and covered by a fifth. Sometimes the sides may consist of more than one slab, as may the cover, while walling is not unknown as a method of constructing the sides. Such cists may be set in a grave or upon the ancient surface beneath a barrow mound or cairn. In the north of Britain, numbers of cists have been found with no definite trace of mound or cairn above them.

Whether or not stone cists were a substitute for timber coffins in regions where suitable stone was plentiful is not clear. They have been found in places far removed from suitable stone, which had had to be transported. On the other hand certain cists, one of them to be seen on Samson still, have side slabs which have been skilfully grooved to receive the end slabs. These suggest the perpetuation in stone of features more normal to timber. Thus substitution may have been customary in certain places.

Within the British Isles stone cists frequently house contracted inhumation burials, sometimes with beakers, food vessels, daggers, battle-axes and other grave-furniture of the Early Bronze Age. A number also enclose cremations similarly furnished (Ashbee, 1960, 92). In the South West, cist-grave cemeteries, notably at Harlyn Bay, near Padstow, Mount Batten, Plymouth and Trelan Bahow, St Keverne, have been found to contain furnished burials of the so-called Celtic Iron Age (Hencken, 1932, 115–21; Fox, 1964, 113). At Harlyn Bay the grave furniture included a bronze swan-necked pin and two iron ring-headed

Page 121 9a Halangy Down, St Mary's. The lower slope building complex during excavation

9b Halangy Down, St Mary's. The circular chamber of the courtyard house, 1969

Page 122 10a Nornour: detail of hearth in main chamber
10b Nornour: detail of walling in antechamber of main installation

pins, two La Tène I bronze brooches recalling Iberian styles, earrings and a bracelet, all of which date from the late fourth and third centuries BC. From the cemeteries at Mount Batten and Trelan Bahow came bracelets, beads and La Tène III brooches, with decorated mirrors and imported glass vessels, an assemblage which suggests interment early in the first century AD. Not dissimilar cemeteries, with inhumation burials surrounded by rectangles of stone slabs set on edge have been encountered in Brittany (Giot, 1960, 184–6) and the Channel Islands (Kendrick, 1928, 79).

In the Scillies three categories of stone cist may be distinguished (Fig 19). The first is that of large cists met with beneath stone cairns, notably on Samson. The second is a small series which contained cremated burials apparently in urns. These urns, or the remains thereof, found in such cists are of the same character as the pottery from the numerous chamber tombs such as Bant's Carn. The third is such cist-graves as were found in numbers at Porth Cressa, Hugh Town, St Mary's (Ashbee, 1954; Dudley, 1961), which contained Romano-British pots and brooches.

The first record of the discovery of what appears to have been a stone cist in the Isles of Scilly is from the diligent pen of William Borlase (Borlase, 1758, 322, Pl xxix, Fig 2). In a passage in *The Natural History of Cornwall*, under the heading of 'Antiquities which have occurred in Cornwall since the year 1753', he writes:

A plain urn, inclosing human bones, found in Mr. T. Smith's garden at Newfort, in the isle of St. Mary's Scilly: it stood upon the natural clay, inclosed in a vault four feet six inches long, two feet three inches wide, about one foot three inches deep; the sides of the vault were faced with stone, its covering, flat stones; the run of the vault N.N.E. This is inserted as the only one yet discovered in the Isles of Scilly, to shew that these Islanders had the same way of burning the dead, and preserving what the fire left unconsumed, as other ancient nations.

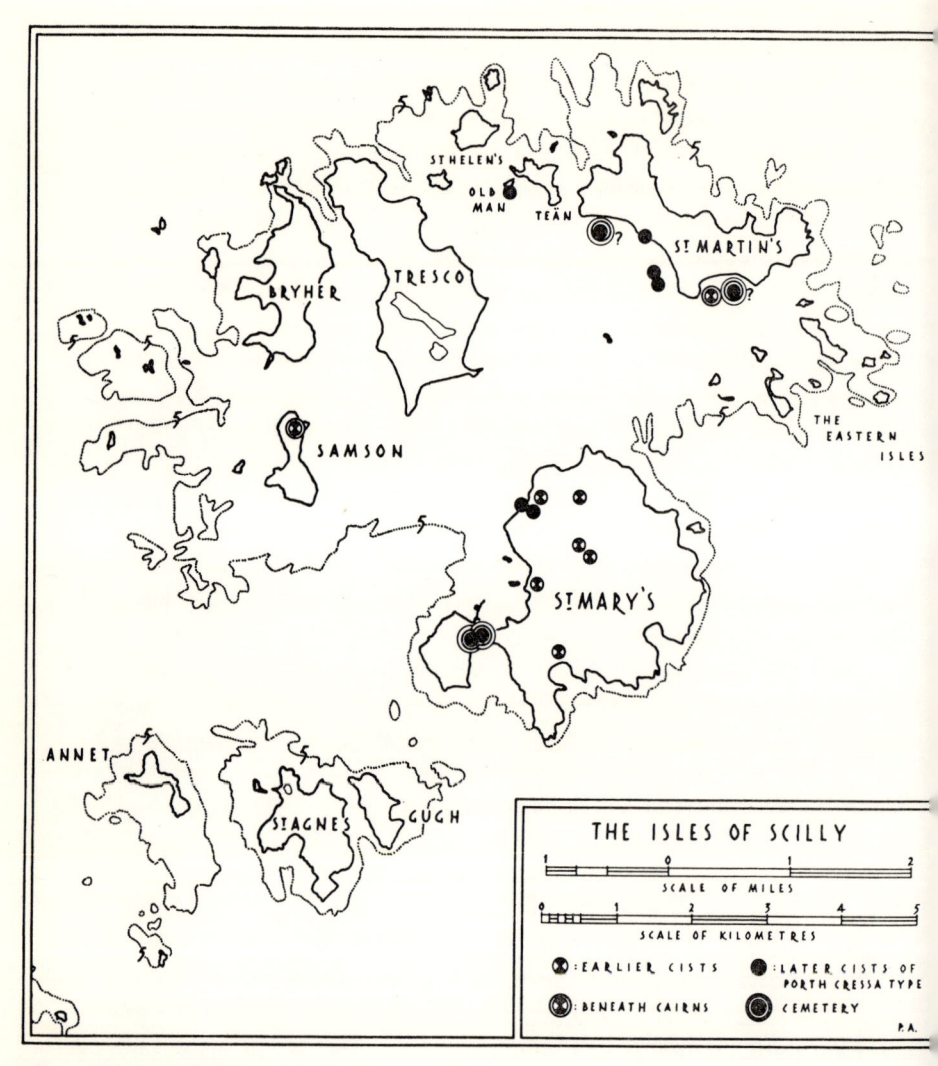

Fig 19 Cists on the Isles of Scilly

While it is possible that his 'vault' was the chamber of a small chamber tomb such as has been observed upon Middle Arthur (O'Neil, 1954), Borlase seems at pains to depict a rectangular structure. Indeed, by his use of the term 'vault' it would appear that he had something different in mind from the chambers of the chamber tombs which he refers regularly to as 'caves'.

There is only one certain example known in the Isles of Scilly of a large cist beneath a barrow or cairn, the first category. This, as described in the first chapter (page 26), was disclosed as the result of a barrow excavation conducted by Augustus Smith on Samson in 1862. A chamber on Buzza Hill, above Hugh Town, has been inspected by probing and as far as can be seen without excavation, is a large stone cist. It is probable that a cairn formerly surrounded and covered it. From the undulations which may well betoken the one-time cairn, it would seem likely that the cist had been set into the ground. A small barrow now ruinous on Helvear Down, St Mary's, seems to have had a small cist set near its top. On Normandy Down, the existence of vertical blocks at both ends of a chamber could suggest a closed chamber or cist.

Great care must be exercised in the diagnosis of stone cists in barrows and cairns on the Isles of Scilly. With the exception of such a patent example as the Samson cist, the mere morphological approach may fail. It will be remembered that certain chamber tombs were seemingly closed by a block. Thus with a relatively simple chamber, had the coverstones and some of the cairn material been robbed, and the blocking stone left *in situ*, the remaining structure would closely resemble a cist. This is a problem that can only be resolved by sympathetic excavation.

The cist on the North Hill of Samson (Plate 6a; Fig 20) is in the barrow opened under the direction of Augustus Smith, for the benefit of the 'select party of Cambrian archaeologists' on 3 September 1862. They levered off the great single cover-stone and found, in the cist beneath, a deposit of burnt bones and nothing else although it was large enough to have housed an inhumation burial. A most remarkable feature of this cist is the grooves in the side-stones which house the end-stones. Such grooves could have been made in granite with, for example, hard

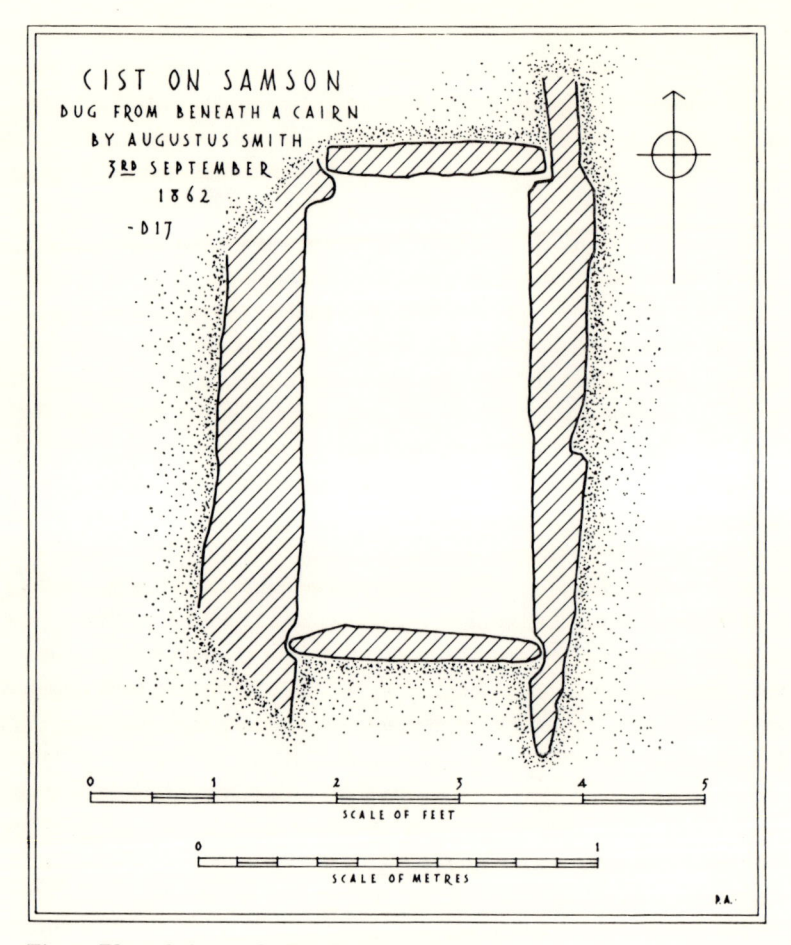

Fig 20 Plan of cist on the North Hill of Samson

quartz tools and the use of a peck and percussion technique. On the other hand it has been mooted that they are selected weathered stones gleaned from beach or outcrop on account of their form. Three flat irregular stones floored this cist while clay mortar secured them, luted the joints and the cover-stone. Its internal dimensions are 3ft 9in long

STONE CISTS AND CIST-GRAVE CEMETERIES

by 2ft wide and 2ft 3in deep; the cover-stone is 4ft by 5ft 7in. Piggott (1941) has described this cist on Samson in detail, comparing it with a series of similarly grooved cists, all within a radius of one mile of Poltalloch in Argyll (Craw, 1930). At the same time he emphasised that these grooved cists could be renderings in stone of timber coffins, the grooves in the side-slabs being the reflection of similar jointing in more easily worked wood. By comparison he was able to imply an Early Bronze Age date for the group.

Augustus Smith, as mentioned in Chapter 1, read an account of his barrow opening on Samson at a meeting of the Royal Institution of Cornwall on 29 May 1863. In his own words, which are quoted at length by W. C. Borlase in his *Naenia Cornubiae* (Borlase W. C., 1872, 159–62):

> The mound, in its outer circumference, measured about 58 yards giving, therefore, a distance of near upon thirty feet to its centre, from where the excavation was commenced. For about eighteen or twenty feet the mound appeared entirely composed of fine earth, when an inner covering, first of smaller and then of larger rugged stones, was revealed. These were carefully uncovered before being disturbed, and were one by one displaced till a large upright stone was reached, covered by another of still more ponderous dimensions, which projected partially over the edges of the other. At length this top covering, of irregular shape, but measuring about 5 feet 6 inches in its largest diameter, was throughly cleared of the superincumbent stones and earth, and showed itself evidently to be the lid to some mysterious vault or chamber beneath.

When the stone of 'more ponderous dimensions' was raised, there was 'disclosed to view an oblong chest or sarcophagus beneath'. In the cist Smith and the Cambrian archaeologists 'in paleto and crinoline gathered round in reverential and earnest expectation' and 'in a small patch, a little heap of bones, the fragmentary framework of some denizen of earth, perhaps a former proprietor of the Islands—were discovered piled together in one corner'.

The work continued and

The bones were carefully taken out, and the more prominent fragments, on subsequent examination by a medical gentleman, were found to give the following particulars: Part of an upper jawbone presented the alveolae of all the incisors, the canines, two cuspids, and three molars, and the roots of two teeth, very white, still remaining in the sockets. Another fragment gave part of the lower jaw with similar remains of teeth in the sockets. All the bones had been under the action of fire, and must have been carefully collected together after the burning of the body. They are considered to have belonged to a man about 50 years of age.

Presumably after the removal of the 'little heap of bones', they scrutinised the cist, for its characteristics and construction are commented upon in good detail: 'The bottom of the sarcophagus was neatly fitted with a pavement of three flat irregular-shaped stones, the joints fitted with clay mortar, as were also the interstices where the stones forming the upright sides were joined together, as also the lid, which was very neatly and closely fitted down with the same plaster.' On its construction he observes: 'Two long slabs, from seven to nine feet in length, and two feet in depth form the sides, while the short stones fitted in between them make the ends, being about three-and-half feet apart, and to fix which firmly in their places, grooves had been roughly worked in the larger stones.' In conclusion, he notes how the paving stones were 'embedded immediately upon the natural surface of the granite of which the hill consists'.

One other cist covered by a barrow is known in the Isles of Scilly. During 1949 B. H. StJ. O'Neil excavated a small cist covered in this manner, on an ancient surface overwhelmed by the sea on Par Beach, St Martin's. No direct evidence of date was found but a sherd of Scillonian 'Bronze Age' pottery lay close by.

From time to time, other cists, to be grouped in the second category, containing either pottery comparable with that from the chamber tombs or cremations, have come to light. One or two of these seem to have contained nothing identifiable but, on account of their size and general character they should be considered as belonging to the series.

A cist perhaps found in the vicinity of Halangy Porth many years ago produced pottery pronounced by R. A. Smith, who was at that time Keeper of British and Mediaeval Antiquities at the British Museum, as being of the 'Megalithic Period' of Scilly (Dowie, 1928–9, 243). From the brief and only record of it: 'The sides and bottom of the cist were each composed of single slabs, the top by 5 separate slabs, all of granite. The internal dimensions were 3ft. by 1ft. by 1ft. 6in. high. Some of the sherds were decorated with incised and impressed motives.' This discovery is matched by another cist uncovered during building operations at Old Town, St Mary's, during 1964 (Mackenzie, 1965). Fragments of bone were recovered from it but whether they were contained in the pot, also found in the cist, is not known. These fragments of bone were only partly calcined and warped and this would seem to result from a rather inefficient cremation. Such partly burned bones have been met with from time to time elsewhere and can only result from a lack, real or contrived, of suitable fuel when the body was burned.

Two small cists, each built of flat stones and covered by a single large slab have long been known on St Mary's. One at Content Farm (Ashbee, 1952) (Plate 6b) was 2ft 2in in length, 1ft 5in wide and 1ft 2in in depth. In it was the base of a pot (Fig 21). Details of the cist's discovery as related in 1950 by Mr J. Treneary of Telegraph Hill suggest that it might have been covered by a small cairn. From the soil around it he collected eight worked flints; which included a barbed-and-tanged arrowhead, a small almost circular scraper and a blade with side retouch. The technique on the last is reminiscent of the plano-convex knife series (Clark, 1932). The flints need not, however, have been associated with this cist, since surface industries occur on the neighbouring fields (Ashbee, 1954, 125–6). An almost identical cist was found at the close of the nineteenth century in the Klondyke Field (Plate 6c) just west of

STONE CISTS AND CIST-GRAVE CEMETERIES

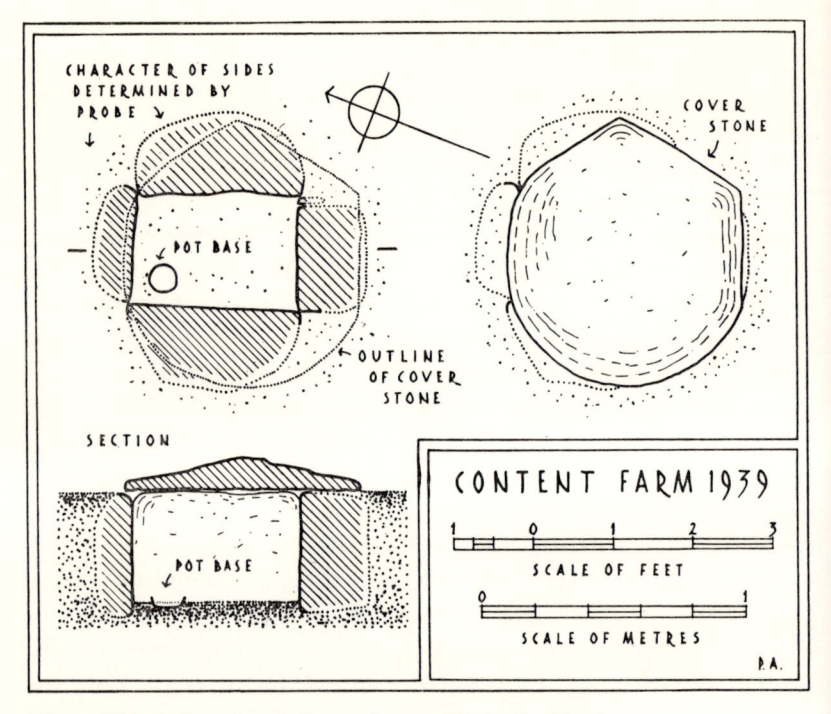

Fig 21 Plan and section of cist on Content Farm, St Mary's

the Coastguard Tower on Telegraph Hill. A photograph was taken of it by Mr Alexander Gibson but it is not known what its contents, if any, were. Yet another cist of this type, some 2ft square was found on Par Beach, St Martin's (O'Neil, 1949, 164).

The internal dimensions of the Content Farm cist make it unlikely that it contained an adult contracted burial although, perhaps, bones could have been packed into it. No trace of cremated bone was seen and it seems unlikely that such could have disappeared completely. It might be thought that the quarrymen interfered with it when it was found but since, presumably, they overlooked the pot base, and Mr Treneary was present shortly afterwards, this seems unlikely. Both this and the Klondyke Field cist could, however, have contained the inhumation burials of children which would have left little trace in the lime-hungry soil.

When O. G. S. Crawford visited the Isles of Scilly in 1926 he saw a rectangular cist which had long been exposed in the surface of Town Lane, St Mary's (Crawford, 1928, 420, Pl III). This cist, noted as 'about midway between Holy Vale and the Marconi Station' was about 3ft in length and 2ft in width. From its character and dimensions it could be considered as comparable with that found, not far distant, on Content Farm. Crawford observed that 'Nothing is known about it, but presumably it was found when the road was made by Mr. Augustus Smith more than 80 years ago' and 'There is said to have been another near it, but Mr. Gibson has searched without success'. Since these words were written, the road has been metalled and there is nothing now to be seen. However, as far as is known this cist was not disturbed, so that it remains *in situ* below the modern road. If the precise spot were located, a future remaking of the road might allow investigation.

A cist of size commensurate with Borlase's Newfort example, and that on Samson, was exposed by a cliff fall on St Martin's in 1946 (Lewis, 1949). The site was on the southern side of the island opposite St Martin's Flats and between Knackyboy Cairn and Yellow Rock Carn. One end of it had fallen on to the beach, but the rest of its structure remained in the cliff. It was some 4ft below the modern surface and had been built in a pit dug into the subsoil to the rabb, which was its floor. In length it was about 4ft, but it was only rather more than 12in in depth below its cover-stones. Slabs on edge with smaller stones formed the sides. Upon scraping clean the floor of this cist two flat-oblate amber beads of about 1cm diameter were found, together with what appears to have been a curiously fibulate iron concretion. On account of its amber beads it could well be considered with the second category of cists.

An urn allegedly found in a natural cleft in the rocks near Yellow Rock Carn (Lewis, 1948, 8), of which a photograph was taken by Alexander Gibson, might also be considered in this series. Such a mode of burial recalls certain of the chamber tombs, the builders of

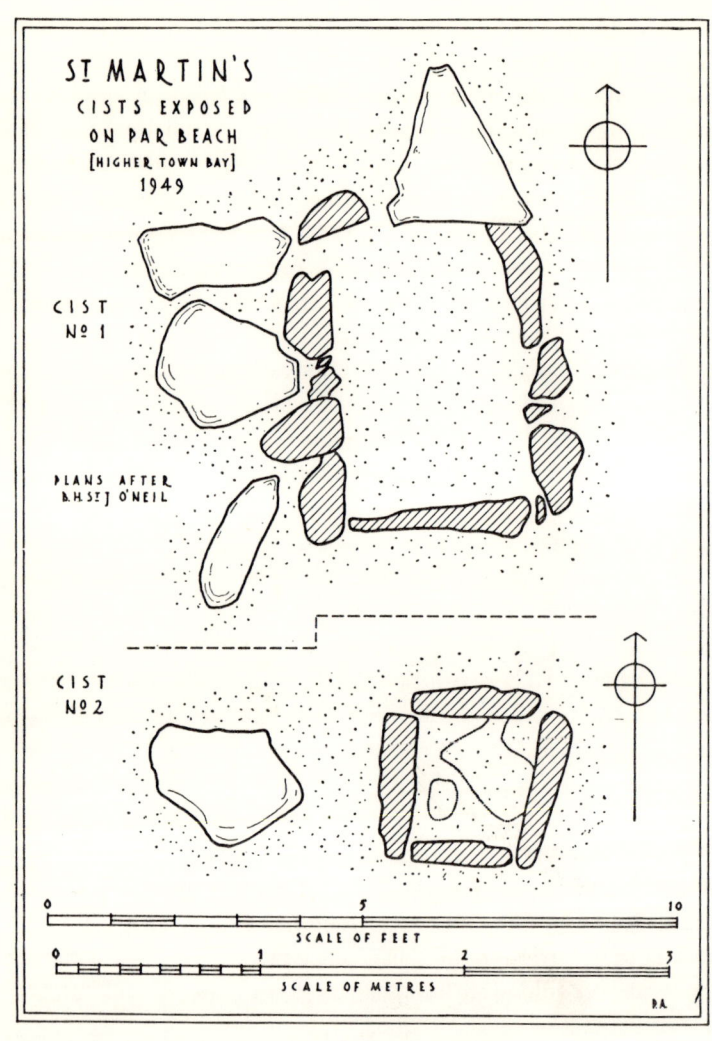

Fig 22 Plans of cists on Par Beach, Higher Town Bay, St Martin's

STONE CISTS AND CIST-GRAVE CEMETERIES

which have frequently incorporated into their structures natural outcrops and protuberances of rock.

We now come to the third category of stone cists—cist-graves. Cists have from time to time been exposed by the continual inroads of the sea (Fig 22). Troutbeck (1794, 112) tells of what may well have been cist-graves found, shortly before his time, under sand washed away by high tides near Middle Town, St Martin's. Indeed, Lewis (1948, 8) was of the view that his description suggests contracted burials.

It was the encroachment of the sea that revealed a cist in a bay,

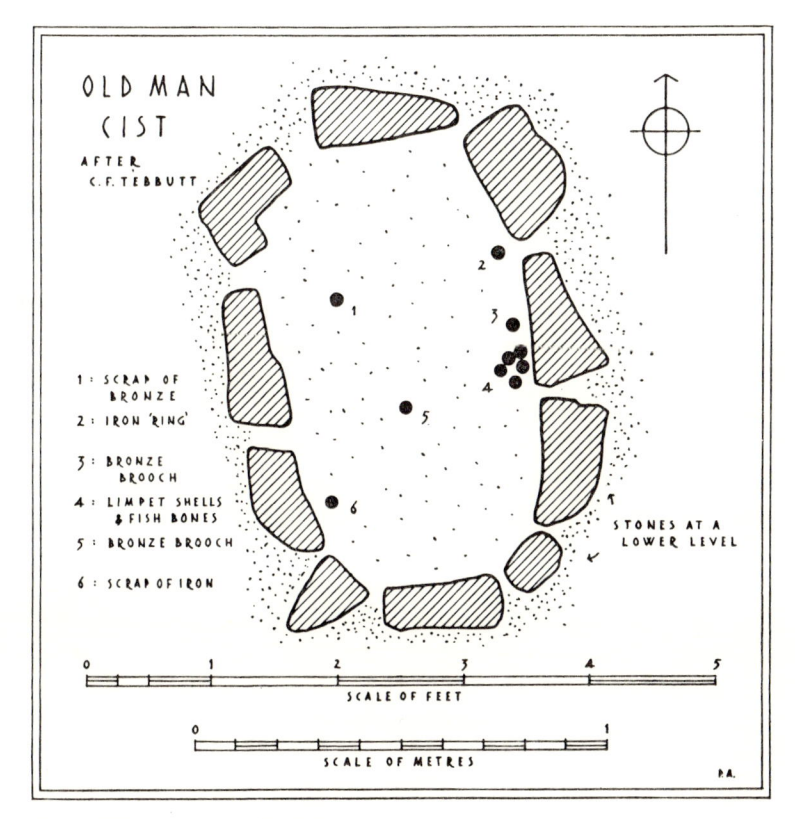

Fig 23 Plan of cist on Old Man

broken through by the sea, on the west side of the small island of Old Man, Teän (Fig 23). This cist was first seen, and excavated, during June 1933 by C. F. Tebbutt (Tebbutt, 1934). Selected boulders enclosed an oval area 3ft 6in long and 2ft wide but no cover-stones were found. In it were two bronze brooches, remains of another disintegrated bronze object, a scrap of iron, part of an iron ring and what was considered as a food deposit—a few limpet shells and fish bones. In Mr Tebbutt's own words:

> The stones were unworked but obviously chosen with a view to making the required oval shape. There appeared at first to be a gap at the SE end of the cist, but actually it was complete, the tops of stones 1 and 2 being 7in. below the tops of the others, and covered by sand.
>
> On clearing away the sand that had accumulated inside, a layer of dark grey clay was found at an average depth of 10in. below the tops of the enclosing stones. At the north end several thin slabs of stone lay in the cist.
>
> The layer of grey clay was an inch thick and contained much charcoal, several larger pieces of carbonised wood [identified as Common oak *Q. robur*], and all the objects found. Below it was a layer, an inch thick, of very black oily clay that was sterile of objects and lay directly on undisturbed yellow clay.
>
> No traces of bone or other human remains were found, and I am inclined to regard it as an inhumation (if a burial at all), as it is unlikely that cremated bones would have entirely disappeared ... The large amount of charcoal in the layer of grey clay had the appearance of a grave lining of brushwood or coarse matting.
>
> ... All the metal objects were in a bad state owing to contact with sea-water. The two fragments of brooches are difficult to parallel, but appear to be amongst the latest examples of the La Tène style, and probably date from the first century A.D.

When in October 1949, the present writer travelled for the first time to the Isles of Scilly he had been provided by Mr G. C. Dunning, at that time Inspector of Ancient Monuments for the Ministry of Works, with a copy of the published report on the Teän, Old Man, cist. In view of the news of cists at Porth Cressa, by Hugh Town, St Mary's, that had reached the ministry, this seemed the most relevant in the circumstances. The discovery of cists had been made during the digging of trenches for the foundations of houses on the Isles of Scilly's council housing estate. The trench for the dividing wall between two houses revealed one cist and the end of another. Excavations (Plate 7a) were continuous from the latter part of October 1949 to January 1950 and revealed ten cists and a boulder-covered grave. Some of the cists contained bronze brooches, comparable to those found on Old Man, while two were furnished with Romano-British pots. In one the greater part of a contracted inhumation burial was found. Thus the situation apparent upon the Old Man, Teän, discovery was substantiated, that cist-graves of the Romano-British era existed in numbers in Scilly. As has been observed by Radford (1958) there is a contrast with the well-built rectangular cists of the Harlyn Bay cemetery but the rite is the same. A comprehensive report of the excavation was published in 1954 (Ashbee, 1954).

A decade later, in 1960, further cists were encountered in Poynter's Garden, Hugh Town, a plot not far distant from the site of the Porth Cressa cemetery. Excavations were carried out by Miss D. M. Dudley (Dudley, 1961). Although there were signs of recent disturbance, cist-graves comparable to those examined at Porth Cressa were unearthed together with boulder-covered graves. From eight of these identifiable bones were recovered testifying to a contracted inhumation rite.

The Porth Cressa cist-grave cemetery (Fig 24) lay just to the south of Hugh Town, in what was until recently termed the 'Parson's Field'. This field was the southern extremity of the middle and lower part of the slope from the eminence of the Garrison to the low ground which separates Porth Cressa from St Mary's Pool. The greater part of Hugh Town stands upon this isthmus. The cemetery contained ten boulder-built and composite-covered cist-graves (Plate 7b) and one boulder-covered grave. The cists had been built, in pits dug into the subsoil, of

STONE CISTS AND CIST-GRAVE CEMETERIES

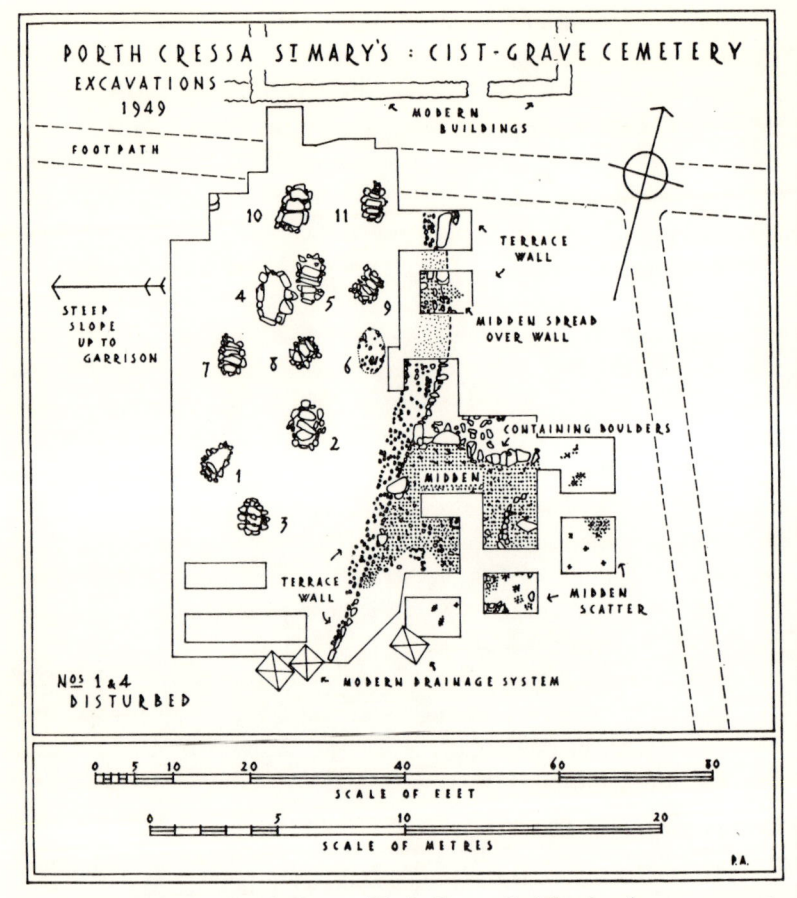

Fig 24 Excavation at Porth Cressa, Hugh Town, St Mary's, cist-grave cemetery

selected granite blocks and slabs, and were similarly covered (Fig 25). Of the ten cists in the cemetery, eight were of approximately uniform size and form. Two, however, were larger and of more massive construction. They were built of selected boulders such as would result from the weathering of sea-cliffs or carns. For the most part tabular weathered material was employed, but there were a small number of beach-worn blocks also. Five of the ten cists were oval in plan, three

STONE CISTS AND CIST-GRAVE CEMETERIES

could be described as coffin-shaped, while two more were rectangular. The two rectangular cists were larger than the remainder, and were of more massive construction. These oval and coffin-shaped cists have been termed Type I; the more massive and rectangular, Type II.

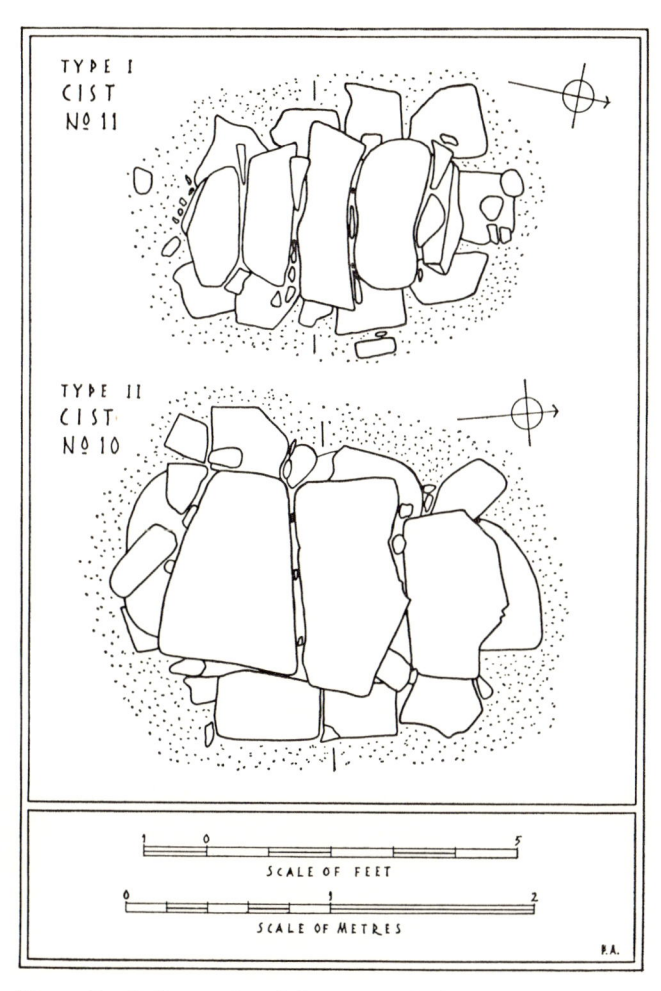

Fig 25 Porth Cressa cists, before removal of cover-stones

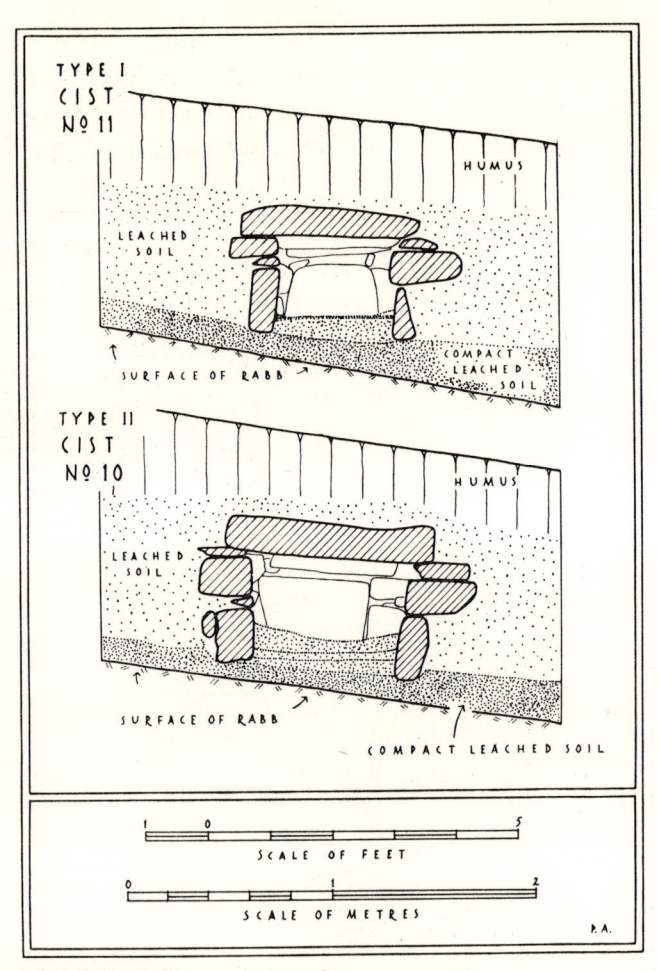

Fig 26 Porth Cressa cists, sections

The method of construction of the Type I cist sides and ends varied. For some, standing slabs had been used; for others, stone walling; while others again were built of a combination of standing slabs and stone walling (Fig 26). Each cist-grave had been covered by three or four capstones. These were selected slab or bolster form stones, set upon the

Page 139 11a Granite Roman altar, now at Tresco Abbey

11b Stone column base preserved in a garden opposite the Atlantic Hotel, Hugh Town, St Mary's

Page 140 12a St Helen's, the Oratory, east wall and altar

12b Saddle quern from Halangy Down, St Mary's

12c Bowl quern found on the beach Halangy Porth, St Mary's

cists at right-angles to the long axes. The cover-stones varied in number according to the size of the cist, and as to whether slabs or bolsters were used. There were two slabs and a bolster on one and five bolster-stones on another. It did not appear that a definite form of cover-stone was allied to any specific style of construction. Rather, it would seem, available stones had been collected and used as needed. Where cover-stones were not long enough to span a cist interior, oversailing courses had been arranged to lessen the gap.

The massively constructed Type II cists were built of large granite blocks, too large in one instance for two, or even three, men to carry with ease. In one of these larger cists the lower course of one side was one entire rock. Their internal dimensions were almost twice those of the remainder.

In cist-graves built of standing stones or large blocks the interstices of the sides were filled up with small broken pieces of granite bedded in the bright yellow sandy clay. In almost every instance where cover-stones were undisturbed it was clear that this procedure had been used to seal off the gap between them. Larger gaps were filled by the insertion of convenient blocks. With the passage of time much of this yellow sandy clay has washed into their interiors forming a layer on the bottom and mantling the remains found in them (Fig 27).

Packing blocks behind the standing slabs of the side of one cist showed that they had been built in pits dug into the subsoil. They had been inserted to secure the stones in an upright position. In the leached soil it was almost impossible to detect these pits visually. However, the compact character of the pit fillings, with occasional humic clods beneath overhanging stones allowed some observation of their character. In each case the cists appeared to have been set directly on the rabb.

The long bones and skull found in a relatively well-preserved condition in one cist show that the rite of burial in the Porth Cressa cist-graves, and by implication in others of their type (for example the Old Man, Teän cist), was contracted inhumation. The skull, on its right side, might point to the body having been laid in that position. A long bone fragment found in another cist reinforces this conclusion, as do the

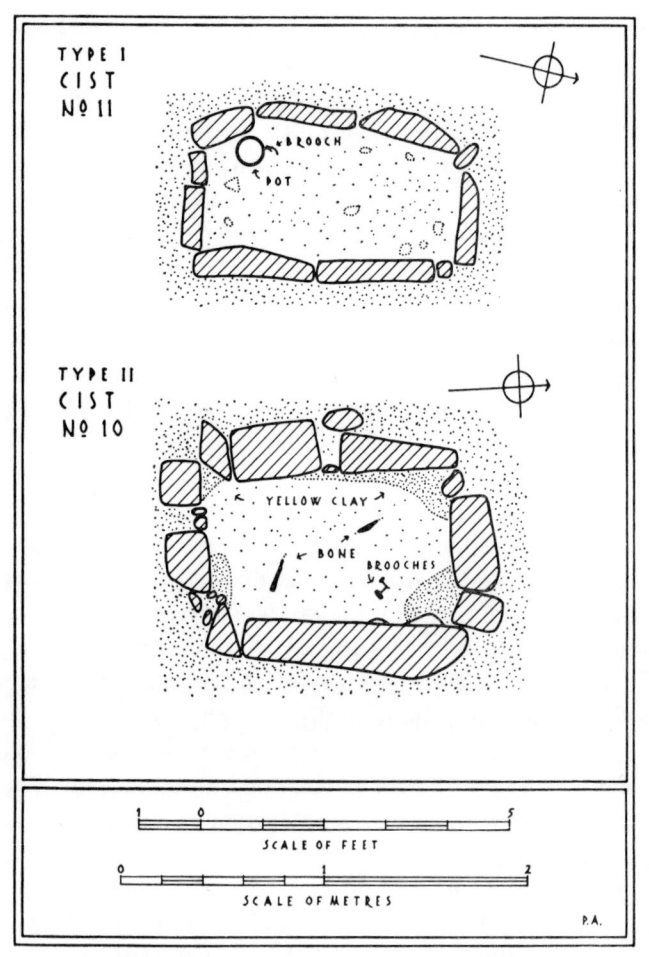

Fig 27 Porth Cressa cists after removal of cover-stones

long bones found beneath stones which were all that remained of the uncisted burial.

In three instances, two brooches had accompanied the deceased to the grave; in another instance one only. In two more instances there was a brooch and a pot, plus an oblate glass bead in one. Thus in 9 cist-graves (excluding 2 disturbed ones which with the boulder-covered grave make a total of 11), 6 were furnished, while 3 were unfurnished. These bronze brooches may well have fastened cloaks or shrouds.

Where it was possible to assign approximate dates, based upon approximate parallels from southern England, the bronze brooches, with one exception, fell within the first century AD. The exception is a disc brooch which has affinities with later Romano-British brooches. The two pots from the cists would not be out of place in a Late Iron Age or earlier Roman context in the South West. The striking point with regard to the series of brooches is the difficulty which Mr M. R. Hull, who made an especial study of them, had in finding counterparts among the very large number of Roman brooches known to him. It may be that parallels should be sought in Gaul. On the other hand when the now quite large number of brooches known from the Isles of Scilly, a number augmented by the recent excavations on Nornour, be considered, a specific Scillonian form seems apparent.

The two different types of cist-grave, the smaller (Type I) and the larger (Type II) must be noted. As far as can be seen, however, the grave furniture, where present, was much the same in each. The larger ones built of bigger rocks would have entailed more labour in their construction than the smaller, and it would be possible to describe the smaller cists as built around the larger, although at a distance. Can it be that here there were the more substantial and elaborate cists of more prominent members of the community, whose interment accordingly demanded more labour than that of the remainder? An alternative interpretation would be that in view of their greater size, the larger cists were intended for double burials, a contention that is difficult to prove in the absence of skeletal remains. Admittedly the records of cist cemeteries, cists and graves elsewhere do not provide many examples of double burial, but they are known. Differentiation between male and female graves is also difficult; the presence of a bead might denote a female grave. Examination of skeletal material suggested that the burial beneath boulders might have been that of a female.

The relatively level area in which the cist-grave cemetery had been sited was found to be one of deep soil retained by a massive dry-stone wall which ran across the hill-slope. In the soil were numerous worn sherds of pottery and a few flint flakes. The wall retaining this depth of soil would seem to antedate the cist-grave cemetery, and it seems likely that it was because of the soil-depth the terrace offered that it was chosen to house the cists. Its original function would seem to have been a cultivation terrace.

At one point, above the robbed remains of the terrace-retaining wall there was an extensive midden, comprised almost entirely of limpet shells. A spread of these shells was also above the wall in one place where it was intact. The main midden was confined on one side by large granite boulders, perhaps robbed from the terrace wall. In addition to limpet shells, the midden contained bones of ox, horse, pig and sheep, fish-bones and above, in, and below it, a small number of sherds of distinctive 'grass-marked' pottery. This is found extensively in the South West (Thomas, 1968) and may range in date from the sixth to tenth centuries AD.

Poynter's Garden, Hugh Town (Dudley, 1961), was a stone-walled enclosure not far to the north of the erstwhile Parson's Field at Porth Cressa and, like it, was part of the slope from the Garrison's height to the lower ground. Foundation trenches dug for building early in 1960 allowed five cist-graves to be examined by excavation. Four of these, all oval in shape, were of Porth Cressa Type I form, while one, although not appreciably larger than the others, was built more massively and was of Type II. A point of difference was that in building the oval cist-graves in Poynter's Garden, more and smaller boulders were used than in the Parson's Field.

As a result of the excavation she conducted Miss Dudley (Dudley, 1960–1, 224) was able to comment upon cist-grave construction. She considered that a pit of average depth of about 12in was first of all dug. Thereupon blocks of granite and beach-boulders were collected and set around the edge of the pit. Although the stones were not very large they were selected as possessing at least two flat sides, one to facilitate housing in the pit and the other for a neat internal finish. In the vertical plane the stones were set closely and were often wedged for stability. Both the walling and the vertical slab method of building were observed, but there was no evidence of clay rendering or luting. On account of their size it was thought that the cover-stones must originally have been visible above ground level. One of the Parson's Field, Porth Cressa, cist-graves had a heap of stones above its fallen-in cover-stones, so small covering cairns may, when they were first built, have marked each one. Indeed, this may have obtained in Poynter's Garden also.

Unlike the Parson's Field cists, few things had accompanied the Poynter's Garden burials. In one of the cist-graves a few fragments of a bronze pin lay by the skeleton, while pieces of an iron pin were found vertically near the neck. As Miss Dudley observed, it might have been expected that metal would have survived in conditions that favoured bone.

Two of the Poynter's Garden cist-graves had in them the greater part of complete skeletons, while there was a considerable amount of bone in another. Examination of the bones from all the eight burials under laboratory conditions allowed tentative identification of sex to the extent of four males, a female and a child.

The cemetery was dated by association with a nearby habitation site and by analogy with the Parson's Field, Porth Cressa, cemetery. It was considered by Miss Dudley how the general time-range of these cemeteries is in accord with the occupation of the homestead excavated on Halangy Down in 1950 (Ashbee, 1955).

Down the years obstructions to cultivation have been met with in the bulb gardens which fringe Toll's Porth at the foot of Halangy Down. It has often been said locally that here lies the cemetery that might be associated with the settlement. Although a truncated cist of Porth Cressa Type I has long been visible in the cliff close by (Ashbee, 1955) it was only in May 1965 that a fall-in of soil in one of the bulb gardens betrayed the presence of a cist-grave. This turned out to be a well-built example of the Porth Cressa Type I series, like that exposed in the cliff close by. Four slab cover-stones remained, while a fifth had, at an earlier juncture, been removed and timber and smaller stones substituted. The timber had rotted but its presence was revealed by earth subsidence. An excavation was carried out by members of the Isles of Scilly Museum Association (Mackenzie, 1967) which showed that the cist was built of walling with carefully selected blocks and was of well-proportioned oval form with a length of 4ft 5in, a breadth of 2ft 5in and a depth of 1ft 8in. Nothing however was found in it.

Over a long period of time cists have been revealed by the sea on the inner beaches of St Martin's. As mentioned on page 58, Troutbeck (1794, 112) reports what could well have been cist-graves which were found shortly before his time, exposed at low tide, near Middle Town. They might well have contained contracted inhumation burials. The Rev H. A. Lewis (Lewis, 1948, 8) searched for this site but could find no trace. Crawford illustrates a cist (Crawford, 1928, 420, Pl II) visible on the shore at St Martin's which he presumably saw when he visited the islands.

> ... between Crethus Hill and English Island Point, about 20 yards from the edge of the rushy bank, and approximately high-water mark. It is oriented north and south and is 3 feet long by 2 wide. It has now no capstone. The cist when found was full of coarse, gravelly sand and stones, which were cleared out; amongst this were parts of leg-bones (the joint-ends missing) and smaller fragments; then a piece of a human jaw, without teeth, and finally the skull. The facial portion was missing. The skull fell to pieces on removal but it and all the other pieces were preserved and the cist filled in again. Near by, to the west, were two or three other cists of the same type, and many years ago yet others were observed, both round this bay and at Lawrence's to the west of Crethus Hill.

These cists on Par Beach, St Martin's, which from their contents seem to have been of Porth Cressa type were, like those in Poynter's Garden, St Mary's, at no great distance from a contemporary habitation site (O'Neil, 1949, 164), while there are also traces of such habitation on the hill-slope above at May's Hill and Laurences' Brow. This close relationship of cemetery and dwelling also obtains at Halangy Down.

It emerges that there were two periods when cists were used for burials on the Isles of Scilly. The first may be put, to judge from the pottery and the use of the rite of cremation, at a time contemporary with the chamber tombs. The character of this relationship is difficult to define, and it is tempting to see a pattern of devolution and consider the first cists as succeeding the chamber tombs (Grimes, 1960, 178). Such a conclusion should be resisted for we do not know with any precision what was the relationship of cists to chamber tombs. A similar situation with regard to cists and chamber tombs can be seen on the mainland, in Cornwall. Thomas and Wailes (1967, 20) in their discussion of Penwith chamber tombs have sought to isolate an early mainland form of the evolved pottery of the Scillonian chamber tombs. They drew attention to a simple pot found in a cist at Trevedra Common, St Just in Penwith, in a field which had previously produced another cist containing a long-necked beaker (Thomas, 1961). These Penwith chamber tombs emerge as broadly parallel to the Scillonian series and it could be that cists were current at the earlier end of their usage.

The second, the now quite numerous range of cist-graves of Porth Cressa type, cannot be other than an insular Scillonian version, in Romano-Scillonian times, of the stone coffins or cists attested in the Cornish Iron Age. As Radford (1958, 58) pointed out, the burial rite is the same. Their sometimes rough structure was determined by the granite of the islands, but the distinctive coffin shape was a matter of deliberation for, as at Porth Cressa, it was possible to build a rectangular cist when this was desired. The Scillonian erratic polygonal form has been considered as a survival in isolation of a megalithic tradition (Thomas, 1961, 192).

CHAPTER 6

Standing Stones

Standing stones, sometimes termed menhirs or even menhiron, are found in a variety of circumstances. They can occur singly and in pairs, in circles and alignments while sometimes they stand around barrows and cairns. They have been found above and beside burials, which can be either inhumations or cremations, furnished or unfurnished (Lewis, 1965). In regions where suitable stone is rare their equivalents, found by burials, were massive timber posts (Pitt Rivers, 1898, 49; Piggott, 1936, 229). The first timber posts marking burials, and some of the standing stones, appear as field monuments of our Neolithic and earlier Bronze Age communities. The practice of posts and stones continued, however, into Celtic Iron Age times (Piggott, 1965, 232).

It seems unlikely that the timber posts would have been bare trunks; they may well have been carved and embellished, like those seen by early travellers in temperate North America (Wright, ed, 1947, 222), in a manner recalling the wooden figures that have come to light in our bogs and marshes (Piggott and Daniel, 1951, Plates 30–3). Standing stones, if not in anthropomorphic form, may have been adorned with portable and possibly perishable objects. What may have been an Irish circle of standing stones appears in the Tripartite Life of St Patrick, a ninth-century compilation recording early fifth-century events, which is preserved in an eleventh-century manuscript. In this the principal idol of Ireland is described as richly clad in gold and silver with twelve other idols covered with bronze ornaments around it. Stripped of the metal trappings, the description might be that of a stone circle with a central monolith (Kendrick, *The Druids*, 1928, 191).

Hencken (1932, 59) remarked that single standing stones are very numerous in Cornwall and, on the whole, undated. He cited the larger examples, those ranging from 10ft to about 18ft in height, and drew attention to a handled cinerary urn and accessory vessel found more than a century ago at the foot of the tallest, the stone at Tresvennack, in the parish of Paul, Penwith. The recent excavation (Russell and Pool, 1964, 15–26) about a standing stone at Try Farm, Gulval, showed that it stood by a cairn of stones which covered a rectangular cist built from four slabs of stone and covered by another. In the cist was a handled beaker and two unburnt bones, while its infill contained scattered calcined bone fragments. As an adjunct to their account the excavators summarised matters pertaining to menhirs in West Penwith and found that more than eighty are recorded or inferred. Some forty are still standing and seventeen have been the subject of investigation. From the details available they seem referable to the earlier Bronze Age. What must have been the largest single standing stone in the south-west was recorded by Borlase (1769, 162). It stood at Mên-Perhen in the parish of Constantine and was 24ft in length. Of this length, 20ft stood above the ground, while it had been set 4ft into the soil. When it was felled 'it made above twenty Stone Posts for gates, when it was clove up by the farmer'.

Borlase (1756, 34, 40), as a result of his visit to the Isles of Scilly, has given us details of the three undoubted standing stones still to be seen (Fig 28). He termed them 'Rude Stone Pillars' and wrote regarding the two on St Mary's: '... there are two still standing in this island; one on the summit of a round hill, on a little *Tumulus* near *Harry's Battery*, ten feet above the ground, by two feet nine inches wide; another, near *Bant's Karn*, nine feet three inches high, by two feet six inches square at a medium.' Of the standing stone on Gugh he wrote that 'Here, on a plain we found a large stone-erect nine feet high by two feet six inches wide'.

Above Porth Mellon on Mount Flagon, the stone (Plate 8a) seen by Borlase still stands 'near *Harry's Battery*'. From seaward it is obscured by the nearby white windmill-sailed daymark, after which it is often

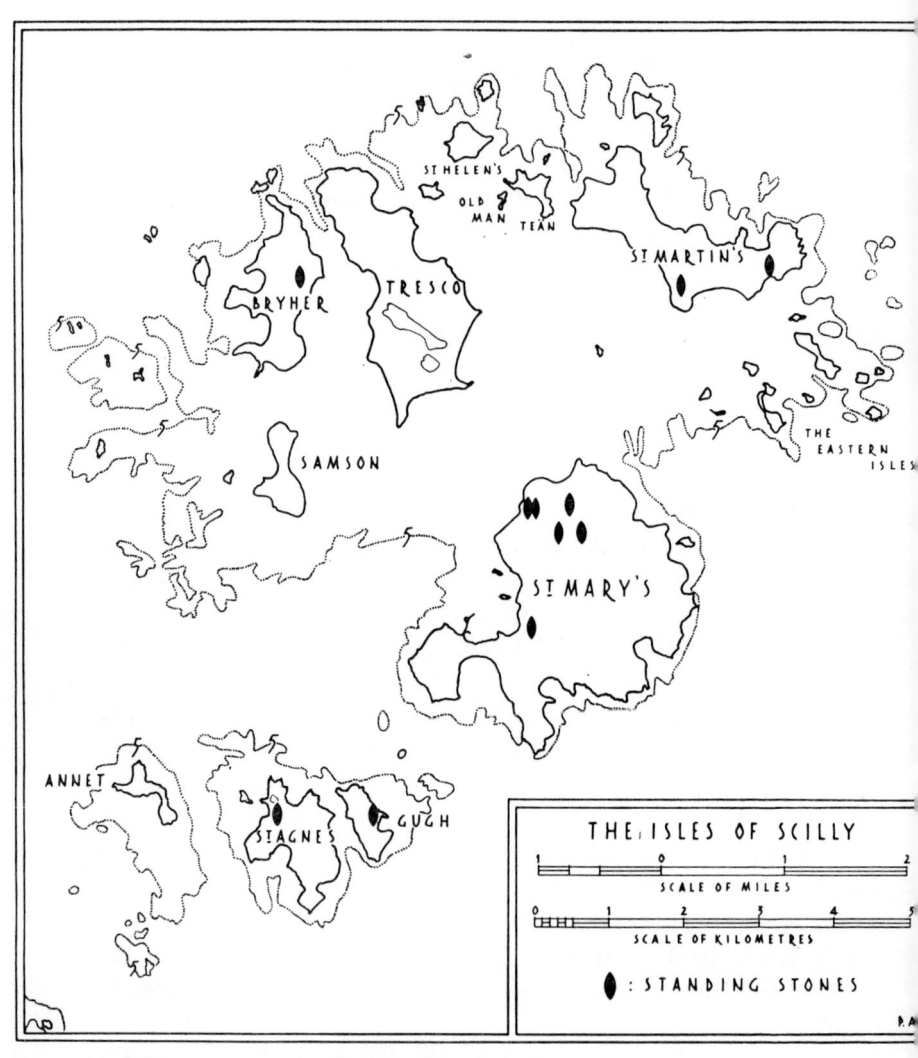

Fig 28 Standing stones on the Isles of Scilly

called. It has been in recent years secured in position, but traces of a small cairn can still be seen about it. Its slender angular, slightly irregular form suggests that it might originally have been split from a larger block. Although the mis-sited and uncompleted Harry's Walls were built close by during the sixteenth century (Saunders, 1962), this stone seems to have stood unscathed and presumably survived the demand for building stone that this structure must have entailed. The stone 'near *Bant's Karn*', from the dimensions given, is the 'Long Rock' which stands, slightly slanting, in a belt of pine trees just to the east of McFarland's Down (Plate 8b). It is of approximately square section and is regular, but slightly tapering. Indeed, its even surface might result from dressing at some distant date. A feature that the stone on Mount Flagon, by Harry's Walls, and the Long Rock have in common is that they are both slightly bulbous at the top distantly recalling Cornish crosses. This gives them both a rather anthropomorphic aspect. Indeed, the top of the Long Rock, although much weathered, might originally have borne a schematic face representation. Another standing stone referred to as 'in the corner of a field called Pungies is a square stone pillar' (Troutbeck, 1794, 101) may be a reference to the Long Rock.

Borlase's standing stone on Gugh, just to the south-east of Kittern Hill, now leaning eastwards at an angle of about sixty degrees, is, when seen in profile, slender and tapering, but has a broad flat face-side and rounded rear. It is much weathered and any features that it carried have long since disappeared from view. The lower part where it emerges from the ground may have been dressed to emphasise the broad face-side. Although there is a ruined chamber tomb close by, it stands at a distance from the concentration on Kittern Hill. Like the stone by Harry's Walls, on St Mary's, there are some signs that it might have had a small cairn close by it. Bonsor, however, dug around it to a depth of 3ft without finding anything (Hencken, 1933, 20).

It might be thought that these stones could be the remaining stones of erstwhile circles. The topography of Mount Flagon would seem to preclude this as far as the stone there is concerned. It must be remembered that Borlase saw these stones as single standing stones when he explored the islands during the eighteenth century. He was much concerned with stone circles, having studied the Cornish examples and, indeed, he considered that certain conjunctions of stones on St Mary's, were such circles. Had he seen other stones, even fallen ones, by these single standing stones he would have been likely to have commented upon them.

In addition to these standing stones Borlase refers to 'circles of Stones-erect' and illustrates both a circle (Borlase, 1756, Pl II, Fig ii) and a standing stone (Borlase, 1756, Pl II, Fig iii). The circle that he saw was on Salakee Down, St Mary's, 'On a Karn adjoining to the Giant's Castle', while the stone that he termed 'The High Stone', adjacent to some 'Basons' and 'thin, pyramidal, twelve feet at the base, and thirty feet high, not improbably an object of Druid Devotion', was at Peninnis. The circle may have been no more than a juxtaposition of natural boulders and the stone at Peninnis a fossil stack. This last stone Borlase was careful to separate from the 'Rude Stone Pillars' which he saw as 'sometimes idols, sometimes sepulchral Monuments, and at other times of various other uses amongst the ancients'.

Concerning the stone circle on Salakee Down, St Mary's, in Borlase's (1769, 198) own words:

> On a Karn adjoining to the Giant's Castle in St. Mary's Scilly we found the back of the Rock clear'd, as it seem'd of all unevenness, and making one plane of Rock. This Area is of a circular figure, 172 feet from North to South and 138 feet from East to West; on the edges of it are nine vast stones still remaining planted in a circular line, several others perfected the round, but from time to time have been remov'd, and some of them within these few years. There is no uniformity in the shape of the Stones that remain, neither do they seem to have been plac'd at any calculated, equal distances. The Stone [Borlase, 1769, Pl XI, Fig ii] plac'd among the Rock-idols makes one of the ring; the front of it, towards the center, is 20 foot long; a rude Pillar fallen down lies before it, about five paces distant, inwards. The rock stands East of the Central Point, and in a line

from it somewhat to the North of the West, are three large flat Stones which have Basons on the top of them, but pieces of them are broke and carry'd off. This was a great work of its kind, the floor of one Rock, and the Stones round the edges of an extraordinary size.

Whether or not Borlase 'constructed' this stone circle from the weathered stones that he found scattered in the vicinity of Giant's Castle we cannot know. However, he was a careful and consistent observer and thus some credence can be given to his description. It must suffice to say that a stone circle or, for that matter, circles of the character of the Cornish range (Hencken, 1932, 49–63) would not be out of place in the Isles of Scilly.

A stone 'pillar' is recorded on St Agnes by Gibson (1932, 98) who notes how 'A stone pillar called the "Priest Rock", about 9ft high can be seen on the shore near the Churchyard' while Hencken (1933, 17, fn) details that 'Mr. S. A. Opie of Redruth has lately reported a hitherto unnoticed stone circle on St. Agnes'. Borlase (1756, 52) remarks how he saw, when he landed on St Martin's, 'On the top of the adjoining Karn a large long stone (now fallen) stood upright, seven feet six inches long.' Of all these no trace can now be found.

A single large vertical stone (Ashbee, 1965, Pl IV, A) has for long been visible at the western limit of the hut complex at Halangy Down, St Mary's. Excavation has shown that it is most probably a corner stone of the rectangular annexe built on to an earlier oval hut (Ashbee, 1966, Fig 2). Scrutiny of this stone has discovered, low on its uphill surface, what could well be a stylised face representation of the same character as might conceivably have existed on the Long Rock. It is to be suspected that it might have been brought to Halangy Down from some other place and utilised as a standing corner stone on account of its sturdy character.

Excavation at Halangy Down during 1966, in the oval hut mentioned above, disclosed another stone which may well have originally stood elsewhere. Around the arc of the interior uphill wall of this oval hut were a series of large blocks of stone. Their weight and size suggest that they would not have fallen accidentally had they been upon the existent lower course. Beside these stones and coinciding with a gap in the remaining lower course (Ashbee, 1966, Pl VII, A), lay a stone some 7ft long and about 1ft 6in broad, triangular in section with dressed pointed ends, its flat face-side lying on the rabb floor of the hut. From its position it would seem to have fallen, face-side downwards from a vertical position in the wall. While this long stone could well have fallen in the course of time, as its pointed base had not been dug into the rabb, the fact that its neighbouring bottom-course stone was out of position suggested that the felling of this stone, and removal of heavy wall-stones was part of a programme of deliberate slighting. The face-side of this long stone had been carefully dressed to a plane surface, only a small roughly rectilinear area, longitudinal to the stone, being left in relief (Ashbee, 1966, Pl VII, B). Two clear circles delineated by a slight lowering of the plane surface are adjacent to the upper corners of a rounded relief rectangle. These features could well be all that is left of a more complex device removed by dressing. The possibility must be considered that this long stone was a standing stone, or a statue-menhir, for some reason incorporated into this hut wall.

During 1967 further excavation disclosed yet another large stone, which, by reason of its characteristics, could also be considered as an erstwhile standing stone of, indeed, an earlier age than the hut complex. It is a broad natural irregular block some 6ft in length, of flat lenticular section and about $3\frac{1}{2}$ tons in weight. Two side projections, one now broken from the block, would have given it a crude cruciform appearance when standing. It was found in the interior and well below the floor level of a sub-rectangular hut, immediately downhill of that excavated during 1950 (Ashbee, 1966, Fig 2), and just by the great fallen corner stones. Close by it, previously, a large fire-marked rectangular block, with a perforation, broken in antiquity, had come to light. The upper surface of this stone has in it a juxtaposition of deep clear cup-marks and a slot, some 9in in length and 3in in breadth (Ashbee, 1968, 24). Although a number of cup-marked stones are preserved in various Scillonian gardens as ornaments (Ashbee, 1953, 77), the only other undoubted cup-marked stone in an early archaeological context was found on St Martin's when, during his excavation of the Bronze Age hut on English Island Carn, O'Neil (1949) found a large stone with cup-markings at its base. A great stone set on edge was a feature of the hut foundations that O'Neil investigated on Par Beach.

A stone of much the same lineaments as this great Halangy Down boulder once stood in a hedge on Bryher (Gibson, 1932, 87). It had two perforations in its longer axis, set some 1ft 3in apart. Another stone, squared, but with similar perforations may be viewed in Tresco Abbey gardens. Neither of these stones need necessarily be of prehistoric origin. Indeed, perforations are regularly made even today, in granite jamb-stones, gate-posts and the like. They are, however, something other than the stones normally taken for such use, thus their having been taken from an earlier monument might be considered. Just below the present-day path which leads to the foot of Halangy Down from the lane which descends to Pendrathen Quay, stands a great tabular boulder. This has, on account of its isolation, often been thought of as a standing stone. It would seem possible that this large isolated stone is all that remains of an outlier of the Halangy Down stone-walled enclosure system and that it has survived on account of its size and solidity.

CHAPTER 7

Houses and Settlements

The first record of the location of an early house on the Isles of Scilly was by Borlase who described (1756, 40) where high tides bared walls on the shore of Annet. He also remarked that ruins were similarly disclosed on Samson Flats although he did not specify the form that they took. During the past half-century cliff erosion and archaeological fieldwork on the islands have brought to light extensive evidence of early dwelling (Fig 29). Apart from the Halangy Down 'Ancient Village', long known on account of its substantial hut remains, the clue that has frequently pointed to the presence of early habitation has been a midden. Quantities of limpet shells, bones, dark soil and broken pottery have been seen and all too frequently there are records of such middens, but details of the houses close by them are all too often not known.

Scillonian dwelling sites which have been detected through the discovery of middens or the foundations of stone-built houses and other structures, fall into three clear-cut categories according to the associated pottery. First, there are those characterised by sherds of pottery of the same kind as those from the chamber tombs. Secondly, there are those which have produced sherds of native Iron Age or imported Romano-British wares. Thirdly, a small series has yielded pieces of pottery and other objects which point to a period from immediate post-Roman times to a millennium later.

EARLIER HOUSE SITES

One stone-built house, within the first category, by English Island

Page 157 13 Urns from (a) Knackyboy Cairn, St Martin's (D8), and (b) from Obadiah's Barrow, Gugh, photo *c* 1900 (HI:D5). Both display comb-stamp ornament
(a) height 8in
(b) height 7½in

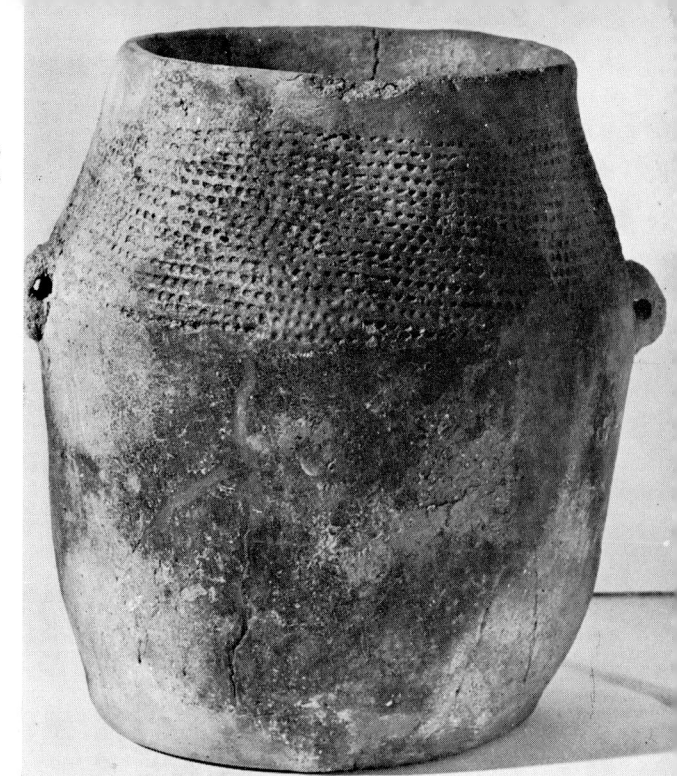

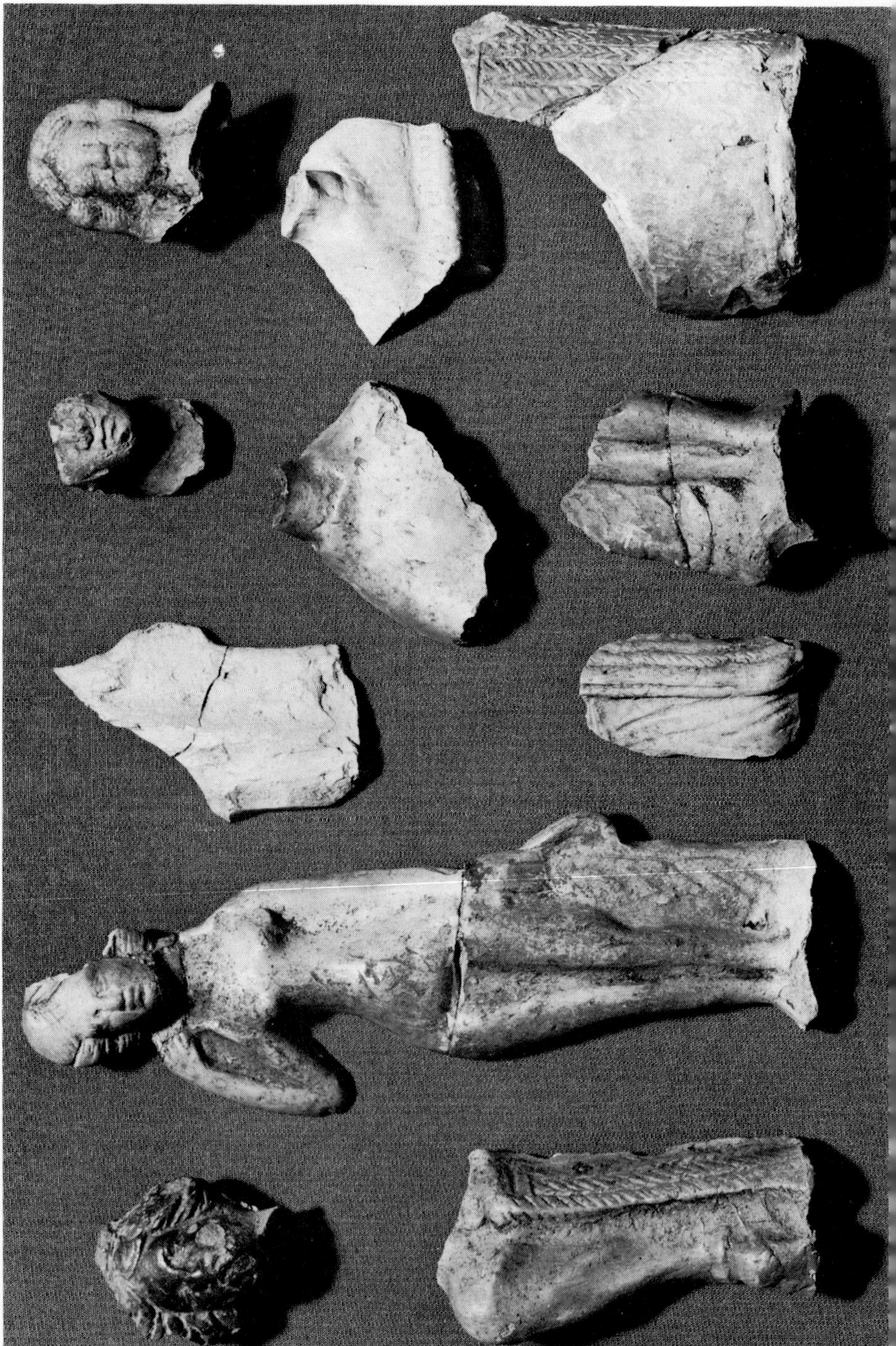

Carn, St Martin's, was shown by excavation to have been roughly rectangular in plan, unlike the Iron Age and para-Romano-British houses which are round or oval, as at Halangy Down (Ashbee, 1955). In this case, however, these forms have been progressively modified and the end result is a house plan closely resembling the Cornish courtyard houses (Hencken, 1933, *Archaeologia*). An oval or sub-rectangular house on Teän was not abandoned until the late sixth or seventh centuries AD.

By far the best known and recorded midden exposure in Scilly is that at Halangy Porth, St Mary's, drawn by George Bonsor (Hencken, 1932, 30, Fig 10C; 1933, 16, Fig 4) (Fig 30). Most of it has now been carried away by the sea and only the remains of sand-blanketed stone buildings still stand in the cliff, but at one time there was an enormous mass of limpet shells covered by an even greater mass of charcoal and burnt material. Among the shells were animal bones, substantial pieces of broken pottery, almost identical to those from the chamber tombs, as well as saddle querns. Excavations were conducted by Mr Alec Gray, between 1934 and 1936, in the then newly laid-out bulb garden to landward of this cliff exposure. From his work and from scrutiny of the cliff-exposed remains of buildings still visible it is possible to establish something of the character of this site.

The huts had been built in a declivity running, in a roughly south-westerly direction, to seaward and the masonry still to be seen in the cliff was the best preserved. The digging to landward revealed only the footings of a building and great quantities of loose stone rubble. Of the two buildings in the cliff-face, the northernmost was described by Gray as 'a small structure probably oval or circular in shape', and at one time was suggested as a possible chamber tomb (Ashbee, 1963, 15). Two sides remain, one built of large blocks, the other of small stones. It is possible that this was a narrow rectangular building, perhaps part of a complex. On the other hand the visible remains might represent the juncture of structures built one against the other. Between these walls was found the famous midden recorded by Bonsor and published by Hencken (1933). Regrettably this had for the most part gone by 1934

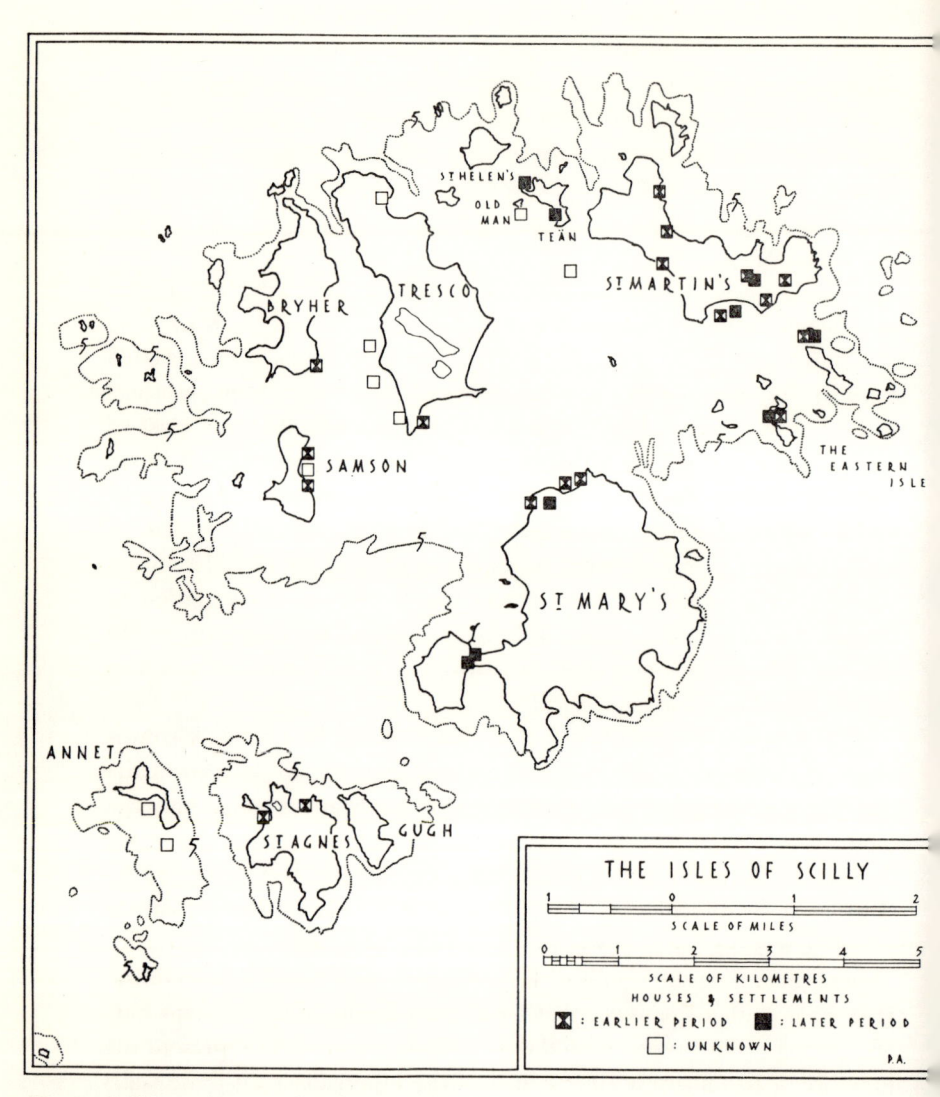

Fig 29 Scillianon house and settlement sites

HOUSES AND SETTLEMENTS

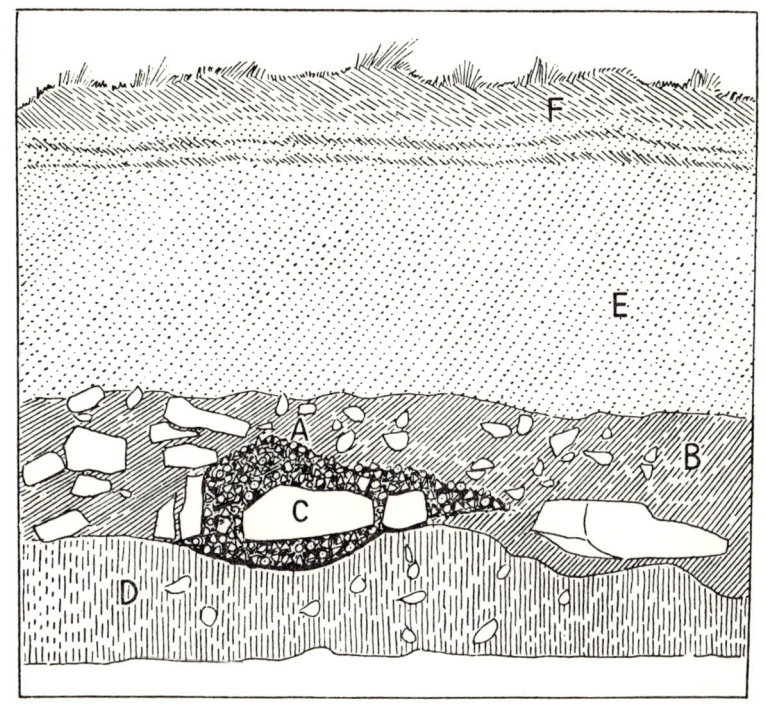

Fig 30 George Bonsor's section of Halangy Porth midden, showing layers observed (after Hencken, 1933)

when Gray investigated the site, although it is not known who dug this midden away and bared the walls which had housed it. Gray was able, however, to identify some of the contents for he describes limpet shells packed tightly together and lists bones that he found—split, broken and cut—of sheep, seal, horse, red deer and a small deer.

Close by and to the south is the remaining wall, with two rounded corners, of a sub-rectangular hut. Even today this stands to a height of about 5ft and the hut, of which this formed a part, would have been about 12ft long. The wall is built of good-sized tabular blocks of stone and tends to be relatively massive at the corners. A pivot stone was found built into this wall as were some beach stones. From what must have been the interior of this house came two barbed and tanged arrowheads while from here, and close by, Gray recovered about a hundredweight of pottery. These potsherds were closely comparable with the large series of roughly biconical, barrel-form and globular urns from Knackyboy Cairn, St Martin's (O'Neil, 1952) and the urns and sherds from the other chamber tombs (Hencken, 1932; 1933). Other pottery from Halangy Porth is now in the museum at Hugh Town (page 255).

Adjacent to the remains of the hut in Halangy Porth there is still to be seen the end of a stone-built drain, referred to locally as a 'Tobacco-man's Hole'. Its interior is about 9in in height with flat stones piled on the cover-stones. This drain, for stone drains are a regular feature of Scillonian stone houses, lies between the hut and the side of the declivity in which it stands. Beyond it the cliff presents a natural profile.

In 1934 and 1935, Mr Alec Gray excavated two areas about 30ft to landward of the cliff-exposed remains. He concluded that it was difficult to say how far to landward, or for that matter to seaward, the structures had extended and his work disclosed what appears to have been a considerable area of loose stone rubble. Indeed, he refers specifically to the air-spaces between the stones; among these was an immense quantity of pottery, all of the same character as that from the cliff below, in addition to limpet shells, animal bones, flints, both flakes and implements, as well as what appears to have been a circular mace-head with an hour-glass perforation. Further excavation was undertaken in 1936 as the result of the sinking of post-holes for the boundary fence of the bulb garden. Still more loose stone rubble and even pottery was encountered. Two areas of the rabb, one dished, which were burnt red and hard, point to continued exposure to fire. By one of these burnt areas was a pit cut into the rabb in which was found the greater part of a large storage pot (Fig 31). This pot was at least the second one to be set into this pit for it intruded upon the diameter of another of the same character, the first having been broken away to facilitate the insertion of the second. The later pot was packed about with whitish clay and contained a miscellany of black soil, stones, small sherds, charcoal and

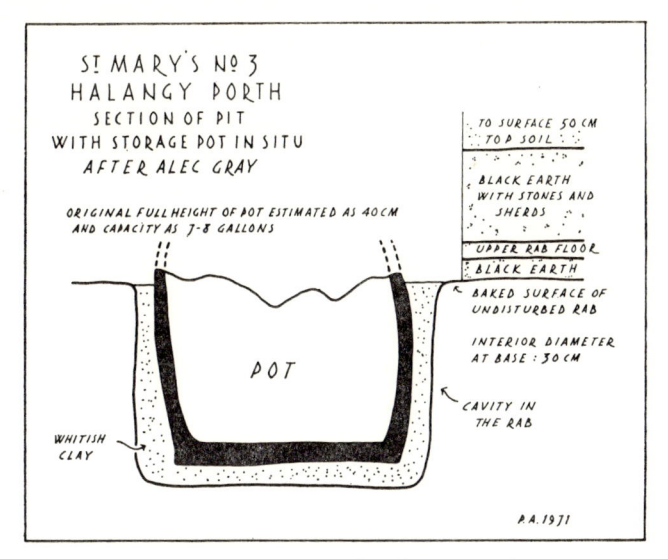

Fig 31 Storage pot from Halangy Porth, St Mary's

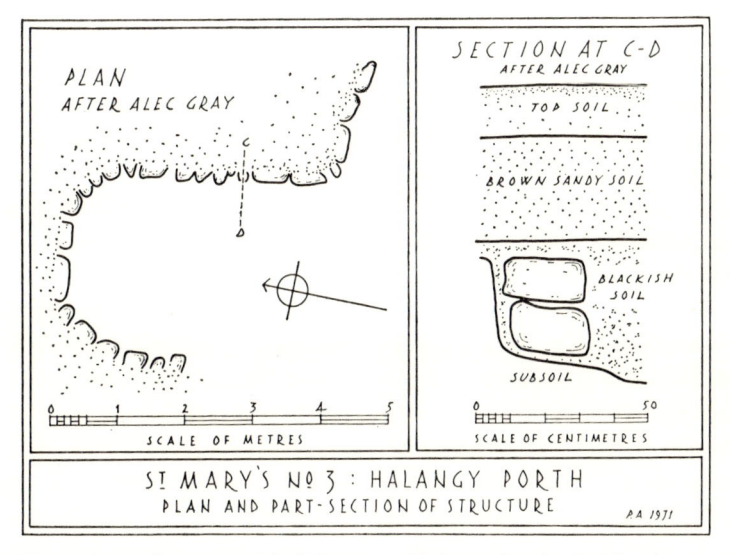

Fig 32 Plan of remains of building near Halangy Porth, St Mary's

pieces of bone. There was no rim, although some of the thicker rims found round about could have belonged to such a pot and its base diameter was some 13in. Originally this pot could hardly have been less than about 1½ft in height and its capacity some 8 or 9 gallons. The upper part, where it stood above the pit which housed it, was weathered suggesting exposure, while Gray described how the clay packing filled every indentation of its patterned base. It was eventually reconstructed and is now housed in Penzance Museum. In his report he recalls how during his earlier digging he had found the base of a pot of the same size.

Gray also found the foundation courses of a building beneath the bulb field (Fig 32). There had been a cut into the rabb of the slope and a seating made for the stones. The building seems to have been sub-rectangular in plan and some 14ft in length and 9ft in width. At one point the turn of the wall was found suggesting a thickness of 6ft. Within these footings he came upon numerous sherds of large plain pots, flint scrapers, flakes and cores as well as some burned clay. The great storage jar was apparently found close by.

Unlike these buildings the hut at English Island Carn, St Martin's, found by the Rev H. A. Lewis (Lewis, 1948, 9) who detected the midden, and excavated by O'Neil (1949, *SM*, 164–5), was a composite structure of timber and stone (Fig 33). It was completely excavated and its form clearly exposed. Roughly rectangular, but with the longer walls converging to a point at the southern end, this house is said to have recalled certain chamber-tomb plans. It had thick walls of small stones tied together on one side with a few large orthostats and on the other by wooden posts, the holes of which were found in the walls. These posts must have sloped at a considerable angle and it is thought that they may have been the mainstays of a ridged roof. Within these walls O'Neil found three levels of occupation. The lowest, which may have been earlier than the walls, was for the most part black soil, adjacent to a hearth. By this were found a few sherds of a black cordoned vessel which, it was observed, was a form not previously met with in Scilly. Also in this layer was a loom or net weight, a bone point and seven flint

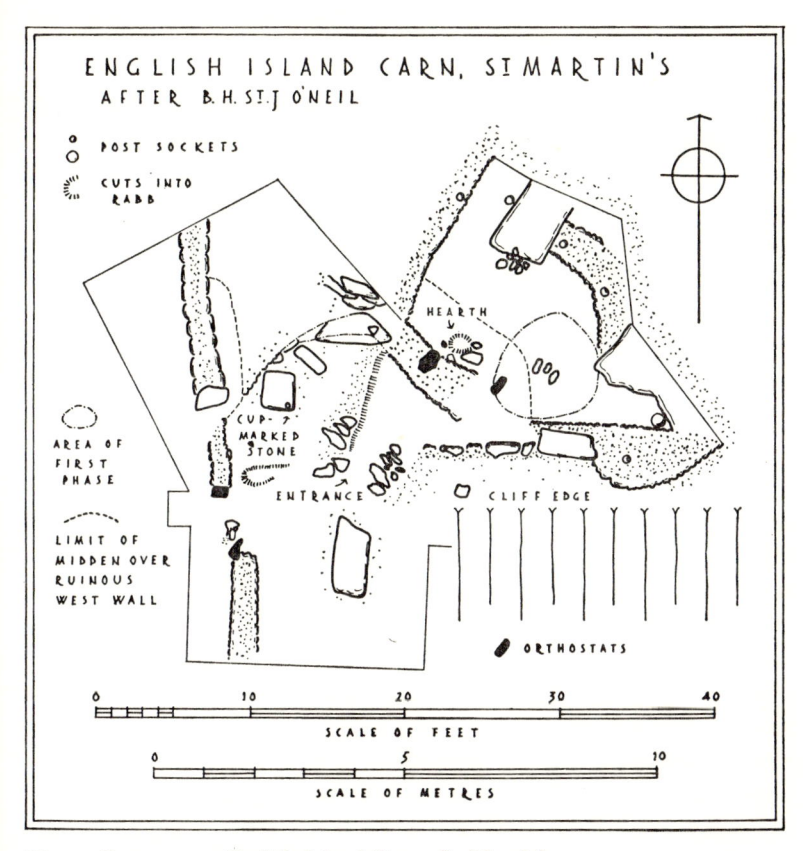

Fig 33 Structure at English Island Carn, St Martin's

scrapers. A second dark layer covered the whole area inside the walls of this house and covered paving stones as well as concealing the earlier layer. There was a hearth built in a slight hollow in the floor as well as a considerable quantity of pottery and a number of flint flakes. These potsherds were all of fine ware and included about a hundred of one vessel, the decoration of which was a series of rows of impressed dots. On account of its form and decoration O'Neil compared it with some of the pots found in the chamber tomb at Knackyboy Cairn, on the same island, which he had excavated a year previously (O'Neil, 1952). He also took the view that, because of its substantial nature, this layer represented a long period of occupation in the history of the structure. The third occupation layer was above as was more paving, in which were a few sherds of rough pottery. Blown sand intruded at this juncture and on the sand, which sealed the last occupation, was a midden of limpet shells and animal bones. These clearly came from another house, just to the north-west, which still awaits examination.

Besides his detailed work at English Island Carn, O'Neil found on St Martin's as a result of his own fieldwork and that of Lewis, a number of related sites. Excavations carried out during 1950, 1951 and 1952, revealed their character and often showed that only a vestige remained.

Excavation, during 1950, of the remnant of a massive stone-built native Romano-British hut on May's Hill (Fig 34) disclosed that it had been built over the debris of earlier occupation. Pottery similar to that from English Island Carn and Knackyboy Cairn, animal bones and limpet shells, all contained within brown soil, lay in a hollow in the rabb, thought to be artificial. Among them was 'a small bar of bronze', perhaps an awl. Associated with the layer was a circular, or semi-circular stone structure of just under 4ft in diameter, but of this only the inner face remained, to a height of 1ft. It was built of small stones set mostly as headers, a method reminiscent of the stone-set pits which were a feature of the so-called workshop area of the complex on Nornour (Dudley, 1967, 9, Fig 2).

Also during 1950, O'Neil was able to investigate the cliff at Lawrence's Brow where he came upon, in dark soil, some twenty-five sherds of pottery, some of them cord-ornamented, and all of them comparable with the English Island Carn and Knackyboy Cairn assemblages. Lewis had previously recovered from here some fifty sherds including a large piece of an urn. This site may well be one of the exposures noted by Gray, which are mentioned below. Lying loose in the blown sand on top of the dark soil was part of a saddle-quern rubber while close by was a triangular granite stone bearing a large cup-mark on one face. One or

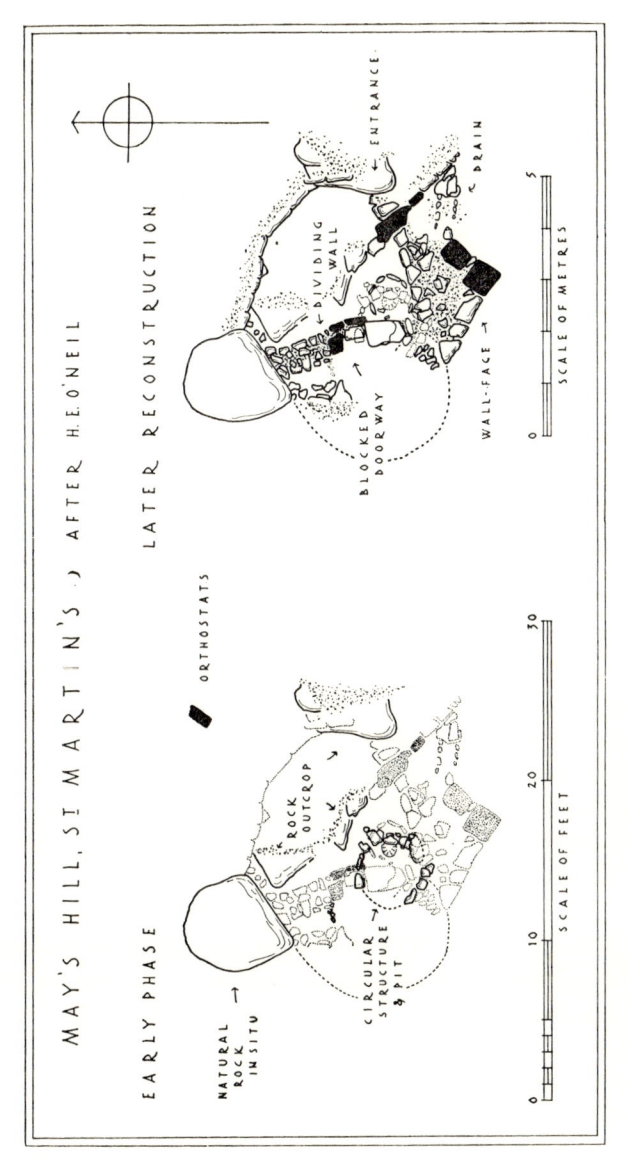

Fig 34 *Structures at May's Hill, St Martin's*

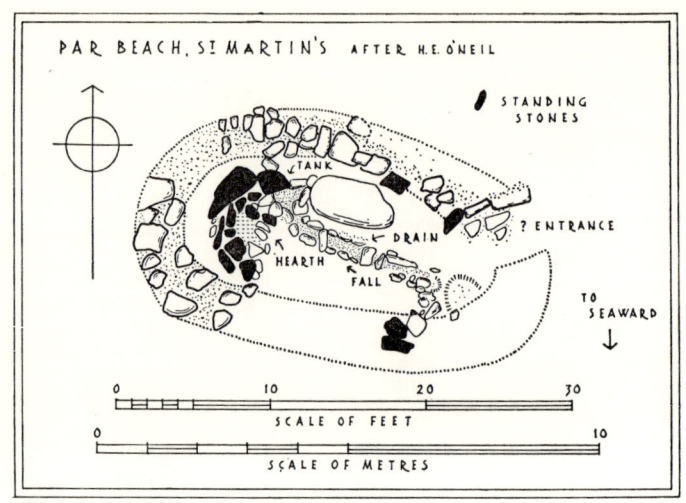

Fig 35 Oval hut on Par Beach, Higher Town Bay, St Martin's

two flint flakes were also present. Clearly there is or had been a building close at hand, but digging into the cliff was not possible while, towards the sea, erosion had removed all trace of a building.

The Rev H. A. Lewis found, in 1951, stones bearing the patent marks of burning below the high-water mark on Par Beach (Fig 35). During July of that year O'Neil conducted excavations. The structure revealed, which seems to have been part of a larger complex, had been oval. Walls, some 3ft in thickness, enclosed an oval area 20ft by 9ft. At the western end was a hearth backed and bounded by substantial standing stones. Adjacent to this was a stone-lined pit or sump fed by a well-built stone drain which ran along the longer axis of the building. This drain fell towards the sump, and was apparently fed by a hollow in the rabb. Two pieces of pottery were found close by this drain; both, on account of their character, can be associated with the earlier sites on St Martin's.

In the same season O'Neil also investigated the ruins of a hut at Perpitch (Fig 36). This appears to have been built into an ancient cultivation terrace; indeed, O'Neil was of the view that there could have

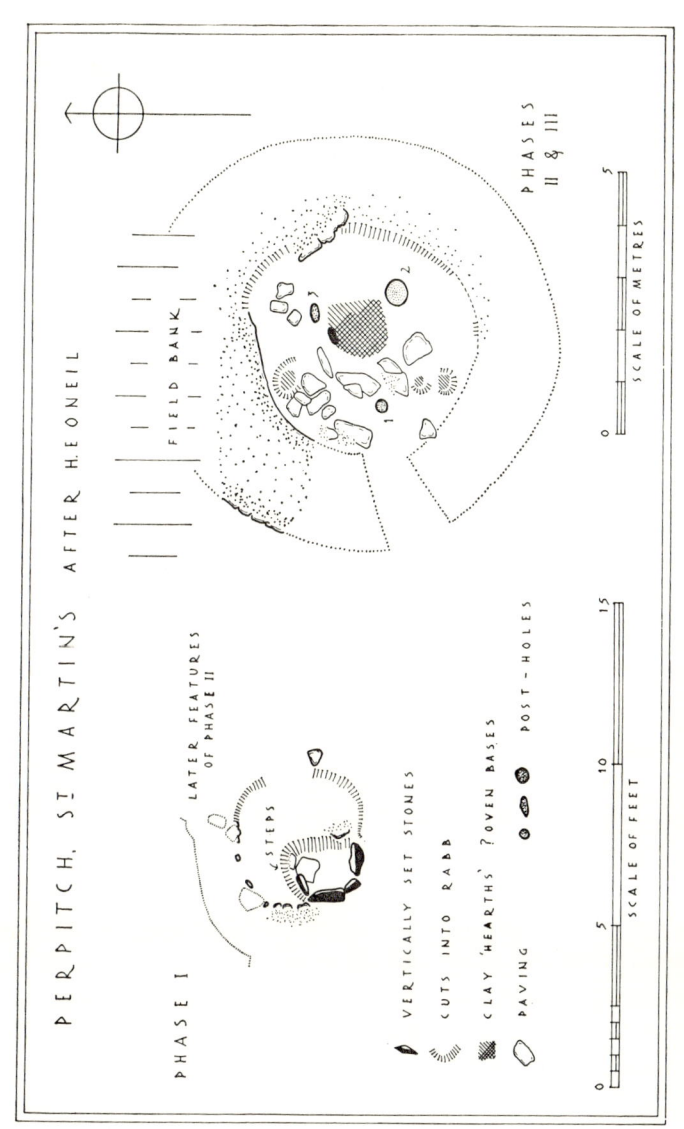

Fig 36 Modified hut with corn-drying ovens at Perpitch, St Martin's

been little doubt that the bank and hut were contemporary. In the circumstances it is possible to consider it as, perhaps, an 'out-field' structure. Excavation showed that it had been progressively enlarged and its internal features modified. A first phase was represented by an area 8 to 9ft in diameter, defined for the most part by a shallow excavation into the rabb. To one side was a deep hollow, slab-lined, into which two slab-steps descended. Neither hearth nor post-holes were found. The view was expressed that a remnant of walling recalled that of the English Island Carn hut. This stone-lined pit had been infilled with soil in which were sherds of early pottery. Above it was found what was thought to be a clay hearth, which could well have been the remains of a corn-drying oven such as Gray encountered at Halangy Porth. A thick wall, a part of which was bared, standing to a height of 2ft 6in replaced the earlier small-stone built walling of the first phase of this hut. This points to a structure, roughly circular and about 14ft in diameter. Another oven may have been in the interior beside where the walling still remained. A central clay 'hearth', also perhaps an oven, was a feature of this phase. A third phase involved another central clay 'hearth', with traces of a kerb about it. The surface, hard and black, cracked and broken with use, was bared and it bore a close pattern of finger smears. These followed the edge in parallel lines, their regularity showing that they were not accidental. There were also structural features belonging to this phase although the second-phase main wall remained in use, the stretches of paving by the wall and about the hearth. Three post-holes were around the central hearth. Quantities of early pottery were associated with both the later phases. In addition to sherds of pottery, there was found an object of baked clay, shaped like a small flangeless cotton reel. It is 1in in diameter and 1in high, decorated with dots which resemble the motifs on many of the Knackyboy Cairn urns, and since the perforation is small, it does not seem to have been a spindle whorl.

A length of wall, seen in the sand-hills of Great Bay, was investigated during July 1952. A 5ft length was bared and the wall was found to be

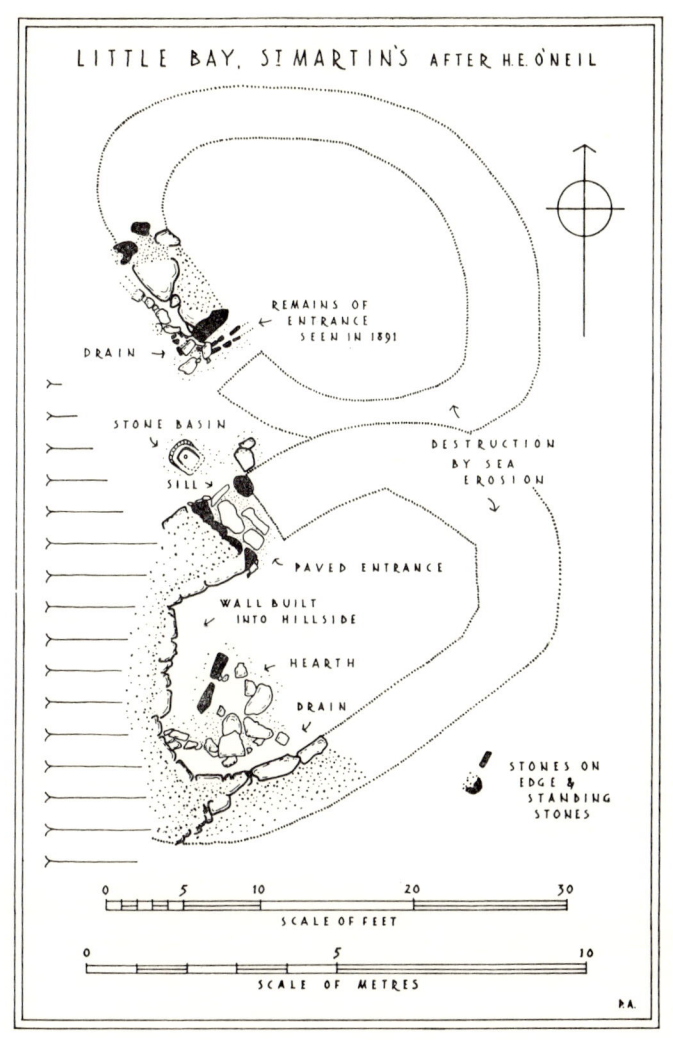

Fig 37 Remains of structures in Little Bay, St Martin's

standing to a height of 2ft. There was no occupation layer contiguous to it but early pottery was found in dark soil above a scree of boulders against it.

The great storm of 1891 caused considerable destruction along the coastline of St Martin's Bay on the north-east side of that island. In the northern part of Little Bay it exposed ancient walls and an entrance-way (Fig 37). Storms covered them with sand again until they were found by the Rev H. A. Lewis years later. Subsequently O'Neil excavated at this site during 1952 and 1953. He found, first of all, the remains of a component of a much larger complex of buildings. This was a chamber or 'hut', oval or 'curved rectangular' in plan. It had been built into the hillside and the inner wall faces were of substantial coursed masonry, an outer face to the hillside wall seemed unlikely; elsewhere it was some 5ft in thickness with a core of stones and soil. The entrance had been lined with large upended stones, four of which were remaining on the side still preserved, the other having been removed by the sea. These corner stones were larger than the others, which had walling above them. There were paving stones in the entrance and a sill-stone at the outside. Inside was a massive drain built against one wall while by this, towards the middle, there had been a stone-built hearth. The floor was of black soil which yielded numerous flint flakes, cores and early pottery. About 10ft distant from the entrance to this 'hut' were the remains of the entrance-way seen in 1891. One great lining stone still stood with a length of walling running from it. A stone-built drain had passed through it, the cover-stones of which had acted as paving. A cup-marked stone was in the wall-filling. Between the two entrances lay a large block of granite which had been hollowed out for use as a trough. A large piece of a saddle quern and a complete saddle-quern rubber were found in the stone debris. More pottery, embedded in dark soil, lay in the general area between the two ruined structures. O'Neil was of the view that the site originally consisted of two small round, or approximately round, huts, linked by a yard or garden wall.

While Halangy Porth, St Mary's, English Island Carn and the series on St Martin's are the better attested sites of the earlier phase, there exist several others which were located by Gray during the inter-war years on shores or as cliff-exposures. In his account of his work he refers frequently to pottery 'of the usual kind'. This phrase denotes that he found pottery comparable with that from Halangy Porth which was his constant comparative yardstick. Another narrative, by Jackson, for example, of huts on the shore at Pendrathen, a small anchorage with a quay, just to the north of Halangy Point, describes the discovery of a burial urn among them. Gray failed to find them, but Pendrathen is, perhaps, best described in its observer's own words (Jackson, 1947; 1948). He wrote: 'I well remember the "Bee-hive" prehistoric huts at Pendrethen [sic] and found the remains of several more on the shore at low water, proving that a great subsidence of the land must have occurred. Among the huts on the land I found a perfect burial urn but on removing it it fell to pieces. My daughter also found one; this we coated with "white of egg" and let it dry, secreted in the bushes, before removing it. She took it with her to Brighton, but on leaving that place she presented it to the British Museum where it is now.'

On the west side, and just to the south of Bar Point, St Mary's, Gray found exposed in the cliff an ancient surface upon which could be seen quantities of stone rubble. The only visible structure was the end of a small stone-built drain, like that at Halangy Porth, for which he used the term 'Tobaccoman's Hole'. Stray sherds of early pottery were found on the ancient surface beneath the sand dunes, while 'fair quantities of pottery' were mixed with the stones and soil by the drain although flint and bone were rare. Gray suggested that it is possible that further extensive traces of occupation might exist beneath the sand at Bar Point, both above and below high-water mark, and in fact a further cycle of erosion, since 1969, has revealed more walling, part of a square stone-built hearth and a drain, and more pottery.

Gray's fieldwork on the off-islands detected six cliff-exposed sites where he saw the positive remains of structures and from which he collected pottery. Two other sites turned out to be only middens of shells with bones and pottery.

On Tresco, just to the north-east of the landing slip at Carn Near, an

HOUSES AND SETTLEMENTS

ancient surface was exposed beneath the sand dunes. Walling about 3ft in height was seen while from the soil came a quantity of flint and pieces of the 'usual rough pottery'. Gray described it as 'an ancient habitation site' which he compared with Halangy Porth, the two places being easily intervisible across the Road. As at Halangy Porth, blown sand could have been the cause of its final abandonment. Pottery and flints were also found in the cliff-face on the west side of Carn Near, in the corner of Apple Tree Bay.

On Bryher, just below Bonfire Carn at the extreme south-eastern point of that island, a section of what was considered to be a hut floor was seen exposed in the cliff-face. The 'floor' consisted of a thin band of black soil about 2in in depth and 7ft in length, bounded by stones at each end. Near one end were the remains of a large pot, the base of which was bedded below the black soil; which Gray considered to closely resemble the large pot from Halangy Porth. More pottery was found scattered on and below the surface of this layer and, indeed, sherds of pottery were found in the cliff for nearly 300ft in either direction. Many of these sherds were at the base of the soil profile and almost in the top of the rabb. Flint flakes were numerous, but few showed any signs of retouch. Below this layer of dark soil, Gray found a small piece of corroded iron. He also records small sherds of a hard, fine-grained ware containing a liberal admixture of quartz.

The remains of stone structures in the East Porth of Samson were beneath blown sand. On the northern side of the porth flints and pottery, most of which was 'of the usual type' appear to have been associated with an ancient sand-covered surface. Here and there, flints and pottery were found right from East Porth to Bar Point at the north-eastern extremity of this island. Sections of this soil were seen to be as much as 3ft in depth in places while at one unspecified point there was walling thought to be the remains of a circular hut. If the walls of this hut could be located it might, perhaps, be fitted into the patterns of walling, discussed in a previous chapter, which extend seawards across the sand-flats.

Flint implements and a few sherds of pottery were found in the cliff on the southern side of St Martin's, between Yellow Rock and the Old

175 15 Sherd, (a) [exterior] (b) interior, from [Ti]ngy Porth, St Mary's. [Be]ars upwards of fifty [grain] impressions

Page 176 16a Limpet-shell midden at Halangy Down, St Mary's. Exposed and examined during the excavations in 1967
16b Faience and glass beads from Knackyboy Cairn, St Martin's (D8)

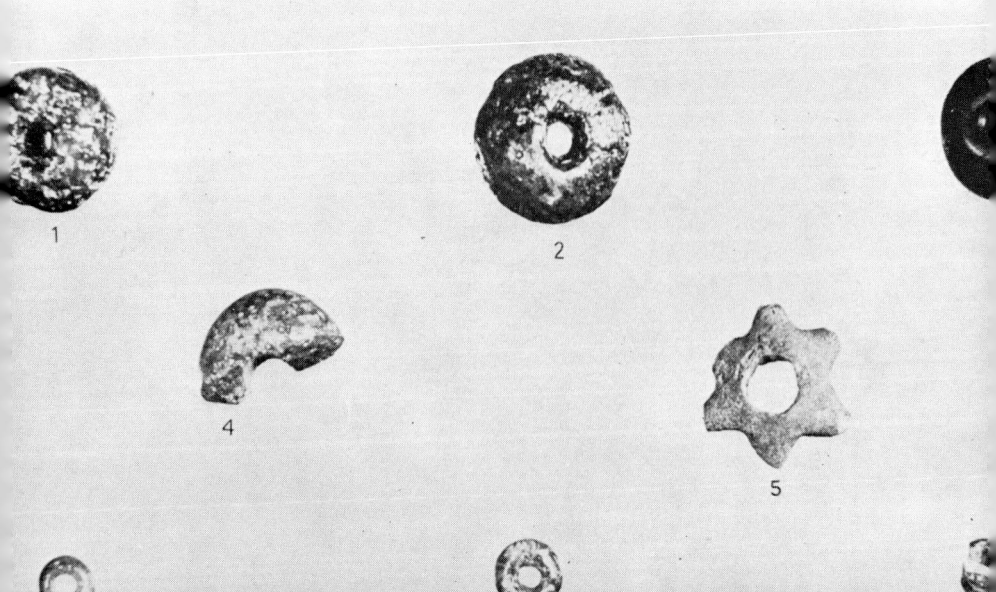

Quay. At one place there were a number of boulders which Gray thought might have been part of a hut. Lewis (1948, 9) found by Pernagie Carn, at the north-westerly corner of this island, a considerable amount of pottery which also included half of a complete pot. He also refers to 'imported clay ... made up into balls ... some bearing a distinct impress'. He also commented, after his experiences with Knackyboy Cairn, that it seemed unusual to find such a quantity of pottery except in a burial chamber.

Digging during 1935 disclosed a great quantity of decomposed bones and limpet shells beneath the sand and rocks of the neck which links Little and Middle Arthur, for bubbles rising through the sand at low water had revealed the presence of ancient remains. A buried soil, relatively stone-free, was disclosed. With the bones and shells were ash and charcoal fragments, lying around a large flat stone. Besides flints and a fragment of coarse pottery, Gray found a bone point resembling those found in the chamber of Obadiah's Barrow on Gugh (Hencken, 1932, 28, Fig 12A). The good state of preservation of this bone point compared markedly with the decomposed character of the bones in this midden deposit.

Immediately below the lifeboat house, at Periglis on the western side of St Agnes, is an exposure of black ancient soil some 3ft in depth. From its lower level, Gray collected bones and a quantity 'of pottery of the usual type'. No trace of structures was seen and the low cliff here is masked by a recent make-up of rubble and rubbish. In the southern corner of Porth Killier, which opens to the north and looks across to Samson, Bryher and Tresco, an extensive area of ancient surface was exposed in the early 1930s. It was masked by sand upon which a modern grassed soil had developed. Scattered through its entire depth Gray found great quantities of pottery, many bones and limpet shells, charcoal, lumps of clay and a number of flints. A circular granite rubbing stone was also recovered. On the eastern side of Porth Killier is a small bay and here, on what was thought to be a raised beach, was also a mounded midden of limpet shells among which were bones and sherds of an unspecified character. The pottery from the main site in Porth

HOUSES AND SETTLEMENTS

Killier seemed to be of a finer and harder ware than that from Halangy Porth, but this may have been an accident of preservation.

Gray had the bones from Porth Killier identified and all of them proved to be seal. Thus in the absence of traces of buildings this site was considered as a seasonal station for sealing and, perhaps, fishing.

LATER HOUSE SITES

Mr Alec Gray's excavation of the most prominent 'hut' on Halangy Down, St Mary's, during 1935 (Fig 38) established the character of that complex. His account was unfortunately not published and the 'hut' remained for subsequent exploration (Ashbee, 1955; 1965; 1966; 1968; 1970). Yet his careful fieldwork resulted also in the discovery of traces

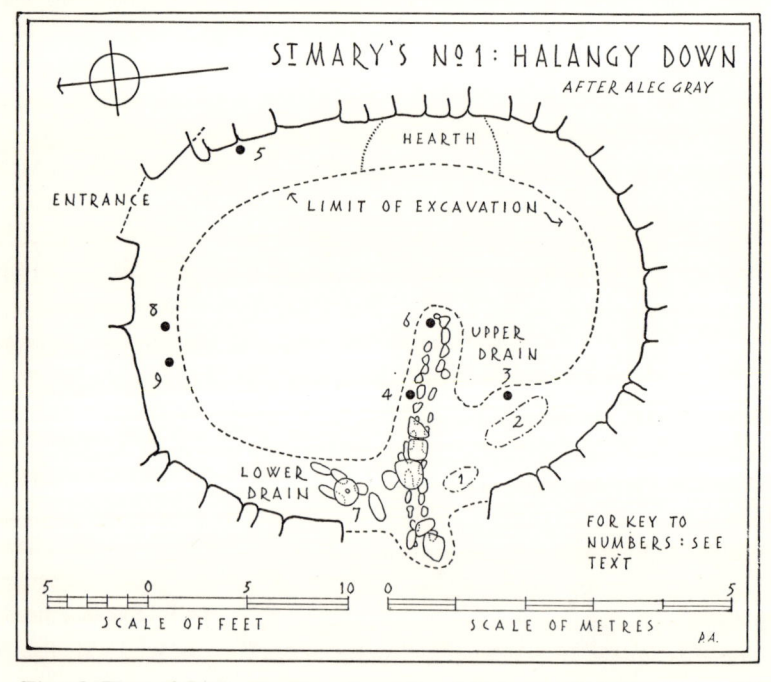

Fig 38 Plan of large chamber of courtyard house on Halangy Down, St Mary's

of structures of the second category, of Iron Age and Romano-British times, bordering Gimble Bay, Tresco. Of the same period were the researches on St Martin's of the Rev H. A. Lewis and B. H. StJ. O'Neil which resulted in the excavation of the remains of three huts of Iron Age and Romano-British times. All of these were oval or more-or-less round in plan and were much larger than those of the earlier phase of house building. At Halangy Down, excavation has shown that, far from being simple single-chambered buildings, the huts there had subsidiary chambers and rectangular annexes and were the result of progressive modification over a considerable period of time. O'Neil's excavations on Par Beach, St Martin's, have shown that the egregious remains there are almost certainly of a complex building of Halangy Down character. Indeed, were his work continued and extended on the other sites that he located and worked upon, something of their complexity, seemingly the hallmark of permanent settlement, would emerge. For, while simple small round and oval huts, sometimes associated with walled field systems and enclosures are known in the South West (Dudley, 1957) and suspected in Scilly, the basic permanent unit appears to be a Scillonian counterpart of the courtyard houses best known at Chysauster (Hencken, 1933, *Archaeologia*) in Cornwall.

Two of the house foundations investigated by O'Neil (1949, 163; 1950, 9) were on Par Beach in situations normally covered at full tide. This aspect has been discussed in the preceding chapter treating Scillonian submergence. Another was on a hill-slope comparable with Halangy Down, and a further foundation was on Little Arthur.

O'Neil's Iron Age hut on Par Beach (Fig 39) was stone-walled and oval, some 17ft by 15ft. Three post-holes were thought to denote supports for the roof. The doorway opened to the west while paving stones were about the inner face of the wall. O'Neil noted that it was of far more substantial construction than the earlier house excavated at English Island Carn on the same island. Apart from potsherds and flint implements, however, nothing was found in it. A later grave had been dug into its floor destroying, perhaps, one of a square setting of post-holes.

HOUSES AND SETTLEMENTS

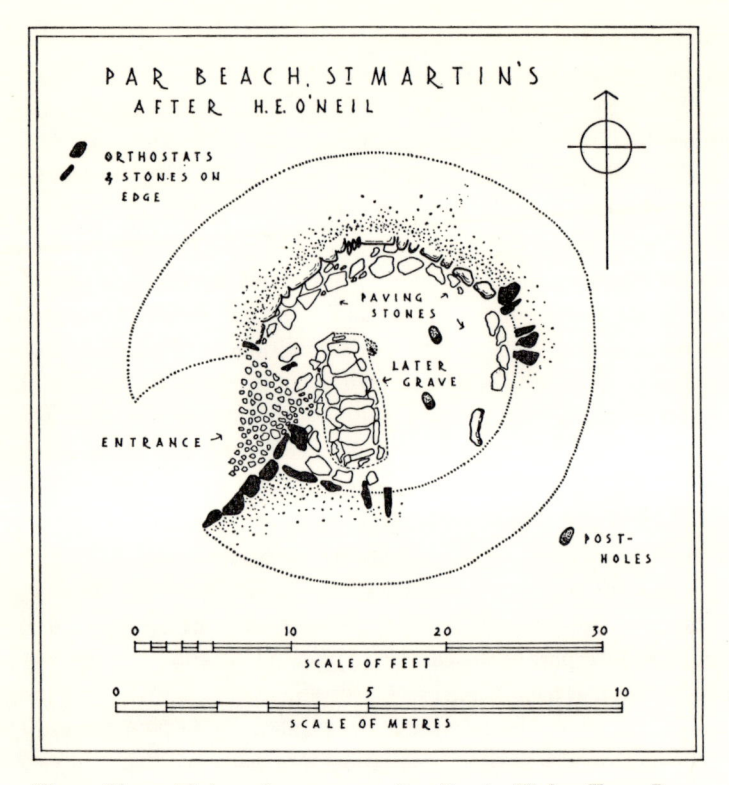

Fig 39 Hut, with intrusive grave, on Par Beach, Higher Town Bay, St Martin's

Mr Alan Goddard of St Martin's noticed good walling in the cliff edge of Little Arthur (Fig 40) a few feet above high-water mark, and the Rev H. A. Lewis collected pottery from the site. O'Neil carried out a small excavation in July 1951. This showed that there had been a stone-built hut here roughly pentagonal in plan, 13ft wide in one direction and 11ft in the other. A standing stone at one point was thought to denote an entrance. Paving stones were on the floor and there were traces of a bench against the wall. One stone associated with this had a cup-mark in it as had a large boulder which seems to have been in-

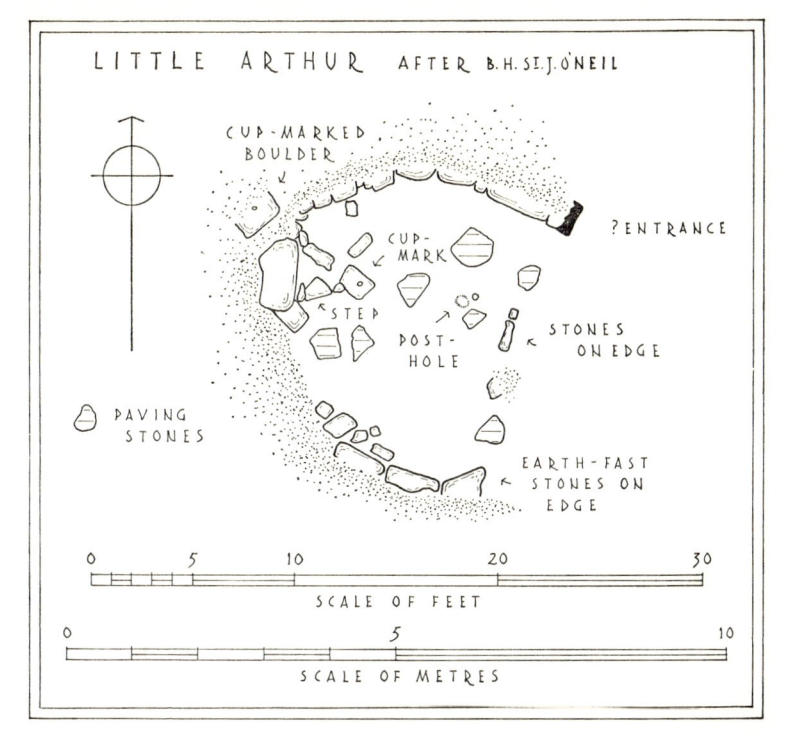

Fig 40 Remains of hut on Little Arthur

corporated in the wall. A well-defined post-hole was situated near the middle of the structure; while there was no especially constructed hearth, in the middle there was a great accumulation of black soil and in places the rabb was burned red. A broken mortar or saddle quern, a dressed squared stone, an unfinished loom or thatch weight and some utilised pebbles were found besides a considerable quantity of Iron Age potsherds. Flint flakes and scrapers were also present. Indications of another house close by were observed.

Excavation of the round native Romano-British hut on Par Beach was begun by the Rev H. A. Lewis, but as with the Iron Age hut, work could only be carried out, piecemeal, between tides and involved the

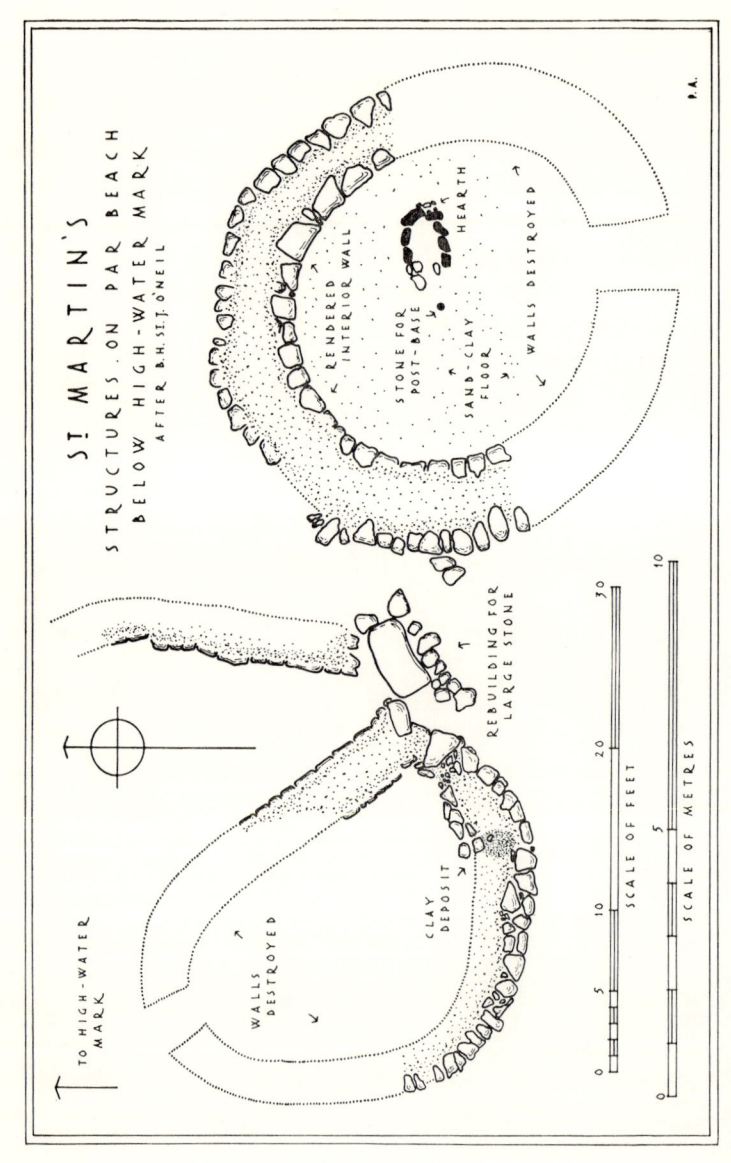

Fig 41 Structures below high-water mark on Par Beach, Higher Town Bay, St Martin's

clearance of enveloping shore sand. Much of the building had been destroyed by the sea and only a half of the main structure remained (Fig 41). It had a stone wall upwards of 6ft in thickness, which together with the part lost, had enclosed an area about 20ft in diameter. The walls had been set upon sand but the area within had a substantial clay floor. The inner face of the wall had been rendered with clay-mortar which had been forced into the interstices of the stonework. A flat slab of granite with a circular hollow pecked into it such as those found at Halangy Down and Chysauster, was discovered near the middle of the hut, and was considered to have housed the butt of a roofing post. Also in about the middle was a large hearth retained by small upright stones. In the dark soil of this were pieces of Romano-British pottery and a fragment of cassiterite—tin ore. O'Neil was of the view that this hut had been destroyed by fire, since he observed that the floor was covered with a layer of black soil, thicker than would have been derived from the hearth, and that on it were pieces of the clay-mortar rendering from the walls, burnt hard and black or red in colour. This observation is of importance as one of the ruined oval-hut phases at Halangy Down (Ashbee, 1966, 24) has markedly reddened wall-stones and pieces of burnt rendering were found.

A few yards to the west of this were other structures which did not seem to have been parts of actual dwellings. There were two converging walls, standing in one place as much as seven courses in height, and almost as well-constructed as the main building, while farther west still there was a long narrow area bounded on one side by only a thin wall. This would seem to correspond with the rectangular annexes which were a feature of Halangy Down (Ashbee, 1966, 23, Fig 2). There were considerable traces of burning together with many pieces of what were described as 'crude pottery'. This could be the remains of corn-drying ovens such as have been found on Teän and Halangy Down. Where the two well-coursed converging walls came almost together evidence was found of rebuilding to incorporate a very large stone, 4ft 8in in length and 2ft 4in in breadth, set on edge. It was thought from its character to have served as an earlier stone cist cover-slab. Why this was utilised in

HOUSES AND SETTLEMENTS

this manner is not clear but a long stone, taken perhaps from an earlier monument, was found buried below the floor level of an oval building at Halangy Down (Ashbee, 1966, 24).

Removal of stone for wall-building during the last century had mutilated the remains of a house on May's Hill, St Martin's (Fig 34), although they were still substantial. O'Neil's excavation showed that it had been oval in plan, some 16ft by 10ft, and divided by a party wall into two parts of unequal size, through which was a doorway. The main entrance into the house was on the eastern side and was monumental in conception. At some juncture during the use-life of the building the doorway through the party wall had been blocked and paving laid over earlier debris, while the main entrance was expanded. The pottery from this hut was entirely of Romano-British type and included two very small pieces of Samian ware, the first from Scilly. Evidence of earlier occupation, mentioned on page 166, contemporary with the chamber tombs and the Halangy Porth settlement, was found beneath.

The site at Gimble Porth, Tresco, found during fieldwork by Gray in 1937, would seem to resemble in principle the Halangy Down complex on account of the fact that it is on an eastward facing slope and is conjoined with an early field or enclosure system. The latter would seem to have its upper limits on Castle Down, which rises to a height of just over 100ft, above Gimble Porth. The walls, which may have been laid out between some of the barrows here, extend down the slope to the porth. Two fields are on the level ground between the slope from the Down and the sea. At the northern end of the area there is a confused mass of ruined structures obscured by furze, brambles and bracken.

As a result of exploration and fieldwork Gray had arrived at the conclusion that the 'settlement' on Halangy Down was of a far more substantial nature than Hencken's view (1932, 30) allowed. He believed there were the foundations of several huts, together with walls and terraces with large stones scattered around seemingly at random. Much of it had been destroyed by the removal of stone, so that only bare hollows indicated where some of the huts had stood for no stone remained in them. Gray's prospecting led him to the view, which has proved correct, that some of the structures were oval, others round and that at least one was rectangular. A round 'hut', about 12ft in diameter, with a doorway facing west and presumably the structure photographed by Alexander Gibson at the beginning of the century was, however, easy to find and the larger oval 'hut' to the south-west of this was the focus of his attention.

When the present writer first saw Halangy Down in 1949, a considerable growth of bracken and bushes effectively concealed almost everything on the hill-slope. In spite of this it was possible to locate Gray's 'large oval hut' (Fig 38) as it was adjacent to a narrow path which descended from the chamber tomb above to the track below. Although overgrown, the walls could be seen as well as drains which led to a south-west facing entrance. When, the following year, extensive clearance prior to excavation (Ashbee, 1955) had been carried out, the trenches dug by Gray in 1935 were clearly visible. A narrow trench followed and exposed the internal wall-face while another exposed the entire length of a stone drain which led from the interior.

Gray's 1935 excavation is best summarised in his own words:

Before I partially cleared this building in 1935, it was completely buried, the exposed corner of one stone being the only indication that anything of interest lay beneath the soil ...

An inexplicable feature of the filling of the hut was the number of large blocks of granite it contained. These were in all sorts of positions and at all depths, and were much too large to have fallen from the walls or to have formed part of a partition. There were traces of hearths close to the wall at two places; these contained ash and burnt earth but nothing else, and were just hollows in the natural ram ...

The only large stone of any interest which was found, was a slab of granite, more or less square, having across the centre of one of its edges a deep groove, obviously made by friction. The stone was not in situ ...

The only covering stone of the lower drain which remained in place, proved to be the lower stone of a beehive quern in excellent preservation ...

The filling [of the hut interior] was much disturbed, and the disturbance had probably taken place in ancient times. There were definite floor levels or stratification ...

In the course of his work, Gray found 'several fragments of iron' which included 'an object some 10cm. long' and others 'in the form of a disc an inch or so in diameter, with sometimes a stalk or shank in the centre, and were perhaps studs of some kind'. He observed, doubtlessly with the profusion of pieces on earlier sites in mind, that pottery was scarce. Apart from a few small rough hand-made pieces, only two rim fragments of wheel-turned ware came to light. Worked flints, lumps of flint, granite rubbing-stones and a sandstone hone complete his inventory.

The existence of an ancient settlement site on Halangy Down had long been known and down the years it had been a convenient source of building stone, as is evident by split stones, lost stone-breakers' 'feathers' and evidence of the pulling down of walls. At the close of the last century Alexander Gibson cleared away the underbrush from a hut chamber, rebuilding part of its wall in the process, and made a photographic record of it. It is not known whether or not Bonsor visited it; he only records the abundant traces of early occupation in the cliff of Halangy Porth below (Hencken, 1933, 16). Hencken, having noted Bonsor's description of the midden, and as nothing was known of the material culture of the site, associated the two (Hencken, 1932, 30). His search through the thick underbrush gave him the impression of the foundations of a number of small round huts, which he compared with huts known to him on Bodmin Moor and Dartmoor. He thought them 'insignificant and unsubstantial' and contrasted them with the massive Scillonian chamber tombs. As has been shown above it was the pioneer work of Gray that initially disclosed something of the extent and character of the Halangy Down settlement.

B. H. StJ. O'Neil visited Halangy Down in 1947 and 1948 and shortly after this the Ministry of Works took the site, and the chamber tomb at the top of the slope, into their guardianship. Late in 1949, when the underbrush was low, the present writer was, guided by Mr J. Treneary, enabled to see its size and something of its disposition. Excavation for the Ministry of Works was undertaken in the summer of 1950. The selected component was the structure partially examined by Gray more than a decade previously, and in the course of the excavation the interior, a subsidiary chamber, the lower wall and entrance were revealed (Ashbee, 1955). At the same time clear indications were observed of adjacent structures. Their general character gave grounds for comparison with the courtyard houses of the Cornish mainland. Over the years the Ministry of Works cleared the enshrouding brambles and bracken from the site. Also, a fire revealed, close by, a range of stone-walled terraced fields. Gray had traced these but in 1950 they were not visible due to the prolific vegetation.

The writer visited this and other Scillonian sites in 1963 and a programme of excavation was subsequently undertaken beginning in 1964 and continuing until recently (1970). At the outset of the work the well-built oval structure on Halangy Down, termed a 'homestead' in 1950, stood alone in a changed landscape. Adjacent, to the south-west was a turf-mantled chamber which gave on to an annexe or courtyard which bracketed the entrance of this and the structure examined in 1950 (Ashbee, 1965, 37, Fig). Just to the north-east was the hut, that had been the subject of Alexander Gibson's photograph, seen as all that remained of a near-completely destroyed building. Above, a turf-clad slope extended to the crest of the hill. Downhill, from the 1950 'homestead' to the track leading to Halangy Porth, was an area strewn with a great confused quantity of stones of all sizes. Many of these displayed patent signs of recent breaking while one large cavity on the site pointed to quarrying. The first task carried out was the clearance of all non-earthfast rocks and their conveyance to a distance from the site.

Apart from an examination of the small 'Alexander Gibson' structure, excavation, from 1964 to 1967, was confined to the area below the so-called 'homestead' examined in 1950 (Ashbee, 1965; 1966). Only recently (Ashbee, 1968) was it possible to examine the structures

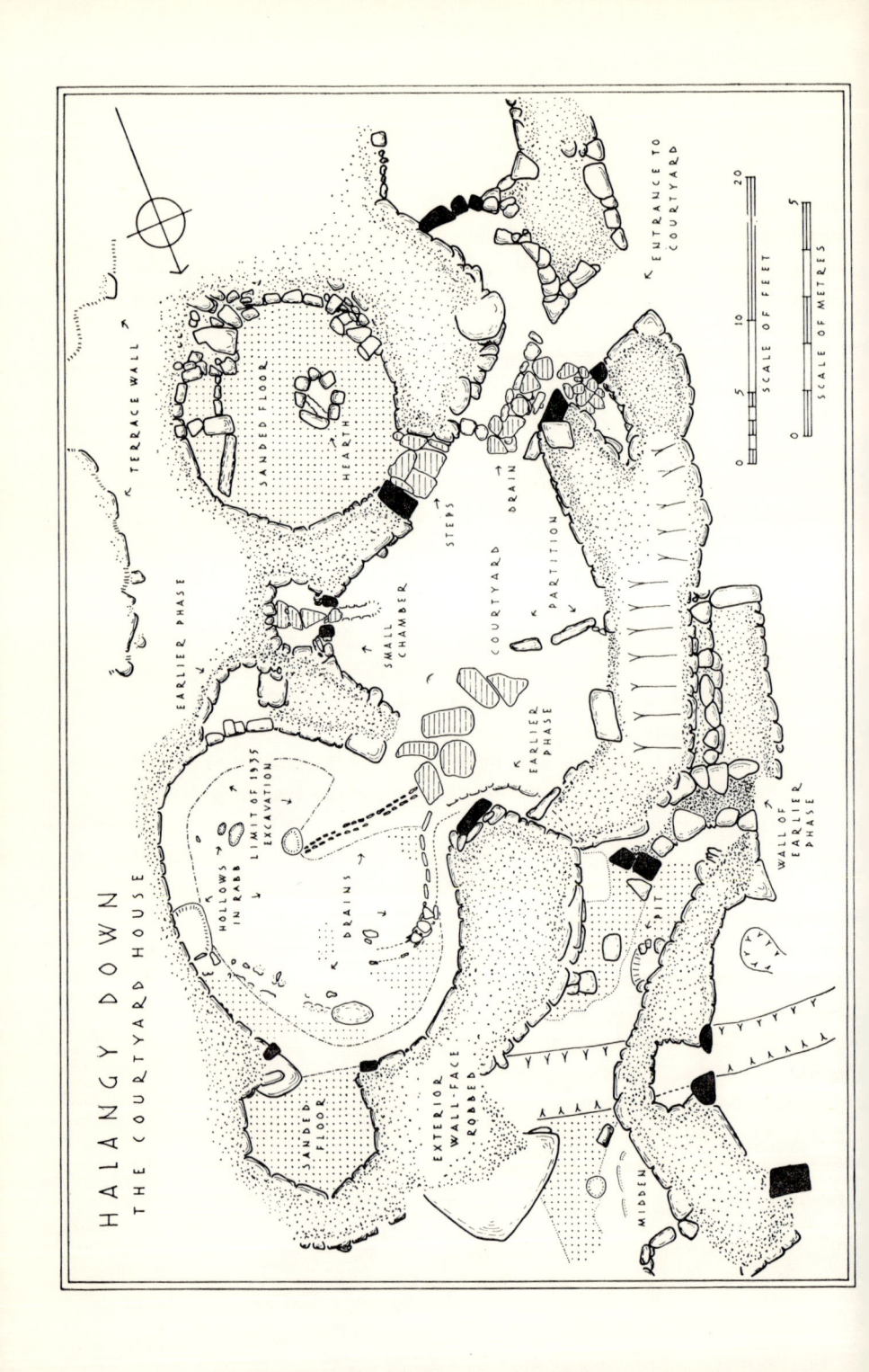

HALANGY DOWN
THE COURTYARD HOUSE

adjacent to the 1950 excavation. As the result of this and work in 1968 it has emerged that these, the uppermost as yet revealed on the hillslope, are the best preserved, and that elsewhere only footings remain. Notwithstanding, excavation has shown that there was an extensive complex of interconnected stone-built huts on Halangy Down developed and modified during the course of some half-millennium, set into an extensive range of cultivation terraces. Indeed, it is reasonable to suppose that the remains on the Down and those in and about the Porth below, demonstrating a continuity of settlement in the same immediate area, represent aspects of the development of the same complex. The reasons for abandonment of the lower and much earlier phase of the settlement, described at the beginning of this chapter, are to be seen in the accumulation of blown sand above it. This blown sand, the product of the considerable marine transgression which has taken place in Scilly (Chapter 3), must have ultimately made it untenable, so that the focus of settlement had to move to the hill-slope above.

The associated structures revealed as the result of the excavations in 1950, 1968 and 1969, are considered to comprise a 'courtyard house' (Fig 42) as, indeed, was suspected earlier. The units appear to be the product of progressive building, for the substantial wall limiting the space which is termed the 'courtyard' butts on to the end of the lower wall of the 'homestead' examined in 1950. However, the structures do, elsewhere, appear as interjoined, though with stone architecture of this nature a rebuilding can often be far from obvious. Despite the shared characteristics no direct comparison can be made with any specific example within the Penwith series, for although all have characteristics in common the buildings differ and thus are peculiar in matters of dimension and arrangement.

Excavations on Halangy Down since 1964 (Ashbee, 1965; 1966; 1968) have revealed something of the complex of buildings set into that hill-slope. While the courtyard house is the uppermost, there are other buildings, conjoined and related to one another, lower down (Plate 9a), which were probably ruined and abandoned towards the end of the occupation of the courtyard house (Fig 43). These features are a large

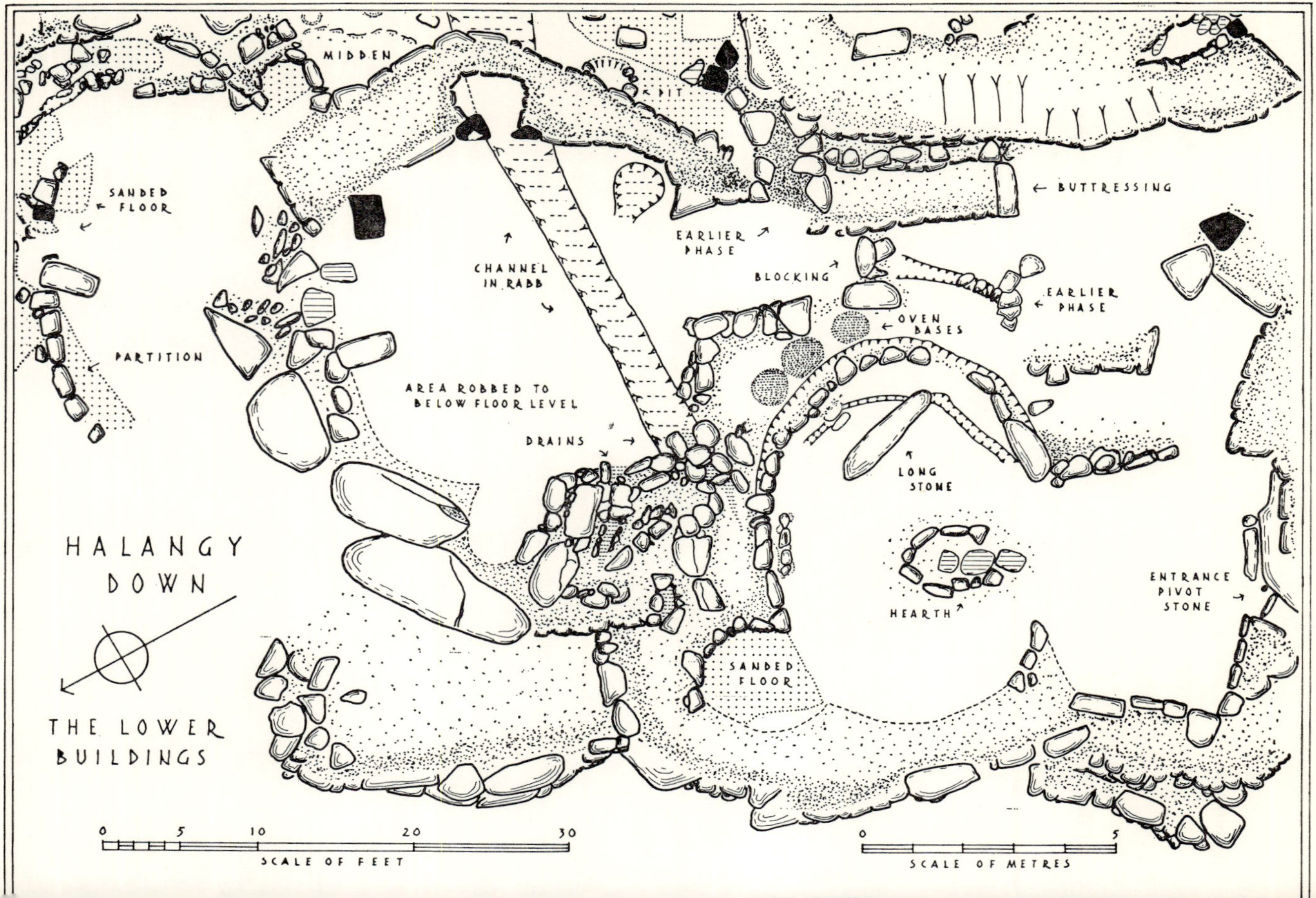
HALANGY
DOWN
THE LOWER
BUILDINGS
MIDDEN
PIT
BUTTRESSING
SANDED FLOOR
EARLIER PHASE
BLOCKING
EARLIER PHASE
CHANNEL IN RABB
OVEN BASES
PARTITION
AREA ROBBED TO BELOW FLOOR LEVEL
DRAINS
LONG STONE
HEARTH
ENTRANCE PIVOT STONE
SANDED FLOOR
0
5
10
20
30
SCALE OF FEET
0
5
SCALE OF METRES

oval and much ruined chamber and an oval hut with a rectangular annexe subsequently added, which employ much the same structural techniques as the courtyard house. The large oval chamber might be a component of a larger complex of which little appears to remain.

The courtyard of the courtyard house is bounded on the downhill side by a massive wall. Giving on to it are the entrances to a large oval chamber (the 1950 'homestead'), a small one-time stone-roofed storage chamber and a circular chamber with a central hearth. This courtyard is entered by a relatively narrow 'corridor', defined by large standing stones from which there is access, on one side, to modified and ruined buildings, possibly circular or oval chambers, and on the other to a small intra-mural recess. A drain from the circular chamber runs out through the entrance, which has a considerable gradient. It is likely that this 'corridor' was paved but no positive trace remained of the stones, which would have been an obvious prey for stone robbers. On the uphill side the surface of the courtyard was sporadic cobbles set into a matrix of soil over the rabb. To obtain a level surface there was a considerable build-up of soil against the interior of the massive lower wall. It seems probable that this became soft, or even at intervals waterlogged, for the middle area was patched with cobbles and occasional flat stones. Some of these had sunk and others had been put upon them and thus here and there successive surfaces were detected during excavation. Odd pieces of pottery and broken quern stones were amongst this patching and infilling.

Entry to the large oval chamber was over large flagstones. Its earthen floor had been sanded in the same way as was practised in the eighteenth century when Heath (1750, 26) observed how sand (from Porth Mellon) was used in houses in Hugh Town while he was on St Mary's. A system of stone drains led under the main entrance and beneath the courtyard. One of these drains led from a hollow in the rabb which may have served for water collection. A smaller circular chamber, distant from the entrance, also had a sanded earthen floor. As far as can be seen the uphill wall was but a single face of boulders built into the hillside while the downhill wall, like that of the courtyard, was some 5ft in thickness and built of large boulders. As with the courtyard, a level interior had been obtained by a build-up of soil against the lower wall. There was no trace of a central hearth.

The walls of this oval chamber are built of selected blocks of granite and to the right of the entrance sharp angled stones show clearly how reconstruction may have converted a circular plan into an oval. This would have been carried out when part of a small chamber was demolished to give extra space. Several techniques may be observed in such construction: breakage of joints; panels formed by massive vertical stones, the space between being filled up with lighter work; and massive 'grounders' which would have carried lighter masonry. Outside, the face of the downhill wall can be seen to be of this more massive material. One of the grounders here is a great block, some 6ft in length and 3ft in height as well as being, so far as can be ascertained, of proportionate thickness. The resulting wall is built with a slight uphill batter. Such massive construction is quite understandable on account of the great weight borne by the lower courses of the downhill wall. A considerable length of this still stands intact although part has been badly robbed. The original filling of this downhill wall seems to have been soil or turf. Traces of mortar were observed between some of the stones of the main and the smaller chamber. More was adhering to one or two stones in the fallen rubble, but this may represent the remains of applied rendering rather than evidence of binding. On the floor of this oval chamber a number of sherds of Romano-British pottery were found while spindle-whorls and a perforated slate disc or button were found in the soil filling of the drains.

The entrance to the small stone-roofed chamber was through jamb-stones which are the centre-piece of a concave façade. This has walls of irregular bonded masonry which stand some 3ft in height and have, at one point, the oversailing courses, building up to the stone roof, still in position. Its floor was a line of flat slabs which covered a drain. This may continue uphill beyond this chamber.

Adjacent to this small chamber, and between its wall and the wall of the large oval chamber, part of an identical structure was detected in

1968 and excavated in 1969. It had been in part demolished; the wall of the oval hut cutting across it and sealing it off from use.

Access to the circular hut from the courtyard is via steps of massive slabs. On one side they are bounded by a substantial jamb-stone, on the other by coursed masonry. In the middle of the sanded floor there is a hearth of horse-shoe form with a drain running beneath it. The hearth when found, was packed with dark soil and stones. The walls are built of selected tabular blocks of granite. On one side they are carefully coursed and bonded, extra stability being secured by the device of alternating large boulders with 'panels' infilled with coursed work. The basal wall-stones are the more massive. On the other side the wall is predominantly of large vertically-set blocks. Here also there are indications of re-building. The uphill side of this approximately circular hut (Plate 9b) is cut by a straight wall parallel to the general slope of the hillside, closing off an arc. An entrance leads through this partition to a rear entrance to the chamber. From this, a path leads out to the rear. This is sloping and the resulting gulley had been filled in with stone rubble and the way blocked. On one side of the partition is a large vertical slab, on the other massive coursed work.

It is probable that this entire house, both chambers and courtyard, was roofed. Presuming headroom in both, of about 5ft 6in, the lower wall faces would have stood to a height of some 16ft. The thick walls could have carried roofing spars pitched from their inner edges and supported in the middle by posts, the butts of which might have been housed in large dished stones. At least one of these has been found. These spars could have carried a thatch of reeds or straw, held in position by reed or straw ropes or netting secured to wooden pegs or weights. Heath (1750, 29) writes of straw thatcd bound by straw ropes on stone-built houses, while many perforated stones which may have done duty as weights have been collected to ornament present-day Scillonian gardens. About the wall-top there would have been a platform leaving room for a man to walk and work during the periodic repair or renewal of the thatch. Such a system has been seen in practice in the 'black houses' of the Hebrides (Curwen, 1938).

Only the uphill wall and the modified southern entrance of a large single chamber remain, filling the area downhill from the oval chamber of the courtyard house. Even its floor was destroyed, while of the remaining lower walling only the footings still exist. This upper wall's interior face is partly of coursed stones and partly of boulders. The extant southern entrance, found filled with soil covered by an extensive midden of limpet shells, exhibits in its uphill wall some of the finest stone-walling extant on Halangy Down. Massive blocks define the angles, the space between being filled with coursed work. On the lower side there are large blocks. It is possible that this entrance, like the entrance to the courtyard, was roofed with stone, a long tie-stone being found here amongst the stone debris. Another entrance opposes this one at the other end of the chamber. The uphill side still stands, defined by a great angular upright block. By it, and downhill, was found a worn and fallen jamb-stone while traces of stone paving were still *in situ*. Beneath the mass of soil, needed for a level floor, a deep channel, cut into the rabb, may have aided hillslope drainage. Three stone drains ran through the footings of the lower wall, each leading from the area above the deep-buried channel. Large blocks, still in place above these footings, may remain from a downhill entrance. The lower exterior corner of this chamber is defined by a series of huge isolated boulders, all that remain after stone-robbing. This chamber appears to have been almost square in plan, with rounded corners. One well-turned example remains. It could have been roofed in the same manner as the courtyard house higher up the slope.

Adjacent to this sub-rectangular chamber, and occupying the area of the hill-slope immediately below the courtyard of the courtyard house, is an oval hut with a rectangular annexe appended to it. To begin with, this oval hut, and its small circular chamber, similar to that to be seen attached to the large oval chamber of the courtyard house, may have been an entity with a long corridor entrance or even part of a complex now destroyed. At some juncture in its history, the downhill wall of its corridor entrance and much of one side was demolished and the rectangular annexe built on to it. A horse-shoe hearth, with the open end facing the entrance for a draught, was built close against the erstwhile entrance. While the original oval hut had been built with carefully coursed stones, of which only the basal courses remain, the basic building style of the annexe was vertical stones which may, in turn, have carried coursed work. A narrow, oblique entrance occupies the middle of the longer wall of the annexe, while its uphill side is defined by a huge recumbent block. Its threshold stone is still in position and by this was found a fallen jamb-stone and a door pivot-stone. Uphill from the rectangular annexe is a square supplementary chamber, notable for its huge end-stone. One wall of this has been robbed. Recent excavation (1969) has disclosed a few stones, and various cuts into the rabb, plus a drain, which may point to this oval hut having been the principal element of a complex of round and oval chambers of courtyard-house character. A common factor of both the larger sub-rectangular chamber and the modified oval hut was the large stones found beneath the floor-level of each. These, described in detail on page 152, appear to have been incorporated either from earlier structures or on account of the peculiar qualities inherent in them.

Traces of activity on the hill-slope before the stone buildings were erected have been found. These are a series of clay-built corn-drying ovens. A clutch of these were partly beneath the downhill wall of the southern entrance to the sub-rectangular chamber and had been cut into so that the stones of the wall of the oval hut could be housed. Another such oven has been detected below, and thus earlier than, the uphill wall of this sub-rectangular chamber.

All about the buildings on Halangy Down described in the preceding paragraphs there are vestiges of others. To the north-east there is a chaos of stone-breakers' debris among which one chamber still stands and others can be detected. Up the hill, beyond the courtyard house, a large chamber may exist below the accumulation of soil which in great measure protected the courtyard house. On the south-western side the site is bounded by a field-wall running down the hill. This may at one point incorporate part of a hut while also forming a rough limit to the range of buildings.

A series of small terraced fields are associated with the Halangy Down buildings. One massive wall, which seems to be an extension of one of the main walls of the system, retains the lower series of excavated buildings. This seems in great part to be an original massive terrace wall, designed to support a considerable depth of soil. At the same time it displays traces of progressive modification to incorporate it with the structures that it supported.

The material culture of those who lived in the buildings on Halangy Down, and those in the Porth below, is discussed in Chapter 10. Unfortunately little of this is significant, except in a general sense, because of the digging of the stone-robbers. However, sufficient has been found in places to allow association with specific aspects of the structures. The pottery, all fragmentary, consists for the most part of native Romano-British wares, but several splinters of imported Samian ware and one or two pieces of Castor ware have come to light. A number of pieces of burnished pottery recall Cornish Iron Age pottery.

Quantities of what is termed grass-marked pottery are also a feature of the site. It bears the negative impression of finely-chopped grass or hay which has been fired out. Several sherds were quite large and can be seen to be pieces of jars and platters. In general, much of the Romano-British pottery is intimately associated with the courtyard house or the large lower rectangular annexe. However, the courtyard house continued in use into the period when grass-marked wares were current, for pieces of this post-Roman pottery were found deep in the infill of the hearth in its circular chamber. Quantities of this grass-marked pottery were found during the excavation of the oval hut and its rectangular annexe, although in large measure in the topsoil of the area.

Numerous flint and quartz implements in the form of scrapers, utilised scraps, points and trimmed pebbles, as well as nodules and granite pebble-hammer and rubbing-stones have been found during the course of the excavations, as have complete, and broken, bowl, saddle and rotary querns. On the other hand metal finds were sparse, apart from a few scraps of iron and some iron slag. However, four bronze brooches, all from the topsoil, link the inhabitants of Halangy Down with the burials in the cist graves (Chapter 5).

While the site on Nornour (Dudley, 1967; Dudley and Butcher, 1968) has much that makes it necessary to consider it as a possible cult centre (page 221), many other factors show that the buildings were inhabited. This site was found, following a storm-damage cliff fall, in 1962, and excavations were carried out between 1962 and 1966. The buildings lie at the foot of the slope on the south side of the small island and extend for some distance into the beach, embodying the results of more than a millennium of occupation and progressive modification. The excavations uncovered three basic elements that made up the structures. First of all two conjoined chambers (Fig 44) with massive, high-standing, double-faced, walls, called by the excavator Rooms I and II. Secondly, adjacent to these, an extensive midden which covered the remaining internal wall-face of an oval hut. Thirdly, at no great distance up the slope, and built against a natural granite outcrop, a circular hut which, by progressive rebuilding, had been made smaller internally.

Room I, a circular chamber, was found to have been radially partitioned and to have had, besides other internal fitments, a succession of hearths. Room II also had a massive hearth and, on account of the adjacent midden, has been considered to have served as a kitchen. The interior of the small hut under the midden was featureless, but inside the circular hut, up the slope, was a massive hearth and a stone-lined pit or tank. Three other such stone-lined pits or tanks, protected by a stone wall, were just outside.

The evidence for the first phase of occupation is difficult to disentangle although its existence cannot be denied. In general terms, it is claimed that Rooms I and II were built over a 'Bronze Age' living site which seems to have extended along the present shore line. Beneath Room I were post-holes, presumably cut into the rabb, which appear to be covered in part by elements of later internal structures. A 'lower' hearth was found which contained charcoal, and another hearth detected partly under the wall of Room II which 'belongs to the area which is considered to be of Bronze Age date'. The small hut beneath the midden

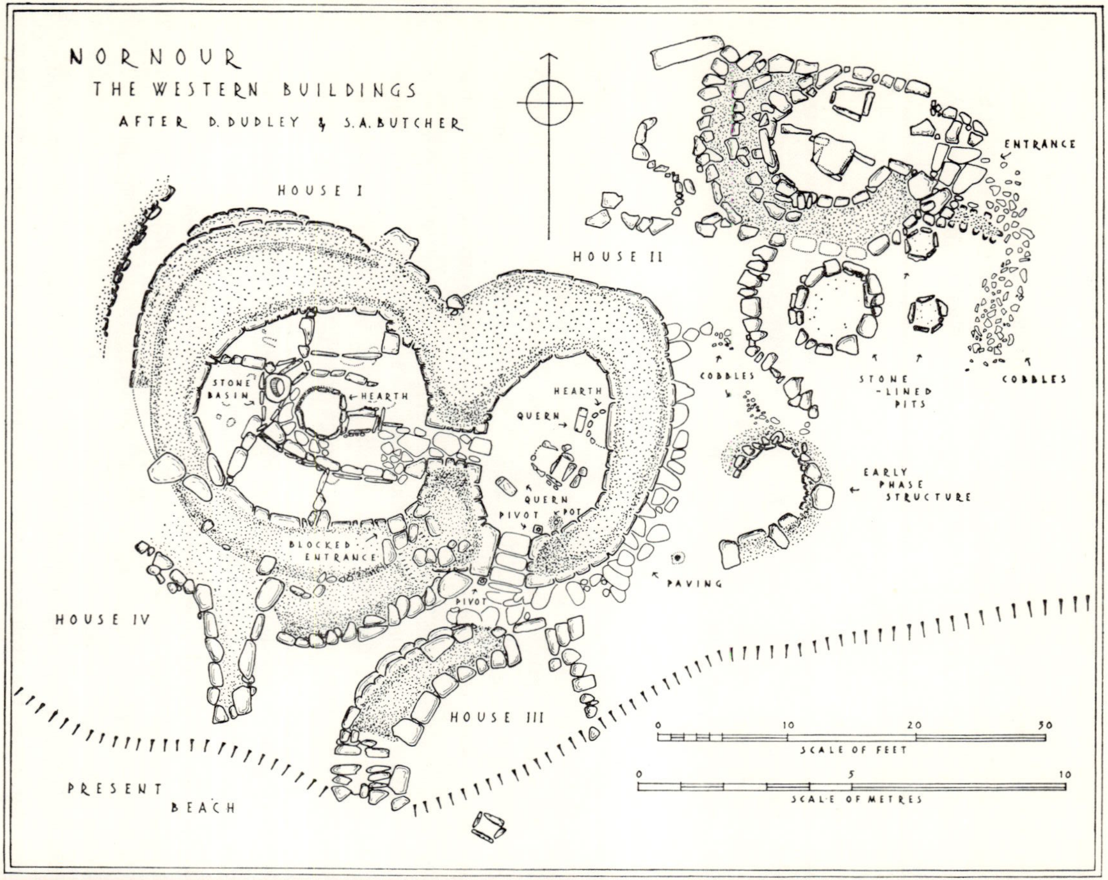
NORNOUR
THE WESTERN BUILDINGS
AFTER D. DUDLEY & S. A. BUTCHER
HOUSE I
HOUSE II
HOUSE III
HOUSE IV
ENTRANCE
STONE BASIN
HEARTH
QUERN
PIVOT
POT
BLOCKED ENTRANCE
PAVING
COBBLES
STONE -LINED PITS
EARLY PHASE STRUCTURE
PRESENT BEACH
0 10 20 30
SCALE OF FEET
0 5 10
SCALE OF METRES

is also considered to belong to this phase. Any structure which existed, however, was obviously demolished before Room I was built.

The structure termed Room I is near-round in internal plan and access to it was by an entrance through its flattened eastern side. It would seem to have been at least 7ft in height and, where not damaged, was still standing to that height when excavated. Its walls, at least internally, have as basal courses well-matched vertically set stones. Above this is irregular coursed work. Externally 'strong revetment', strengthened at some point by a buttress, was used. This room 'built in the deeply-rooted tradition of the Scillonian Chamber Tombs' is difficult to separate from the early phase. Indeed, the three post-holes, set symmetrically in its interior might have been related directly to it. Pottery, strikingly similar to that from Knackyboy Cairn (O'Neil, 1952), stone balls, a petit-tranchet derivative arrowhead, small stone discs, a quartz pendant and a grooved hammer-stone are the artifacts associated with the 'Bronze Age' phase.

A third phase in the development of the Nornour buildings is the addition of Room II, the construction of the complex interior fitments within Room I and, seemingly, the erection of the adjacent round hut with its hearth, pits and tanks. The walling style employed for the construction of Room II is coursed and bonded work. It is claimed (Dudley, 1967, 7) that 'the walls throughout are of normal Iron Age construction'. Presumably, were this structure, at some juncture, built on to an already existing building, there would have been re-bonding. That this may not have been entirely successful is suggested by a modification of the corners of the narrow corridor giving access to Room I. In plan Room II is a flattened oval, with a narrow paved corridor giving access to Room I and there is a similar external entrance. Inside there is a hearth of open-ended form. Its external wall-face stands in great measure upon paving stones. When it was constructed a midden was cut into. Sherds of Iron Age pottery and, for that matter, Bronze Age pottery, were found in the filling, in the walls and in the lower level of the floors. It is thought (Dudley and Butcher, 1968, 6) that a burning roof had fallen on them. Such burning might account for the over-all reddening of the walls of this chamber.

The fitments of the interior of Room I have caused it to be called a 'wheel-house'. The internal area was divided into at least five compartments by radial piers or partitions. These piers or partitions are built of horizontally laid blocks of granite and stand, at the present time, to a height of some 3 or 4ft. It is thought that they were originally built to the full height of the chamber to support the roof. They butt against the internal wall although none of them are bonded into it. This suggestion that these piers are a modification of the original chamber is strengthened by their relationship with the chamber entrance. This is not symmetrical and thus these partitions cannot be regarded as an integral part of the structure. A large bowl, fashioned from a block of granite, is a prominent feature of the interior. Because of its awkward positioning in relation to the later phases it is considered that it was introduced at an earlier juncture and continued in use over a long period. Each of the compartments can only be entered from the central area, from which it is separated by low vertically set stones and a flat granite shelf or seat set above the floor. The space between this and the hearth is paved. A large central circular stone hearth (Plate 10a) was found to be filled with limpet shells and burnt soil. By it, towards the entrance, is another square hearth built of granite slabs. In the circular hearth were found seven miniature vessels, 2in in height, with internally bevelled lips and cord ornament. An Iron Age pot was encountered in one corner of the square hearth. At the distal end of the chamber and adjacent to the hearth are two slab boxes or tanks. A drain is mentioned in the account of the excavation (Dudley, 1967, 5). When excavated, these chambers were found to be filled with stones and sand and it is from here that the great quantity of metal objects, mainly brooches, and the figurines came. A considerable number of Roman coins, spanning the period AD 70 to AD 380 was found also.

The other round hut termed the workshop, with its massive hearth, pits and tanks, is considered to belong to this third phase on account of 'some Iron Age sherds' found 'on top of the wall'. This hut, some 8ft

Fig 45 Nornour: the eastern buildings

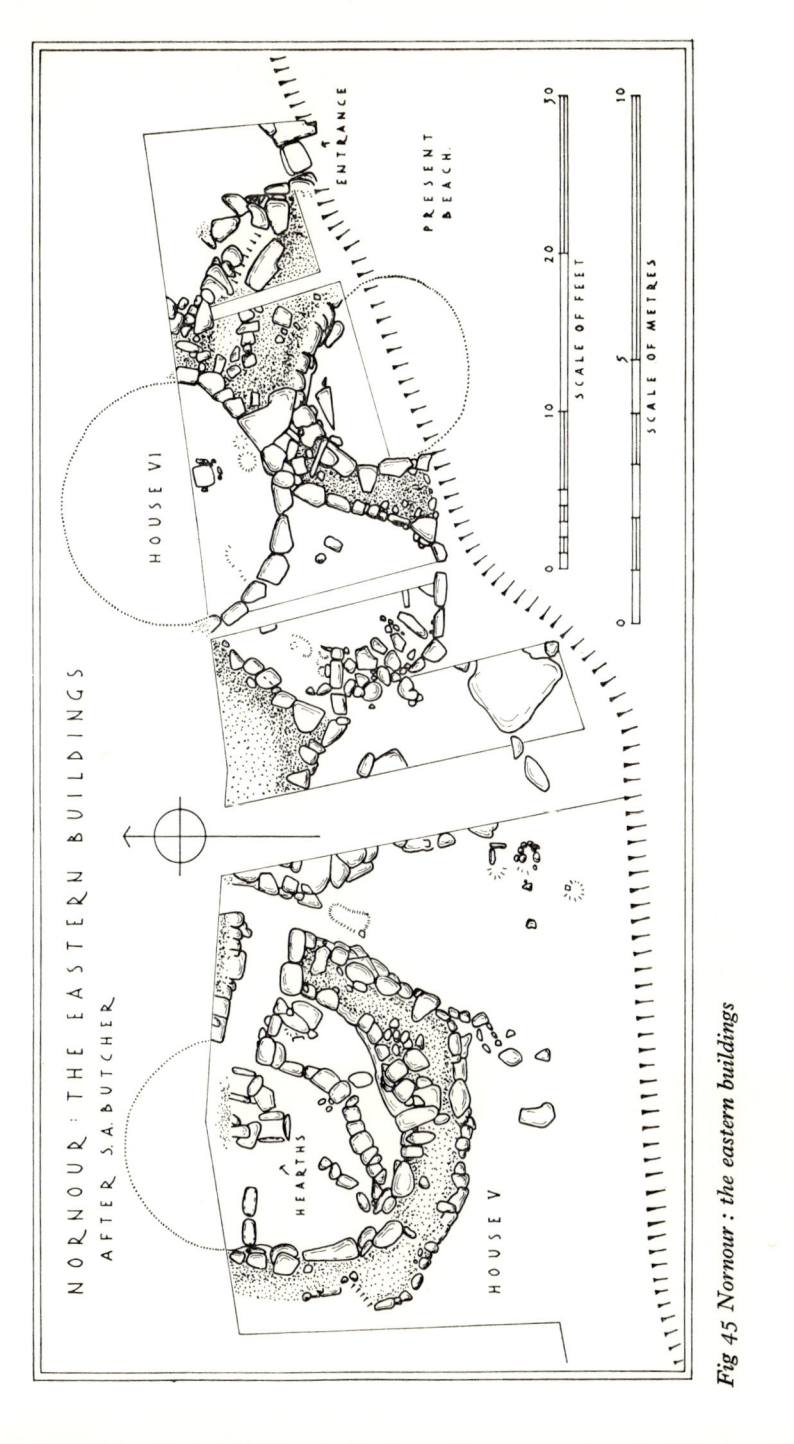

in diameter in its final form, has a broad, paved corridor entrance which was approached by a cobbled path. It had been built against a considerable natural granite outcrop which had, to some extent, dictated its site and form. What are described as 'other walls' appear to be the phased footings of a thick, presumably soil-filled wall. A single spur, perhaps remaining from a more substantial wall runs down the slope, while there is another ruined structure just to the west. Inside this hut, just to the left of the entrance, was a stone-built, near horse-shoe form, hearth. When found it was covered by a huge slab of stone, perhaps a fallen fire-back. To the right of the entrance is a sub-rectangular pit lined with slabs of granite, but nothing was found in it. Outside the hut, down the slope, are one large and two smaller stone-lined pits. The larger, some 6ft by 4ft 6in, is oval and when excavated was found to contain quantities of light-coloured clay while more lay around it. It seems not unlikely that this results from the washing out of luting or lining. The two smaller pits are almost identical to each other, each being built with size-selected and matched stones and each having a flat stone bottom. It was observed that the stones of one of these pits was marked by fire. More recently further buildings have been unearthed (Fig 45).

For all these abundant traces of domestic economy it is not easy to see Nornour as only a settlement, because of the question of the significance of the wealth of the, sometimes exotic, objects found there. Besides pottery and equipment of flint, chert and granite, these included Roman brooches, rings and other bronze objects, Romano-Gaulish clay figurines, Roman coins and glass beads. The only plausible suggestion that accounts for the unique features of the buildings and the artifacts is that Nornour was a votive site with, perhaps, a workshop on its premises, as will be argued in Chapter 9. In the circumstances no other explanation wholly and satisfactorily explains these buildings (Plate 10b), and their associations, on Nornour.

Excavations on Teän in 1956, carried out by Professor Charles Thomas, disclosed the inner face of a small stone-built hut of oval or, perhaps, sub-rectangular form. Of this only some three courses remained; the interior being partly choked with large stones, perhaps from the ruined wall. It is possible that this structure was dug into a pre-existing midden on account of the absence of an outer wall-face. The absence of an outer wall-face, with the material from the midden, suggest that this structure may be compared to the single-walled buildings, with some form of outer cloaking, which seem to be a feature of sub-Roman Cornwall. This hut was the earliest feature revealed during the excavation of a series of buildings, one possibly a chapel, which is discussed below.

SUMMARY

This account of the remains of almost two millennia of houses and settlements on the Isles of Scilly has isolated several distinct problems that require consideration. First there is the question of continuity of occupation of more or less the same site for a long period of time; occupation which begins in the early second, or late third, millennium BC and often continues into post-Roman times. Secondly there are the problems surrounding the planning and structure of Scillonian houses during this long period of time. Thirdly, not all of the known buildings may have been dwellings in a permanent sense; they were either temporary or for some specific economic or industrial purpose. Finally there are questions of the significance of the siting and size of each unit, which extend into socio-economic matters as to what size the territory which belonged to each homestead or settlement was, and what sort of social structure created them.

It is reasonable to suppose that the extensive remains in Halangy Porth belong, by the quantities of pottery, to the chamber-tomb phase, and those on Halangy Down, shown by pottery to have been inhabited during Iron Age, Roman and post-Roman times, represent aspects of the development of the same complex. The sites thus demonstrate continuity of settlement within a confined area. The lower, earlier, phase was obviously abandoned because of the encroachment of blown sand, itself a preliminary to marine transgression. Following the abandonment of the lower buildings, the focus of settlement moved to the hill-slope above. The same conditions must also have dictated a similar shift at Pendrathen. Here the earlier phase, observed by Jackson, has in great measure been destroyed by the sea, while traces of a later phase have been detected as still surviving inland.

Further direct evidence of continuity has been detected on St Martin's and on Nornour. At May's Hill, St Martin's, it was found that a stone-built native Romano-British hut had been built over the debris of earlier occupation. This debris, which was mainly midden material, yielded pottery similar to that from the hut at English Island Carn and the chamber tomb, Knackyboy Cairn. The Nornour complex has provided even more direct evidence, for here traces of structures were found beneath, and even perhaps incorporated into, a later Iron Age and Roman phase.

In the first two examples cited, the reasons for the move were self-evident, but on May's Hill and on Nornour the reasons for demolition and rebuilding would seem to have been both social and economic. On Nornour, blown sand can only have been a contributory factor to abandonment at a late juncture. Within the land area that is the present-day Isles of Scilly and within the range of the relatively large number of sites known there are certainly other examples of continuity to be detected, for example in the close juxtaposition of earlier and later sites on Par Beach, St Martin's, or on the flats by Arthur. There are also grounds for suspecting similar relationships on Samson and Bryher. Probably excavation of later sites would in many instances disclose traces of earlier occupation in the same location.

The houses built by the first immigrants to the Isles of Scilly may have been entirely of timber. If this is so, no trace has been found. However, some of the earlier buildings can be termed composite, that is timber featured more prominently in their construction than in later structures.

As has emerged earlier in this chapter, sufficient is known of Scillonian huts and houses of both the earlier and later phases, to permit general observations regarding their form and fabric. In the earlier phase, termed the Bronze Age by O'Neil (1949, *SM* 164–5) and Dudley (1967), a number of buildings were rectangular, or sub-rectangular, while some

HOUSES AND SETTLEMENTS

were oval or circular. During the later phase, which is broadly Iron Age, Roman and post-Roman times, huts, or chambers which are components of courtyard houses, are normally oval or circular. Notwithstanding, square structures are not unknown, as is shown for example by the square-planned extension to an oval hut on Halangy Down.

Of the excavated structures of the early phase, O'Neil's hut at English Island Carn (O'Neil, 1949, *SM* 164–5) was described as roughly rectangular in plan, but with the walls converging to a point at the southern end. It is difficult to determine whether this form was dictated by certain large natural boulders which were incorporated into it or if it results from progressive modification. The footings of a hut bared by Gray at Halangy Porth, St Mary's, appear to have been roughly rectangular, their dimension being 14ft by 9ft. As far as can be seen from the substantial hut wall still standing in the cliff of Halangy Porth, this also was a square or rectangle. If Room I of the substantial building on Nornour was built at the time, that also tends to the rectangular, the wall which contains the entrance being straight. Another hut, allegedly 'Bronze Age' on Nornour may be only the remaining circular end of a more-or-less rectangular building. Other huts of this early phase, on St Martin's at Great Bay, Perpitch, and Par Beach appear to have been circular as do the alleged 'bee-hive' huts on the beach at Pendrathen, St Mary's.

Halangy Down, on account of the relatively large area that has now been excavated, has given us near-complete structure plans of the later phase. Together with these are the possibly atypical buildings on Nornour. A good part of an oval structure has been examined on Teän while there was a round hut, with other buildings attached to it, on Par Beach, St Martin's.

The two principal chambers of the Halangy Down courtyard house are respectively oval and circular in plan, with the small, sub-circular cells between. One other hut is oval but has a markedly rectangular annexe built on to it, making a composite unit. The remaining hut, perhaps part of a larger unit, is best described as sub-rectangular. Although the D-form of one of the Nornour huts was dictated by the circumstances of a massive rock outcrop, the D-form of Room II at this site appears to have been a matter of deliberate choice. Only a part of the Teän hut was bared, the remains there were of a small hut of oval or perhaps sub-rectangular form. The hut on Par Beach, St Martin's, was round although half had been eroded by the sea. Another small structure, close by, may also have originally been circular although here fragmentary remains may point to an erstwhile rectangular building.

At English Island Carn there were thick walls built of small stones and only a few orthostats were used. One wall appears to have been composite, combining timber posts and masonry. The walling exposed in Halangy Porth is well-coursed and bonded, the stones seemingly selected for their purpose. There is also the use of very large stones for walling, to be seen at one point in this cliff. Room I at Nornour was built of orthostats with coursed walling above them. Such walling can be seen in the chamber tombs of the Isles of Scilly and West Penwith, and was also employed to build the square annexe to an oval hut at a late juncture on Halangy Down. The round hut at Perpitch had walling that resembled English Island Carn and posts, set into dug sockets, supported the roof. The alleged 'bee-hive' huts at Pendrathen may have been roofed by corbelling. The surviving courses of corbelling were found in the small intra-mural chamber at Halangy Down. At Halangy Down the walling of the later phases is for the most part coursed work carried out with carefully selected stones. Orthostats are employed and, sometimes, there are panels of coursed walling between them. As noted above, the technique of basal orthostats was used also at this time. Great boulders are used for external angles and at entrances. The coursed walling of Room II at Nornour was preserved to a height of almost 7ft.

It is presumed, for there is no direct evidence, that from the first, early Scillonian houses and other buildings had thatched roofs, as described in connection with Halangy Down. Indeed, burning thatch may have reddened the internal wall-faces of Room II at Nornour. Internally the timbers of the roof framing must have been supported by posts. This is attested by dug post-sockets, as for example at Perpitch. Such sockets have not been found in later structures where, often, quite large spans were involved. Here it is thought that vertical supporting posts had their butts housed in large dished slabs of stone, such as that found *in situ* on St Martin's.

The entrances to buildings at all times were normally paved with flat slabs and flanked with substantial jamb-stones. Small friction-marked cupped stones are found in entrances and point to side-pivoting timber doors. Floors frequently appear to have been sanded, and when sand was not employed they were of earth. Now and again stones or slabs seem to have been used for patching. Most of the earlier and the later buildings had systems of drains, sometimes well below their floors. These were of stone slabs, used for sides and covers. They usually led out of entrances. The early hearth at Nornour may have been circular. Apart from this most hearths were horse-shoes of substantial standing stones. Pits, exemplified by the Nornour series, were of orthostats or coursed stones, but no precise evidence has been forthcoming as to the use of such stone-lined pits.

Almost all of the early buildings detected and examined on the Isles of Scilly have been termed huts or homesteads and by this domestic occupation has been implied. It would seem possible from the number of 'hearths', that is areas of clay 'baked with fire' that were a feature of the later phases in the Perpitch hut, that this building was used for a specialised purpose. As it is in an early enclosure system it is possible that the baked clay represents the remains of corn-drying ovens. The large oval chamber of the Halangy Down courtyard house is notable for its complex system of drains and hollows. Unlike the smaller circular chamber, it lacks a central hearth, although Gray found traces of burning against the uphill wall. It is not impossible that this, from time to time, accommodated animals rather than human beings, a contention principally supported by its uneven floor. There is also the question of the internal fitments of the two main rooms of the buildings on Nornour. Do these denote domestic circumstances or was this a workshop connected with this possible cult centre?

At the present time the buildings in Halangy Porth and on Halangy Down, taken together, comprise what would seem to be the most substantial domestic site on the islands. However, the extent of sites where only small-scale clearance and excavation has taken place is not known, while also it is uncertain how much, as for instance on Par Beach, has been destroyed by the sea. Assuming that the various buildings in Halangy Porth extended to about twice their seeming size, range and area, they would not, perhaps, have accommodated more than about one or two extended families. Later on, when the focus of the settlement had moved up on to the hill-slope that is Halangy Down, the buildings there, both excavated and unexcavated, might at the most have housed about four such families.

It can be seen that each domestic site is roughly associated with a tract of land. The Halangy Down site has a clear relationship with the area about it although it is far from clear what its relationship was to the similar site at Pendrathen. Again, on St Martin's there is the site up on May's Hill and the site on Par Beach. Likewise there is the site on the eastern side of Tresco at Gimble Porth which, like Halangy Down, is associated with a field system.

Here and there on the islands, middens have been found without, as yet, any traces of associated structures. For example there is the large midden, found by Gray at Porth Killier on St Agnes, containing pottery, charcoal and seal bones. It would seem that such accumulations may represent only seasonal successions and, in the circumstances, the dwellings may only have been temporary. For until relatively recently some Scillonian cottages were not built of stones at all. As in Ireland, their walls were of turf, their roofs of spars and thatch. If such a mode of building was employed in early times little more than a hearth would mark the site.

How far the houses, and the modes of life lived within them, are products of local circumstances or whether they owe anything to external stimuli are the obvious questions that one might ask. Local circumstances certainly dictated materials as they would also have done in the similar western highland regions of the British Isles. As far as the distinctive courtyard house at Halangy Down is concerned, however, there is the parallel in the localised series in Penwith, Cornwall. Beyond general resemblances to cellular buildings in, for example, Wales, little can be said.

CHAPTER 8

Forts and Enclosures

Such Scillonian sites as can be termed forts (Fig 46), some six in number, come within the category called promontory forts or cliff castles. Apart from these there is one penannular walled hill-top enclosure of uncertain function. Other enclosures are the remnants of ancient field-systems. Cliff castles were made by building ramparts, which appear today as banks and ditches, across the neck of a peninsula. Such ramparts were straight, in out-flung arcs or in combinations of the two techniques. Thus on two or more sides, sea-cliffs or the sea, for there are low-lying estuarine sites, serve as natural defences. In many instances a single rampart sufficed, in others more than one was deemed necessary while, again, even more complex systems suggest more than one period of building.

For the most part cliff castles are found about cliff-girt coasts; there are nearly fifty of various forms, sizes and strengths on the coastline of Cornwall. Most of these have complex rampart systems, seemingly multi-period and, where excavation has been carried out, they have been shown to have been inhabited centres. Some fifteen or so of these promontory forts or cliff castles enclose from 3 to 15 acres although one walls off an even greater area. Besides Cornwall and the Isles of Scilly, promontory forts are found, in Britain, about the coasts of Devon, Somerset, Wales, the Isle of Man and Scotland. In Ireland more than 200 have been identified. On the mainland of Europe the best known are in France on the coasts of Loire Inférieure, Morbihan and Finistère. They are also to be found in the Channel Islands.

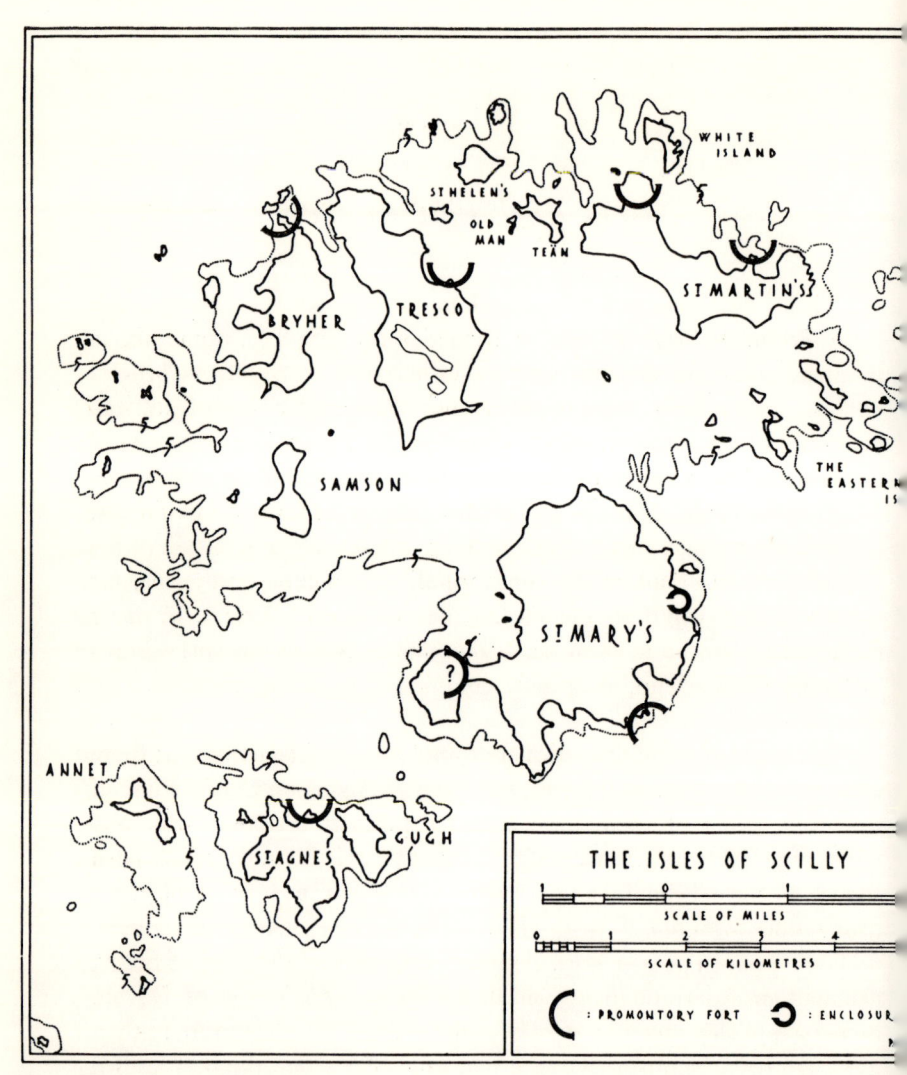

Fig 46 Scillonian promontory forts

FORTS AND ENCLOSURES

Of the promontory forts of the Isles of Scilly, the multi-vallate Giant's Castle on the eastern side of St Mary's is the best known. It excited the attention of Borlase (1756, 11) on the occasion of his memorable visit and it seems that he coined the term 'cliff castle'. He commented upon the fortifications that were to be seen on St Mary's and concluded by observing that 'what they call here the Giant's Castle is certainly prior to the Norman Conquest'. Borlase also wrote:

> This *Castle* is situated on a promontory, which towards the sea is an immense crag of rocks, as if heaped on each other: this heap or turret of rocks declines also quick, but not so rough towards the land, and spreads to join the downs, where at the foot of this knoll it has first a ditch crossing the neck of land from sea to sea; then a low *Vallum* of the same direction; next, a second ditch and a higher *Vallum*; lastly, near the top of this crag, it had a wall of stone encompassing every part, but where the natural rocks were a sufficient security; this wall by the ruins appears to have been very high and thick. It is call'd as I have said but now, the *Giant's Castle*, the common people in these islands as well as elsewhere, attributing all extraordinary works to giants.

The ruins of a wall of some height were seen by Borlase. Something of the erstwhile stone-walling system can still be seen and it is clear that great quantities of stone must have been taken away down the years. Its proximity to Old Town might account for this or it could have been a ready source of stone for Old Castle, which was in earlier times styled the Castle of Ennor.

Hencken (1932, 31) briefly described Giant's Castle and considered that its small size might be accounted for by erosion of the cliffs. The solid granite character of the cliffs makes it unlikely that there has been any appreciable change to alter in any great measure its total area. Indeed, for reasons detailed in the next chapter (page 218), the function of its ramparts may have been to demarcate the prominent rock-stack.

Gray (Ashbee, 1972, 38) saw the earth and stone character of one of the ramparts but could find no trace of huts or other structures within. There is, however, some slight evidence of date. O'Neil (1949, 9) records that during the war a few sherds of pottery were found in a cutting made by the army at the outer edge. It has been said that some of these sherds bore 'duck' ornament (Hencken, T. C., 1938, 88); their present whereabouts is not known.

Shipman Head, the precipitous northern extremity of Bryher, was defended by a massive wall of selected granite blocks. It ran from Boat Carn on the east side to the steep sea-cliff on the west and had a narrow entrance with a guard-chamber but no ditches. The facing stones of the footings can still be seen, much massive masonry still in position, as can the entrance and guard-chamber (O'Neil, 1949, 9). Cliff erosion has accounted for a considerable length of wall on the west side and has reduced the area of this promontory fort. One or two level areas on the slope within the wall may be hut platforms. No evidence of association or date has been forthcoming from this site.

A large apparent earthwork, which may be turf-enshrouded stone walling, cuts off the promontory on the eastern side of Tresco on which stands the Old Blockhouse (O'Neil, 1949, 9). The inner rampart is roughly semi-circular in plan and, as at Shipman Head, there is no trace of a ditch. A gap on the southern side may denote an entrance. Two other banks can be seen, each with an entrance-gap, further down the slope. There would seem to have been here a multi-vallate promontory fort in the style of Giant's Castle but of walling without ditches.

On St Martin's, Burnt Hill, a large rectangular area with steep cliffs on the northern coast, bears traces of a stone wall separating it from the remainder of the island (Lewis, 1948, 9; O'Neil, 1949, 9). This, again, seems to have been a walled, ditchless, promontory fort of some strength and, inside, there are clear traces of stone-built huts. At the north-western end of this island there are the remains of a rampart and ditch running from Little Bay on the east to Porth Seal on the west, dividing Top Rock Hill. In places the ditch and rampart is of some size

FORTS AND ENCLOSURES

and it cuts off a large area which would also have included White Island, prior to its break-off.

Mount Todden Battery, on St Mary's, which Troutbeck (1794, 94) called a 'sod-battery' and described the semi-megalithic structure inside it as 'a bomb-proof watch house', seems to have been originally an enclosure of an age commensurate with that of the promontory forts. O'Neil (1949, 9) remarks that it encloses a roughly circular area on top of a hill, not on the edge of the sea, and that, at the entrance, one end of the rampart is turned inwards in a manner which is very common in camps of the early Iron Age. Mount Todden allows an excellent view of the Cornish cliffs and consideration could be given to the possibility that this modest enclosure might be the remains of a native-built signal station copying the Roman system (Fox, 1964, 139) of the mainland.

Early enclosures, either on slopes and terraced or on level ground and walled, are to be seen on a number of islands and their shores. The best known and preserved, as well as the most extensive, series of terraced plots are those associated with the stone-built houses on Halangy Down, St Mary's. They have not as yet been surveyed in detail but it can be said that plots on the hillside, each about a third of an acre in size, are retained by walls built of massive boulders which in places are associated with spreads of smaller stones. These smaller stones were either cleared at the time of the initial layout or during the course of agricultural operations. Tracks bound certain parts of the system which is set about the chamber tombs, while here and there the patent remains of out-field structures can be detected. Lengths of walling can be seen linking some chamber tombs on Gugh, Samson and Bryher and recall the main tomb-aligned terraces of the Halangy Down system. These may be the remains of erstwhile early field-systems or the basic walls of a plan never fully developed. On St Martin's at Perpitch, the foundations of a hut, which may have housed a battery of corn-drying ovens, were found to have been built into an ancient cultivation terrace.

The renowned submerged walls, the circumstances of which have been described in detail in Chapter 3, are for the most part fragmentary or have perhaps been only partly observed and investigated. Those on

Samson Flats are probably the best known and here several are a good many hundred feet in length which contrasts with the modest size of the quite well-preserved walls on the shores of Teän. Charles Thomas has suggested that the counterparts of the lengthy Samson submerged walls lie in the later Bronze Age cattle-ranching systems of the Wessex chalklands (Hawkes, 1939, 146, Fig 1). He has also compared the construction of the two systems and sees the walls on Samson Flats as of cruder construction than those on Teän which exhibit coursed facework with selected boulders bound by rubble coring.

Besides observing and describing submerged walls, Borlase (1756, 26) noticed the remains of hedges and ancient enclosures on both inhabited and uninhabited islands. Of St Martin's he wrote 'This island seems to have been entirely cultivated in former times, for everywhere as we went (through the whole length of it) we could trace Hedges so plainly crossing the ridge and descending to the sea on either hand of us, that there can be no doubt but that the land was inclosed and divided into fields anciently, though now for the most part incapable of cultivation, because over-run as it is with sand, the soil is quite buried.' When commenting upon the Eastern Islands he remarked that 'on one of them called Arthur', there are 'three *Burrows* and the remains of Hedges, but nothing else remarkable'.

As O. G. S. Crawford (1936, 163) said, when writing on the field-walls of Cornwall, 'Walls in the West age quickly but live long.' Everywhere on the Isles of Scilly, on the downs and wastes of the inhabited and uninhabited islands, the patterns of enclosures, unrelated to present usages, can be seen. On St Mary's, for example, many of them must mark the extent of those squalid crofts that were combined into economic holdings by the improving zeal of Augustus Smith (Inglis-Jones, 1969, 77). Only on Samson is there an enclosure pattern preserved from before Augustus Smith's wholesale changes. Other walls, like the terrace bared by excavation at Porth Cressa (Ashbee, 1954, 6), or those on Halangy Down, remain from earlier times. Intensive fieldwork and patient detailed survey might well unravel relative patterns, but the craft of 'hedging' has lasted unbroken without great change since the Samson

FORTS AND ENCLOSURES

Walls were set down on the low-lying central plain of a larger island. Thus, unless there is direct association with earlier habitation, all merge into a pattern of lichen-clad, weather-induced, deceptive antiquity.

CHAPTER 9

Cult Sites and Early Christians

Consideration of cult sites and objects makes necessary some excursion on to the quicksands of early barbarian religion. The egregious evidence which can be marshalled in the Isles of Scilly points to common ground with the mainland, that is Britain and beyond.

Recently, a measure of order has come to the British scene (Ross, 1967); archaeological method, backed by critical consideration of classical and early vernacular literary sources, has been brought to bear upon the diverse mass of 'cult' material: miscellaneous metal objects, stones, structures and sites, that have accumulated down the years. All this has involved equation with allusions contained in the early vernacular literature of Britain and Ireland, with essential factors in folklore and tradition and with accounts by those writers of the classical world who came into contact with the northern barbarians beyond its boundaries. Archaeological evidence for religion in the European Celtic realm has been summarised by Piggott (1965, 229-35). It is not abundant but, as in Britain, a constant recurring pattern emerges. Surrounding almost every archaeological manifestation of Celtic religion there is an aura of archaism. Almost everything has its counterpart in much earlier times. It was this factor, combined with the especial regional aspects of the native pantheon, that posed such difficulties to Roman writers and administrators who tried so hard to mould them into the imperial matrix.

Cult sites were actual structures or natural features of especial significance: hills or the sources of rivers, wells and springs. These last sometimes had buildings close by them. In Roman times many earlier sites were formulated into temples and skilled excavation has revealed the original form beneath. Certain cult figures have been identified; these range from complex stone statuary to crude boulders. Many such stones recall the wooden figures which have long since perished. Barrow and cairn cemeteries were also cult centres where tribal rites took place to invoke the ancestors. From time to time, either by accident or excavation, assemblages of votive objects have come to light and these, by their character, are sometimes suggestive of offerings at a shrine. The antiquity of the practice of shafts and wells having cults centred about them has been shown by excavation (Ashbee, 1966, 227-8). Another ubiquitous cult was concerned with the human head. This can be discerned already in Mesolithic times and is manifest in the numerous heads of stone or representations of heads on stone pillars.

Cult sites must have had attendant priests and recognition of this leads to the vexed question of the Druids (Kendrick, 1928; Tierney, 1960; Chadwick, 1966; Piggott, 1968). As a result of the works of William Stukeley (Piggott, 1950, 92-135) and his followers in the eighteenth century these have passed into popular imagination. Indeed, they have become near synonymous with 'Ancient Britons' and thus lurk, even in these days of popular televised archaeology, in the vicinity of almost every prehistoric monument or even cave, ruin or grotto. Neo-Druidism is not without its exceptional English charm but, apart from its influence upon the development of our studies (Borlase was a disciple of Druidism), it is irrelevant in this context. The evidence for a priesthood among the peoples of pre-Roman Europe and Britain is both tenuous and prosaic. There are the comments of the classical writers coupled with such inferences as can be drawn from prehistoric archaeology. In general such writers show little interest, for the Roman Raj was both tolerant and accommodating except when cult practices became identified with political and practical opposition to its civilising mission. Caesar's propagandising makes more mention of them than any other writer and he was of the view that they had their origin in Britain. Tacitus makes much of them in Anglesey in AD 61 for here

Paulinus had to urge his troops to the attack in the face of their fury. At present archaeology can give us little more than insight into the structure, character and surround of cult sites and nothing of this nature is direct evidence of Druids. For good political reasons the classical writers endowed them with a degree of sophistication that the general balance of probability does not allow. One might see them rather as barbarian shamen concerned with the appropriate observances which were geared to the propitiation of the shadowy *genii loci* of forest glade, rocky carn, shaft, spring or rustic shrine.

Apart from the possibility of certain standing stones, discussed in a previous chapter, having had cult significance, little or nothing to mark this aspect of the earlier stages of Scillonian life, has been detected. There are, however, a few relevant possibilities.

Giant's Castle, the seemingly trivallate cliff-castle situated on the eastern side of St Mary's, has some claim to be considered as a possible cult site. This promontory fort, which is, above all else, in Wheeler's words (1957, 5) 'suspended in an enduring sea-mist between the mournful screaming of the sea-birds and the relentless crashing of the breakers', is but a rocky carn. The ramparts enclose a minimal habitable area: there are but few level spaces, scarcely large enough for a small hut, and it does not seem likely that there has been any appreciable erosion. Indeed, the purpose of the ramparts would seem to be the demarcation of the prominent and distinctive rock-stack. It is feasible that in Romano-British times a cult building, perhaps even a native Scillonian version of a Roman temple, existed on the Garrison or on a point of the slope at the southern end of Hugh Town. Inferential evidence of this is the granite Roman altar (Plate 11a), now at Tresco Abbey, said to have been found either on the Garrison (Hencken, 1932, 195) or opposite the Atlantic Hotel (O'Neil, 1949, 11), in Hugh Town. A note illustrating and briefly describing it was published in 1921 (Anon, 1921, 239). This, from an unnamed correspondent, is as follows:

> There is but little history attached to what seems to be a Roman altar now preserved among the figure-heads of wrecked ships in the

Valhalla of Tresco Abbey. Two views are here given ... from photographs kindly supplied by Messrs Gibson and Son of Mount's Bay Studio; and these show a sacrificial knife and axe on the two sides, but there are no traces of an inscription on the front. The altar is of coarse granite, 32 in. high, 17 in. across the base, and 15 in. square at the top. The owner, Major Dorrien Smith, is convinced that it is no recent importation from the mainland, and his predecessor, Mr. Augustus Smith, brought it from the island of St. Mary's in 1870, where it used to stand near the Garrison Hill, beside an old masonic lodge. Mr. George Bonsor thinks that it came originally from Old Town (the ancient capital of St. Mary's before the Elizabethen Star Castle was built in 1593), that being the only place where Roman antiquities have been discovered in the islands; but he himself has found earlier relics, and promises a report on his excavations carried out in 1899–1902.

Axes, as on the left side of this altar, are not unknown among the numbers that have come to light in Britain. The so-called 'sacrificial knife' on the right side could also be regarded as the outline of a long-shafted votive axe.

Two bottom parts of well-finished granite columns (Plate 11b) are preserved in a small garden opposite to the Atlantic Hotel, in Hugh Town. Their precise origin is not known. They are of flattened oval-rectangular section with chamfered edges. Each stands upon a rectangular base. Each base has a broad chamfered upper edge. The face of one, visible towards the road at the present time, might have borne a relief device. This is weathered and its character cannot be defined with any precision. These columns were apparently placed in their present position as garden ornaments during the refurbishing of Hugh Town that went on in the last, and during the earlier years of this, century. It is possible that a scrutiny of Scillonian garden ornaments might yield other comparable pieces. Down the years, querns, cup-marked and other 'featured' stones have been collected in various places for such use. Indeed, one very large assemblage still stands in a garden, at a house called Rocky Hill, just to landward of Harry's Walls, on St Mary's.

The site of such a structure as has been inferred may well be impossible to locate. The building of Star Castle, the Old Quay and the Garrison Walls would have accounted for any readily portable stone in the immediate vicinity, at an early stage. A possible clue lies in Borlase's account of St Mary's (1756, 12). He writes that 'Just below the *lines* are the remains of an old Fort (Pl. III, No. 10): It is a round hillock and seems to have had a *Keep* on top of it, in the same manner as *Trematon* and *Launceston* Castles, in *Cornwall*, but smaller; the walls of it have been stripp'd to build the *Lines*; tis call'd *Mount Holles*.' Borlase's Pl. III is 'Fort, Town Pier & Harbour of St. Mary's in Scilly with the Northern Islands taken from Bosu [Buzza] Hill June 5, 1752'. By implication this was a circular tower-like building and part of it, in spite of stripping, seemingly still remained when Borlase saw it. Its siting seems unconnected with the later topography of the island, for it lies below Star Castle and outside the Garrison, while the eminence at the back of the town, yet at a distance from Porth Cressa, excludes it from the Civil War fortifications. There is also a possibility that it may have been an expedient of Thomas Godolphin who, when appointed deputy to John Killigrew, Governor of Pendennis Castle, Falmouth, was charged to direct the construction of a fort at the eastern end of St Mary's harbour (Matthews, 1960, 10). Yet there is evidence (Saunders, 1962, 88) that, although garrisons had been established by 1549, little had been done to build fortifications. In the circumstances it might be that Borlase's 'old Fort' was the remains of a much earlier structure and that it is from Mount Holles that the altar and columns come. At the present time the site is covered by the spread of Hugh Town, although the name is perpetuated by a house. If, as surmised, this was a circular cult structure on Mount Holles, it could be of significance that the sites of the Porth Cressa (Ashbee, 1954) and Poynter's Garden (Dudley, 1961) cist-grave cemeteries are just at the foot of the 'round hillock' on which this enigmatic structure stood.

Although work upon the excavation of the sea-exposed site on

CULT SITES AND EARLY CHRISTIANS

Nornour (Dudley, 1967) is, perhaps, not yet complete, the possibility that it was a cult site should be entertained. The initial work disclosed the two well-built rooms, one with a central hearth, while subsequent work has exposed a series of stone-lined pits and earlier structures. Excavation assembled a remarkable collection of brooches, rings, bracelets, coins ranging from AD 69 to 371, bead, glass fragments and numerous pipe-clay figurines, broken and entire, of 'pseudo Venus' and *dea nutrix* character as well as a series of small archaic votive pots. Taken together, this material could be considered to have a votive character (Ross, 1967, 44-52). The three prominent peaks or carns of Nornour might be significant in this context; their distinctive triple character, which sets them apart from others, might have influenced the siting of a shrine at this spot at a time when the Eastern Isles were a part of the remaining land mass.

There is considerable evidence in British prehistory for cults centred upon wells, pools and lakes (Ross, 1967, 22). They were elsewhere seemingly later harnessed to the Christian cause (Hencken, 1932, 142, 259; Thomas, 1967, 120-5). An echo of such a well or spring may linger in St Warna's Well on St Agnes. From the detritus of myth and legend that surrounds this well two elements emerge. First, in spite of Christianisation, Warna, in common with other Celtic saints, appears as allegedly capable of malevolence to some in that she could attract wrecks. Secondly, this power could be invoked by votive offerings in the form of crooked pins. These pins recall the quantity of votive offerings recovered from, for example, the well-known Coventina's Well (Smith, 1962) in Northumberland, which included pins and a great number of coins.

Any consideration of cult sites on the Isles of Scilly would be incomplete without mention of the earlier phases of Christianity. While no one can tell who were the first to bring news of this new religion to the islands, it is recorded that two Christian bishops, albeit heretics, were exiled to the isles in AD 387. In that year the Emperor Magnus Maximus crushed the Spanish Priscillian heresy, executing its innovator and banishing his followers. Sulpicius Severus (Hist Sacr II, 51) states that Instantius and Tibericus or Tiberianus were to be sent to *sylina insula*, described by Solinus, in about AD 240, as separated from the coast occupied by the British tribe of the Dumnonii by a tempestuous channel. This use of the singular, for what is now an archipelago, has been discussed on page 62. At about this time most of the islands, excluding St Agnes, Annet and, perhaps, Samson and Bryher, were still one roughly horse-shoe shaped, sand-dune linked, entity. This identification of the Isles of Scilly as the place of banishment of the Priscillians is, in some measure, substantiated by the reflection of *sylina* in the Orkneyinga Saga. This, a twelfth-century compilation, records the plundering of a vessel owned by the monks of the *Syllingar* isles.

This naming of Scilly as the place of exile is a clear indication that the Imperial organisation regarded it as forming part, if a most desolate one, of the Empire, and that there must have been some recognised path of communication, even though the pattern of direct links between it and Gaul and the rest of the Empire is somewhat thin. This pattern, apart from the question of chamber tombs in earlier times, can be seen perhaps a little earlier than the first century BC in the multi-vallate Giant's Castle, on St Mary's, and at least three other similar structures. These seem disproportionate for so small a region and could be evidence of a link with north-western France. Following upon this it will be remembered that in the description on page 143 of the bronze brooches from the Porth Cressa cist-grave cemetery (Ashbee, 1954, 24), M. R. Hull had great difficulty in finding counterparts among the very large number of Roman brooches known to him. At the time it was suggested that the like should be sought in Gaul. There is also evidence from excavation of Roman and post-Roman structures that pottery, which includes wine and oil vessels, came to Scilly. That the islands should be within this prosperous western mart (Thomas, 1958, 67; Fox, 1964, 162–5) seems remarkable. The six silver coins from Samson, of Constantine II, Julian and, the latest, Honorius (AD 393–423) (Hencken, 1932, 195) may have derived from this source also. On the other hand, these may have been a votive deposit to the ancestors in the many chamber tombs on Samson.

CULT SITES AND EARLY CHRISTIANS

It would have been very surprising if the Priscillianists had left any tangible remains of their presence in Scilly. Monuments and relics of the Early Christians are sparse throughout the mainland of Britain, where there is known to have been an organised and widespread church. But since the Priscillianists, who were considered doctrinally very little in error when their case was reviewed in AD 400 but who had influential enemies, renounced earthly honour and practised asceticism, they are particularly unlikely to have left any ostentatious signs of their domicile in Scilly. It is perhaps of interest, however, that one of the islands should be called St Martin's presumably because of some dedication, the object of which is now lost to memory. The Priscillianists did have contact with St Martin of Tours and had reason to venerate him: he opposed the passing of the death sentence on Priscillian and his six companions. As has already been mentioned, there are house sites of the Romano-British period on St Martin's, and other buildings have been buried by sand and inundated by the sea. There are no undoubted church buildings in Britain from this time, but house-churches (Toynbee, 1968, 186) are known to have been in use. So no especial building would have been required for Christian worship and Christian graves may well remain to be found. However, the dedication could equally be of a much later date.

A century or more later, Scilly could have been affected by movements from Wales and Ireland. Towards the end of the fifth century there was an influx of a considerable number of Irish into Wales and, later, Cornwall (Thomas, 1958, 66, Fig 4). This seems to have been to some extent warlike and to have led to the removal of the Cornish royal seat further to the south (Thomas, 1958, 64), although the later spread of the Irish along the north coast of West Cornwall as far as Land's End appears to have been achieved relatively peacefully and been followed by intermingling of the peoples (Thomas, 1958, 66, Fig 4). While the Irish were at this time nominally Christian, there is little historical or archaeological evidence for missionary activity on the part of these newcomers to Cornwall and nothing certain, except pottery, to connect them with the Isles of Scilly. The movement of Britons from Wales and elsewhere towards Armorica and Galicia brought in its wake a wave of saints, travelling, in a fairly leisurely fashion, in the same direction, who were destined to minister to their spiritual needs. The disciples of St Illtyd, and others, left a trail of place-names and legends across Cornwall, too strong to be dismissed as entirely fable. Celtic-founded churches were normally indentified by the names of their founders rather than from dedications to some more eminent but distant saint. Missioners to lapsed Christians rather than missionaries to the heathen, in intention, it is possible that they found themselves in a region where Christianity was little understood, once they entered Cornwall. The best authenticated is St Samson, of whom an early life is extant. He is said to have spent some time in Cornwall, where there are several ancient churches dedicated to him, before establishing his famous monastery at Dol, in Brittany. He, of all the eponymous saints of the Isles of Scilly, and by this time the islands would have taken on much their present form, could possibly have personally been associated with the place. A few things have been found that would suggest a chapel or oratory on the island of Samson. Claims have been made regarding foundations allegedly exposed on the east side of the neck of Samson and attention has already been drawn to a very large granite post-base or mortar (Plate 8c), apparently associated. This has been claimed as a possible font. A square structure close by, the foundations of which were recorded by Gray, might have been a hermit's cell. Recently the site of an early cemetery has come to light and a bronze buckle and bone object have been recorded. There is, however, nothing as yet to date these remains to quite so early a period.

Early Christian remains there are on the Isles of Scilly, but they are not such as can be readily attributed to any precise source or period. On Tresco were discovered a memorial stone and three early graves. The stone, incorporated into the later fabric, reads '... THI FILI ... COG (?)' (Macalister, 1945, 462–4) which would be, broadly, '(The stone of) ... son of Cog (?)', in not too unrecognisable Roman capitals. The graves, close by, are about 9in in depth and some 15in wide, covered by stone slabs. The best preserved is only about 4ft in length, but may have been longer. All are oriented somewhat south of east. Near one of them was a stone, approximately 6in in diameter, which had a simple cross cut into it. Christian graves would be set east-west, with the head at the west and be without grave furniture. Commemorative stones, with inscriptions giving the name and parentage in Latin capital letters, have been found in North Britain, Wales and Cornwall and been dated from the fifth to the eighth centuries, and have affinities with memorials in Gaul and the Mediterranean lands in both wording and style (Thomas, 1971, 106).

The island of St Helen's was known in the later Middle Ages as *Insula Sancti Elidii*—the island of St Lide or St Elidius. Nothing is known or reliably rumoured of a holy man of this name, though this does not mean he did not exist, merely that he failed to acquire a hagiographer. The earliest description of the buildings on St Helen's was by Borlase (1756, 51, Pl IV, Fig III) who considered the church 'the most ancient Christian building in all the Isles'. A sketch that he made shows round arches with developed Romanesque detail of twelfth-century date. During the last war a German incendiary bomb set this island alight and revealed the ruins, at which juncture a plan was made of all that was visible (Radford, 1941). Subsequently, excavation (O'Neil, 1964) was undertaken in 1954 by B. H. StJ. O'Neil and in 1956 and 1958 by H. E. O'Neil (Fig 47).

A round hut and a rectangular 'oratory' were the first Christian buildings on the island. Whether or not the precinct wall was a contemporary feature is uncertain. Subsequent additions were the chapel, seen ruined in its later form by Borlase, and three rectangular domestic buildings. This round hut, about 12ft in diameter and with walls 3ft in thickness, was built of selected dry-stone granite masonry. In it, and against the wall on the east side was a hearth on a large flat stone, behind which was a draught hole through the wall. Flooring was large granite slabs placed on the natural rabb. Numerous thin, slab-like stones, might point to this structure having been a clochán as, for example, on Skellig Michael or Inishmurray (Leask, 1955, 12). The oratory, of cruder and more massive construction than the round hut, was a single

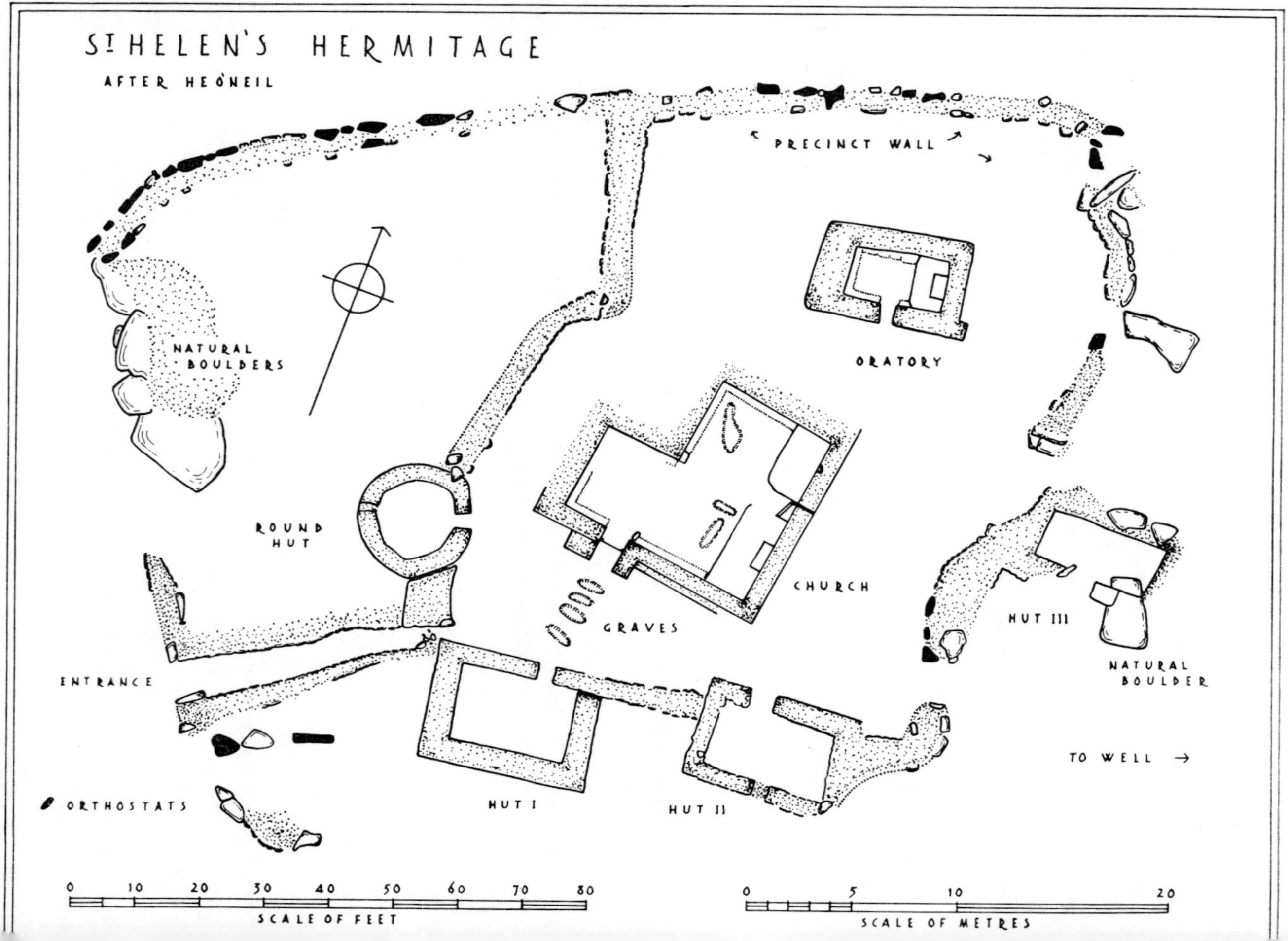
ST HELEN'S HERMITAGE
AFTER HE O'NEIL
PRECINCT WALL
NATURAL BOULDERS
ORATORY
ROUND HUT
CHURCH
GRAVES
HUT III
NATURAL BOULDER
ENTRANCE
TO WELL →
ORTHOSTATS
HUT I
HUT II
0 10 20 30 40 50 60 70 80
SCALE OF FEET
0 5 10 20
SCALE OF METRES

rectangular structure, almost 16ft long and 8ft in width, oriented east to west. Its entrance was through the southern wall, while the floor level within was on the natural rabb. Five feet of the eastern end was raised one step above the floor to form a sanctuary, while a further slight step led up to a stone altar placed against the eastern wall (Plate 12a). This altar was built externally with standing stones and appeared to be packed with flat slabs inside. A stone seat occupied the space on the north side of the altar, the other side being left vacant. On top of the altar, at its southern end, was a narrow recess, built of three upright stones, thought to have been for relics. A low stone bench, 1ft in height, ran around the nave. There was no indication of the mode of roofing, but a stone roof is a possibility. Four graves, comparable with those on Tresco, were found in the cashel enclosure. Grass-marked pottery from the lowest level of occupation within the round hut and from one of the rectangular buildings represents the debris of the earlier stage of occupation.

Excavations by Charles Thomas (Thomas, 1960, 159) during 1956, on Teän, disclosed the foundations of what must have been St Theona's chapel or oratory. This was a rectangular building, internally 16ft in length and 8ft in width, with walling on its west side just over 2ft in thickness. There was an entrance through the long, southern side. It is almost the precise counterpart of the oratory on St Helen's in both dimension and character. Early oratories in Ireland, on the other hand, of the Gallarus type, have their entrances in one of the short sides (Leask, 1955, 22). This structure on Teän overlay slab-built graves, as on Tresco and St Helen's, which had been dug into a midden. Materials recovered from this point to a third- to late sixth-century date which could imply about AD 700 for the foundation of the chapel. The sophisticated layout of the St Helen's chapel or oratory could, perhaps, indicate a later date of the order of about AD 800.

There is a tradition that after Athelstan had subdued the South West, in 931, he visited Scilly, and founded the monastery on Tresco, presumably after donating the islands to the Abbey of Tavistock, in Devon, which is later known to have held the patronage. There is no actual record of the date of the founding of the abbey, although it seems likely to have been pre-Conquest. Henry I issued a charter confirming the abbey's possession of the churches of Scilly and their land. The establishment on Tresco appears to have, during the later Middle Ages, developed into a place of some substance judging from the outline of the nave and chancel which can still be traced. Some insight into an earlier stage of Tresco's fortunes may be contained in that passage of the Orkneyinga Saga, already referred to, which recounts the seizing of a vessel belonging to the monks of *Syllingar* and a raid on, presumably, a satellite installation on St Mary's.

The most important event in the history of the Isles of Scilly was the conversion of Olaf Tryggvason, the Viking raider, later to become King of Norway, towards the end of the tenth century. The saga, written down some 200 years later, recalls that while in Scilly, Olaf encountered a Christian soothsayer. This man impressed Olaf, firstly by failing to be deceived by an impressive imposter sent wearing kingly clothes to test him and secondly by foretelling an ambush in which Olaf would be wounded on his return to his ship. He had at the same time promised Olaf future glory and so the latter, on recovering from his wounds, returned, eager to learn the source of the man's wisdom. This led to an informal course of instruction in the Christian faith and the baptism of Olaf and all his followers. On his departure from the islands, Olaf took with him 'priests and other learned men'. The wise man, who after all would not have required great second sight to tell the Viking two things both of which must have been known by all those involved in their planning, is reminiscent of the 'holy and wise man who used to live amongst them as an anchorite' consulted by the British bishops at the monastery of Bangor during their confrontation with St Augustine (Bede, 731, II, 2). In the same episode Bede refers to 'Bishops and very learned men'. Anchorites living within a religious community, and the distinction of a class of 'learned men' are features unremarkable in a Celtic monastery but unusual among the Benedictines, and so it seems likely that Olaf had encountered part of the community on St Helen's, whose way of life was as yet largely unaffected by the Benedictine Rule.

CULT SITES AND EARLY CHRISTIANS

There are later Christian remains of various kinds on several of the islands, but little is known about any of them. However, fieldwork and excavation could be undertaken with a view to testing the claims of the sites involved. A chapel or oratory stood on Chapel Brow, St Martin's, possibly on the site of the later watch-house, the ruins of which adjoin the daymark (Lewis, 1948, 14). It would have provided a source of material for this structure when it was built. A 'Chapell' is depicted on Chapel Brow on the first printed map of the islands, that dedicated to Henry, Duke of Grafton, and published in 1689. On St Agnes nothing has been traced; only the name St Warna remains attached to a well. Here the sites of churches might repay investigation. Although it is not possible to say when the first church was built here, two had already done service by the end of the eighteenth century (Matthews, 1960, 77). That drawn by Borlase (1756, Pl IV, Fig VIII) is noted as 'from twenty-four to thirty-two feet long by fourteen wide' and would appear to have had a Romanesque door in its long southern side.

On St Mary's, and within living memory, a stone cross stood on a wall in High Cross Lane, which leads to Salakee Down. Its approximate site (remains of) is marked on the Ordnance Survey Maps (Sheet LXXXVII, SE, surveyed 1887-8, revised 1906). The Rev S. M. Mayhew visited the islands during the nineteenth century (Mayhew, 1877, 193) and describes how he 'set up' the, then presumably fallen, cross at 'Silakee'. Gibson (1932, 30) observes that 'The cross on the gable of the Church [Old Town Church] came from the hill the opposite side of Old Town Bay, from a spot called "High Cross", where no doubt was a religious house and village. There was, but a generation ago, a second cross there, but no trace of it can now be found.' It is possible that this cross or those crosses do denote, as Gibson suggests, the site of an Early Christian establishment on St Mary's, but it should be remembered that throughout the Middle Ages, and later, crosses were used to indicate many things besides the existence of religious houses. Of note is his observation regarding Carn Friars, a house just to the north of Porth Hellick. He remarks (Gibson, 1932, 50) that 'we can see today arched doorways and worked stone remains, evidences of ecclesiastical buildings.' It would seem possible that at High Cross and Carn Friars there may have been early churches but all trace has long since vanished. Here again excavation might provide an answer. Another early cross of unknown provenance is in the centre of the gable-end of Newman House in Hugh Town while Troutbeck (1794, 60) mentions what may have been a cross-base by the quay.

With the possibility of an early ecclesiastical site at no great distance from Old Town—a site which could have provided building material at all times—an origin for the great granite 'trough', which still lies by the shore, is suggested. This trough has been described by Gibson (1932, 32). He wrote that 'Near the crude little quay where a few boats are moored, we find a huge stone box made out of a single rock, over 7ft. long and nearly 4ft. high, its rectangular interior about 30in. deep, and holding eighteen Winchester bushells ... During the last century it was utilised for the communal salting of fish.' This well-wrought granite 'box', locally made judging from the granite, might possibly be a stone coffin taken from an Early Christian site.

CHAPTER 10

Material Culture and Equipment

Flint implements, singly, in small numbers and in considerable assemblages, have been found on various islands, on submerged surfaces, in chamber tombs and associated with houses or settlement sites. For the most part they are various forms of scrapers and other kinds of light equipment. Only rarely are axes and heavy tools found.

All the flint used in Scilly appears to have come from the thin glacial deposits which mantle the higher downs of St Martin's and the northern parts of Bryher and Tresco. The origins and affinities of this flint are discussed in Chapter 2. Beach pebbles are another source, for pieces of flint are to be found all around the shores and porths of the islands. Lest it be thought that the lightweight flint industries of the prehistoric Scillonians were brought about by the limitations of raw material, it must be stressed that flint suitable even for axes was available. That beach pebbles were a source of raw-material supply is attested by the many implements which retain rolled cortex upon them.

Flint implements from the Isles of Scilly (Fig 48) were noted during the nineteenth century (Whitley, 1865, 48-9; Brent, 1889, 60) and examples were collected from both Tresco and St Mary's. O. G. S. Crawford (1927, 6) recounts of Samson Flats, upon the occasion of his memorable fieldwork, how 'While Mr. Gibson was taking photographs, I wandered about on the sands and picked up a few flint flakes. Most of these were lying on the tide-scoured sand below the ordinary *low* water mark. Their edges, originally sharp, have been smoothed by the action of the sand and water, so that they have the appearance of gravel-rolled

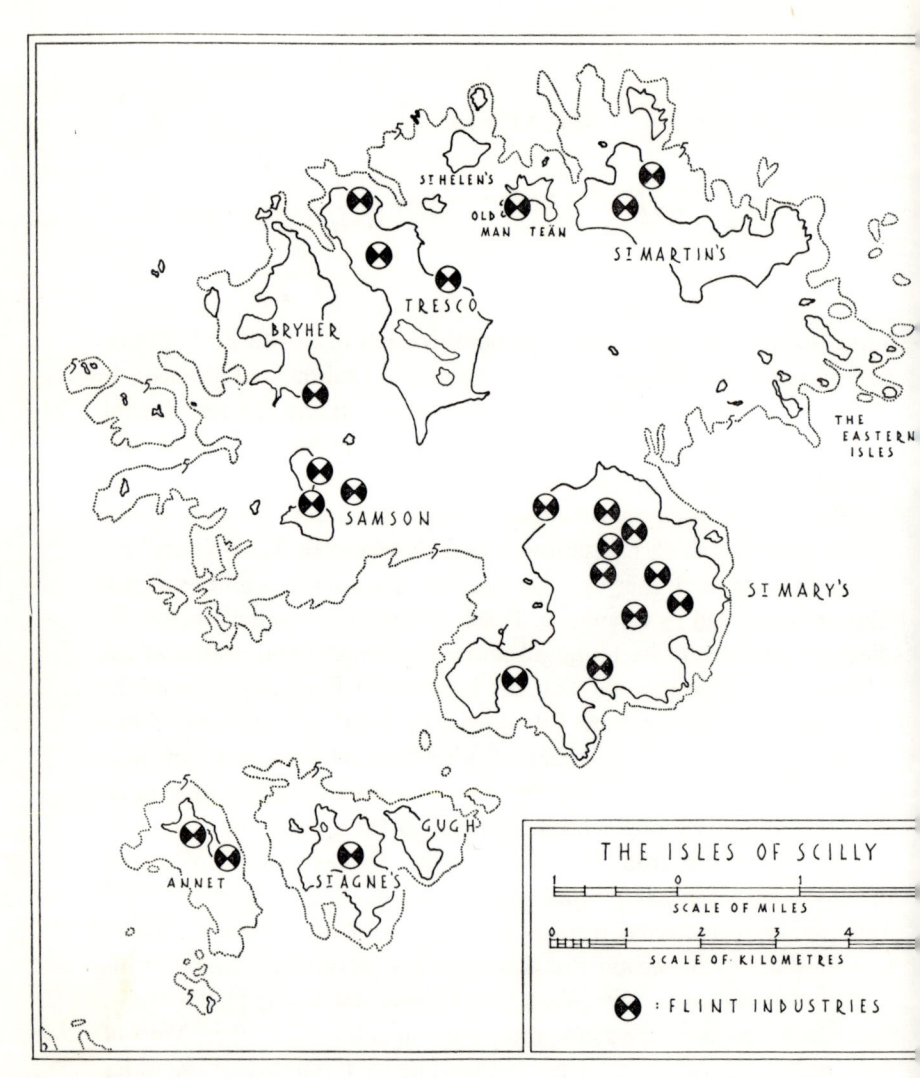

Fig 48 Surface flint industries on the Isles of Scilly

flints. They are quite white and the surface is matte. A few are illustrated here' (Crawford, 1927, 6, Fig 1).

The occurrence of surface industries on St Mary's is particularly well known (Ashbee, 1954) and considerable collections have been amassed by the late Mr J. Treneary of Telegraph Hill, Mr R. Symons of Hugh Town and others. Such industries are usually confined to a relatively small area. The one from which Mr Symons has gleaned so many implements is restricted to a few fields close by Normandy Farm. Over the years some 114 implements have been picked up. Of these 64 are small, near-circular, scrapers while 6 more have a broad and marked tang. Parallel-sided blades were present here, usually with neat side retouch. There were also awls and hollow scrapers from this site. The collection also includes three arrowheads, one barbed and tanged, with a broad tang and poorly finished barbs, another of lozenge form and the third a broken hollow-based triangle. Many other bulb farmers have similar collections from their fields. During 1949, some fields south of the junction of High Lane and Town Lane were indicated by Mr Treneary as being the site of a flint industry similar to the one described above. The freshly turned soil was scrutinised in the half-light of a dusky winter's day and 6 circular scrapers, 3 cores, 8 retouched flakes, 6 waste flakes and 1 blade were found.

In recent years (Minett-Smith, 1968) a great number of implements and waste flakes have been collected from the foreshore of Bryher, just below Samson Hill. A petit-tranchet derivative arrowhead (Clark, 1935) has been observed (Mackenzie, 1971) in this assemblage. Here the industry was concentrated in an area of about one hundred square yards. Indeed, collections of flint artifacts have been made from time to time in the areas around the submerged walls and other structures adjacent to both Teän and Samson, and it is possible to say that these industries also appeared to be devoted almost exclusively to scraper production. A series of such scrapers, from various provenances, is now housed in the museum at Hugh Town (P. Z. Mackenzie, 1967) and the ingenious suggestion that they may have been mounted together to form composite tools has been made.

When, during 1939, Mr Treneary examined the stone cist by the old quarry on Content Farm (Ashbee, 1952, 28), he collected eight worked flints from the soil around it. These included a barbed and tanged arrowhead, a small, almost circular, scraper and a blade with side retouch. The flaking technique on the last is reminiscent of the plano-convex flint knife series. These flints were not, however, necessarily associated with the cist, since surface industries are known in neighbouring fields.

Hencken (1933, 27) found a lump of battered flint by the northern jamb-stone of the chamber tomb that he examined on Samson (H1:D5). Excavation of Knackyboy Cairn (O'Neil, 1952, 22), on St Martin's, recovered a flint axe or adze from beneath a remaining portion of the original cairn material. It is unpolished, 5·125in in length, 2·25in in breadth and retains part of the original flint cortex.

The rectangular hut at English Island Carn, St Martin's, which yielded pottery comparable with that from the chamber tombs (O'Neil, 1949, *SM*, 164–5), had seven flint scrapers associated with it. A barbed and tanged arrowhead, flakes and scrapers, were collected from the site of the earlier phase of occupation beneath the bulb garden behind the cliff at Halangy Porth, St Mary's, by Mr Alec Gray (Ashbee, 1966, 21), while flint and chert implements were in use during the earlier phase of the complex site on Nornour (Dudley, 1967, 7). It was observed that a likely source would have been St Martin's which is at no great distance from Nornour. Excavation of the cultivation terrace, the site of the cist-grave cemetery at Porth Cressa, produced a number of flint flakes and cores (Ashbee, 1954, 6), presumably associated with earlier occupation in that locality. Flint and chert scrapers, awls and blades, have been found on Halangy Down (Ashbee, 1955; 1965; 1966; 1968; 1970) associated with all phases of the range of buildings which have been examined during the past decade and, for that matter, associated with the ecclesiastical site on St Helen's (O'Neil, 1964, 67).

Since the establishment of the Isles of Scilly museum, it has been possible to order, and store for reference, the very considerable quantities of flint implements that once formed the collections of a number of individuals. For the most part these consist of miscellanies of flakes, scrapers of various kinds, and arrowheads in all stages of manufacture, from the settled and cultivated areas of the main islands, supplemented by the products of sporadic gathering from the shores and cliff exposures of various smaller, uninhabited islands. All too frequently the collections represent periodic collecting from specific areas; there are groups from Samson Flats—indeed, some of these may be those collected by O. G. S. Crawford on his visit (Crawford, 1927, 6)—while the shores and cliffs of Annet are similarly well represented. In terms of quantity, more than a half of the assemblage represents the activities of Alexander Gibson who, in 1933, had a museum at his Lyonesse Studio; almost all of this material being without location on the islands.

These collections of flint artifacts amplify such observations as can be made from the published accounts, namely, that scraper production played a very large part and that heavy tools, such as axes, are conspicuous by their absence. Hollow scrapers are present while there is a hitherto unsuspected profusion of barbed and tanged arrowheads. These last are represented in all stages of manufacture, though finely finished examples are rare. Another element is a considerable number of substantial trimmed flakes and blades, some of which are as much as 3.5in in length and 2in in breadth, of 'Larnian' character (Mitchell, 1949; 1971). There are also heavy points of triangular section as well as numerous smaller points, presumably for perforation.

Quartz has been used for a whole range of heavy equipment in early Scilly. For quartz occurs naturally and widely in veins in both Scilly and Cornwall. Indeed, a whole range of scrapers and flakes are claimed (Lacaille, 1942, 215) from the region. It must be emphasised that reliable and objective criteria for determining workmanship in quartz scarcely exist. Quartz possesses inherently the property of conchoidal fracture yet most varieties respond so erratically to treatment that the separated surfaces, of what are considered as artifacts, are usually irregular. Nevertheless, the regularity of intentional working and the patent marks of use leave almost unmistakable traces while the regular occurrence of pieces of quartz, side by side with flint implements, makes for their acceptance.

A number of quartz implements were found during the excavation of the larger chamber of the courtyard house on Halangy Down (Ashbee, 1955, 195–7) in 1950. They were either crude choppers or rounded blocks bearing percussion bruises at various points. Subsequent work has collected further material (Ashbee, 1965, 40; 1966, 26; 1968, 31; 1970, 75) which includes many rough scrapers, crude hand-axe-like points and trimmed pebbles.

As is to be expected in a stone region such as Scilly, local granite is used for a wide range of heavy tools and equipment. Together with this there is the question of the use of imported fine-grained stones. Certain tools and equipment can be associated, either by implication or direct association, with the earlier prehistoric Scillonian period, the chamber tombs and settlement sites. Other material is associated with the later period, the Iron Age sites and Romano-British establishments such as Halangy Down.

Hencken (1932, 8) mentions a group of polished stone axes from Scilly, adding that their value and, indeed, the value of certain Cornish groups, is dubious, as they correspond with the activities of collectors. Mr Alexander Gibson was active on Scilly at this time. Hencken (1932, 12, Fig 6) on his distribution map of 'Stone Age' Cornwall and Scilly, indicates three axes from St Mary's, one from St Martin's and, possibly, one from Gugh, and their locations are listed in his archaeological gazetteer. Some of these axes are now preserved in the Isles of Scilly museum in Hugh Town. A pointed-butt, apparently greenstone, axe from Gugh, formerly in the possession of Major A. Dorrien Smith is there, as is a battle-axe (Roe, 1966, 199) from Normandy, St Mary's. This last may be the 'mace-head' formerly in the Gibson Collection at Penzance. Hencken (1932, 67, Fig 18 G) illustrates an edged-cushion macehead (Ashbee, 1960, 107) from Bryher which he said 'takes the form of an adze with the blade at right-angles to the handle'. An incidental discovery at Porth Cressa (Ashbee, 1954, 22, Fig 8, 13) was a discoidal pebble of fine-grained granite with an incomplete 'hour-glass' perforation. A half of a tourmaline battle-axe, with a complete perforation from the collection of Mr R. Symons in the museum, was found in the vicinity of Normandy (Ashbee, 1954, 126) on St Mary's. The work on Nornour (Dudley, 1967, 4) has found stone balls, discs and a quartz pendant as well as a grooved hammer-stone.

Thanks to the work of the sub-committee of the South-Western Group of Museums a range of Scillonian stone implements have now been thin-sectioned and petrologically identified (Evens, Smith and Wallis, 1972, 239, 262, 266, 272). The bulk of these, mostly pebble-hammers and pounders from Nornour and Normandy Farm, St Mary's, are of ungrouped rocks such as could have been gleaned from island beaches. Two implements are, however, of note and cannot but be imports from Cornwall. The half of a battle-axe from Normandy Farm is of tourmaline granite while a stone ball or pounder from Nornour is of Group I greenstone.

Excavation of the chamber tomb on Samson (H1:D5) produced the upper stone of a saddle quern (Hencken, 1933, 29, Fig 13). It had been utilised as part of the paving beneath the larger of the surviving capstones. Also associated with this chamber tomb was a smooth pebble of fine-grained granite with its rounded end 'roughened as if by pounding'. Two saddle querns (Plate 12b) have been found with the midden and structures exposed in the cliff of Halangy Porth (Hencken, 1932, 30) and others may have been found there from time to time. Indeed, a large bowl quern (Plate 12c) was visible on the beach in 1968. Excavations on Halangy Down (Ashbee, 1965; 1966; 1968; 1970) have brought to light numerous querns, both complete and broken, of saddle, bowl and rotary types. Indeed, the numerous pieces of broken querns lead one to speculate upon the reasons for such breakage and subsequent incorporation in structures, as such massive objects would hardly be broken by accident. Saddle querns were found *in situ* beside hearths in Room II on Nornour (Dudley, 1967, 7) and upper stones, normally termed 'riders', were a regular feature of the site. A large stone bowl, possibly a mortar, was by the hearth in Room I there also. A comparable stone bowl (page 224) has recently been found on Samson. Part of another large granite bowl was found in what has been termed the 'workshop' area at Nornour (Dudley, 1967, 10) and close by were a number of heavy pounders. Indeed, such 'pounders', normally large elongated smooth beach-boulders bearing end-battering have also been found in considerable numbers at Halangy Down. They are difficult to distinguish from naturally bruised beach-boulders; only their numbers and regularity of size point to their having been used. These deep stone bowls should not be confused with the well-finished depressions worked into flat granite stones which may have housed roofing-post butts (Hencken, 1933, 276) as at Chysauster in Cornwall or the even smaller pivot-stones of the same character.

Rotary querns appear to have remained in use until relatively recently. Heath (1750, 26) observes that while he was on the islands there were 'many Hand-Mills for grinding upon Emergency, in all the islands, but a Wind-Mill upon a Tract called Peninnis, grinds the larger quantities'. It would seem that the upper stone was turned by a long rod, fixed in a hollow near the circumference, turning in a roof-beam above. These querns, or hand-mills, appear to have been mounted upon a bench and their pitch controlled by a spindle from the upper stone down to a stone socket upon an adjustable timber transom. Indeed, many of the so-called pivot-stones from Scillonian and Cornish sites may derive from such devices. Their use until an advanced stage in the nineteenth century is attested by a photograph of a drawing in the Gibson photographic archive, while their efficacy has been demonstrated by experiment, a reconstruction having been made and used at Gwithian (Thomas, 1971, 121, Fig 96) in Cornwall.

Collections of querns, saddle, bowl and rotary, as well as granite stones of various sizes, perforated, grooved or cup-marked, have been made by several people on St Mary's. Something of the extent and character of Alexander Gibson's one-time collection can be seen in a photograph exhibited in the museum in Hugh Town. The heavy stone objects, which included querns and various perforated and grooved boulders, now lie in the public gardens adjacent to the Town Hall. During 1950 the present writer was invited to Seaways, Porthloo, by

MATERIAL CULTURE AND EQUIPMENT

Mrs Birkenshaw, at that time the owner, to inspect a small collection of stones ranged upon the terrace there (Ashbee, 1953, 77). There were, among them, five true saddle querns, two of which were reputed to be from Halangy Porth and may be those noted by Hencken (1932, 30). Mr J. Treneary, of Telegraph Hill, had in his possession two saddle querns found in the debris of a stone wall close by his house. Deep trenching for the Hugh Town cinema in 1950 brought to light well-made rotary querns, possibly of recent date and which could have been mounted in the manner described above. Mr Treneary was able to demonstrate their function at a small exhibition of local curiosities, both artificial and natural, held in Hugh Town during 1950. A considerable collection of querns and other wrought stones, including a number of perforated boulders which may have been thatch weights, as well as a perforated monolith of some size, are housed in a garden at Rocky Hill, St Mary's. A large flat stone with a pecked-out hollow in one of its surfaces lies in a garden just below Buzza Hill on the outskirts of Hugh Town and doubtless there are many more massive stone artifacts of early origin to be found in many more gardens. Indeed, it is probable that a systematic scrutiny of Scillonian garden ornaments would provide at least quantitative evidence of heavy stone equipment, although in almost every instance provenance is forgotten or unknown.

Slate, either imported from Cornwall or taken from the remaining portion of Scilly's erstwhile cover, has been used for light stone equipment and there is a number of chisel-like edge tools in the museum collections. A spindle-whorl and a bevel-edged disc, with three perforations and a partial fourth, were found at Halangy Down in 1950 (Ashbee, 1955, 195, Fig 5). A hone from Nornour (Dudley, 1967, 25, Fig 10, 52) may have been of such material, although a hone from St Helen's (O'Neil, 1964, 66) is of a fine-grained micaceous sandstone and would appear to have been imported. The shale mould for casting small bronze box- or book-cover attachments from Porth Cressa (Ashbee, 1954, 22) and the bracelet from Nornour (Dudley, 1967, 25) were either imported as manufactured objects or, were they made on the islands, as raw material.

MATERIAL CULTURE AND EQUIPMENT

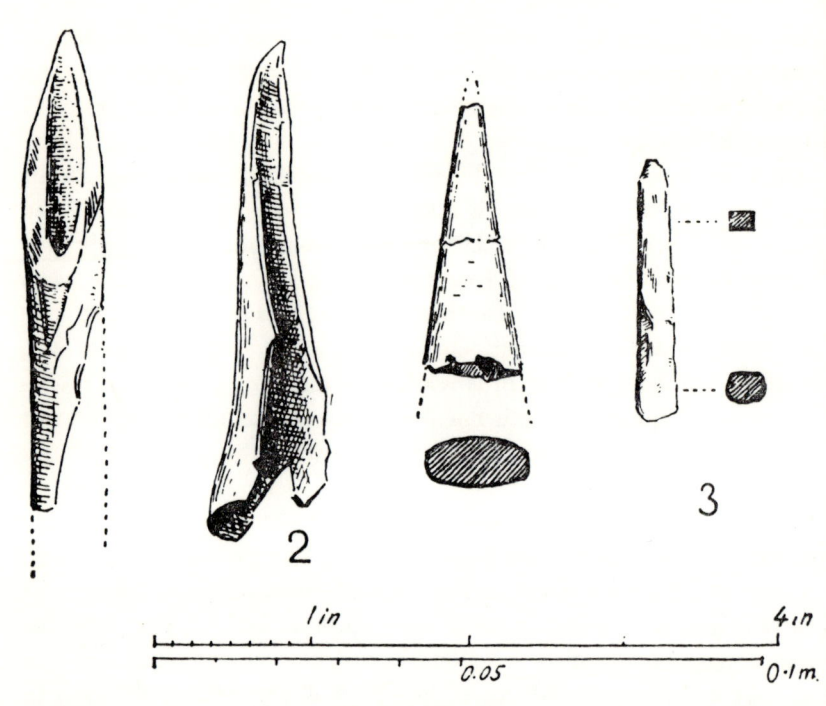

Fig 49 Bone points and bronze awl from Obadiah's Barrow, Gugh (from Hencken, 1933)

There are a few patent bone implements from Scilly. Two points were found in the chamber of Obadiah's Barrow (Fig 49) (Hencken, 1933, 24, Fig 9b, 2) on Gugh, while another has been found with early pottery on Annet. A whalebone tool was found during the excavation of the Celtic hermitage on St Helen's (O'Neil, 1964, 67) and a piece of a bone comb on Teän. Bone was probably used regularly for tools and appliances but by its nature it has rarely survived in what are frequently acid soil contexts.

Bronze objects are attested from primary positions in at least two Scillonian chamber tombs. Bonsor's excavation of Obadiah's Barrow on Gugh (H1:D5) recovered a fragment of a square-sectioned awl about 1·5in in length (Hencken, 1932, 27, Fig 12 B). This was analysed by Dr

MATERIAL CULTURE AND EQUIPMENT

Plenderleith at the British Museum and proved to be bronze very poor in tin (Hencken, 1933, 23 fn). O'Neil's excavation of Knackyboy Cairn on St Martin's unearthed what he described as 'pieces of bronze—a hook, and perhaps a handle from a brass-bound wooden box or bucket' (O'Neil, 1952, 30), from the chamber. The hook may be from a bronze earring and comparable examples are known (Ashbee, 1960, 110) while the 'handle' could well be a bracelet end not dissimilar to the ends of that from Garton Slack (Clarke, 1970, 397, Fig 946d) in Yorkshire.

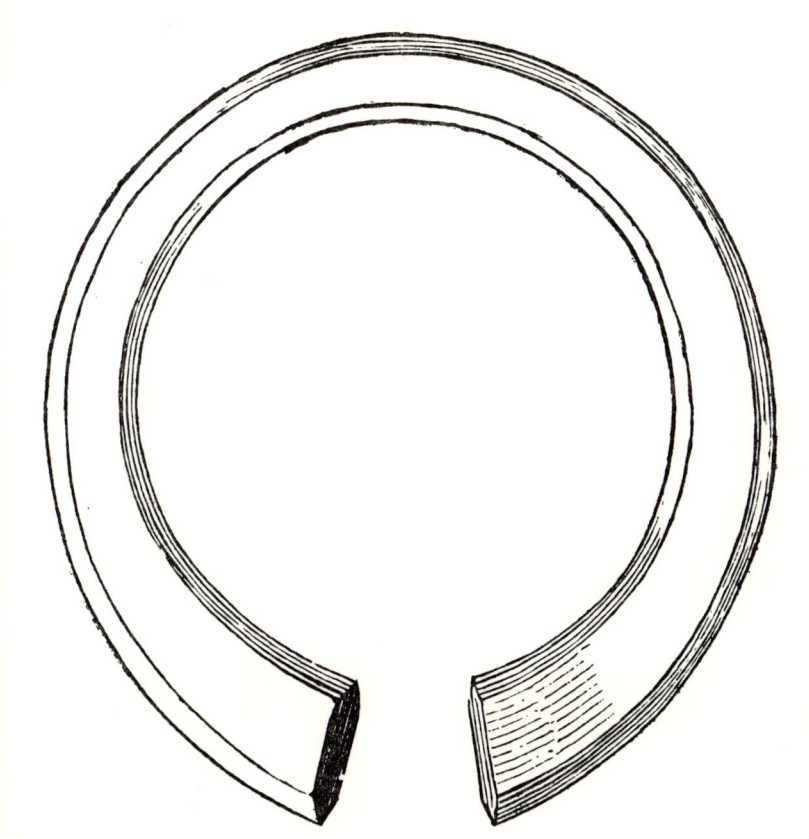

Fig 50 William Copeland Borlase's line drawing of one of the torques found in a barrow on Peninnis Head, St Mary's ($\frac{1}{4}$)

Pieces, or a piece, of a bronze dagger have long been alleged from either a cist or a chambered barrow on St Martin's (Hencken, 1932, 21; Daniel, 1950, 125). O'Neil (1952, 21) relates how enquiries showed that the site, dug into by Alexander and James Gibson, was in fact Knackyboy Cairn. The 'bronze dagger' (now lost) is thought to have been a small triangular plate off a box! This could well have been another piece of the bracelet indicated above. Recently, however, the museum has acquired a dagger said to be from Carron Rocks, St Martin's.

Two heavy bronze torques (Fig 50) (Ashbee, 1960, 114), which might

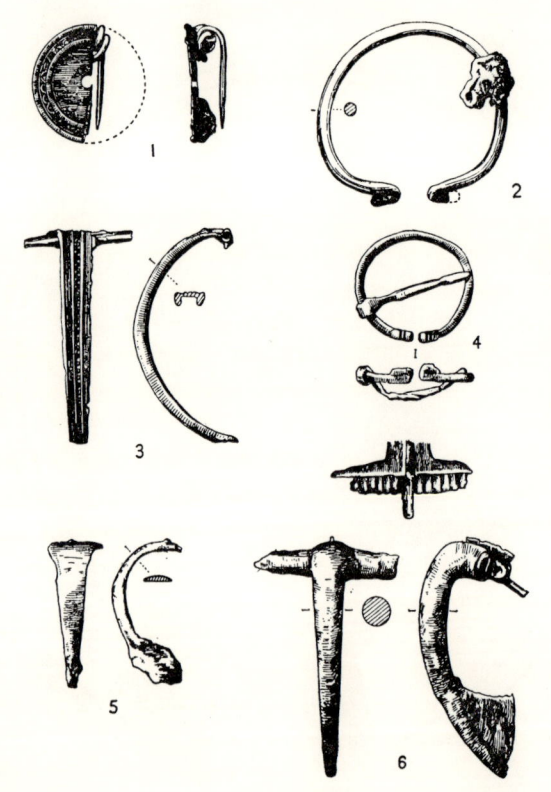

Fig 51 Bronze brooches from Porth Cressa, Hugh Town, St Mary's, cist-grave cemetery ($\frac{1}{2}$)

well be a specific version of massive ingot torques, perhaps unfinished versions of some more normal ornament form, were found during the demolition of what appears to have been a chambered barrow on Peninnis Head (Douch, 1962, 97). It is difficult, if not impossible, to point to precise counterparts. They are not unreminiscent of the heavy Northern series (Forssander, 1936, Taf XXXVII, 1), while Butler (1963, 139) has isolated a small series of British neckrings characterised by thickness, a cast technique, which he calls the West Buckland type. Apart from the foregoing the only other early bronze from Scilly is a 'Breton' socketed axe, seemingly a stray find on St Mary's, which was housed in Plymouth Museum when Hencken (1932, 307) visited it.

The use of bronze continued into later prehistoric and early historic times for a large number of objects and appliances, other than tools and weapons. At Porth Cressa, St Mary's, the excavation of the cist-grave cemetery in 1949 (Ashbee, 1954) discovered a number of provincial Roman brooches (Fig 51) of that metal. All were of early types, except perhaps one, a disc brooch that could well be placed in the third century AD. As mentioned on page 143, the striking point with regard to this brooch series is the difficulty which M. R. Hull, who most kindly examined them, had in locating similar examples among the very large number from Roman Britain known to him. Two broadly comparable bronze brooches were in the cist on the small island of Old Man (Tebbutt, 1934), although the cists found in Poynter's Garden, Hugh Town (Dudley, 1961), yielded only a few fragments of a bronze pin. Four bronze brooches were found among rock rubble during the excavation of the Halangy Down, St Mary's (Ashbee, 1966, 25), stone-built hut complex. As at Porth Cressa, precise counterparts are difficult to locate, indeed they could be seen as an extension of that series.

On Nornour a great number of Roman bronze objects, possibly votive offerings at a shrine, were found in the infill of the two principal chambers and in the upper layers of the accumulation outside (Dudley, 1967). There were pieces of some 30 finger-rings, 6 bracelets, miscellaneous ornamental mounts and pieces of thin sheet bronze, and almost 300 brooches! The rings, and other objects, such as seal-box lids and discs, the use of which is not apparent, bear the same decorative techniques as many of the brooches, particularly in the use of enamel. It is considered that all comprise an homogeneous group and that they are the products of a single workshop. If they were votive offerings this would account for the range of date within the assemblage; raw materials could have been brought from Cornwall and, at best, traces of manufacture would be slight and could well have been removed by the sea. Thus, devotees of the Nornour cult, beneath the shadow of the curious tripartite rocky carn, may have obtained their offerings close by.

With the exception of the one disc brooch from Porth Cressa, all the Scillonian bronze brooches, excepting the Nornour series, are of the 'bow' variety. That is they consist of a curved bar, the 'bow', with a cross-piece at one end, housing the spring or hinge by which the pin is attached, and the fastener at the other. 'Plate' brooches, the other variety, which were found in considerable numbers on Nornour, are those which exhibit a flat surface, which may be circular, square or representational in outline. For the most part they are less efficient, the pin cannot gather and secure cloth in the manner of a bow-brooch. It would seem likely that their prime function was display; a flat surface allows considerable scope for ornamental development, particularly enamels.

Bow-brooches have a long history. Their origins lie in the European Late Bronze Age and the Mediterranean world and they were current, in various and sometimes massively ornamented forms, during the Iron Age. Plate brooches have similarly early origins and the two types are closely related. Their ultimate origins may well lie in Late Bronze Age spectacle-brooches and ornament-bearing leaf-shaped bows. Their function was to secure a fabric cloak about the body and to this end they were worn singly or in pairs. Indeed, representational art (eg Pobe and Roubier, 1961, Pls 236–7) often depicts what must be prominent plate brooches worn on the shoulder. Carried in such a manner, many of the more elaborate Nornour disc brooches would have been both distinctive and prestigious.

An enamelled penannular brooch (Fig 52) found while breaking fields just after World War I on St Martin's (O'Neil, 1953), has Irish affinities.

MATERIAL CULTURE AND EQUIPMENT

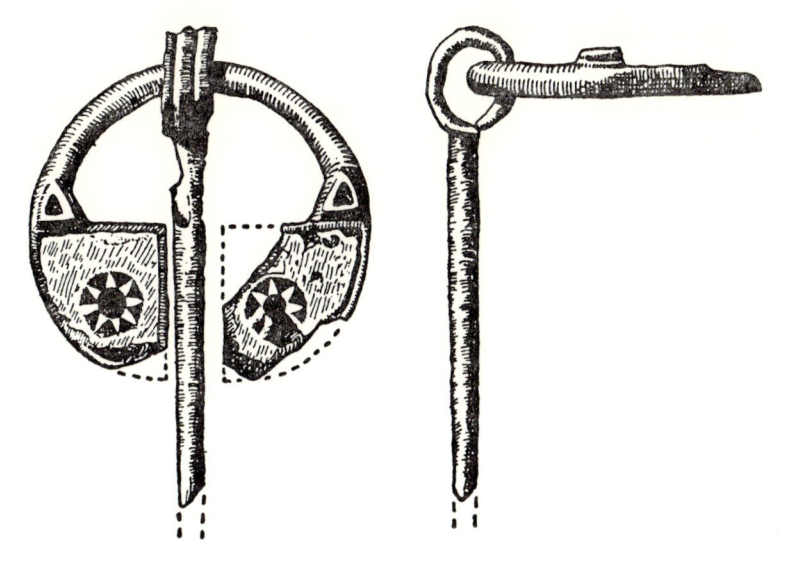

Fig 52 Enamelled penannular brooch from St Martin's (2/7) (from O'Neil, 1953)

Its form is that which has been termed zoomorphic, although the resemblance to an animal's head in this example is distant. One terminal plate is intact, the other damaged and it lacks the end of its pin. Remains of enamel in the portion which would be considered as the ears of an animal's head may have been green, which appears to have been the general background colour of both terminals. The 'eye' is a blue circle carrying a yellow star. Its date of manufacture has been estimated at *c* AD 650 and in the light of much of the later archaeology of Scilly its presence on St Martin's should cause no surprise. This later history and archaeology of the islands is also represented by the scraps of bronze, some as late as *c* AD 1400, brought to light during the excavations on St Helen's.

Evidence of the use of iron has been forthcoming from most of the later Scillonian sites, usually in the form of egregious and featureless scraps or, now and again, pieces of slag. Gray found a few scraps of iron in the main chamber of the courtyard house on Halangy Down during the course of his work there. Nornour was rather more productive (Dudley, 1967, 25): pieces of four iron knives, a point, what seems to have been an iron arrowhead, a ferrule with traces of wood in its interior and with a loop set into its end, and some boot-nails. A much corroded scrap of iron, perhaps a worn-out knife blade, was found in the midden at Porth Cressa (Ashbee, 1954, 21, Fig 8, 11) while a scrap from the St Helen's hermitage (O'Neil, 1965, 66) is considered to be the rim of a cauldron.

Iron objects have been found in two cist-graves. The cist exposed by an inroad of the sea on Old Man, Teän (Tebbutt, 1934) had in it a scrap of iron and what was described as an 'iron ring'. This 'ring' was an iron penannular brooch (Fowler, 1960, 176) similar to the examples of bronze from Porth Cressa, one of which may have had an iron pin. Such brooches appear to have been a specifically British development in the third century BC and, with progressive modification, they persisted into post-Roman times. The brooch from the St Martin's cist-grave has many forbears: the 'concretion or object of iron' (Lewis, 1949) was described as 'fibula-shaped' and may well be the corroded remains of a bow-brooch. It was accompanied by two amber beads.

A number of pieces of iron slag were found at Halangy Down (Ashbee, 1955, 197) both during the 1950 excavations and subsequently. In the circumstances the occasional domestic preparation of iron seems likely and iron-pan or the nodules from the rabb would be a likely source.

Eight oblate beads of blue glass and one six-rayed star bead of faience (Plate 16b) were in the burial deposit of the Knackyboy Cairn (O'Neil, 1952, 30–4) on St Martin's. As evidence for glass manufacture prior to the Iron Age, as far as the British Isles was concerned, is lacking, the inference was that they were imports to the islands, perhaps even from the Mediterranean. J. F. S. Stone, who described the beads in O'Neil's report, was able to indicate a number of glass beads in commensurate contexts to the Knackyboy Cairn while stressing the late date of the star faience bead.

During the later period of Scilly's prehistory, glass was also current. A bluish-green flattened glass globular bead was in one of the Porth

Cressa cist-graves (Ashbee, 1954, 17, Fig 6, 10) while a similar bead has been found on Halangy Down (Ashbee, 1965, 40). On Nornour (Dudley, 1967, 25–7) both pieces of glass and glass beads were found. The pieces of glass consisted of fragments of bottles and other containers and one of window-glass. It has been suggested that this glass is the residue of a supply of raw material brought to the site for the production of enamel. Indeed, one piece of a decorated vessel had been re-cut for use in place of a gemstone in a finger-ring. Some sixteen beads of various types, some ornamented and almost all with counterparts in Roman Britain were found during the excavation of the two principal chambers.

It is possible to make two broad divisions in the ceramic record of the Isles of Scilly. There is, first of all, the early pottery: the urns and fragments from chamber tombs and similar material from settlement sites. Secondly, there is the later pottery: of Iron Age, Roman and post-Roman times. Within this latter category there is a wide range of wares. A series of sherds from Halangy Down and Nornour are comparable with the considered range of Cornish Iron Age pottery. From these two sites, and from certain sites on St Martin's investigated by B. H. StJ. O'Neil, as well as the Porth Cressa cemetery there is what can be broadly termed 'Roman' pottery. This consists of, on the one hand, fragments of fine vessels, of Samian and Castor wares, and, on the other, a wide range of coarse wares in various provincial Roman styles. If not products of the islands, they were made in the West Country, for almost every fragment exhibits glittering micas. There are also, from a number of sites, modest quantities of grass-marked pottery, bearing the negative impression of finely-chopped grass or hay, impressed on the damp clay and fired out. As a native pottery of Scilly, and for that matter Cornwall, it had a long life, from immediate post-Roman times to the tenth or even the eleventh centuries AD. Apart from sherds from Teän (Thomas, 1958, 71) there are as yet few pieces of the imported wheel-made pottery that characterises these centuries. To conclude the later sequence, some pieces of c tenth century AD squat flat-based sooted cooking pots with 'bar-lugs' or 'bar-lips' have been found in a midden on St Martin's.

Hencken (1932; 1933) was the first to describe the earlier Scillonian

MATERIAL CULTURE AND EQUIPMENT

pottery in any detail, calling attention to the biconical form of the urns 'in shape like two truncated cones placed base to base' and saying that 'Most of the pottery is an extremely coarse blackish ware, very thick, micaceous, and gravelly'. He was at pains to describe and illustrate the material dug from chamber tombs on Gugh and St Mary's as well as that collected from the cliff exposure in Halangy Porth. To this we can add the material collected from domestic sites collected by Gray, from the chamber tomb on Salakee Down examined during the war-years by W. F. Grimes and the considerable assemblage from Knackyboy Cairn.

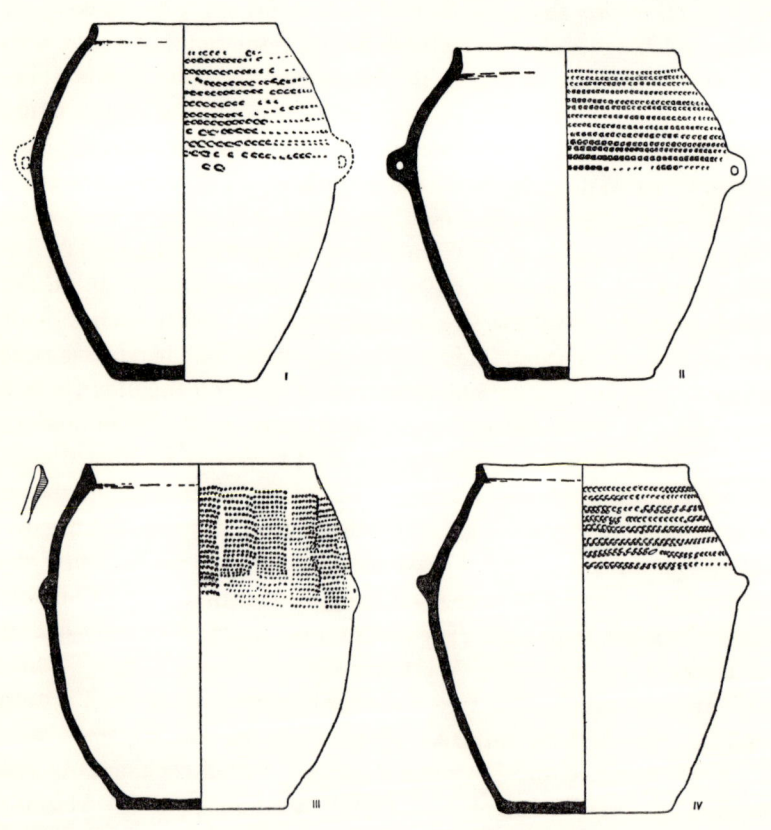

Fig 53 Urns from Knackyboy Cairn, St Martin's ($\frac{1}{6}$) (from O'Neil, 1952)

As well as this, there is the pottery from English Island Carn and other sites on St Martin's, a collection from Halangy Porth made by Alexander and James Gibson in the early 1920s, which is now housed in the museum at Hugh Town, and a small assemblage dug under controlled conditions from Bant's Carn, Halangy Down, during the recent restoration of the cover-stone and jamb-stone. It must be stressed that, up to the present, there has not been a detailed study of the pottery, its decoration or its affinities, nor is but a tithe of the available material published.

Apart from Hencken's outstanding pioneer work there is but one comprehensive study of early Scillonian pottery and that is the preliminary report on the great assemblage from the Knackyboy Cairn (O'Neil, 1952, 25-9), on St Martin's (Figs 53, 54). As an aid to the disentanglement of the complex contents of the chamber, O'Neil used a system of numeration for the urns, or rather for the more intact and restorable examples, which is referred to in Chapter 4. In terms of basic shape there are three clear forms in the assemblage; barrel, biconical and bucket. Notwithstanding, an inspection of the restored urns and sherds, often substantial, from this and other sites, shows that the series shade one into another and that the firm forms are but extremes of the general principle. Decoration is invariably restricted to the upper half of such pots as bear it, while lugs, normally in opposed pairs, imperforate or horizontally perforate, are usually set upon the maximum girth. Although much of the 4cwt of sherds, which included about a hundred rims, from this site is coarse and full of granite grits, certain pots have thin hard walls and no visible trace of lamination or coil manufacture. Some fine, hard sherds have been noticed from other sites, notably Bant's Carn and Halangy Porth, while the assemblage from Porth Killier, St Agnes, described by Gray, was entirely of fine, hard, wares. This differentiation between fine and coarse wares may be false for soil weathering can destroy surfaces.

The decoration of the Knackyboy pottery was subjected to especial attention by O'Neil. It was established by experiment that specific effects on certain vessels had been executed by impressing linen threads

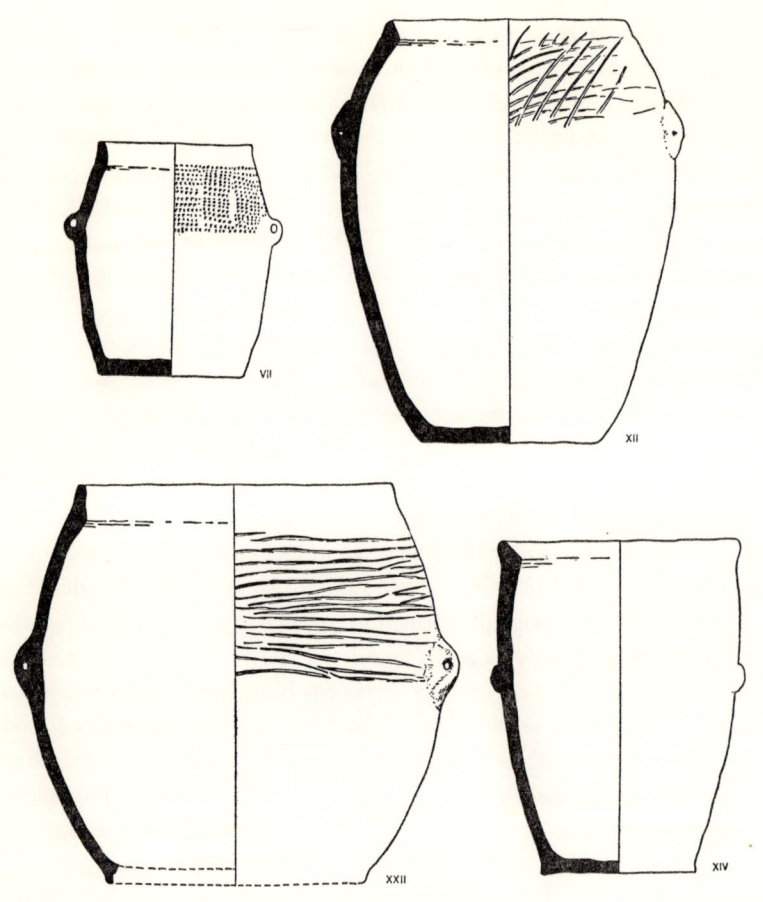

Fig 54 Urns from Knackyboy Cairn, St Martin's ($\frac{1}{6}$) (from O'Neil 1952)

on to the unfired clay. Also certain bases bore the imprint of woven textiles or, perhaps, of rush-matting. Such decoration was, however, reserved for but a small proportion of the pottery. By far the most common form of decoration is that borne by Urn III, horizontal rows and vertical zones of eight- or nine-toothed comb impressions (Plate 13a). Indeed, such comb impressions are reminiscent of the techniques employed upon beakers (Clarke, 1970, 9). Stroke ornamentation is also to be seen (Urns XII, XXII); such modes of incision are not unknown in later beaker assemblages. Rims are almost always bevelled and are frequently thickened to a near club-form. A variation is a marked verticality of rolled or squared rim, particularly on barrel-form vessels. This range of rim is also to be seen in the sherds from Halangy Porth, on St Mary's, assembled by Gray. Many lugs are but lumps of clay, poorly affixed and imperforate. However, some of the perforated lugs are horizontally elongated and well-turned, approximating, occasionally, to the renowned Neolithic trumpet lugs from Hembury in Devon (Piggott, 1954, 68, Fig 9, 1). Indeed, such an observation was made by Grimes (1960, 177) when discussing the pottery from Obadiah's Barrow, on Gugh, in the light of the material from Salakee Down.

From his excavation of Obadiah's Barrow (H1:D5), Bonsor (Hencken, 1933, 24) recovered sufficient sherds of pottery to fill a large basket, but only one near-intact urn (Plate 13b). This, for long in the possession of Major A. Dorrien Smith at Tresco Abbey, is now housed in the museum at Hugh Town, while some of the sherds are in the British Museum. It is barrel-shaped, although slightly angular, and its rim is missing. The

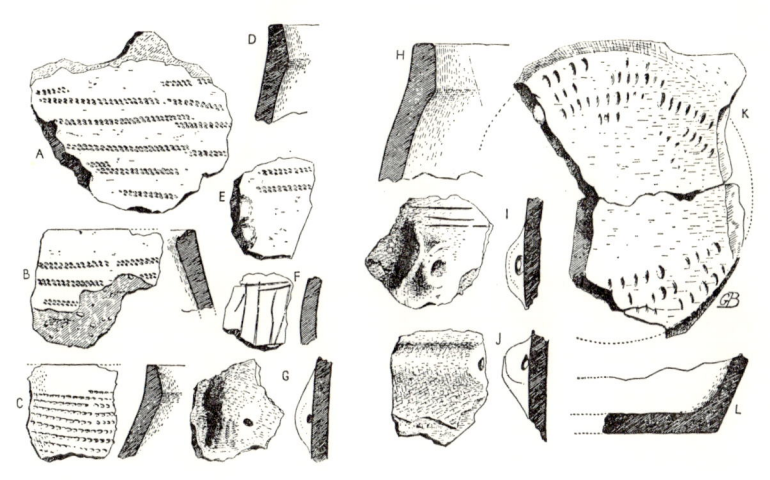

Fig 55 Pottery from Obadiah's Barrow, Gugh (¼) (from Hencken, 1933)

upper part is decorated with parallel lines of square-toothed comb impressions. A sample of the quantity of pottery (Fig 55), which should be compared with the great assemblage from the Knackyboy Cairn, was painstakingly and accurately drawn by Bonsor and has been reproduced by Hencken (1933, Fig 10). There depicted is a base and some lugs, as well as rim and body sherds. The base may well bear the impression of a mat or the like in the manner of the Knackyboy bases, the lugs can all be matched in the Knackyboy series, as can the bevelled rims, although the elongation of the particular lug noted by Grimes (1960, 177) is exceptional. One bevelled rim-sherd which bears continuous even lines of square-toothed comb impressions, is reddish and of a better quality ware than the remainder and is again closely reminiscent of beaker in decoration. A body sherd bears possible incised-line zoning, while others are decorated with double horizontal lines of what may well be cord-ornament.

The pottery from the passage grave (H1:D7) on Porth Hellick Down, St Mary's, was described as several sherds (Hencken, 1932, 20), which were accompanied by a fragment of pumice. Hencken (1932, 22, Fig 9) illustrates two sherds, one substantial, both bearing cord-ornament. The larger, from a lugged barrel-urn, has its ornament in the form of roughly equidistant vertical zig-zag lines. Each zig or zag consists of about five or six twist impressions, not all conjoined. The smaller, a bevelled rim-sherd, carries a similar motif, bounded by horizontal lines. Cord-ornament employed in this manner is not unknown upon Cornish Bronze Age pottery (Patchett, 1944, 30, Fig 6; 1952, 61, Fig 4, B24) and, further afield, in comb-stamping on Beaker bowls (Clarke, 1970, 306, 323).

Hencken (1933, 16, Fig 3) reproduces Bonsor's sensitive drawings of the sherds (Fig 56) that he found in the passage, just outside the chamber, of Bant's Carn (H2:D3), on the brow of Halangy Down, St Mary's. Confirmation of this was found in 1970 when a small area was excavated to re-seat the displaced jamb-stone and pottery was found upon the ancient surface at the entrance to an apparent side chamber. Neither Hencken nor the present writer have been able to

MATERIAL CULTURE AND EQUIPMENT

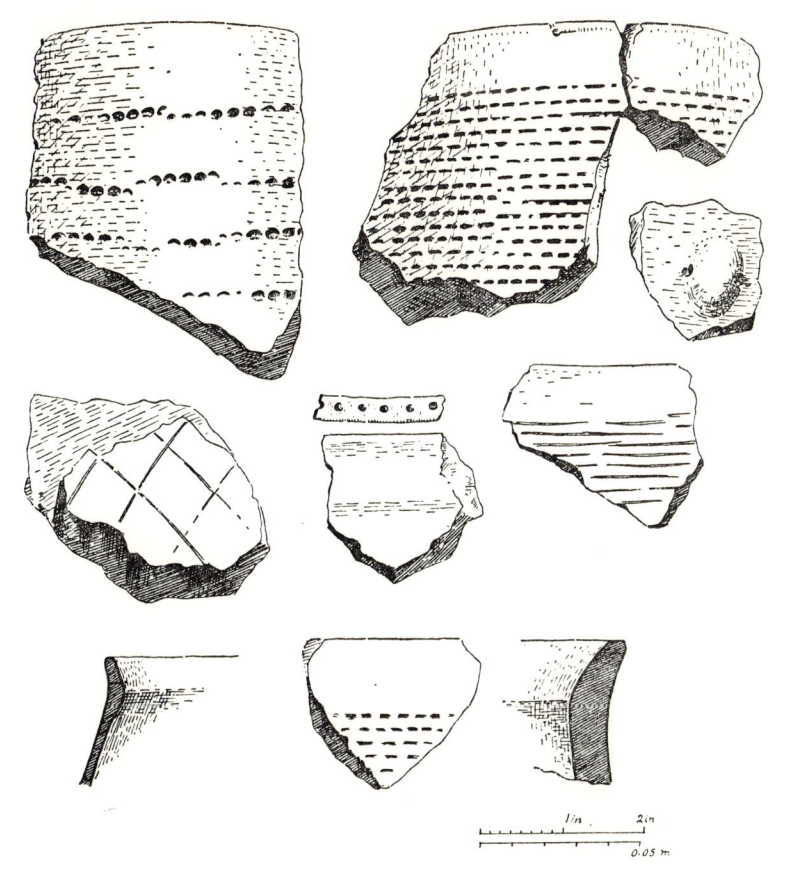

Fig 56 Pottery from Bant's Carn, St Mary's (from Hencken, 1933)

locate Bonsor's pottery, so comments are based upon his drawings, which depict rim-sherds, a horizontally perforated lug and a body sherd. One substantial rim-sherd bears short horizontal lines of small semi-circular impressions, their repetitive character suggesting a form of comb-stamping. Two others have horizontal 'hyphenated lines', also seemingly from comb-stamping, one more has short parallel incised lines upon it, and another has a system of saltires in incised outline, while a rim carries upon its top edge recurring equally-spaced circular impressions. The pottery found in 1970, some eighty sherds, includes a good part of a plain bucket-urn with everted, bevelled rim and intermittent finger-tip impressions below it. One worn base bears traces of radial line ornament, while the decorated body sherds bear either well-finished round-bottomed grooving, or incised lines. There are two imperforate lugs, one is detached from its parent pot and still retains the peg which secured it. There is also a considerable number of thin, hard, undecorated body sherds. This hard ware may well be the pottery which has given rise to the consideration of the possibility of a bowl 'with a round base like the usual neolithic pottery of Britain' (Hencken, 1932, 24).

Grimes (1960, 174–6) was able to reconstruct two urns from the chamber tomb on Salakee Down, St Mary's, that he excavated during the early months of 1942. From the disturbed area of the chamber came pieces that suggested a near-biconical, imperforate-lugged, bucket-like jar, with a bevelled rim, which had a height of about 7in and a shoulder diameter of 5·5in. The ware is heavily gritted to the extent of giving an irregular surface to it, although it is well-finished. A well-marked foot is possible, although it is not possible to join the base fragments to the body. In the north side of the chamber there were thin, hard-fired, externally dark red-brown sherds, which allowed the reconstruction of a markedly biconical, bevel-rimmed, also imperforate-lugged urn, 9·5in in height and with a shoulder diameter of 10·5in. Similar vessels were seen in Scilly, in the Knackyboy assemblage and from Par Beach, St Mary's (Ashbee, 1955), and comparisons were made with vessels from Cornwall and the Deverel-Rimbury range.

It was Hencken (1932, 29–30) who was the first to call attention to the similarity between the pottery from the cliff-exposed domestic site in Halangy Porth and that from the chamber tombs. He wrote, regarding this pottery from Halangy Porth:

> Among the fragments of pottery from it are some that were decorated with rows of small semi-circular marks like those from the neigh-

bouring passage-grave at Bant's Carn and from No. 1 on Samson ... Other fragments had decoration similar to that on some of the pottery from Obadiah's Barrow, and pieces of the same kind of thick gravelly ware found in that tomb also came from the midden. Some of the pottery from both the midden and the chambers is much finer however, and in this respect is more like the neolithic pottery of the British mainland. The rubbish heap also yielded some rims of pots like those from the megalithic graves, and it would thus seem fairly certain that the pile of refuse was made by the tomb-builders.

Subsequently, Hencken (1933, 16–17, Fig 4) published Bonsor's sectional drawing of the midden exposed in the cliff in Halangy Porth saying that it 'yielded sherds of much the same kind as those from the neighbouring passage-grave'. In the initial account, Hencken (1932, 23, Fig 10B) illustrates the sherd that he alludes to, together with three rims, one plain and two bevelled.

It was left to Gray to carry investigation of Halangy Porth further (Chapter 7). During 1934 and 1935 he appears to have collected about a hundredweight of pottery. Much of it was unornamented, comparatively thin, and often of a plain brown or biscuit colour. Such ornament as was present consisted of lines of comb-stamping and cord-ornament. Indeed, in the account of his work, Gray illustrates a biconical, lugged pot, with a zone of cord-ornament consisting of two continuous horizontal lines, joined by diagonals about its girth, as well as a series of rims. The last of all have their counterparts in both the Knackyboy Cairn assemblage and the pottery from other chamber tombs. Of especial note are the large storage jars found in pits.

Alexander Gibson knew Halangy Porth and a few years ago a collection (Ashbee, 1966, 21) of large, heavily sooted, decorated sherds from there, after having been for long housed in Tresco Abbey, came into the possession of the museum in Hugh Town. The record accompanying the material was 'Found Lingy Cliff James and self 1924' [*sic*]. 'Lingy' (=Halangy) is the local usage for the formal Ordnance Survey name. These sherds are of barrel-urns with horizontally perforated lugs as well as of markedly angular biconical pots. Ornament is lines of comb-stamping and lines of circular impressions between lines in relief, presumably brought about by incision before the application of the cylindrical implement. One substantial sherd, bearing a horizontally perforated lug and decorated with horizontal incised lines, has, in its surfaces, interior and exterior, some fifty clear grain impressions. Pottery similar to that from Halangy Porth has been collected from the cliff between Pendrathen and Bar Point, St Mary's. A pot recovered by Mr J. Treneary (Ashbee, 1954–5, 123) is biconical, bevel-rimmed, and has two imperforate lugs on its shoulders.

Full details of the pottery from English Island Carn, St Martin's (O'Neil, 1949) are not available but it is possible to say that considerable quantities were found. In O'Neil's own words 'The potsherds, all of fine ware ... included about one hundred of one vessel, which has decoration in the form of rows of impressed dots. In this way and in its shape the vessel closely resembles several found in 1948 at Knackyboy Cairn, about a mile away ...'

Regrettably few details are available of the pottery found by Gray, associated with the considerable number of early domestic sites that he located. It appears (Ashbee, 1972, 21) that the pottery from Halangy Porth, St Mary's, is his basis for comparison for all other sites. At the same time he compared his pottery with Hencken's (1932, Pl VI, 1, 2, 3) illustrations of vessels taken from chamber tombs while reference is usually made to pottery 'which appeared to be exactly similar to that from St. Mary's No. 3 [Halangy Porth]'. Comparisons with that from other sites are sometimes made. Also, as already stressed, such expressions as 'usual type' or 'typical' are sometimes used of the pottery. However, Gray does enter into detail regarding pottery from a shore exposure at Porth Killier, on St Agnes, described on page 177. He wrote:

> The pottery and bones from this site are in a very good state of preservation, and this makes the pottery seem to be of a better and finer paste than that from St. Mary's No. 3, etc., but, with the exception of one rim which certainly seems finer ware, a close examination

leads me to think that it is only its better condition which makes it seem different.

The most important find is a considerable portion of a pot about 30cm. in diameter at its centre. From the position of the fragments it was clear that they had all been united when thrown away, and that breakage had been caused by the weight of the earth which accumulated over it. The pot is of unusual design, and comes as near to the beaker in shape as anything which has come to light in Scilly. Unfortunately, although a fragment of the base was found, this did not connect with the upper portion, and it was too small for it to be possible to determine the basic diameter. Assuming, however, that the relation between width and height are the same, this jar bears an extraordinary resemblance to one found in a Megalithic grave at Quelvezin in Brittany [Kendrick, 1925, 33, Fig 8].

Early pottery, comparable with that from the chamber tombs, was collected during the progress of the excavations on Nornour (Dudley, 1967, 12, Fig 5). The view has been expressed that some of the sherds are from burial urns, with the rider that there are no tombs on the island, although there are some at no great distance, and that possibly similar wares were used for both domestic and funerary purposes. Many of these sherds are coarse and contain stones of some size and are yellowish-red in colour. Decoration is considered to be in the form of stab marks, incised lines either 'plainly or in chevron patterns' while cord-ornament is present. As far as can be seen, certain sherds bear lines of square-toothed comb stamping. Fine ware was also present; it was smooth, reddish and undecorated, and its use was apparently for small pots. On Nornour it would seem that the pots, represented by the sherds, had been used for cooking and storage purposes.

A number of stone cists on the Isles of Scilly contained early pottery, although the details available are few. Notwithstanding, its form and affinities can be clearly seen. Borlase (1758, 322) records 'A plain urn, inclosing human bones' from a boulder-built cist in the garden of a Mr T. Smith, at Newfort, St Mary's. A cist, found somewhere in the vicinity of Halangy Porth, produced pottery pronounced by R. A. Smith of the British Museum as being of the 'Megalithic Period' of Scilly. All that is known of this pottery, which up to World War II was preserved in the museum of the Torquay Natural History Society, is that 'Some of the sherds were decorated with incised and impressed motives ...' (Downie, 1928-9). The cist at Old Town (Mackenzie, 1965) was found during building operations and only a piece of the urn that it contained was saved. This pot was hand-made, its fabric containing granitic micas, and would appear to have been biconical in form. It is not known whether or not it was lugged and decorated. A pot-base was present in the cist on Content Farm (Ashbee, 1953), the remainder had presumably disintegrated. It was of dark-brown ware containing many granite grits, closely comparable with the small biconical urn from Par Beach (Ashbee, 1954-5). Mention must also be made of an urn allegedly found in a natural rock cleft, near Yellow Rock Carn on St Martin's (Lewis, 1948, 8). This urn, and a plain biconical lugged example, have been illustrated by Hencken (1932, 21, Pl VI, 2, 3) and it is likely that they were discovered when Knackyboy Cairn was dug into by Alexander Gibson (O'Neil, 1952, 21fn).

Turning now to the second broad division, the later period, for long the only Iron Age pottery known from the Isles of Scilly was the allegedly 'duck' ornamented sherds found during the digging of a war-time trench on Giant's Castle, St Mary's (O'Neil, 1949, 9). However, a quantity was recovered from the remains of a hut exposed in the cliff of Little Arthur by O'Neil in 1951. Since then excavations on Nornour have produced an associated assemblage as has the continuing work on Halangy Down, St Mary's.

While much Cornish and, certainly, all Scillonian Iron Age pottery might be seen at the best as distant and atypical members of a nebulous Southwestern amalgam with native additives, it is not really practicable to discuss such Scillonian pottery within the omnibus of Hodson's 'Woodbury Culture' (Hodson, 1964, 108, Fig 1). The alphabetical groupings of Hawkes' system of Iron Age A, B, and C are here retained (Hawkes, 1959).

MATERIAL CULTURE AND EQUIPMENT

The pottery from the cliff-exposed hut on Little Arthur was remarkable for the quantity concentrated within the remains of a comparatively small structure. Eighty-six sherds were in the black soil that was a floor, while, in the debris above, some 380 more were found. No precise details are available but it is possible to say that this assemblage can be compared with the Nornour series (Dudley, 1967, Figs 5, 6, 7).

Both the initial series of excavations (Dudley, 1967) and subsequent work (Butcher 1970) on Nornour have produced Iron Age pottery. Iron Age A on Nornour is represented by two groups of sherds. One is of a number of angular-shouldered vessels, although in many instances the shoulder is no more than a curvilinear profile. The other is of a range of coarse wares, distinguished by their rough, uneven fabrication and the incidence of finger-printing. Lugs are also present. Certain pieces, distinguished by their light-ochre colour, are considered to resemble the flat-rimmed, angular bowls of light brown ware from Bodrifty (Dudley, 1956, 22–8, Fig 9, 20), in Cornwall. Well-made wide bowls with upright necks, a few of which bear hatched designs have counterparts at Castle Dore, Cornwall (Radford, 1951) and, together with some bead-rims and countersunk handles, are assignable to the category of Southwestern Second B. Well-finished wheel-turned wares with occasional cordons could be considered to represent Southwestern Third C. A number of sherds of hard, red, wheel-turned ware with lattice ornamentation and markedly everted rims might, perhaps, also be considered with the last category. Excavation of buildings to the east of those initially examined on Nornour (Butcher, 1970, 78, Fig 24) recovered yet more Iron Age A pottery. The wares from one building (Butcher, 1970, 79) seem a local product for they are coarse, soft, and filled with large granite grits. For the most part, large, fairly straight-sided, ring-built jars with upright, squared, or even everted rims are represented although there were some gently curved bowls. It was observed that some jars carried curious vestigial lugs, made separately and secured by insertion. From another building came pieces of coarse jars which can, in a general sense, be compared with the coarse pottery from numerous other earlier Iron Age sites in Britain.

MATERIAL CULTURE AND EQUIPMENT

The Iron Age sherds from Halangy Down (Ashbee, 1968, 31), St Mary's, are all small and worn. They were found in disturbed soil amongst stone-breaker's debris, juxtaposed with later pottery. As far as comparisons can be made with such egregious material, certain pieces could be compared with the well-made earlier series from Bodrifty in Cornwall.

Two wheel-turned, complete vessels were found in cist-graves at Porth Cressa (Ashbee, 1954, 18) in Hugh Town (Fig 57). One was of a general form, with angular neck and slightly flared, rolled rim, such as might be found on Romano-British sites as far distant as Colchester or Richborough. The other, a bowl of reddish-brown ware with traces of a darker brown slip, had a beaded rim and a base slightly convex, incised with three concentric circles. Its affinities appear to lie with the Iron Age B series of the South West rather than with provincial Roman pottery.

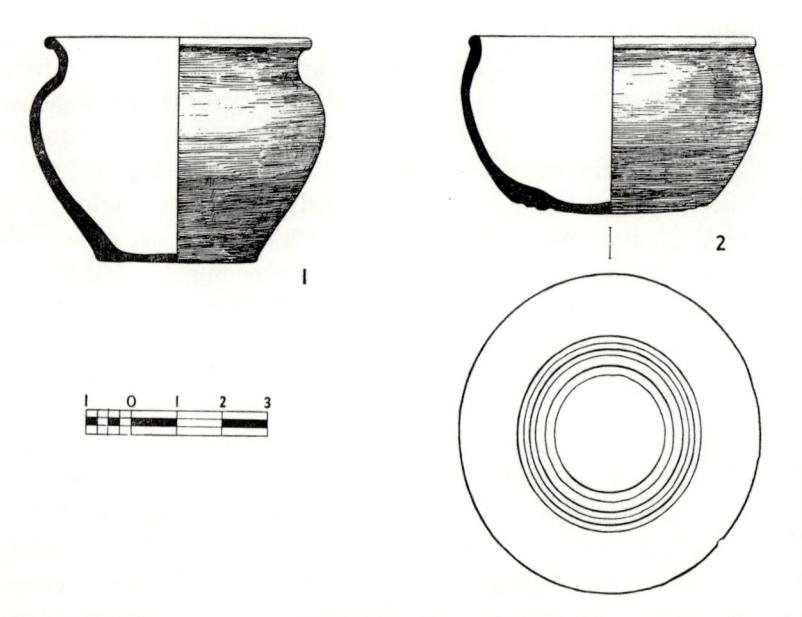

Fig 57 Romano-British pots from Porth Cressa, Hugh Town, St Mary's, cist-grave cemetery

MATERIAL CULTURE AND EQUIPMENT

Provincial Romano-British wheel-made coarse pottery has been found on a number of domestic sites in Scilly (see Chapter 7). Indeed, they serve as an approximate indication of age and affinity, for other artifacts and the remains of stone structures tell one little. In many instances they may be local products or, at least, from the granitic regions of the South West, for they regularly contain comminuted mica. Now and again, as on St Martin's or at Halangy Down, small worn fragments of Samian and other imported pottery have been found. Sherds of coarse Romano-British pottery were found at Halangy Down by Gray, and during excavations in 1950 (Ashbee, 1955, 194), and their affinities with those from such sites as Chysauster (Hencken, 1933) has been shown. Indeed, further excavations, since 1964, have substantiated and extended this pattern. Similar pottery has also been found on Nornour (Dudley, 1967, 13, Fig 6, 38; 15, Fig 7, 62, 66, 67, 68) including a Samian sherd.

Two ceramic products from Nornour stand apart from the rustic life-style implied by the coarse pottery usage. On the circular hearth in Room I (Dudley, 1967, 5) were seven small pots (Dudley, 1967, 15, Fig 7, 72), 2in in height, with internally bevelled rims and cord ornament. Indeed, in general appearance they resemble diminutive 'Trevisker style' (ApSimon and Greenfield, 1972, 365) Bronze Age urns. They are unique in the South West and their function is far from clear. It has been suggested that they were crucibles connected with the manufacture of brooches and other ornaments. Their only direct counterparts are the small vessels of similar size associated with the Triangular Temple at Verulamium (Wheeler, 1936, 190-2, Fig 32, 45; Pl LIX, 2) considered as having been used to contain oil for ritual usage. Among the stones and sand infilling Rooms I and II were a number of fine fired-clay moulded female figurines, for the most part fragmentary (Dudley, 1967, Pl IV B). They are of two types, the *dea nutrix* and 'pseudo-Venus' respectively (Plate 14). The first represents a seated female in the act of suckling either one or two infants, the second a standing female nude clutching at draperies with one hand and adjusting a tress of her hair with the other. Frank Jenkins, who has studied the

Nornour series (in Dudley, 1967) has shown that they were numerous in Gaul, their place of origin, where they were products of an industry analagous to that which produced the *terra sigillata* near the middle of the second century AD. They were popular votive products and appear to have been substitutes for the more elaborate, and presumably more costly, statuary.

Grass-marked pottery (Thomas, 1968), the post-Roman pots and plates that bear the negative impressions of burnt-out chopped grass, is represented by sherds from Porth Cressa, Halangy Down, Teän and St Helens. The sherds from Porth Cressa were from a midden of limpet shells and animal bones piled against the wall of the terraced field in which was the cist-grave cemetery (Ashbee, 1954, 13). On Halangy Down the sherds were scattered in the top-soil and associated with earlier pottery. They are thick, coarse, and contain large grits, the grass impressions being upon their outer surfaces and bases. Indeed, their reddened fragmentary character suggests that they may have been refired. Rather more grass-marked pottery was found by Charles Thomas during his excavation on Teän in 1956. Some sixty sherds emerged, all exhibiting the basic characteristics of the range, while affinities with native Romano-British styles were also present. It was from this site on Teän that pieces of imported wheel-made wares of Mediterranean origin were recovered. The grass-marked pottery from St Helen's (O'Neil, 1964, 55) was of considerable importance and interest as it allowed a study of methods of manufacture to be made. After manipulation into the required shape by hand the vessels remained upon the grass-strewn work-surface to dry. It is thought that the sagging bases were produced by pressing out from the interior after lifting.

Nothing is known of the circumstances surrounding the discovery of substantial pieces of bar-lipped or lugged ware on St Martin's. They were shown to the present writer by Mr J. Treneary a few years ago when it was said that they had been found during the construction of a house. Indeed, for many years pottery has been collected from the Isles of Scilly but brief notices say nothing of its character or place of origin. At the second meeting of the Prehistoric Society, held on

MATERIAL CULTURE AND EQUIPMENT

Wednesday, 9 October 1935, in the rooms of the Society of Antiquaries, Burlington House, London, Mr E. H. N. Skrimshire exhibited 'Sherds from a midden on St. Martin's site, Scilly Isles' (*Proceedings of the Prehistoric Society*, I, 1935, 163).

CHAPTER 11

Subsistence Economy and Trade

Surrounded as they were by the sea, early Scillonians sought sustenance from it. Shellfish were collected, fish, birds and mammals were caught, and all were eaten and their bones discarded. At the same time the resources proffered by the land were not neglected. Certain mammals were hunted, probably to local extinction, while with farming new animal species were introduced, tended and exploited. Similarly cereals were brought to the islands and clearances were made to grow them. By farming, the biosystem was being progressively modified to man's needs and in the train of this process came ecological change. Although there must have been both good and bad seasons, there could not have been privation or starvation at any time for the sea appears as an alternative to the land as a source of food. It would seem that a combined land-sea subsistence economy evolved and, as the considerable number of domestic sites at no great distance one from another suggest, a slightly above average population density may have obtained right through the second and into the first millennium BC. Indeed, even in recent times recourse had to be made to the sea, for on Samson, the island from which Augustus Smith expelled the inhabitants in 1839, a ruined cottage still has a vast heap of limpet shells beside it.

By far the best-known ancient limpet-shell midden on the Isles of Scilly was that seen and recorded by Bonsor (Hencken, 1932, 30; 1933, 17, Fig 4), seventy years ago in Halangy Porth. As described in a previous chapter, pottery of much the same kind as that from the chamber tombs was associated with it. Today, only the remains of stone buildings still

SUBSISTENCE ECONOMY AND TRADE

project from the cliff and the midden has been completely washed away. Such shell middens are invariably an indication of early occupation (Appendix 4) and have long been recognised as such (Mothersole, 1919, 72-3). Sometimes, besides pottery as at Halangy Porth, they contain fish and animal bones as well as discarded stone tools. Excavation of the cist-grave cemetery at Porth Cressa, St Mary's (Ashbee, 1954, 13), disclosed a midden adjacent to a field terrace wall, while in nearby Poynter's Garden (Dudley, 1960-1) another extensive shell-midden, bounded by a wall, lay upon an ancient surface. Sherds of pottery amongst the shells suggested Romano-British affinities. The midden on Teän was also upon an ancient surface and was contained in black crumbly soil. Besides limpet and other shells, it produced the bones of animals, birds and fish, pieces of granite, pebbles, charcoal and lumps of clay. A limpet-shell midden, containing quantities of animal bones and broken pottery, was found to have covered an earlier structure on Nornour (Dudley, 1967, 9) as did the midden found during the course of the excavations on Halangy Down (Ashbee, 1968, 30).

This midden on Halangy Down (Plate 16a) was found to contain some 110,000 limpet shells and this may be but the remains of accumulations which were periodically removed and used for land fertilisation. Indeed, some of the buildings stand upon earlier terraces and excavation in depth has produced quantities of rotted limpet shells, pointing to such a practice. It would appear from the great number of limpets, both here and on other Scillonian sites, that they had an important role in supplying protein in the diet of the early communities.

A study of the common limpet (*Patella vulgata*) as a source of protein, with especial reference to those found in the Halangy Down midden, has been undertaken (Townsend, 1967). Assessment of those univalve conical-shaped shell-fish, which cling firmly to rocks, involved the investigation of a size-ranged series from a Welsh shore. It was found that the Scillonian samples consisted mainly of small shells, and this may well be an indication that they were gathered too frequently for them to grow to large size. A concentration of small shells could point to excessive collection, while the appearance of larger ones could indicate the end of a cycle when other food resources had been exhausted or the use of a new collection area.

It may be asked why the Halangy Down and other early Scillonians concentrated upon limpets; and why the shells of other molluscs, or for that matter fish-bones, are not present in comparable quantities? This could be explained by the fact that, once the mechanical nuances of limpet collection have been mastered, they can be collected rapidly and are thus a bounty of protein, albeit rather gritty, for the expenditure of not too long a period of labour. The end-battered beach pebbles, a considerable number of which have been found on Halangy Down and many other Scillonian sites, may have been the tools employed for the task. These have their counterparts in other early communities which ate limpets (Breuil, 1921-2, 268, Fig 4). Scottish Azilian elongated end-battered beach pebbles have been shown by experiment to be ideal for use as punches for detaching limpets from rocks (Atkinson, 1962, 3). The process entails a single, swift, sweeping blow, for if it is not precisely delivered the limpet clings and a further blow only smashes the shell.

The early Scillonians may well have consumed their limpets in conjunction with other foodstuffs, and thus it is clearly impossible to know how many constituted a meal or how frequently they were eaten. There are, however, certain possibilities to be considered. Consumption of animal protein is normally considered as 9g per head, per day for the undernourished countries of the world, 36 for Europe and 66 in the United States of America. To supply protein to the ideal American standard for a family consisting of father, mother, a boy, a girl and an infant, 756 Scillonian midden-type limpets would be required daily. It is doubtful whether the limpet population, even of a considerable stretch of rocky shore, could support such daily demands for very long. A more modest estimate is the World Food and Agriculture's target *per capita* consumption by the undernourished of 16g of protein, the equivalent of 250 Scillonian limpets daily. This could possibly have been met if the collecting area had been fairly extensive. With the circumstances of the mixed economy that seems to have obtained on most Scillonian sites in mind, it would seem that limpet consumption was probably geared to the availabilities of other commodities, and modulated by the growth of limpets on specific shores. Indeed, the small size of the Halangy Down limpet shells might well reflect controlled collecting circumstances. Communities which consumed, at appropriate times, limpets for three or more millennia would doubtlessly have learned the lessons of over-exploitation of such a staple.

Evidence of sea-fishing is in the fish-bones found in certain midden accumulations. Such bones are frequently fragile and are often difficult to observe and preserve, even in the conditions obtaining on a present-day excavation. Thus many more middens, other than those which have been the subject of careful investigation, may well have contained quantities of fish-bones. At Porth Cressa (Ashbee, 1954, 14) about 2lb weight of fish-bones, mainly wrasse, were recovered. On Teän fish jawbones were of a species like a ballan wrasse and it was felt fair to assume that the rest of the fish-bones belonged to the same species. Fish-bones were fairly numerous on Nornour (Turk, 1967, 265) but only the remains of wrasse, conger eel and, possibly, hake have so far been identified. Wrasse jaw and other bones have been found in incidental accumulations in the midden at Halangy Down. Nothing, so far, has come to light from the early settlements of Scilly which would indicate methods of fishing, although it has been plausibly suggested that certain conveniently sized grooved, or perforated, stones were net-sinkers.

Seal bones were found by Gray at Halangy Porth and on St Agnes. Seal bones were also present on Nornour (Turk, 1967; 1968), only a little fewer than those of the sheep. Gray had the bones from Porth Killier, on St Agnes, identified—he had previously sent bones from Halangy Porth to the British Museum (Natural History) and to the Fitzwilliam Museum, Cambridge, for identification—and all of them proved to be those of seals, grey seal (Atlantic seal), *Halichoerus grypus* (Fab) or common seal (harbour seal), *Phoca vitulina* (L). In the absence of traces of buildings, this site was considered as a seasonal station for sealing and, perhaps, fishing. Porpoise bones were also present on

Nornour (Turk, 1967, 261) and St Agnes (Turk, 1968, 78) while an artifact of whalebone was found during the excavation of the monastic enceinte on St Helen's (O'Neil, 1964, 67).

Seals (Clark, 1952, 72–83) would have been a valuable source of oil, meat and skins. Indeed, the oil, besides its uses as a fuel for illumination, even has medicinal properties! The collection and conveyance of the oil would have needed fine-ware jars, such as were seemingly present at Porth Killier, while the lumps of clay, a feature of the site, could have been used to secure such containers. Flints and rubbing stones, such as were also found, would have played their part in such an installation. Porpoises appear to have been exploited for meat in early historical times (Clark, 1947, 98) the north-western French coast being a centre. Thus porpoise bones in a Scillonian midden are not surprising. Whalebone could have been obtained from a stranded creature, for strandings must have taken place in early times as they do today on the islands, for instance on Samson where bones still lie.

Sea-bird bones were numerous in the Nornour midden and razorbill (*Alca torda*), guillemot (*Uria aalge*) and puffin (*Fratercula arctica*) appeared to be by far the commonest (Turk, 1967, 263). All these birds could have been used for food as well as feathers. It is frequently quoted that Scilly, for some time after the reign of Edward I, was held at a rent of 300 puffins. They were scarce in Troutbeck's time (Troutbeck, 1794, 12) and he comments how, on account of the rent, there must have been great numbers of them formerly. Borlase (1756, 31) speaks of sea-birds, especially puffins, and comments on their fishy taste, saying that the birds which went for rent may have been wanted for their feathers rather than their flesh.

Even in the circumstances of the present-day islands forming a continuous land tract, a larger island or islands in early times, it scarcely seems possible that wild animals of any size or food potential would have long survived the attentions of man. Gray records the bones of red deer and a 'small deer' from the early site at Halangy Porth. Red deer bones have been found on St Agnes (Turk, 1968, 78) while antler was found on Nornour (Turk, 1967, 260) and it seems that both a large and a small species were present. There is, of course, the possibility that these bones represent creatures brought to the islands, dead or alive. For such animals have, in such an environment as Scilly, no other enemy but man, so that they are, to some extent, tractable and some varieties have, from time to time, been brought to specific Scottish islands (Ritchie, 1920, 280).

The bones of small mammals, fox and, perhaps, hare, were in the midden at Porth Cressa (Ashbee, 1954, 14), while curlew and wild duck were recorded from Teän. Here the considerations of fur, feathers and flesh are all possible. It should be observed in passing that the bones of rabbits, rats and voles in the Nornour midden may be recent intrusions (Turk, 1967, 261–2).

A number of carefully collected assemblages of domestic animal bones, usually smashed and bearing cut-marks suggesting butchery, provide further evidence of food and farming practices. Nothing is known of the character of the pig's jawbone from the chamber tomb at the foot of Halangy Down, St Mary's, (H2a:D14) but Gray records bones of ox, sheep and a horse from his bulb-garden site by Halangy Porth. From Halangy Down quantities of ox, sheep, pig and horse bones and teeth have come to light during the course of the excavations in recent years (Ashbee, 1966, 26). The midden on Nornour (Turk, 1967, 252–9) contained ox, sheep, goat and pig remains. It was remarked, however, that these bones bore little evidence of any butchery practice, only a few bones had knife or hatchet marks. Many, seemingly, had been roughly used and others had apparently been burned. Ox, horse, sheep and pig were present in the Early Christian midden investigated at Porth Cressa (Ashbee, 1954, 14). A quantity amounting to a half-wheelbarrow's content were recovered. They had all been smashed into small fragments, indeed there were few complete articular ends or readily identifiable fragments, excepting teeth. Many pieces had been burned. Several of the larger pieces of bone showed regular incisions, made in removing the flesh, while other, smaller pieces of long bones showed bruises, made perhaps in smashing them for their marrow content. The somewhat later midden on Teän (Turk, 1968, 75–9) had in it bones of ox, sheep, goat and pig. It was felt that there was a probability that the domestic animals on Teän at this later period may have been a little larger than those from Nornour, although it was admitted that the evidence was scanty. The positively identifiable goat bones were few in number. It was thought that few were kept and that those were probably away from the main settlement.

The record of domestic animal remains from Scillonian habitation sites of all periods is uneven, to say the least, and thus conclusive comparison must be tempered with caution. The general pattern shows little change from the earlier to the later sites. Besides meat, the animals would, when alive, have been a source of milk as well as hair and wool, while dried excrement can be used as fuel. By-products of slaughtering would have been hides, sinews, bone and fat. Indeed, the considerable numbers of flint scrapers which are a feature of the earlier sites may reflect the importance of hides to these early communities. At an early stage in Scillonian ecological history, domestic animals would have been, with man, agents of deforestation and change, on account of their browsing habits. Such changes may have opened up grazing areas but, even were the land areas larger than today, there would have been inevitable limitations. However, it is possible that these limitations of land area and grazing were circumvented by recourse to the sea, for cattle can be foddered upon seaweed and even fish!

Direct evidence of cereal cultivation is the sherd (Plate 15) from Halangy Porth (Ashbee, 1966, 21) which has, upon both interior and exterior, some fifty very clear grain impressions. Indirect evidence is in the terraced hillside plots, as on Halangy Down or Porth Cressa, and the enclosures elsewhere, both on land and beneath the sea. There is the very considerable number of querns, saddle, bowl and rotary, found whole and broken on numerous sites, and the corn-drying ovens as identified on Teän and at Halangy Down. With this there is the evidence for pits and storage pots besides, possibly, areas for grain-drying, resulting from Gray's work at Halangy Porth.

It is doubtful if archaeological methods could demonstrate conclusively the character of the crops grown upon such cultivation terraces as those lining Halangy Down. Notwithstanding, their importance to those who initially constructed them is shown by the labour that the process must have entailed. These plots on Halangy Down can, in some measure, be related to the settlement. It is an open question as to whether they would have sufficed for a large community. However, using Bersu's (1940, 104–5) basic annual consumption-harvest figures for Little Woodbury, Wiltshire, and the presumption of a similar sized occupation of the courtyard house, they could be seen as fulfilling a good measure of the demand. Yield, however, would be conditioned by the efficiency of shell, bone and organic rubbish fertilisation. If more than one house had been occupied during the use-life of the site the extant fields would have been too few. Then greater demands would have been made upon other aspects of the, quite broad-based, land-sea subsistence economy.

Little can be said about the querns except to emphasise their number. With the fragments found by excavation, and taking cognizance of those now in use as garden ornaments, almost a hundred are known from St Mary's. This number does not include any estimate of those that may be lurking in walls or that may have been destroyed. The saddle and bowl querns may reflect different processes for different crops. With the bowl querns one must consider the large granite bowls, such as the example from Nornour. These may have functioned as mortars, adding yet another dimension to our presumptions regarding early Scillonian dietetic usages.

The presence of corn-drying ovens on the Isles of Scilly was first noticed on Teän in 1956. Areas of porth clay lay across the surface of the midden and within their compass were circular burnt areas. Spread over a wide radius were fragments of burnt daub which frequently contained the negative impressions of rush wattling. Burned areas detected by Gray, during 1934 and 1935, below the bulb garden behind the structures in the cliff of Halangy Porth, may also point to the erstwhile presence of corn-drying ovens. Such a view would be supported by the large storage pots, one of which was found in a pit. Indeed, it was from this site that the large grain-impressed sherd came. Numerous 'clay hearths', surely the bases of corn-drying ovens, were found in the hut set in an early field system at Perpitch, St Martin's, excavated by B. H. StJ. O'Neil in 1951.

On Halangy Down (Ashbee, 1970, 72, Pl VIb) the substantial remains of the bases of three corn-drying ovens have been revealed, and beneath one of them were ephemeral traces of two others. The greater parts of these circular bases were underneath a jumble of pieces of burnt clay daub, many of which had impressions of reeds or straw. The best preserved showed that the interiors had been some 2ft 3in in diameter, with sides some 10in in thickness. The bases were dark burned, resting upon a raft of small stones, and it could be seen that the interiors had been smoothed. This clutch of ovens, after their abandonment, had been cut through by the bedding trench of a later wall.

This inferential evidence of early grain-drying in Scilly is commensurate with the discovery of carbonised grain at Itford Hill, Sussex (Burstow and Holleyman, 1957, 206-9), a site of the Middle Bronze Age of southern England. The burnt flints, sooted soil and burned clay fragments found by Bersu (1940, 61-2) at Little Woodbury attest to the practice during the Iron Age. Romano-British T-shaped drying ovens were considered by Goodchild (1943, 148) while Curwen (1946, 101-4) has contributed a general account. Parching corn is necessary to avoid germination when it is stored in pots set in pits or in such small chambers as those in the thickness of the walls of Halangy Down. Indeed, many of the pieces of quite large vessels from later Scillonian sites may be of storage jars which could have been covered with stone discs such as have been found on Nornour. Corn roasting not only improves flavour but makes the grains more brittle and less liable to crushing or flattening during grinding. Curwen (1946, 104) has shown by experiment that it is possible to grind a pound of roasted wheat to fine flow in a few minutes while undried wheat takes much longer and needs repeated regrinding.

With the foregoing data in mind, what then of the development of the prehistoric and early historic subsistence economy of the Isles of Scilly? There must have been an initial *landnam* (which means simply landwinning), or 'breaking' as it is so often called on the islands. This means that people came from the mainland and after, presumably, preliminary exploration, they made land-fall with their seed-corn and kine. As Case (1969) has so cogently demonstrated, such settlement implies the establishment, in new territory, of a primitive farming system by stone-using people with such transport as was available to them, and it is clear that positive archaeological evidence of such early enterprise may continue to elude us, except inferentially. For what we see all about us are established cultures, the circumstances that Case (1969, 183) has termed stable adjustments to new environments. The pottery with grain impressions, traces of corn-drying, great storage pots in pits and saddle querns, found down by the shore at Halangy Porth, on St Mary's, show a well-established Neolithic mode of life.

The settlement by Halangy Porth reflects, however, much more than a mere land-based economy. In a topographical sense, land and sea merge, one into another, in the Scillonian scene. These inseparable dimensions are ever present in the subsistence economy. From the first, side-by-side with grain growing and the keeping of kine, swine and flocks, themselves complementary, there was catching, gathering and, indeed, hunting, the products of the sea. Thus from an early stage, a mixed land-sea economy evolved. With such advantages, it is even possible, bearing in mind the relative profusion of early remains on the islands, that a slightly above-average population density could have obtained right through the second and into the first millennium BC.

At this stage the question must be posed as to the degree of isolation that obtained for the early Scillonian communities. It has been argued with force and conviction (Thomas, 1966) that in Roman times the South West, and this must include Scilly, was an area beyond the limits of civilisation, enshrouded in its own particular benightment. Yet the long south-western peninsula, and Scilly, looks towards Brittany, Ireland and South Wales and, given good weather, the sea can conjoin and unite as well as separate and divide. The extent to which early Scillonian society was stimulated by intercourse with other contemporary societies can, in some measure, be assessed by evaluation of what can be termed 'trade', that is, objects brought from an external source to a region where quite distinct local types were current. In other words, objects which have been brought to the islands and which have been found by archaeological investigation and recognised as imports.

Confusion concerning early trade all too frequently arises from the application of current connotations of the term to the conditions of early society. Archaeology can demonstrate the presence of objects foreign to local culture but it cannot define the nature of the transactions involved. The peaceful and systematic exchange of goods (Clark, 1965) can function by a variety of methods. In a pre-monetary society, barter or gift-giving and exchange may have been the mode. At a later stage, given a community in which some divisions of labour may have obtained, the earlier media would have persisted side-by-side with monetary transaction.

During the earlier period there are a number of patent imports into the islands that can be earmarked as having been obtained from external sources. Taken together they make a pattern of paucity. This may be due to certain exchanges having been in the form of commodities, such as oil or skins, that have left no trace in the archaeological record. At the same time this pattern does emphasise the inherent conservative nature of local material culture. The greenstone axe from Gugh could well be an import from a Cornish source (Ashbee, 1970, 10), while the raw material of which the Normandy battle-axe is made may be from the same place, although the focus for the type seems far removed (Roe, 1966, 216, Map 1). Stray metal objects do not warrant use of the term 'Bronze Age' (Childe, 1956, 91) for the builders of the chamber tombs were basically a stone-using people. It is more than likely that the bronze awl from Obadiah's Barrow, on Gugh (Hencken, 1932, 28, Fig 12B), is an import to the islands as are the other few pieces. Indeed, the massive bronze torques from Peninnis, St Mary's (Ashbee, 1960, 114) may even have come to Scilly from northern Europe. This possibility could be countenanced when one recalls the ribbed bracelet, from a similar source, from Cornwall (Butler, 1963, 155).

The star-shaped faience bead (Plate 16b) from the Knackyboy

Cairn (O'Neil, 1952, Pl XI, 5) probably did not, as was initially thought, come from the Near East. Indeed, the whole question of the Mediterranean origins of these beads is now in question. Only one star-bead comparable with the Knackyboy example is known from the mainland of Europe; their predominantly Scottish distribution not too far from a source of copper salts has been adduced as grounds for suggesting that this was their place of manufacture (Newton and Renfrew, 1970, 203). If, therefore, this six-rayed star-bead was brought to Scilly from Scotland, it would underline the implied connection with that region brought forward as a result of the excavation of the White Cairn, Bargrennan, Galloway (Piggott and Powell, 1948-9, 144-53) which closely resembles a Scillonian chamber tomb. The same writers also consider that the celebrated glass beads from the Knackyboy Cairn (O'Neil, 1952, Pl XI) form a separate group and can at present be presumed to be of local manufacture. Whether this means manufacture on Scilly or at a mainland centre where, perhaps, metalworking was undertaken, is not clear. In view of the sparse occurrence of metal, as has been stressed above, one cannot speak of a Scillonian 'Bronze Age'; a mainland or more distant source seems more likely.

Two amber disc-beads were found in the cist exposed during 1946 in the cliff, between Knackyboy Cairn and Yellow Rock Carn, on St Martin's (Lewis, 1949, Pl Xb). As there seems little likelihood of sea-borne amber reaching Scilly, they could be considered as imports, as can the oblate glass beads from Porth Cressa (Ashbee, 1954, 17, Fig 6, 10), Halangy Down (Ashbee, 1965, 40) and Nornour (Dudley, 1967, 26-7). Indeed, many of the Nornour beads have counterparts in both Britain and Gaul.

During Roman times a range of products found their way to Scilly. Splinters of Samian ware have been found on St Mary's, St Martin's and Nornour, while fragments of Castor ware have been found on Halangy Down. The celebrated Nornour brooches may well be a local manufacture and, if this is so, there is the possibility that many of the small, broken bronze objects and broken pieces of glass were assembled for this purpose.

Surprisingly enough, a considerable range of Roman coinage has been found on the islands. A group of six silver coins of Constantine II, Julian and Honorius have been found on Samson. Hencken (1932, 195) suggests that this points to deposition in about the reign of Honorius, AD 393–423. Three small bronze Roman coins were in the midden layer on Teän. One bears traces of an attempted attachment. They were respectively two *sestertii* of Marcus Aurelius (AD 161–86), and a *sestertius* of Septimus Severus (AD 193–211). Miss Anne S. Robertson, of the Hunter coin cabinet, Hunterian Museum, who examined these coins, expressed the view that they were not as worn as Roman bronze coins frequently are and that they would not have been in circulation after about the middle of the third century AD. Nearly seventy coins came to light on Nornour (Dudley, 1967, 27–8) and they range from Vespasian (AD 69–79) to Gratian (AD 367–83), the greater number being of the House of Constantine.

It is considered (Dudley and Butcher, 1968, 15) that the presence of Imperial Roman coins and imported pottery show that Scilly was on well-used routes in Roman times. On the other hand, with the possible character of the Nornour installations in mind, it is feasible that a range of materials found their way to the islands by the agencies of intercourse with the Cornish mainland of which Scilly is an appendage. In such circumstances one should consider the mode by which artifacts, pottery, metal and even stone, are circulated amongst communities in a specific region, which may well have quite different motives than those that we term trade.

Besides the splinters of fine Roman wares, all from places of origin a considerable distance from the islands, every site of the period has produced quantities of coarse wares. These are normally sherds, often of small size, although two near-complete pots were unearthed in the Porth Cressa, St Mary's cemetery (Ashbee, 1954, 19, Fig 7). Scrutiny of these considerable assemblages shows that they were for the most part locally made, the indicator being the glistening micas in their fabric, showing the granitic origin of their clays. By use of the term 'locally made' to designate pottery, one cannot be certain whether this

SUBSISTENCE ECONOMY AND TRADE

pottery was in fact manufactured in Scilly or in appropriate granitic regions of Cornwall. Undoubtedly the impetus to change of fashion in pottery forms came via imported vessels from the Romanised regions of England and only by painstaking examination of fabrics can coarse wares from a distance be separated from those locally made.

In post-Roman times, wheel-made wares of Mediterranean origin were brought to the islands, a number of sherds of various kinds being found during the excavation of the Early Christian site on Teän (Thomas, 1958). The grass-marked pottery, considered to resemble closely the 'souterrain ware' of Early Christian Ulster (Thomas, 1971, 65), is in the main a local product, although it may have been introduced by Irish settlers. The enamelled penannular brooch, found many years ago on St Martin's (O'Neil, 1953), is a type fairly common in Ireland and is further evidence of connections with that country.

By the later Middle Ages a wide range of products was reaching the islands. Excavation of the monastic installation on St Helen's (O'Neil, 1965) unearthed a range of glazed and other pottery from a number of English and French sources, as well as roofing slates, Purbeck marble and ornamental ridge tiles. In the circumstances, it seems inescapable that Scilly was involved during the thirteenth century, seemingly the most flourishing period of St Helen's, in the complex patterns of western European trade.

A number of topographical writers (eg Kay, 1956, 59) have claimed that the Isles of Scilly were the fabled Cassiterides, the Phoenician tin islands. It was William Camden, more than three centuries ago who identified the tin islands of the classical writers (Rice Holmes, 1936, 483-514) with Scilly and propounded the picturesque idea of Phoenician trading voyages to Britain. As William Borlase was at great pains to point out, the tin resources of Scilly, egregious veins on St Mary's and Tresco, are slight. Indeed, it is impossible that Scillonian tin could have been of any consequence in the ancient world. This is not to deny the possibility of transhipment or knowledge of the commodity. A piece of cassiterite was found during the excavation of the hut floor on Par Beach, St Martin's (O'Neil, 1949, 163). It seems likely, as Hencken (1932, 168) stressed, that the name Cassiterides was given to the Atlantic tin source-lands before these areas, probably the mouth of the Guadalquivir in Spain, became a part of the Roman Empire. As Rome advanced, the fabulous islands vanished into the obfuscating sea-mist.

CHAPTER 12

Scillonian Communities: Origins and Affinities

The prehistory and protohistory of the Isles of Scilly expressed as an archaeological sequence can be seen as follows:

c 2000 BC–400 BC
Long-lasting Beaker/Late Neolithic communities with flint, stone, bone and antler equipment, making barrel, biconical and bucket-form urns and pots, the upper half of which frequently bear stamped or incised ornamentation. Eighteen habitation sites, some with the remains of stone-built houses, have been identified, while about eighty chamber tombs, often termed entrance-graves, in regular cemeteries are known, as are several cist-burials. The burial rite was cremation, either unurned or inurned, although there is one instance of inhumation. A bronze awl was in one chamber tomb and pieces of an armlet in another, while a further awl has been found on a settlement site; two massive bronze torques were found in what may well have been a barrow; a socketed axe was a stray find.

c 400 BC–AD 250
Several stone-built huts have produced 'Iron Age' pottery commensurate with that from the Cornish mainland and four or five promontory forts have been identified.

c AD 250–AD 400
Romano-British pottery, both locally made and imported, has been found on six sites and at one of these there stood a demonstrable

courtyard house. Another range of buildings, possibly of ritual character, yielded a great number of brooches and other bronze pieces, besides coins and pipe-clay figurines. Burial was by contracted inhumation in stone-built cists, often with brooches.

c AD *400*–AD *1000*

Grass-marked pottery, imported and bar-lip wares, have come from four or five sites. A number of ecclesiastical establishments, including one unambiguous monastic enceinte, are a feature of this phase. An inscribed stone, some possible crosses, and a few extended burials can also be considered.

Although an artifactual sequence set down in such terms may be thought of as fossilised human behaviour (Childe, 1929, vi), it should not be overlooked that it must, perforce, contain the equipment, in the broadest sense, necessary to deal with the specific environment that was the Isles of Scilly. This is not to say that this environment determined the precise pattern that early Scillonian society followed, for there is good evidence that, within its limits, certain limited choices were exercised. For example, for food the all-pervading limpets were a preference, winkles were available although, perhaps, not so easily collected.

The early stages of the material cultural pattern of these early Scillonians may, as has been set out above, owe much to Late Neolithic and Beaker sources, but the archaic, although seemingly successful, economy does raise the question of a contribution, ultimately, from indigenous Mesolithic stocks. In other words, a possible explanation for much of the character of the long-continuing Scillonian Late Neolithic could be that it developed as the result of a process of acculturation between hunter-fishers and the developed Late Neolithic and Beaker societies that had emerged in the South West. As a catalystic process, bringing about what can be seen in the archaeological record as a distinctive insular Scillonian manifestation, it would seem little different from the factors that brought about other specific communities as, for example, in Northern Ireland (Case, 1969, 16).

SCILLONIAN COMMUNITIES: ORIGINS AND AFFINITIES

Apart from the presence, among the flint implement collections, of numbers of flakes of Larnian character, nothing that could be considered as Mesolithic has come to light on Scilly. There are, however, many features that can only stem from this source. This is illustrated by settlements, certain houses of which could even reflect the ancient circumpolar world, which were frequently adjacent to shores, and the abundant evidence of fishing and the hunting of seals and land fauna as well as, not least, the persistence of the limpet economy. Many of the flakes with pronounced side and end retouch may echo the elegant non-geometric assemblage which was seen as a feature of the Mesolithic South West at Dozmare Pool (Wainwright, 1960, 201) as may the numerous scrapers, many of which are on blades. The profusion of arrowheads, which could have been used in the pursuit of sea mammals as well as those of land, show the importance of hunting. Indeed, in the earlier stages cereal cultivation and stock-raising may have been but an adjunct to the hunting and collecting practices. Further to this, with the range of stamped decoration on the Knackyboy and other Scillonian pottery in mind, there are grounds for considering the early Scillonian phase as part of a wider Western, Atlantic-Irish Sea process where an indigenous population adopted, at various stages, such Neolithic traits as pottery making and cereal cultivation.

At the risk of repetition, the early Scillonian economy must be briefly mentioned again. Seemingly, society, in terms of material culture and thus structure, changed; the land-sea subsistence economy remained apparently unchanged throughout. The importance of limpets in this circumstance is that they were an easily obtainable supply of protein in advance of that produced by the land-based economy. With such an advantage it is even possible, bearing in mind the number of sites both domestic and funerary on the islands, that an above-mainland average population density was built up and obtained right through the second and into the first millennium BC. Indeed, insular self-containment could have brought about what has been termed (Piggott, 1965, 17) a 'conserving' society. This means one of two things, first of all that the mode of life, once established within the compass of the islands, was deemed satisfactory and thus the communal consciousness was opposed to change or, secondly, that there was such a delicate adjustment to the habitat that this imposed a measure of social rigidity so that change, other than in certain aspects of the spectrum of material culture, was impossible. Presumably, each circumstance affected the other.

The life pattern on the Isles of Scilly was at first a prolonged, stone-using, Neolithic system (for stray imported metal objects do not warrant the term 'Bronze Age'), which lasted until about 700–250 BC (thermo-luminescent date for Nornour early sherds, Zimmerman and Huxtable, 1969). This was followed by the later changes which, although involving what must be termed Iron Age, Romano-British and even post-Roman products, seems to have had little effect upon certain aspects of the basic stone technology nor upon the pursuance of the land-sea subsistence economy.

A constantly recurring feature of such Scillonian settlement sites as have been archaeologically investigated is continuity of habitation. At Halangy Porth, St Mary's, the 'Late Neolithic' settlement was abandoned because of the encroachment of blown sand and, seemingly, the people moved up the hill-side on to their field-system, into new buildings which were used and progressively modified until post-Roman times. On Nornour a similar pattern of continued use and modification can be seen within a closely-knit complex of stone buildings, while much the same situation appears to have obtained on St Martin's.

These Scillonian occupation sites occur at roughly regular intervals about the northern parts of the islands and in instances it is possible to point to an approximate area, as for example the early field-system and downs about Halangy, and consider the possibility of 'territories'. Such territories or catchment areas (Harriss, 1971, 53) could be based upon the eco-geographical concept of limits around a settlement within which it is economically practicable to use available resources. On Scilly such limits would define areas of cultivation, grazing and collection. With material change in mind, against the backcloth of a seemingly constant economy, in an island habitat which is, on the one hand, at a sufficient remove from the mainland to make it isolated and, on the other, close enough to larger land masses to be open to stimuli from quite a wide variety of sources, one can, at an appropriate juncture, examine the nature of the agencies promoting such change. For what we are seeking is the dynamic of this early community in its environmental and historical context.

The material culture of the 'Late Neolithic' phase of the occupation of the Isles of Scilly is characterised, first of all by the chamber tombs and the domestic sites and, secondly, by the associated artifacts, pottery, flintwork, some bone points and the bronze pieces. Closely linked are the flint industries and certain stray objects, the axes and battle-axe. All have been discussed in detail in preceding chapters, but the 'part of a bowl like the usual neolithic pottery of Britain' (Hencken, 1932, 24; Grimes, 1960, 177) has never been traced.

It is not possible, at the present time, to indicate a developmental sequence for the Scillonian chamber tombs for, in spite of differences of size, chamber form and construction, they are of markedly simple uniform plan and appearance. In general, the basic components, common to all the series, show little variation; even when portal stones flank the entrance to chambers they seem only to be a continuation of the principle of a surrounding kerb. Notwithstanding, there are instances where the presence of what has been called an extension 'collar' or 'surround' has led one to suspect that in the course of time specific tombs were modified. It has recently been claimed (Henshall, 1972, 255) that the Scillonian tombs, and their fellows in the Tramore district of Co Waterford, in the south of Ireland, have early features because they are 'minimal' cairns, because of their cairn enlargements which involve 'passage' extensions and on account of their tendency, in instances, to linear grouping. Such a view involves the application to the Scillonian scene of diagnostic criteria developed in distant Scotland and might involve the consideration that further development could have taken place. Indeed, in a society which diverted such a proportion of its energies to tomb building, it is of note that the uniformity of basic design persisted and that progressive developments are so few.

Although the affinities of the overall structure of the Scillonian chamber tombs can be indicated with fair precision, like so many of their kind their origins are not immediately apparent. The outlying Irish counterparts, to which attention was directed in 1941 (Powell, *PPS*, 1941) are five in number and, as just mentioned, are situate in the region inland from Tramore Bay, Co Waterford. Two have been excavated: Harristown (Hawkes, 1941) and Carriglong (Powell, *JCHAS*, 1941). At both sites clear signs of burning, preceding building, were observed, while the pottery sherds from Carriglong were of food vessels, quite different from the Scillonian pottery. When the affinities of this Scilly-Tramore group, as it came to be termed (Daniel and Powell, 1949, 178, Fig 2) were discussed, the possibility of a connection with the Boyne passage graves (Ó Ríordáin and Daniel, 1964) was mooted. Since then this prescient suggestion has received a measure of confirmation; excavations at Townlyhall, Co Louth (Eogan, 1963) and Knowth (Eogan, *Antiquity*, 1963; 1968) have disclosed similar monuments. The Townlyhall chamber was parallel-sided and set within a complex, collar-extended cairn, while certain satellite monuments set around the great passage grave at Knowth (eg Eogan, 1968, 318, Fig 9) seem closely allied to the Scilly-Tramore series. The first chamber to be found in the great passage grave (Eogan, 1967, 303, Fig 1) with its angled passage and sill-stoned chamber, recalls the passage and chamber of the so-called passage grave on Porth Hellick Down, St Mary's (H1:D7). Mention might also be made of the Mound of the Hostages, at Tara (Ó Ríordáin and Daniel, 1964, 97) which has a not-dissimilar chamber segmented by sill-stones. Far to the north, in Scotland, and at a considerable remove from Scilly, there is the White Cairn, Bargrennan, Galloway (Piggott and Powell, 1948-9, 144-53), and other monuments (Henshall, 1972, 449, 539) considered to bear a striking resemblance to the Scillonian series. The pottery from the White Cairn stands apart from southern Scottish wares and, strangely, its stamped and impressed ornament distantly recalls Scillonian pottery.

There are other chamber tombs, beyond Britain and Ireland, not unlike those of the Isles of Scilly. Hencken (1932, 28, 63) refers to Breton and Spanish 'galleries' and comments upon the Spanish character of the large slab, separating passage from chamber, in the passage grave on Porth Hellick Down. Indeed, perusal of Leisner's ordered series (Leisner, G. and V., 1943; 1956) would undoubtedly disclose tombs superficially resembling those of Scilly, while others could be located in Brittany (L'Helgouach, 1965), the Channel Islands (Kendrick, 1928, 104, Fig 36; Hawkes, 1939, 214, Fig 56) and deep in France (Daniel, 1960, 177-87). In this particular context it must be borne in mind that comparisons between chamber tombs in widely separated areas, especially when questions of supposed genetic relationships are sought, are beset with pitfalls and danger. For although aspects of the architecture of the Scillonian chamber tombs are widespread, for example the 'collars' suggesting enlargements have clear counterparts in Brittany (L'Helgouach, 1965, 27), this need indicate nothing more than the apparent homogeneity of the stone-built chamber-tomb tradition imposed by the medium. At the most it could be claimed that the recurrence, in various associations, forms and permutations, of basic elements—the forecourts, façades, passages and chambers, etc—in widely separated areas, could show the underlying European unity of the tomb-builders' forbears.

In the circumstances, a search for the origins of the Scillonian chamber tombs can yield but little. Their components, described in detail in a preceding chapter, are a drum-like kerbed cairn, rarely developed, with chambers which are rectangular, trapezoidal or coffin-shaped in plan, sometimes with passages. For the most part, the rites appear to have adhered to what were Late Neolithic practices in southern England. As seems likely in respect to certain stone-built long barrows (Daniel, 1967), the distinctive Scillonian stone structures might even have their ultimate origins in a memory and appreciation of timber and earthen monuments. Circularity as a concept in domestic and funerary structures appears in Late Neolithic and Beaker contexts and it seems likely that certain of our round barrows were post-revetted (Ashbee, 1957), in a manner similar to some of our earthen long barrows. The drum-shape of a Scillonian stone-bounded cairn would resemble such a timber-revetted round barrow, while the simple rectilinear chambers might equally well be translations into stone of timber mortuary houses. Indeed, long barrow derived and diminished mortuary houses are not unknown in round barrows. Such a mortuary house was a feature of the Crig-a-mennis, Liskey, barrow in Cornwall (Christie, 1960, Pl XVI), while a Beaker grave was in a mortuary house on Earl's Farm Down in Wiltshire (Christie, 1967, 339, 341, Fig 5).

It seems that no great significance can be put upon the rite of cremation, unurned or more rarely inurned, which is a feature of the Scillonian chamber tombs. In England, Late Neolithic usages of the rite were found at Dorchester (Atkinson, et al, 1951), while it was a regular feature of a range of Bronze Age round barrows (Ashbee, 1960). Cremation was, however, a feature of the comparable Tramore chamber tombs at Harristown (Hawkes, 1941) and Carriglong (Powell, *JCHAS*, 1941), probably at two of the satellite tombs at Knowth (Eogan, 1968, 308, 321), and in a pit by the entrance to the chamber of the White Cairn, Bargrennan (Piggott and Powell, 1948–9, 150).

Although the Scillonian chamber tombs can be seen as a Beaker continuum/Late Neolithic phenomenon, they persist, in a temporal sense, into what is termed the Bronze Age elsewhere in Britain. Indeed, in a ceramic and general sense O'Neil (1952) always considered them, and the associated settlement sites, as referable to this archaeological division. For long, the classic burial rite of the Bronze Age (Ashbee, 1960) has been considered as 'single grave' burial, introduced by Beaker immigrants and adopted and developed by native regional groups. Yet, while this brought about furnished 'individual' burials, it is by no means evident that the practice of collective burial ceased. Indeed, furnished burials are a minority and anonymous 'collective' burial, unurned or inurned is widespread. The collective rite of the Neolithic is inherent, and persists, in the 'multiple-cist' cemetery cairns (Savory, 1972), the open and enclosed collared urn, and the 'Deverel-Rimbury' cemeteries (Ashbee, 1960, 81–4). Lynch (1971, 54) has stressed that, although the definition of a cemetery mound is often difficult, there is good ground for considering that the majority of round barrows and cairns in Wales may have been of this character.

Such cairns are not absent in Cornwall, as for example at Crig-a-mennis (Christie, 1960), although here the 'cemetery' aspect was minimal, and Glendorgal (Dudley, 1962) where cists were seemingly the individual repositories. An alternative view, therefore, is that the Scillonian rite is not out of keeping with developments elsewhere upon the mainland of Britain in spite of its apparent archaism. Indeed, the occasional occurrence of inurned cremations would strengthen this affinity.

Two house-plan traditions were current in Scilly during the early stage: the houses at English Island Carn and Halangy Porth were roughly rectangular while the remainder were oval or, apparently, circular in plan. Their small size, the sub-rectangular hut at Halangy Porth was no more than about 12ft in length, and, for the most part, rough construction, makes them comparable with the small series of Late Neolithic and Beaker houses known from both Britain and Ireland (McInnes, 1971; Simpson, 1971). A stone-and-post structure found beneath a cairn at Mount Pleasant, Glamorgan (Savory, 1953) is very similar to the house at English Island Carn, while the remains of the well-built rectangular structure, still visible in the cliff at Halangy Porth recalls, in plan, the mortuary house found beneath a round barrow at Beaulieu, in Hampshire (Piggott, 1943) and its Altheim continental counterparts on the Goldberg (Childe, 1950, 125).

The pottery associated with both chamber tombs and houses is distinctive and clearly of a style which is confined to the islands. Such comparisons as have been made with material from other regions have tended to emphasise this factor. Hencken (1932, 28) saw similarities in the series from Breton chamber tombs and was at pains to emphasise incised decoration, although he considered cord-ornament a 'British' characteristic. O'Neil (1952, 29) invoked 'Deverel-Rimbury', adding that Brittany could have been a potential source of 'influence'. Grimes (1960, 176) looked also to Brittany, via the Cornish ribbon-handled urns (Patchett, 1944, 26ff) and, to him, the Salakee Down sherds were acceptable as a Scillonian version of Deverel-Rimbury pottery and thus, perforce, Late Bronze Age. These were conclusions based upon the pottery and the assumed age of the Deverel-Rimbury 'urnfields' of

Wessex. Such 'urnfields' were assigned to the Late Bronze Age because it was thought that they could not be earlier than their apparent continental counterparts. With the recognition of Late Neolithic cremation cemeteries this doctrine became inoperative. Indeed, as Burgess (1969) has emphasised, little of our Bronze Age pottery is readily datable and the so-called 'Deverel-Rimbury' culture, strictly speaking a Dorset phenomenon, is, upon evidence of association, a feature of the Middle Bronze Age.

The Cornish counterpart of the Deverel-Rimbury group and the Scillonian ceramics is what has been termed Trevisker pottery (ApSimon and Greenfield, 1972). A sequence, supported by stratigraphy, at the type site, Trevisker Round, St Eval, has been offered, while stylistic derivatives are seen as far afield as Wessex. While cord-ornament and superficially similar incised decoration, barrel and bucket shapes and zonal decoration presuppose a positive link with the Scillonian series, both comb-stamped ornament and positive biconical forms are absent, as are basal mat-impressions. Indeed, the only positive tie with the islands is the character of the diminutive vessels from Nornour which are associated with a late phase and could well be of a deliberately conceived archaic nature. The origins of Trevisker pottery must lie in the earlier ceramic traditions of the Cornubian peninsula but a positive lineage is lacking. What does emerge, with substance and clarity, however, is the decorative debt to Bell Beaker sources which could be the common stock from which the Scillonian urns and Trevisker pottery, tempered by other factors, emanates.

As has been stressed, the Scillonian barrel-, biconical-, and bucket-form urns and pots, the upper half of which frequently bears varieties of stamped ornamentation, are restricted to the Isles of Scilly and cannot be considered in isolation. The pottery in a few instances has associations; there were, for example, flint scrapers in the house at English Island Carn, a possible awl from May's Hill, a barbed and tanged arrowhead which was found in the settlement debris at Halangy Porth, while the chamber tombs have produced a flint axe, a recognisable bronze awl and some bone points. In general such flint industries as have been located on the islands include scrapers, some of which are tanged, barbed and tanged arrowheads and blades, some fine-grained rock axes, perforated maces and, significantly, a battle-axe. This general evidence, exiguous though it is, has the appearance of a Late Neolithic or Beaker context. A regular feature of early Scillonian pottery is decoration by means of stamped 'comb' impressions, reminiscent of the technique employed upon beakers. With this characteristic in mind, and the general bias of the material which is directly and indirectly associated, as well as the chamber tombs, their rite, and the nature of the houses, it is possible to consider this particular Scillonian phase as largely a Beaker successor or derived phenomenon. A characteristic of the Beaker groups is the manner in which they adopted elements of material culture and burial rites of indigenous populations. The substance of this process which has been outlined in ceramic terms (Clarke, 1970, 266-75) would seem to be the rule for houses as well (Simpson, 1971, 131-51), and they undoubtedly obtained access to a number of chamber tombs (eg Powell, ed, 1969, 153-61). A particular aspect of this process was seen at Gwithian (Simpson, 1971, 138), on the Cornish mainland, where coarse pottery with chevron cord-ornament, considered to imitate beakers, was found in association with worn Bell Beaker wares. Within the confines of the Channel Islands, Clarke (1970, 138) has shown how beakers have influenced local wares, indeed, the well-known secondary vessels from the La Varde passage grave (Kendrick, 1928, 113) are comparable with specific British beakers. The stray stone battle-axes, and a pendant from Sark, are stressed, and down-Channel movement is suggested. At about the same time a distinctive insular culture emerged in the distant Shetland Islands (Calder, 1955-6). Here the pottery is reminiscent of Beaker and Neolithic styles and there are miniature stone battle-axes and a whetstone which, as in Scilly, indicate an approximate horizon. It is possible that the Scillonian comb-stamp and horizontal-line ornamentation on the distinctive pottery may stem from such a process. In such circumstances the emergence of a distinctive isolated insular Scillonian society, combining characteristics from seemingly diverse Late Neolithic and perhaps, Bell Beaker sources, is not surprising. What is, however, the prime factor is that, once established, it persisted with little or no change for more than a millennium.

The affinities of the 'Iron Age' phase of the Isles of Scilly are those to be found for pottery, a few stone-built huts and the promontory forts. Nornour's Iron Age wares are those of the Cornish mainland and thus relationships with a wide range of sites could be inferred, while the simple huts are similarly widespread in the South West. Save for the new pottery, exiguous traces of iron working and the odd bead, there is nothing to distinguish these structures from the earlier phase. With the exception of some pottery, the whereabouts of which cannot be traced, there is nothing especially indicative of specific relationships for the Scillonian promontory forts with their numerous kin on the western seaboards of Europe.

Although the Scillonian cist graves have Iron Age counterparts in Cornwall (Hencken, 1932, 115–21; Fox, 1964, 113), and apparently early roots in Scilly, they are all of the Roman period, extending up to the third century AD. It is possible to see not unconvincing fellows in Brittany (Giot, 1960, 184) with, making allowances for the mechanism of discovery, a coastal distribution, recalling, in a limited manner, that of the promontory forts. Cemeteries of considerable size, with burials ranging from the Iron Age to Roman times, have been found there. The interments were more or less contracted, and often on their backs, in graves. Most of these graves were lined with slabs on edge or dry-stone walling, and large slabs were sometimes used: this is in essence the constructional modes of the Scillonian cists which are also in cemeteries. Cist cemeteries are also a feature of the Channel Islands (Hawkes, 1939, 173).

As in Cornwall (Thomas, 1966) the 'Iron Age' and 'Roman' times are a continuous process exhibiting little change other than in pottery and the presence of a range of imported objects. Up to the present, the fragmentary material culture of those who lived upon Halangy Down and other such sites has, by reason of its paucity, given an impression of cultural poverty. One can see the Isles of Scilly, the

SCILLONIAN COMMUNITIES: ORIGINS AND AFFINITIES

geographical continuation of Cornwall, as sharing the demonstrable poverty of the Dumnonii (Thomas, 1966, 76, Fig 2). Yet the cellular courtyard houses, as on Halangy Down and suspected elsewhere, were not unsubstantial when seen in terms of time and place. Good imported pottery such as Samian and Castor wares has been found on the islands, as well as the brooches, evidently produced locally, while a mould for the manufacture of metal dishes has been found on Halangy Down. Something of what could be concentrated in terms of material culture, albeit upon an exceptional, possibly ritual, site, has come to light on Nornour, while the fragments garnered from other broadly contemporary house sites on St Martin's supplement this picture. All in all there seems to have been a standard of life not without its veneer of sophistication, nor without communication with Cornwall and beyond. In short, the mores of the Celtic world, a modicum of ostentation in rustic surround, obtained in Scilly. Thus while the islands may seem at first sight merely a remote outpost of a region, itself regarded as beyond Roman Britain, an explanation should be sought as to the circumstances by which such a range of its products were obtained and copied.

Post-Roman times can scarcely be separated from time preceding though expressed almost entirely in terms of pottery types. Post-Roman pottery on Scilly is little more than a series of simplified, and presumably locally made, versions of forms current in the preceding centuries, leavened by the imported wares. Whether they came to Scilly directly from the Cornish mainland, or via various entrepots, is a matter for speculation. Grass-marked pottery (Thomas, 1968) which, in the fulness of time, superseded the ultimate Roman wares, would appear to have had its origins in Northern Ireland and its appearance in Cornwall and Scilly may, in the first instance, be indicative of Irish immigration. Such pottery, known from only four Scillonian sites, is associated with imported eastern Mediterranean wares. This imported pottery is considered to be a reflection of the ramifications of a trade process involving oil and wine, and to be connected, rather tenuously, with early Christianity. The establishment of Early Christian installations upon Scilly, discussed in a previous chapter, may, perhaps, account for its presence. Bar-lip pottery, as found on St Martin's, may result from the journeyings of Frisian traders (Thomas, 1968, 326) and in Cornwall its coastal distribution is marked (Thomas, 1968, 325, Fig 75). A wide range of objects and materials, from far-flung sources, was a feature of the monastic site on St Helen's (O'Neil, 1964); there are links with Wessex and France. Here, however, we are in the Middle Ages.

The continuity of Scillonian economy and settlement has been stressed and something of a succession of archaeological stages has been seen. Such a succession implies change and, in such a circumstance, it is pertinent to enquire of the factors involved: why a particular mode of burial was abandoned and another adopted or why certain promontories were fortified? In aggregate there are few factors in the archaeological record which can be isolated as indicative of the dynamics of change within the available range of material culture. Many of the agencies of cultural change may affect factors in early society, such as 'trade', which are not readily archaeologically detectable.

When the first communities established themselves on Scilly they instigated the pattern of life that built the chamber tombs and used Knackyboy pottery. Little change can be detected during the time-span of this stable adjustment to the character of the particular insular environment. O'Neil (1952, 29), however, from the stratigraphy of the Knackyboy chamber and a considered use-life of half a millennium, considered that plain pottery and that ornamented with horizontal lines represented a later period. If cist-grave burial be considered intrusive, that is introduced by people from another Atlantic region, the cists containing cremations and Knackyboy type pottery could be seen as the adoption of an alien rite. Such cists could, however, represent a compromise between the tenets of the chamber-tomb rite and the single-grave concept. These early cists can be seen as the genesis of the later rite on Scillonian soil. That is, the Porth Cressa cist-grave cemetery rite could well be the product of an indigenous evolutionary process.

Precisely why, in about 400 BC, pottery styles changed and wares, comparable with the Iron Age series of the mainland, became the norm, evades us. There is, again, the question of the promontory forts. The few examples on the headlands of Scilly might conceivably be part of a diffusive process which set these structures in great number right around our Atlantic coasts. However, as Savory (1971, 259) has pointed out, there are a number of promontory forts on the western fringes of France which appear to have been built at some time in the Bronze Age. Thus one could envisage the early establishment of such forts in the South West, if not in Scilly. It seems likely that these forts, even in Scilly, reflect processes long at work, the 'Heroic' society of the Bronze Age (Ashbee, 1960, 172) in a developed form. These defended areas, dominating small separate tracts of land, could well reflect the bellicose territoriality of indigenous early Scillonians.

Roman times and a reversion to undefended structures of substance, as shown by the courtyard-house phase on Halangy Down, would be a change brought about by that Pax Romana which brought slow but perceptible change to Dumnonia (Thomas, 1966, 85–98) and, thus, ultimately to Scilly.

At specific junctures the processes of Scillonian submergence (Chapter 3) could also have exerted pressures upon certain localities and could have been an agent of change. Sand duning, a product of submergence, brought about the final abandonment of the Halangy Porth settlement and the shift to higher ground. Destruction of low-lying land, although a slow process in terms of a given human life, would seem to have diminished the catchment area of Halangy and elsewhere. This would presumably have brought about adjustments between the communities on Scilly and such site catchment area changes would ultimately have had an effect upon patterns of settlement. The processes which eventually separated the islands were in train and the population would have reacted accordingly.

Post-Roman times, imported pottery and Irish immigration would be further agencies of change as would the establishment of Christian enceintes. By this time the islands were separate or near-separate enough to have received individual names and we pass on to the changes that can be inferred from Scilly's written history.

Although changes in material culture, and minor adjustments of essential habitation modes have been shown, it is questionable as to whether, after the initial establishment of permanent communities, there was, during the two-and-a-half millennia treated, any inherent change in the real patterns of Scillonian life. For like so much of the South West, distant from the Celtic urban centres which had emerged by the time of the ultimate Roman Imperial annexation of Britain, Scilly displays a modest range of dispersed rural and repetitive settlement, lacking social focus and related merely to landscape and the all-embracing sea. Only much later and in response to extraneous stimuli—Ennor Castle and Star Castle—did the Old Town and the Hugh Town evolve as modest expressions of mainland dictates, in contrast with the innate island terrain.

To quote William Borlase, who began the processes of systematic Scillonian archaeology, this book could well have been entitled: 'Of the great alterations which the Islands of Scilly have undergone in the time of the Ancients'. Scilly today would still be familiar to William Borlase and, indeed, parts of it at least might not be unfamiliar to the anonymous characters who strode the stage of earlier times. Its besetting problem is whether or not its unique environment can withstand the pressures exerted upon it by the current population explosion in terms of physical impact by visitors, for tourism is now a major industry, and the development that comes in their wake. Like all past change, this is a problem that the Scillonians must face. To return to William Borlase (1756), I can but conclude with the closing words of his *Observations on the Ancient and Present State of the Islands of Scilly* that '… though these Islands are so near to us, they are very little known, and much less valued than in all reason they ought to be'.

APPENDIX 1

Chamber Tombs and Barrows

Note: the chamber tombs of Scilly were initially listed by Hencken (1932, 317–18) who, under the headings of the respective islands, assigned numbers to them. Daniel (1950, 242–50), following fieldwork in 1936 and 1946, modified and extended Hencken's pioneer survey, while giving everywhere references to his numbering. Fieldwork on St Mary's during 1949 and 1950, by the present writer, resulted in a series of sketch plans of sites not illustrated by Hencken together with notices of a number of cairns (Ashbee, 1963), some of which, unbeknown, had been listed by Daniel. A survey of chamber tombs on Teän and Old Man during 1956 (Thomas, 1957) adhered to and extended the Hencken-Daniel system. The following list is by no means exhaustive; it is intended as a basis for further work. Many groups of considerable complexity, for example the concentrations of cairns on Shipman Head Down, Bryher, are largely unexamined and unlisted.

Key to lists: H=Hencken; D=Daniel; A=Ashbee. Where necessary the lists are amplified by notes of specific depositions on various islands.

ARTHUR

H1:D1 On highest point of Great Arthur. Cairn 24ft in diameter, with double concentric stone-block revetment. Chamber 12ft in length, 2ft 6in wide at entrance and 5ft wide at middle. Chamber orientation: NNE/SSW.

H2:D2 On Middle Arthur. Cairn 20ft in diameter, chamber 13ft in

APPENDIX I—CHAMBER TOMBS AND BARROWS

              length and 3ft 6in in width. Chamber orientation: NW/SE. Site much ruined and overgrown.

H3:D3   On Middle Arthur and about 50ft to the south of H2:D2. Cairn 10ft 6in in diameter, chamber 8ft in length, 4ft in width at distal end and 3ft 3in in height. Chamber orientation: NNE/SSW. Excavated in 1953 by B. H. StJ. O'Neil (O'Neil, 1954).

Note: on Little Arthur a linear cairn cemetery running from NW to SE and called, by Daniel, Little Arthur A,B,C,D,E; E being the cairn to the SE.

H4:D4(C) Chamber orientation: NNW/SSE.

H5:D5(D) A small circular chambered cairn on the highest point of the island.

D6   A small chambered cairn to the west of H1:D1 (Great Arthur).

D7(A),
D8(B) and
D9(E)   All appear to be small chambered cairns.

BRYHER

Samson Hill

H1:D1   On south of hill and immediately to south of Carn of Works. Cairn 24ft in diameter and set around with stones. Chamber, coffin-shaped, 19ft 10in in length, 2ft 2in in width at entrance, 4ft 9in in width at middle and 3ft 8in in width at distal end. Chamber orientation: NE/SW.

H2:D7   Immediately to north of Bonfire Carn. Cairn survives but chamber has been destroyed.

H3:D8   To the north of Bonfire Carn. Cairn survives but chamber has been destroyed.

—   On the summit of the hill, just to the NE of Top Rock, the lower courses of a cairn, at least 70ft in diameter, can be seen. It is possible that its chamber was cruciform in the

APPENDIX I—CHAMBER TOMBS AND BARROWS

manner of a passage grave. Only excavation could clarify this possibility.

Gweal Hill

H4:D3   Ruined chambered cairn. Chamber orientation appears to have been SSE/NNW.

H5:D4   Hencken claimed that a second chambered cairn stood on Gweal Hill but none of the numerous small cairns display overt traces of a chamber.

Shipman Head Down

H6:D2   A cairn 60ft in diameter, on the south-western flank of the down, with traces of an erstwhile chamber.

H7:D6   A cairn, with no outward traces of a chamber, on northern flank of down.

H8:D5   A cairn, with no outward traces of a chamber, on the south-eastern side of the down.

Note: there is an extensive system of linear cairn cemeteries on Shipman Head Down. Only a methodical survey and a searching scrutiny would determine their character. A few of the small cairns are in the positions given to them on the 6in OS Map (Sheet LXXXII NW).

GUGH

Kittern Hill

H1:D5   Obadiah's Barrow, excavated by G. Bonsor in 1901 (Hencken, 1933, 20-4), the northerly of two cairns on the south-western flank of Kittern Hill, overlooking the bar from Gugh to St Agnes. Cairn 24ft in diameter, chamber, entered by a short angled passage, 16ft in length, 5ft in width and 3ft 1in in height. Chamber orientation: SE/NW.

H2:D2   The next to the most northerly of the linear cairn cemetery (from the NW: D1,D2,D3,D4,D9,D10,D11) that lines Kittern Hill and is visible from St Mary's. Cairn 35ft in diameter, chamber 12ft in length, 4ft 4in in width and

APPENDIX I—CHAMBER TOMBS AND BARROWS

3ft 6in in height. Chamber orientation: NE/SW (Plan, Hencken, 1933, 19, Fig 6, 20, Fig 7).

H3:D1   The most northerly of the linear cairn cemetery; it lies just to the north of the Trigonometrical Station (100.8) at the northern end of Kittern Hill. A cairn with traces of a chamber.

H4:D9   A circular cairn, with stone surround, that may have contained a chamber.

H5:D10 A circular cairn that may have contained a chamber.

H6:D11 A circular cairn that may have contained a chamber.

H7:D3   A cairn, on the highest point of Kittern Hill, which contained a chamber, orientation: E/W. The covering stones of the chamber had been removed and lay at a distance (Hencken, 1933, 20).

H7a:D12 A cairn, considered to be too small to have contained a chamber. It lies between H7:D3 and H8:D4.

H8:D4   The last, and most south-westerly, chambered cairn of the linear cemetery.

H11:D6 Carn Valla, the southerly companion of Obadiah's Barrow, on the south-western flank of Kittern Hill. The cairn was apparently chambered although, today, it is much ruined.

South Hill

H9:D8   A cairn, 30ft in diameter, with a chamber 4ft 9in wide in the middle, which appears to have occupied almost its whole diameter. Chamber orientation: SE/NW. It is sited on a prominence to the south-west of Carn of Works and adjacent to the shore.

H10:D7 A substantial cairn, 75ft in diameter, with a chamber 4ft 10in in width, sited upon Carn of Works. Chamber orientation: NE/SW.

NORTHWETHEL

H:D   On the hill at the south-eastern end of the island: a cairn

APPENDIX I—CHAMBER TOMBS AND BARROWS

stone-block surrounded, 18ft in diameter, chamber 10ft 2in in length and 4ft 6in in width at its broad end. This chamber has a narrow entrance and is pronouncedly coffin-shaped in plan. Two cover-stones survive. Chamber orientation: E/W (Plan, Hencken, 1932, 25, Fig 11, B).

Note: a number of cairns, comprising a nuclear cemetery, are around the periphery and upon the highest part of this small island.

St Martin's

Cruther's Hill

H1:D2　On the central knoll of Cruther's Hill: a cairn 27ft in diameter, chamber 15ft in length, 2ft 10in in width at the entrance and 4ft 6in in width at the distal end. Chamber orientation: E/W. The floor and part of the side of this chamber is the natural granite rock and some fashioning of this is suspected. Natural outcrops are incorporated in the cairn.

D1　On the northern knoll of Cruther's Hill: cairn 20ft in diameter, demarcated by substantial stone blocks and outcrops of the natural rock. Chamber 18ft in length, orientation: NNE/SSW.

D3　The northernmost of the two cairns on the southern knoll of Cruther's Hill: a cairn 20ft in diameter with a chamber orientated SE/NW.

D4　The southernmost of the two cairns on the southern knoll of Cruther's Hill: a cairn, much ruined, appears to have been about 20ft in diameter and chambered.

Top Rock Hill

D5　There are traces of two cairns on this hill and the northernmost would appear to have been large enough to have contained a chamber.

APPENDIX I—CHAMBER TOMBS AND BARROWS

St Martin's Head

D6 Troutbeck (1794, 108) records a chamber 8ft in length and 3ft in width near St Martin's Head. This was, presumably, near the Day Mark and on the highest point of Chapel Down.

Note: there are traces that suggest the erstwhile existence of a number of cairns on the western side of Chapel Down. They could well have been destroyed for their stone content when the Watch House, adjacent to the Day Mark, was built.

Gun Hill

D7 The site marked as 'Stone Circle' on the 6in OS Map (Sheet LXXXII, NE and SE), and just to the north-east of English Island Carn, appears to be a ruined chambered cairn.

Knackyboy Cairn

D8 Just to the east of Yellow Rock Carn and crossed by the remains of a field-wall: cairn, which incorporates a massive outcrop of natural rock, 50ft in diameter, chamber 12ft in length, 2ft 6in in width at the entrance and 3ft in width at the distal end. Chamber orientation: E/W. Excavated during 1947 by B. H. StJ. O'Neil (O'Neil, 1952). Hencken, (1929, 89) was aware of a chamber tomb on St Martin's from which urns and other objects had been removed by Alexander Gibson. He records that 'On account of a local prejudice Mr. Gibson declines to indicate the exact position of this tomb and I have been unable to find it'. Daniel (1950, 125, 245) observes that it was impossible to obtain exact information as to its location and that it was probably a burial chamber. O'Neil (1952, 21, fn 4) concludes, after careful research on the island, that the site, dug into by Alexander Gibson in 1912, was the Knackyboy Cairn.

APPENDIX I—CHAMBER TOMBS AND BARROWS

White Island
>A cairn, 20ft in diameter, with a chamber 16ft in length, orientated SSE/NNW, lies on the northern hill of this island.

Tinkler's Hill
>Traces of a linear cairn cemetery on the crest of this hill are suggested by the remains of about four cairns.

Note: at least five small cairns lie on the southern slope of White Island's northern hill, which bounds Porth Morran on its northern side.

ST MARY'S

Normandy Down

H14:D5   A large, low cairn, the centre of three in a line running from west to east, 70ft in diameter. Stones, standing in a hollow in the centre of the cairn, suggest a chamber and a SE/NW orientation has been claimed for it. The narrow trench, running from the middle out to the north-western edge of the cairn, may result from an unrecorded excavation.

H15:D6   Cairn 36ft in diameter, the easternmost of the three, with stone-block surround. Chamber, perhaps closed, 14ft in length, 4ft in width at outer and 6ft in width at inner, distal, end. Chamber orientation: NW/SE. Two cover-stones remain. Cairn almost completely removed, chamber and cairn stones deeply weathered.

H6:D4   Cairn 23ft in diameter, the westernmost of the three, with a stone-block surround, a half of which has been removed. The rectangular chamber is 18ft in length and 4ft 8in in width. Chamber orientation: E/W (Plan, Hencken, 1932, 25, Fig 11, E).

Porth Hellick Down

H1:D7   At the northern end of Porth Hellick Down, a cairn 40ft in diameter, originally surrounded by a collar which was destroyed during restoration at the hands of the Ministry of

APPENDIX I—CHAMBER TOMBS AND BARROWS

Works. The chamber is 10ft in length, 4ft 6in in width and 3ft 6in in height. It is approached by an angled passage 14ft in length which is terminated at its distal end by a blocking stone which does not extend to the roof of the chamber. The roof is comprised of four large slab-like cover-stones. Excavated by G. Bonsor, who called it the 'Great Tomb' (Plan, Hencken, 1932, 21, Fig 8).

H3:D9   A cairn, with stone surround, 20ft in diameter, lying about 130yd due south of H1:D7. The rectangular chamber, 13ft in length and 4ft 3in in width, may have had a passage, 4ft 6in in length, leading into it. Chamber orientation: N/S (Plan, Daniel, 1950, 63, Fig 11, 2).

H5:D8   An oval cairn, with only a part of its stone surround remaining, 25ft in breadth and 29ft in length. It has a chamber, coffin-shaped in plan, 22ft long and 4ft 6in wide at its middle. Four cover-stones remain. Chamber orientation: E/W. It is the most westerly of the tombs on Porth Hellick Down (Plan, Daniel, 1950, 63, Fig 11, 4).

H11:D11 A circular cairn, 21ft in diameter, with stone surround and ruined chamber. Chamber orientation: ? NE/SW. It lies near Drum Rock and at about 50ft above sea-level to the west of Porth Hellick.

H12:DE A cairn, horse-shoe form in plan, built around a massive outcrop of natural rock. A chamber, 12ft in length, orientation: NW/SE, is built against and parallel to the outcrop. It lies about 240ft NNW of H13:D10 (Plan, Ashbee, 1963, 14, Fig 4, no 13).

H13:D10 A circular cairn, 20ft in diameter, with many of its surrounding stones missing. Its ruined chamber, orientated N/S, retains its distal end and one cover-stone. It lies about 120ft NNW of Old Rock.

DF   A small, much ruined, cairn, to the west of H12:DE.

DG   A cairn, 19ft in diameter, which is now the site of the Trigonometrical Station at Old Rock.

APPENDIX I—CHAMBER TOMBS AND BARROWS

DH A small cairn which lies between Old Rock and the Batteries.

Porth Hellick West Side

H9:D15 A cairn, the westernmost of three which lie just to the north of Pig Rock. It is 23ft in diameter, its demarcating stones remain and its chamber is 18ft in length. Chamber orientation: NNE/SSW (Plan, Ashbee, 1963, 12, Fig 3, no 9).

H10:D12 A ruined and overgrown cairn, built around an outcrop of natural rock. 31ft in diameter. Chamber orientation: N/S. It is the easternmost of the group (Plan, Ashbee, 1963, 12, Fig 3, no 10).

A25 A cairn, with its surrounding stones still remaining, 19ft in diameter. The chamber is 15ft in length and its orientation is E/W. At extreme eastern end of Salakee Down (Plan, Ashbee, 1963, 12, Fig 3, no 25).

D24 Site marked on 6in OS Map (Sheet LXXXVII SE) as 'Stone Circle' on Ward Hill to north of Salakee Down. Cairn about 40ft in diameter, with stone-block surround, destroyed chamber orientated NE/SW. Excavated by W. F. Grimes during 1942 (Grimes, 1960, 170–80).

D25 A ruined cairn, perhaps originally chambered, just to the north of Church Point.

Note: A number of small cairns are marked on 6in OS Map (Sheet LXXXVII SE) as on the slope just to the north of Church Point. No trace of these can be found but it is possible that they are blanketed by the peaty topsoil which mantles the down. Another cairn, to the east of the 'Stone Circle' is indicated on the OS Map: this could not be found in 1950. A cairn at the junction of three stone hedges, on high ground at the fringe of the marshes, just to the NE of Salakee House, was found during 1949 (Ashbee, 1963, f16).

Inner Blue Carn: it has been claimed that a dilapidated wall (Hencken, 1932, 31) connected these cairns. No trace of such a wall could be found in 1950. Their condition suggests that surrounds and chambers have long since been removed.

Innisidgen

H4:D2 Known often as Innisidgen Carn, it lies just to the west of the rocky carn of that name. The well-preserved stone surrounded cairn is 27ft in diameter. Clear traces of a surrounding collar, as at Bant's Carn, can be seen, although it is masked by the grassed area around it. The chamber, presumably approached by a passage, which would have been about 15ft in length through the collar, is 15ft in length and orientated SE/NW, coffin-shaped in plan and 5ft in width at the widest point and 3ft in width at the chamber entrance. This chamber is 5ft in height and still covered by five blocks of bolster-like character. This chamber height, the same as that of Bant's Carn, is considerably in excess of the average for the Scillonian series. The general character of the Innisidgen Carn, in terms of stone selection and architecture, might point to the work of the same tomb architect who built Bant's Carn (Plan and section by G. Bonsor, Hencken, 1933, 18, Fig 5; see also Daniel, 1950, 62, Fig 10, 4).

H17:D1 Known variously as 'Lower Innisidgen' or 'Innisidgen North', it lies on low ground close to the sea and about 300ft to the north of the Innisidgen Carn. The cairn is about 20ft in diameter, although most of the stone surround is missing, the chamber, trapezoid in plan and orientated E/W, is 3ft in width at the distal end and only 2ft in width at the entrance. Two cover-stones of slab character remain. In 1949 the site was overgrown and the chamber infilled with stones and soil. A clandestine 'excavation' took place in 1950 and the chamber's contents were thrown out and the interior bared. It is not known what, if anything, was found (Plan, Ashbee, 1963, 16, Fig 6).

APPENDIX I—CHAMBER TOMBS AND BARROWS

A21   A high cairn, 25ft in diameter, still stands in a bulb garden on Helvear Down, about 1,000ft to the NE of Higher Trenoweth Farm. Part of the stone surround survives on the eastern side and what may be the upper stones of a high chamber, are visible in the cairn's crown.

Mount Todden

H15a:D19   A cairn of which a few surrounding stones still remain, by the footpath from Mount Todden House to Mount Todden Battery, almost 30ft in diameter, incorporates an elongated natural rock outcrop. Three stones still extant in the robbed cairn suggest a chamber orientated NE/SW.

Pelistry

H16:D18   Near Toll's Hill, which bounds Pelistry Bay on its northern side, Borlase (1756, 28) records a cairn with a chamber 13ft 8in in length, 4ft 6in in width and 3ft 8in in height. It was called the 'Giant's Grave'. No trace remains.

Halangy Down

H2:D3   Bant's Carn stands on the steepest crest of Halangy Down above and just to the east of the Creeb Rocks. A high-standing cairn, retained by coursed walling of large stone blocks, 27ft in diameter, it is surrounded by an extension collar which is also demarcated by stone blocks. Thus the monument has been described (Daniel, 1950, 246) as a 'round barrow 38ft in diameter revetted by two walls of megaliths'. The chamber, 15ft in length and rectangular in plan, has an entrance flanked by substantial jamb-stones, which is approached by a passage, 15ft in length, through the collar surrounding the cairn. The chamber is 5ft in width and 5ft in height and is orientated SE/NW. Chamber height has been secured by the use of oversailing courses on the

APPENDIX I—CHAMBER TOMBS AND BARROWS

corbel principle. Like Innisidgen Carn (H4:D2) this chamber height is considerably more than that of the average height of Scillonian chambers. Four great slabs cover the chamber: until recently the outermost cover-stone was displaced and lay in the passage after an alleged attempt made to pull down the monument in about 1910. The cover-stone replacement operation was undertaken in 1970 (Ashbee, 1970, 70). The chamber was excavated by G. Bonsor and a plan and section made (Hencken, 1932, 22–4, Fig 10; 1933, 14, Figs 1, 2).

H2a:D14 A chamber, in a ruined cairn which is concealed by a substantial lynchet which runs parallel to the bottom of the Halangy Down escarpment. It lies due east of the Creeb Rocks. It is possible that part of the surround of this cairn was straight in a manner similar to H12:DE, for stones, seemingly *in situ*, remain to one side of the entrance. This chamber is 14ft in length and orientated E/W, trapezoidal in plan, 2ft in width at the entrance and 3ft in width at the inner distal end. It is about 3ft in height and two slab cover-stones remain. It was excavated in 1929 by A. Gray (Plan, Ashbee, 1963, 16, Fig 6).

Carn Morval Down

H18:D17 Bonsor observed a chambered cairn on Carn Morval Down (Hencken, 1929, 77), 27ft in diameter with a chamber 17ft in length, 5ft in width and orientated NE/SW. This cairn, which stands upon the crest of the escarpment above Carn Morval, appears to have been destroyed, in great part, by a military installation sited upon it during World War II.

Buzza Hill

H6a:D16 A cairn excavated by Borlase (1756, 29) who records that it housed a chamber, with jamb-stones at its entrance, 22ft in length and orientated NE/SW, 4ft 8in in width and 4ft 10in

APPENDIX I—CHAMBER TOMBS AND BARROWS

in height. Such a height is above the average for Scillonian chambers and thus this site should be compared with Innisidgen and Bant's Carns. It would appear to have been the largest of the three chamber tombs on Buzza Hill and may be the cairn on which the King Edward's Tower, formerly a windmill, stands (Gibson, 1932, 21).

H6b:D16 A smaller cairn, also excavated by Borlase (1756, 29), which contained a chamber, orientated ENE/WSW, 14ft long and 4ft in width 'in the middle' and 2ft in height. There was a circular pit in the floor of the chamber. This cairn lay 42ft to the north of H6a:D16.

H7:D13 Hencken (1932, 317) lists this site as a cairn 30ft in diameter containing a chamber 5ft in width, orientated E/W. Daniel (1950, 247) observes that the chamber is 20ft in length. At the present time the cairn appears to house a substantial closed cist, 8ft in length and 5ft in width. It is possible that a cover-stone has fallen into the chamber, closing off part of it and giving it this appearance. The site lies 150ft due west of the King Edward's Tower.

SAMSON

North Hill
Note: the twelve sites on North Hill are in two linear groups, those to the north of the highest point and those to the south of it. Daniel's numeration (Daniel, 1950, 249-50) progresses from north to south and thus it has been adhered to.

H6:D1 A cairn 20ft in diameter with traces of a chamber orientated NNE/SSW. It is the northernmost of the series and lies on the downward slope of the hill towards Bollard Point.

H7:D2 A cairn 17ft in diameter with a chamber 9ft long and 4ft wide at its middle point. Chamber orientation: E/W. It lies 45ft south of H6:D1.

H1:D5 A cairn 26ft in diameter with a chamber coffin-shaped in plan, 15ft in length and 4ft in width at its widest point and

APPENDIX I—CHAMBER TOMBS AND BARROWS

4ft in height. Two stones at the chamber entrance are larger than the remainder of the surround stones and were, perhaps, jamb-stones. Two cover-stones of slab character remain *in situ*. Chamber orientation: E/W. Excavated by H. O'Neil Hencken in 1930 (Hencken, 1933, 24-9, Fig 11). It lies 75ft to the east of H7:D2.

H8:D3   A cairn 35ft in diameter with a ruined chamber orientated N/S. It is the westernmost of two cairns which are just to the north of the highest point of the North Hill.

H9:D4   A cairn 25ft in diameter with traces of a chamber showing through the turf. It lies just to the south-east of H8:D3.

D17   A large cairn, the crown of which was dug into by Augustus Smith in 1862, to reveal a cist which is tongued and grooved together in a manner recalling timber techniques. Internal dimensions of cist: 3ft 9in by 2ft, cover-stone 4ft by 5ft 7in (Plan, S. Piggott, 1941, 82. This cairn lies 48ft to the south of H9:D4.

D15   A circular cairn with no outward signs of a chamber. It lies 60ft to the south of D17. The northernmost of the series south of the highest point of the North Hill.

H10:D6   A cairn 28ft in diameter with a ruined chamber orientated NE/SW. It lies about 50ft to the east of D15.

H11:D7   A cairn 19ft in diameter with a ruined chamber 3ft 6in in width, orientated SE/NW. It lies about 65ft to the south-west of H10:D6.

H12:D8   A cairn 21ft in diameter, with much of the stone surround missing on the eastern side, containing a chamber 4ft 9in in width. Chamber orientation: N/S. It lies about 75ft to the south-east of H11:D7.

H13:D13   A ruined cairn which may have contained a chamber. It lies about 200ft to the south of H12:D8.

H14:D14   A ruined cairn which may have contained a chamber. It lies about 50ft to the south of H13:D13.

APPENDIX I—CHAMBER TOMBS AND BARROWS

South Hill

H5:D9 A cairn 19ft in diameter containing a chamber 11ft 6in in length and 3ft in width. Chamber orientation: SSE/NNW. This cairn is the northernmost of the linear cemetery on the South Hill of Samson and lies just outside the stone hedge of the large abandoned enclosure.

Note: H4:D10, H3:D11 and H2:D12 are said to be enclosed by a single encircling wall (Hencken, 1932, 26; Daniel, 1950, 249). A visit, in the spring of 1969 when the bracken was low, and an inspection of this feature leads to the belief that it is nothing more than the natural configuration of the carn that is the South Hill. All these cairns are close together and in the above order from north to south.

H4:D10 A cairn with a chamber 12ft in length and 3ft in width. Chamber orientation: S/N.

H3:D11 A cairn with a much ruined chamber.

H2:D12 A cairn with a chamber 10ft 6in in length and 5ft 3in in width at its middle. Chamber orientation: SSE/NNW. The lower part of this chamber may well have been cut into the natural rock.

TEÄN AND OLD MAN

H1:D1 A circular cairn with a ruined chamber. Chamber orientation: E/W. One cover-stone is still in position. It is on the slope on the north side of the bay on the west side of Old Man.

H2:D2 A cairn, seemingly built on an artificially levelled area, about 25ft in diameter, containing a chamber, coffin-shaped in plan, 11ft in length, 3ft in width at its entrance, 7ft in width at the widest point and about 2ft 6in in height. Chamber orientation: NE/SW. A displaced cover-stone lies in the chamber and two others lie outside. They are of slab character. It is on the south side of the Great Hill of Teän, about 100ft below the rocky summit and is overshadowed by a ridge of granite outcrops.

APPENDIX I—CHAMBER TOMBS AND BARROWS

H3:D3   A bun-shaped cairn, 22ft in diameter, with a close-set stone-block surround, intact on the eastern side and built against natural outcrop on the northern side. The chamber is not visible, but two jamb-stone-like blocks on the south-western periphery suggest a chamber orientated SSW/NNE. It lies on the summit of the Great Hill.

Note: the chamber tombs of Teän and Old Man were examined during 1956 (Thomas, 1957), the tomb on Old Man was redesignated Teän 1 and the system, originated by Hencken (1932, 317–18) and extended by Daniel (1950, 242–50) followed.

TRESCO

Note: on Castle Down, the 6in OS Map (Sheet LXXXII, NW and SE) marks a line of about fourteen cairns, with outliers, extending from a point about 250ft south-east of the Gun Hill outcrop, at the northern end, to Beacon Hill. Most of these are small and ruined, although it seems likely that some had chambers. South of Tregarthen Hill, which is to the east of Gimble Point, and within the 100ft contour there are five cairns, four in a line from north-east to south-east, with one outlier to the west. All are chambered or appear to have been chambered. The most southerly is D2 and, to the north of this, there lies H1:D1. Three cairns are on Vane Hill to the north-east of New Grimsby.

H1:D1   A substantial cairn, 50ft in diameter, with a chamber 15ft in length and 5ft in width at its widest point. Chamber orientation: E/W.

D2   A cairn, 25ft in diameter, with the remains of a ruined chamber.

APPENDIX 2

Cists and Cist-grave Cemeteries

THE EARLIER CISTS

Cists beneath barrows

ST MARTIN'S During 1949, B. H. StJ. O'Neil excavated a small cairn-covered cist on Par Beach. A sherd of early pottery was close by, but unstratified.

SAMSON A rectangular tongued and grooved cist beneath a cairn (D17) contained an unurned cremation (Crawford, 1928, 420; Piggott, 1941, 81-3).

Cists without a covering-cairn

ST MARY'S A slab-built cist, near Halangy Porth, produced pottery pronounced by Mr R. A. Smith of the British Museum as belonging to the 'Megalithic Period' of Scilly (Dowie, 1928-9, 243).

ST MARY'S A small, almost rectangular, cist was found in the Klondyke Field, by Telegraph Hill, at the close of the nineteenth century (Ashbee, 1953, 30).

ST MARY'S A cist containing a cremation and pot were found during building operations at Old Town in 1964 (Mackenzie, 1965, 30).

ST MARY'S A cist containing the base of an undecorated pot was found in the field on Content Farm, at the junction of Town Lane and Telegraph Hill, in 1939 (Ashbee, 1953, 29).

APPENDIX 2—CISTS AND CIST-GRAVE CEMETERIES

St Mary's — A cist was for long visible in the surface of Town Lane. Another is said to have existed close by (Crawford, 1928, 420, Pl III).

St Mary's — 'A plain urn, inclosing human bones, found in Mr. T. Smith's garden at Newfort ... in a vault'. Possibly a cist (Borlase, 1758, 322).

LATER CISTS OF PORTH CRESSA TYPE

Old Man — Skeleton had vanished but grave furniture, including brooches, was recovered (Tebbutt, 1934, 302–3).

St Martin's — A cist was found exposed in the cliff between Knackyboy Cairn and Yellow Rock Carn. Two amber beads and a scrap of iron comprised the grave furniture (Lewis, 1949, 84–5).

St Martin's — Perhaps two separate cemeteries? A cist on the shore, between Crethus (Cruther's) Hill and English Island Carn, contained a contracted inhumation burial. Nearby, to the west, were two or three other cists of the same type, and many years ago others were observed both round this bay (Troutbeck, 1794, 112) and at Lawrence's to the west of Crethus Hill (Crawford, 1928, 420).

St Mary's — A half of a cist is exposed in the cliff on the southern side of Halangy Porth (Ashbee, 1954, 25).

St Mary's — A cist discovered in the field to the south-west of Halangy Down during 1965 (Mackenzie, 1967, 111–12).

St Mary's — The cemetery at Porth Cressa. Ten cists and an earth-grave were examined. Grave furniture was bronze brooches in pairs, once singly and twice with pots (Ashbee, 1954, 1–25).

St Mary's — A cist cemetery in Poynter's Garden, near Porth Cressa. A broken bronze pin and some scraps of iron were the only objects from the eight cists found (Dudley, 1961, 221–31).

APPENDIX 3

Standing Stones

BRYHER	A great boulder, with twin axial perforations, which is close by the chapel (Gibson, 1932, 87).
GUGH	Standing stone to the south-east of Kittern Hill (Borlase, 1756, 40; Hencken, 1933, 20).
ST AGNES	A stone pillar called the 'Priest Rock' on the shore near the churchyard (Gibson, 1932, 98).
ST MARTIN'S	A fallen stone, on an 'adjoining Karn', seen by Borlase when he landed on this island (Borlase, 1756, 52).
	Gun Hill. A standing stone, ?modern (Lewis, 1948, 6).
ST MARY'S	*Halangy Down.* A long dressed stone, bearing on one face a relief motif, found beneath a floor in 1966 (Ashbee, 1966, 24, Pls VII, A, B).
	Halangy Down. A lozengiform block, with a heavy base, bearing cup and slot marks on one face, found beneath a floor in 1967 (Ashbee, 1968, 24).
	Harry's Walls. A slender angular stone standing in a small cairn. Often called the 'Day Mark' on account of the mark set to seaward of it (Borlase, 1756, 34).
	The Long Rock. A regular, square-sectioned, stone, leaning slightly, which stands in a belt of pine trees just to the east of Mcfarland's Down (Borlase, 1756, 34).
	Pungies. '... Another good farmhouse called Newford ... From this farmhouse almost in a line with Long Rock, and near the midway, in the corner of a field called

APPENDIX 3—STANDING STONES

Pungies, is a square stone pillar ...' (Troutbeck, 1794, 101).

New House. 'To the S.W. from Long Rock is a stone set upright upon rising ground, which is the highest land in all St. Mary's Island, called New House, where are some ruins, about 20ft in diameter, where is supposed to have been a watch house, as this place commands a prospect of the sea all around, this being the highest land in all the islands of Scilly' (Troutbeck, 1794, 101).

APPENDIX 4

Houses and Settlements

EARLY PERIOD

Sites that have produced pottery identical with that from the chamber tombs. Termed 'Bronze Age' by O'Neil and frequently referred to as 'of the usual kind' by Gray.

LITTLE ARTHUR   During 1935, Gray dug into the sandy neck, below high-water mark, which joins Little and Middle Arthur. He found bones, limpet shells, patches of black clay and a fragment of coarse pottery associated with a flat stone.

BRYHER   Just below Bonfire Carn, at the extreme south-eastern point of the island, Gray found a hut floor exposed in the cliff face. Stones bounded it, while flints and pottery were upon it. Some 10cm of sand, mantled by the modern surface, was above it.

NORNOUR   Early pottery was found in association with specific phases of the complex of buildings (Dudley, 1967, 12).

ST AGNES   Immediately below the lifeboat house at Periglis, Gray discovered an exposure of black earth and a great deal of pottery 'of the usual type', together with bones.

In the south corner of Porth Killier, Gray found an ancient surface which inclined downwards and was thus lost beneath the sand. He obtained from this

APPENDIX 4—HOUSES AND SETTLEMENTS

site a considerable amount of finely made pottery associated with shells, charcoal and seal bones.

ST MARTIN'S *English Island Carn*. Excavations conducted by B. H. StJ. O'Neil during 1948 and 1949. The foundations of a stone-built house of rectilinear plan, but with the longer walls converging. Post-holes were in the walls. There were three levels of occupation. Pottery, shells, animal bones, a loomweight, flint implements and a grain-rubber were found (O'Neil, 1949, 164–5).

Lawrence's Brow. Investigated by O'Neil during 1950. An exposure of dark soil in the sea-cliff which produced a quantity of pottery, some cord-ornamented, a quern-rubber and a cup-marked stone. Gray noted, at this site, boulders which may have been part of a hut and found flint implements and pottery.

May's Hill. Excavated by O'Neil in 1950. A mass of pottery, animal bones and limpet shells among which a bronze awl was found, stratified beneath the remnants of a Romano-British hut.

Par Beach Site F. A site below high-water mark excavated by O'Neil during 1951. The foundations of an oval building had a standing-stone backed and bordered hearth at one end. There was an axial drain leading to a tank by the hearth.

Perpitch. A roughly circular stone-built hut, associated with a cultivation terrace system, was excavated by O'Neil during 1951. Three phases of modification and use were detected. It appears to have housed a series of corn-drying ovens. Pottery and a clay cylindrical object were found.

Great Bay I. A length of wall in the sand hills bordering this bay, was examined by O'Neil during

APPENDIX 4—HOUSES AND SETTLEMENTS

1952. Pottery was found on a series of boulders propped against it.
Little Bay I. The remains of a massive oval hut, and part of another close by, were excavated by O'Neil during 1952 and 1953. The oval hut had a massive drain in it, a hearth and some paving. Black soil in this hut contained numerous flint flakes, cores and much pottery.
Pernagie Carn. Pottery and clay found on a low carn close to the sea (Lewis, 1948, 9).

St Mary's
Halangy Porth. Midden and buildings exposed in cliff face. Excavations by Gray in bulb garden to landward. Pottery, shells, bones, traces of corn-drying ovens as well as storage pots. There was a small circular building beneath the bulb garden (Hencken, 1932, 29–30; 1933, 16; Ashbee, 1953, 76; 1965, 36; 1966, 21; Gray, St Mary's no 3).
Pendrathen. 'Bee-hive' huts and the remains of several more visible on the shore at low water. A 'perfect burial urn' was found 'among the huts' (Jackson, 1947; 1948).
Bar Point. Stone rubble and a stone-built drain found exposed on an ancient surface just to the south and west of Bar Point. Pottery was on the ancient surface and by the drain (Gray, St Mary's no 4).

Samson
Bar Point and East Porth. The remains of stone structures, in the East Porth, beneath blown sand. Flints and pottery were found right round from East Porth to Bar Point. Gray, Samson no 1.

Tresco
Carn Near. Walling exposed on an ancient surface beneath the sand dunes just to the north-east of the landing slip. Flints and pottery were found (Gray, Tresco no 1).

317

APPENDIX 4—HOUSES AND SETTLEMENTS

IRON AGE

Sites that have produced pottery comparable with that from Iron Age sites on the Cornish mainland.

LITTLE ARTHUR Walling noticed in the cliff. Excavations by O'Neil in 1951 disclosed on the beach, not far from the bar which joins Little and Middle Arthur, a hut roughly pentagonal in plan. A considerable quantity of pottery was recovered from its interior.

NORNOUR Iron Age pottery has been found in association with the complex of buildings (Dudley, 1967, 12–13).

ST MARTIN'S *Par Beach*. An oval hut excavated by O'Neil during 1950. Three post-holes were found in its interior, a fourth may have been destroyed by a later intrusive stone-built grave. Paving stones were around the inner wall-face.

ST MARY'S *Halangy Down*. Iron Age pottery has been found during the excavation of the complex of buildings (Ashbee, 1966, 26).

ROMANO-BRITISH

NORNOUR Romano-British pottery, jewellery, coins and figurines are a feature of the floruit of this multi-phase site (Dudley, 1971, 1–64).

ST MARTIN'S *Par Beach Site A*. A round hut excavated during 1949, enclosing an area some 20ft in diameter with a wall 6ft in thickness. A post-stone and a stone-bounded hearth were in the middle. A series of converging walls were found, which did not seem to be parts of dwellings. Pottery was found in the hearth (O'Neil, 1949, 163–4).

May's Hill. The mutilated remains of a substantial stone-built hut, divided by a party wall, into two parts of unequal size, through which was a doorway. The main entrance of this hut was monumental in

APPENDIX 4—HOUSES AND SETTLEMENTS

conception. Quantities of pottery were found which included two small pieces of Samian ware. Evidence of earlier occupation was beneath. The excavation was carried out by O'Neil during 1950.

St Mary's   *Halangy Down.* Excavations in 1950 and from 1964 to 1971 have disclosed a courtyard house and two oval huts, one with a rectangular annexe. The remains of other structures are present. The site is upon the series of cultivation terraces which are a feature of this hill-slope (Hencken, 1932, 30; Ashbee, 1955, 187–98; also Ashbee, 1965 to 1970; Ashbee, 1972; Gray, St Mary's no 1).
Hugh Town. In Poynter's Garden a shell midden yielded sherds which include a flanged rim of the third century AD. A wall was associated (Dudley, 1960–1, 223).

Teän   Excavations by A. C. Thomas on a complex site on the western side of East Porth disclosed a midden with the remains of corn-drying ovens. A hut, of oval or sub-rectangular plan, had been built into it.

EARLY CHRISTIAN

St Mary's   *Porth Cressa.* A shell midden, containing animal bones and sherds of grass-marked pottery, points to a settlement close by (Ashbee, 1954, 13–16).

Teän   The site on the western side of East Porth yielded, from the midden and its scatter, sherds of grass-marked pottery and imported Mediterranean wares.

UNDATED SITES

Annet   High tides bared the walls of a house on the shore of this island 'a few years since' (Borlase, 1756, 40).

Teän   *St Helen's Porth.* An oval hut exposed on the beach.

APPENDIX 4—HOUSES AND SETTLEMENTS

No evidence of association was found. Gray, Teän no 1.

West Broad Ledge. A group of two or more huts of circular plan, some 7ft below mean sea-level, have been observed just to the north of this rock.

APPENDIX 5

Forts and Enclosures

BRYHER — *Shipman Head.* A massive wall, some 20ft in thickness, of which much of the footing and footing-facing stones still survive. It runs from Boat Carn to the steep sea-cliff on the western side of the promontory, and effectively cuts off Shipman Head. There are traces of an entrance and a ? guard-chamber (O'Neil, 1949, 9).

ST AGNES — *Kallimay Point.* There are indications of a double rampart cutting off this headland.

ST MARTIN'S — *Burnt Hill.* There are traces of a stone wall across the northern end of this isolated promontory and indications of stone-built huts within (Lewis, 1948, 9; O'Neil, 1949, 9).
Top Rock Hill. There are indications of a substantial ditch and bank running from Little Bay to Porth Seal, cutting off the northern extremity of the island.

ST MARY'S — *Giant's Castle.* Three curved lines of stone-built rampart and rock-cut ditch, run from cliff to cliff to cut off a small, high-level area and a prominent rocky carn. Pottery was allegedly found in a cutting made during the last war (Borlase, 1756, 11; VCH, 1906, 460; Hencken, 1932, 31; O'Neil, 1949, 9; Cotton, 1958–9, 119).
Mount Todden. A stone-built rampart, with no visible ditch, encloses a small, roughly circular, area at the

APPENDIX 5—FORTS AND ENCLOSURES

top of this hill which is adjacent to the sea and faces the Cornish coast. There is an entrance, one side of which is inturned (O'Neil, 1949, 9).

The Hugh. A wide rock-cut ditch is visible in front of the bastioned curtain-wall built during the early seventeenth century across the neck of land by which the Garrison height is joined to the rest of the island. It is possible that this ditch is of earlier (? Iron Age) origin and that it determined the siting of this curtain-wall (O'Neil, 1949, 22).

TRESCO

Old Blockhouse Promontory. Substantial ramparts cut off this promontory. The inner one is roughly semi-circular, no ditch is visible. A gap in its southern side appears to have been the original entrance. Two other ramparts, lower down the slope, can be traced, each with entrance gaps (O'Neil, 1949, 9).

APPENDIX 6

Flint Industries

Areas from which scrapers, arrowheads, points, trimmed flakes, knapping debris etc have been collected by Alexander Gibson and others. The details of sites are approximate, for much of the material, now stored in the Hugh Town Museum, is unprovenanced and thus locations can only be expressed in terms of Scillonian topography and personalities.

ANNET
South-eastern shore, north of Landing Corner
South side of carn on west shore

BRYHER
On the shore just below Samson Hill (Minett-Smith, 1968)

ST AGNES
No specific location on St Agnes given

ST MARTIN'S
Little Bay within St Martin's Bay
No specific location on St Martin's given

ST MARY'S
Content Farm
GN near George Guy, 1933; GN, 1933, no location (GN=garden)
Halangy Porth

APPENDIX 6—FLINT INDUSTRIES

Longstone (=the Long Rock), Roy Thompson, 1925; Alfred Guy, 1927
Newford, Guy
Normandy
Maypole, Jack Pender
Old Town, 1928, D. K. Phillips
Porth Cressa, on beach in line with Farland's Gate
Porth Cressa, Brow, 1933
Tremelethen

SAMSON
East side of cliff, North Hill
Samson midden (an exposure on the west side of the bar linking the northern and southern hills)
Samson Flats

TRESCO
Beacon Down (=Hill), 1925
East of Old Blockhouse
Tresco Downs, near Piper's Hole

APPENDIX 7

Early Bronze Artifacts

GUGH *Obadiah's Barrow*. Part of an awl from the chamber (Hencken, 1933, 23, Fig 9b, 3).

ST MARTIN'S *Carron Rocks*. The corroded part of a dagger is preserved in the Hugh Town Museum. It came from the Alexander Gibson Collection and its provenance is given as 'Carron Rocks'.

Knackyboy Cairn. Excavation of the chamber unearthed 'pieces of bronze—a hook, and perhaps a handle from a brass-bound wooden box or bucket' (O'Neil, 1952, 30, Pl XI a).

May's Hill. Excavation of the earlier occupation debris beneath the native Romano-British hut produced 'a small bar of bronze', perhaps an awl.

ST MARY'S *Peninnis Head*. Two heavy bronze torques, now in Truro Museum, were found, in about 1812, in a barrow (W. C. Borlase, 1872, 162; Hencken, 1932, 307).

No location. A Breton socketed axe from St Mary's in Plymouth Museum (Hencken, 1932, 307).

No location. 'a circular or oval bronze bracelet ... of the 4th/5th centuries B.C. ... found at St. Mary's ... by Mr. J. H. Treneary ... it came from a circular stone house of that period which was demolished 50 years ago' (SM, no 146, 1961, 89).

Bibliography

The following abbreviations have been used:

AA	*Archaeologia Aeliana*
Arch Camb	*Archaeologia Cambrensis*
Ant J	*Antiquaries Journal*
Arch J	*Archaeological Journal*
BBCS	*Bulletin of the Board of Celtic Studies*
CA	*Cornish Archaeology*
JBAA	*Journal of the British Archaeological Association*
JCHAS	*Journal of the Cork Historical & Archaeological Society*
JRIC	*Journal of the Royal Institution of Cornwall*
JRSAI	*Journal of the Royal Society of Antiquaries of Ireland*
PBUSS	*Proceedings of the Bristol University Spelaeological Society*
PDAES	*Proceedings of the Devon Archaeological Exploration Society*
PPS	*Proceedings of the Prehistoric Society*
PRIA	*Proceedings of the Royal Irish Academy*
PSAS	*Proceedings of the Society of Antiquaries of Scotland*
PWCFC	*Proceedings of the West Cornwall Field Club*
SM	*Scillonian Magazine*
TCNS	*Transactions of the Cardiff Naturalists Society*
UJA	*Ulster Journal of Archaeology*

Anon. 'Roman Altar in Scilly', *Ant J*, I (1921), 239
ApSimon, A. M., Donovan, D. T., and Taylor, H. 'The Stratigraphy

and Archaeology of the Late-Glacial and Post-Glacial Deposits at Brean Down, Somerset', *PBUSS*, IX (1960-1), 67-136

ApSimon, A. M., and Greenfield, E. 'The Excavation of Bronze Age and Iron Age Settlements at Trevisker, St Eval, Cornwall', *PPS*, XXXVIII (1972), 302-81

Ashbee, P. 'Two Stone Cists on St Mary's, Isles of Scilly', *PWCFC*, I (1952-3), 28-30

——. 'Fieldwork in the Isles of Scilly, 1950', *PWCFC*, I no 2 (1953-4), 76-7

——. 'An Urn from Par Beach, St Mary's, Isles of Scilly', *PWCFC*, I no 3 (1954-5), 123-4

——. 'Flint Industries from the Isles of Scilly', *PWCFC*, I no 3 (1954-5), 125-6

——. 'The Excavation of a Cist-grave Cemetery and Associated Structures near Hughtown, St Mary's, Isles of Scilly, 1949-50', *Arch J*, CXI (1954), 1-25

——. 'Excavation of a Homestead of the Roman Era at Halangy Down, St Mary's, Isles of Scilly, 1950', *Ant J*, XXXV (1955), 187-98

——. 'Stake and Post Circles in British Round Barrows', *Arch J*, CXIV (1957), 1-9

——. *The Bronze Age Round Barrow in Britain* (London, 1960)

——. 'The Chambered Tombs on St Mary's, Isles of Scilly', *CA*, 2 (1963), 9-18

——. 'Excavations at Halangy Down, St Mary's, Isles of Scilly, 1964: Interim Report', *CA*, 4 (1965), 36-40

——. 'Excavations at Halangy Down, St Mary's, Isles of Scilly, 1965 and 1966', *CA*, 5 (1966), 20-7

——. 'The Dating of the Wilsford Shaft', *Antiquity*, XL (1966), 227-8

——. 'The Fussell's Lodge Long Barrow Excavations, 1957', *Archaeologia*, C (1966), 1-80

——. 'Excavations at Halangy Down, St Mary's, Isles of Scilly, 1967 and 1968', *CA*, 7 (1968), 24-32

——. 'Problems of the Neolithic and Bronze Age in Cornwall', *CA*, 9 (1970), 5-16

BIBLIOGRAPHY

Ashbee, 'Excavations at Halangy Down, St Mary's, Isles of Scilly, 1969–70', *CA*, 9 (1970), 69–76
——. 'Prehistoric Habitation Sites on the Isles of Scilly by Alec Gray', edited with a commentary by Paul Ashbee, *CA*, 11 (1972), 19–49
Atkinson, R. J. C. et al. *Excavations at Dorchester, Oxon* (Oxford, 1951)
——. 'Fishermen and Farmers', *The Prehistoric Peoples of Scotland*, ed Stuart Piggott (London, 1962), 1–38
Barrow, G. *The Geology of the Isles of Scilly* (London, 1906)
Barton, R. M. *An Introduction to the Geology of Cornwall* (Truro, 1964)
Bersu, G. 'Excavations at Little Woodbury, Wiltshire'. Part I: 'The Settlement as Revealed by Excavation', *PPS*, VI (1940), 30–111
Borlase, W. 'Of the Great Alterations Which the Islands of Scilly Have Undergone since the Time of the Ancients', *Philosophical Transactions of the Royal Society*, XLVIII, pt 1 (1753), 55–67
——. *Observations on the Ancient and Present State of the Islands of Scilly* (Oxford, 1756)
——. *The Natural History of Cornwall* (Oxford, 1758)
——. *Antiquities of Cornwall*, 2nd ed (London, 1769)
Borlase, W. C. *Naenia Cornubiae* (London, 1872)
——. 'Typical Specimens of Cornish Barrows', *Archaeologia*, XLIX (1886), 181–98
Brailsford, J. W. 'Bronze Age Stone Monuments on Dartmoor', *Antiquity*, XII (1938), 444–63
Brent, F. 'Flint Flakes in Cornwall', *JRIC*, IX (1886–9), 58–61
Breuil, H. 'Observations on the Pre-Neolithic Industries of Scotland', *PSAS*, LVI (1921–2), 261–81
Brooks, C. E. P. *Climate through the Ages* (London, 1949)
Brothwell, D. R. 'The Human Remains from the Fussell's Lodge Long Barrow', *Archaeologia*, C (1966), 48–63
Bruce-Mitford, R. L. S. 'A Dark Age Settlement at Mawgan Porth, Cornwall', *Recent Archaeological Excavations in Britain*, ed R. L. S. Bruce-Mitford, 167–96 (London, 1956)
Bullen, R. A. *Harlyn Bay and the Discoveries of Its Prehistoric Remains* (Padstow, 1912)

Burgess, C. B. 'Chronology and Terminology in the British Bronze Age', *Ant J*, XLIX (1969), 22–9

Burstow, G. P. and Holleyman, G. A. 'Late Bronze Age Settlement on Itford Hill, Sussex', *PPS*, XXIII (1957), 167–212

Butcher, S. A. 'Excavations at Nornour, Isles of Scilly, 1969–70; Interim Report', *CA*, 9 (1970), 77–81

Butler, J. J. 'Bronze Age Connections across the North Sea', *Palaeohistoria*, IX (1963), 1–286

Calder, C. S. T. 'Report on the Discovery of Numerous Stone Age House Sites in Scotland', *PSAS*, LXXXIX (1955–6), 340–97

Case, H. J. 'Neolithic Explanations', *Antiquity*, XLIII (1969), 176–86

——. 'Settlement Patterns in the North Irish Neolithic', *UJA*, 32 (1969), 3–27

Chadwick, N. K. *The Druids* (Cardiff, 1966)

Childe, V. G. *The Danube in Prehistory* (Oxford, 1929)

——. *Prehistoric Communities of the British Isles* (London, 1940)

——. *Prehistoric Migrations in Europe* (Oslo, 1950)

——. *Piecing Together the Past* (London, 1956)

Christie, P. M. 'Crig-a-Mennis: a Bronze Age barrow at Liskey, Perranzabuloe, Cornwall', *PPS*, XXVI (1960), 76–97

——. 'A Barrow-cemetery of the Second Millennium BC in Wiltshire, England', *PPS*, XXXIII (1967), 336–66

Clark, J. G. D. 'The Date of the Plano-convex Flint Knife in England and Wales', *Ant J*, XII (1932), 158–62

——. 'Derivative forms of the Petit Tranchet in Britain', *Arch J*, XCI (1935), 32–58

——. 'The Separation of Britain from the Continent', *PPS*, II (1936), 239

——. 'Whales as an Economic Factor in Prehistoric Europe', *Antiquity*, XXI (1947), 84–104

——. *Prehistoric Europe: The Economic Basis* (London, 1952)

——. 'Traffic in Stone Axe and Adze Blades', *Economic History Review*, 18 (1965), 18–21

Clarke, D. C. *Beaker Pottery of Great Britain and Ireland* (Cambridge, 1970)
Collins, A. E. P. and Waterman, D. M. *Millin Bay, a Late Neolithic Cairn in Co Down* (Belfast, *HMSO*, 1955)
Colt Hoare, R. *The History of Ancient Wiltshire* (London, 1810)
Cornish, T. 'The Conversazione', *JRIC*, V (1874), lxvii
Cornwall, I. W. *Soils for the Archaeologist* (London, 1958)
Cotton, M. A. 'Cornish Cliff Castles', *PWCFC*, 2 no 3 (1958–9), 113–21
Craw, J. H. 'Excavations at Dunadd and other Sites', *PSAS*, LXIV (1930), 127–46
Crawford, O. G. S. 'Lyonesse', *Antiquity*, I (1927), 5–14
——. 'Stone Cists', *Antiquity*, II (1928), 418–22
——. 'The Work of Giants', *Antiquity*, X (1936), 162–74
——. *Said and Done, the Autobiography of an Archaeologist* (London, 1955)
Curwen, E. C. 'The Hebrides: A Cultural Backwater', *Antiquity*, XII (1938), 261–89
——. *Plough and Pasture* (London, 1946)
Daniel, G. *The Prehistoric Chamber Tombs of England and Wales* (Cambridge, 1950)
——. ed. *Myth or Legend?* (London, 1955)
——. *The Megalith Builders of Western Europe* (London, 1958)
——. *The Prehistoric Chamber Tombs of France* (London, 1960)
——. 'The Date of the Megalithic Tombs of Western Europe', *L'Europe á la fin de l'age de la Pierre*, ed J. Bohm, and S. J. De Laet (Prague, 1961), 575–83
——. *The Idea of Prehistory* (London, 1962)
——. 'Northmen and Southmen', *Antiquity*, XLI (1967), 313–17
Daniel, G. E. and Powell, T. G. E. 'The Distribution and Date of the Passage-Graves of the British Isles', *PPS*, XV (1949), 169–87
Dewey, H. *South-West England*, British Regional Geology (London, 1935)
Dimbleby, G. W. 'Pollen-Analysis as an Aid to the Dating of Prehistoric Monuments', *PPS*, XX (1955), 231–6

Dimbleby. *Plants and Archaeology* (London, 1967)
Dobson, D. P. *The Archaeology of Somerset* (London, 1931)
Dollar, A. J. *Geological Association Excursion* to the Scilly Isles, *Circular* no 597, 4 (1957-8)
Douch, H. L. 'Archaeological Discoveries Recorded in Cornish Newspapers before 1855', *CA*, 1 (1962), 92-8
Dowie, H. G. 'Recent Archaeological Additions to the Museum', *Torquay Natural History Society Transactions & Proceedings*, V (pt III, 1928-9), 243-4
Dudley, D. 'An Excavation at Bodrifty, Mulfra Hill, Near Penzance, Cornwall', *Arch J*, CXIII (1956), 1-32
——. 'The Early Iron Age in Cornwall', *PWCFC*, 2 no 2 (1957-8), 47-54
——. 'Some Cist-Graves in Poynter's Garden, St Mary's, Isles of Scilly', *PWCFC*, 2 no 5 (1960-1), 221-31
——. 'The Excavation of a Barrow at Glendorgal, Newquay, 1957', *CA*, 1 (1962), 9-17
——. 'Excavations on Nor'nour in the Isles of Scilly, 1962-6', *Arch J*, CXXIV (1967), 1-64
Dudley, D. and Butcher, S. *Nornour*, Isles of Scilly Museum Publication, no 7 (1968)
Duff, A. G. (ed). *The Life-work of Lord Avebury* (London, 1934)
Dunbar, J. *The Lost Land, Underwater Exploration in the Isles of Scilly* (London, 1958)
Eogan, G. 'A Neolithic Habitation-site and Megalithic Tomb in Townleyhall Townland, Co Louth', *JRSAI*, XCIII (1963), 37-81
——. 'A New Passage Grave in Co Meath', *Antiquity*, XXXVII (1963), 226-8
——. 'The Knowth (Co Meath) Excavations', *Antiquity*, XLI (1967), 302-4
——. 'Excavations at Knowth, Co Meath, 1962-1965', *PRIA*, LXVI (1968), 299-400
Evans, J. *The Coins of the Ancient Britons* (London, 1864)
Evens, E. D., Smith, I. F. and Wallis, F. S. 'The Petrological Identifica-

tion of Stone Implements from South-Western England', Fifth Report of the Sub-Committee of the South-Western Federation of Museums and Art Galleries, *PPS*, XXXVIII (1972), 235–75

Forssander, J. E. *Der Ostskandinavische Norden während der Ältesten Metallzeit Europas* (Lund, 1936)

Fowler, E. 'The Origins and Development of the Penannular Brooch in Europe', *PPS*, XXVI (1960), 149–77

Fox, A. *South West England* (London, 1964)

Fox, L. ed. *English Historical Scholarship in the Sixteenth and Seventeenth Centuries* (London, 1956)

Gibson, A. and Gibson, H. *The Isles of Scilly*, 2nd ed (Penzance, 1932)

Giot, P. R. *Brittany* (London, 1960)

Godwin, H. *The History of the British Flora* (Cambridge, 1956)

Goodchild, R. G. 'T-shaped Corn-drying Ovens in Roman Britain', *Ant J*, XXIII (1943), 148–53

Goodwin, A. J. H. 'Prehistoric Fishing Methods in South Africa', *Antiquity*, XX (1946), 134–41

Grimes, W. F. 'Salakee Down Chambered Cairn, St Mary's, Scilly', *Excavations on Defence Sites, 1939–1945*, 1: *Mainly Neolithic–Bronze Age* (London, 1960)

Grinsell, L. V. *The Ancient Burial Mounds of England* (London, 1953)

Harding, J. R. 'Prehistoric Sites on the North Cornish Coast between Newquay and Perranporth', *Ant J*, XXX (1950), 156–69

Harriss, J. C. 'Explanation in Prehistory', *PPS*, XXXVII (1971), 38–55

Hawkes, C. F. C. 'The Excavations at Quarley Hill, 1938', *Proceedings of the Hampshire Field Club and Archaeological Society*, XIV (1939), 136–94

——. 'The A.B.C. of the British Iron Age', *Problems of the Iron Age in Southern Britain*, ed S. S. Frere (London, Council for British Archaeology, 1959)

Hawkes, J. *The Archaeology of the Channel Islands*, vol 2: *The Bailiwick of Jersey* (Société Jersiaise, nd, published 1939)

——. 'The Excavation of a Megalithic Tomb at Harristown, Co Waterford', *JRSAI*, LXXI (1941), 130–47

Heath, R. *A Natural and Historical Account of the Islands of Scilly* (London, 1750)
Hencken, H. O'Neill. *The Bronze and Early Iron Ages in Cornwall and Devon*, Cambridge University PhD Dissertations, University Library, no 343 (1929)
——. *The Archaeology of Cornwall and Scilly* (London, 1932)
——. 'Notes on the Megalithic Monuments in the Isles of Scilly', *Ant J*, XIII (1933), 13–29
——. 'An Excavation for H. M. Office of Works at Chysauster, Cornwall', *Archaeologia*, LXXXIII (1933), 237–84
Hencken, T. C. 'The Excavation of the Iron Age Camp on Bredon Hill, Gloucestershire, 1935–1937', *Arch J*, XCV (1938), 1–111
Henshall, A. S. *The Chambered Tombs of Scotland*, 2 (Edinburgh, 1972)
Higgins, L. S. 'An Investigation into the Problem of the Sand Dune Areas on the South Wales Coast', *Arch Camb*, LXXXVIII (1933), 26–67
Hodson, F. R. 'Cultural Grouping within the British Pre-Roman Iron Age', *PPS*, XXX (1964), 99–110
Inglis-Jones, E. *Augustus Smith of Scilly* (London, 1969)
Jackson, F. W. 'Beehive Huts at Pendrathen', *SM*, XXII (1947), 74
——. 'Beehive Huts at Pendrathen', *SM*, XXIII (1948), 24
Kay, E. *Isles of Flowers* (London, 1956)
Keiller, A. and Piggott, S. 'Excavation of an Untouched Chamber in the Lanhill Long Barrow', *PPS*, IV (1938), 122–50
Kendrick, T. D. *The Axe Age* (London, 1925)
——. *The Archaeology of the Channel Islands*, vol 1: *The Bailiwick of Guernsey* (London, 1928)
——. *The Druids* (London, 1928)
Kingsford-Curram, R. 'Traces of the Roman', *Triton Skin Diving International* (August 1966), 127–9
Lacaille, A. D. 'Flaked Quartz Tools from Cornwall', *Ant J*, XXII (1942), 215–16
Leask, H. G. *Irish Churches and Monastic Buildings*, vol I (Dundalk, 1955)

Leechman, G. F. 'Ancient Causeway from St Mary's to Tresco', *SM*, XX (1946), 44

Leisner, G. and V. *Der Megalithgräber der Iberischen Halbinsel: Der Süden* (Berlin, 1943)

——. *Der Megalithgräber der Iberischen Halbinsel: Der Westen* (Berlin, 1956)

Lewis, H. A. *St Martin's, St Helen's and Teän (Isles of Scilly) in Legend and History* (Truro, 1948)

——. 'Cist at St Martin's, Scilly', *Ant J*, XXIX (1949), 84–5

Lewis, J. M. 'The Excavation of four Standing Stones in South Wales', *BBCS*, XXI (1965), 250–64

L'Helgouach, J. *Les Sépultures Mégalithiques en Armorique* (Rennes, 1965)

Lynch, F. 'Report on the Re-Excavation of two Bronze Age Cairns in Anglesey: Bedd Branwen and Treiorwerth', *Arch Camb*, CXX (1971), 11–83

MacAlister, R. A. S. *Corpus Inscriptionum Insularum Celticarum*, I (Dublin, 1945)

Mackenzie, M. 'Isles of Scilly Museum Association', *CA*, 4 (1965), 30

——. 'Recent Discoveries at St Mary's, Isles of Scilly', *CA*, 6 (1967), 111–12

Mackenzie, P. Z. 'Thumb-nail Scrapers in the Isles of Scilly', *CA*, 6 (1967), 109

——. 'Flint Arrowhead from Bryher, Isles of Scilly', *CA*, 10 (1971), 111

Matheson, C. *Changes in the Fauna of Wales within Historic Times* (Cardiff, 1932)

Matthews, G. F. *The Isles of Scilly* (London, 1960)

Mayhew, S. M. 'Notes on the Scilly Isles together with some Cornish Antiquities,' *JBAA*, XXXIII (1877), 191–4

McInnes, I. J. 'Settlements in Later Neolithic Britain', *Economy Settlement in Neolithic and Early Bronze Age Britain and Europe*, ed D. D. A. Simpson (Leicester, 1971), 113–30

Minett-Smith, H. 'Notes on Flint Industries on Samson, Bryher and Tresco', *SM*, 175 (1968), 186; 176 (1968), 245

Mitchell, G. F. 'The "Larnian Culture": A Review', *JRSAI*, LXXIX (1949), 170–81

——. 'The Pleistocene History of the Irish Sea', *Advancement of Science*, XVII no 68 (November 1960), 313–25

——. 'The Larnian Culture: A Minimal View', *PPS*, XXXVII (1971), 274–83

Mitchell, G. F. and Orme, A. R. 'The Pleistocene Deposits of the Isles of Scilly', *Quarterly Journal of the Geological Society of London*, no 489, vol 123, pt I (15 September 1967), 59–92

Mothersole, J. *The Isles of Scilly* (London, 1919)

Mourant, A. E. 'The Raised Beaches and Other Terraces of the Channel Islands', *Geological Magazine*, 70 (1933), 58–66

——. 'The Pleistocene Deposits of Jersey', *Bulletin Société Jersiaise*, 12 (1935), 489–96

Movius, H. L. *The Irish Stone Age* (Cambridge, 1942)

Newton, R. G. and Renfrew, C. 'British Faience Beads Reconsidered', *Antiquity*, XLIV (1970), 199–206

Oakley, K. P. 'A Note on the Late Post-Glacial Submergence of the Solent Margins', *PPS*, IX (1943), 56–9

O'Neil, B. H. StJ. 'A Romano-British Hut in Scilly', *SM*, XXIV (1949), 163–4

——. 'Excavation of a Bronze Age House in Scilly', *SM*, XXIV (1949), 164–5

——. *Isles of Scilly* (London, HMSO, 1949)

——. *Ancient Monuments of the Isles of Scilly* (London, HMSO, 1950)

——. 'The Excavation of Knackyboy Cairn, St Martin's, Isles of Scilly', *Ant J*, XXXII (1952), 21–34

——. 'An Enamelled Penannular Brooch from the Scilly Isles', *Ant J*, XXXIII (1953). 210–11

——. 'A Triangular Cist in the Isles of Scilly', *Ant J*, XXXIV (1954), 234–7

——. *Ancient Monuments of the Isles of Scilly* (London, HMSO, 1961)

O'Neil, H. E. 'Excavation of a Celtic Hermitage on St Helen's, Isles of Scilly, 1956–58', *Arch J*, CXXI (1964), 40–69

BIBLIOGRAPHY

Ó Ríordáin, S. P. and Daniel, G. E. *New Grange and the Bend of the Boyne* (London, 1964)

Palmer, J. 'Rock Temples of the British Druids', *Antiquity*, XXXVIII (1964), 285-7

de Paor, M. and de Paor, L. *Early Christian Ireland* (London, 1964)

Patchett, F. M. 'Cornish Bronze Age Pottery', *Arch J*, CI (1944), 17-49

——. 'Cornish Bronze Age Pottery (Part II)', *Arch J*, CVII (1952), 44-65

Piggott, C. M. 'Excavation of Fifteen Barrows in the New Forest', *PPS*, IX (1943), 1-27

Piggott, S. 'Handley Hill, Dorset—A Neolithic Bowl and the Date of the Entrenchment', *PPS*, II (1936), 229-30

——. 'Grooved Stone Cists, Scotland and the Scillies', *Antiquity*, XV (1941), 81-3

——. *William Stukeley* (Oxford, 1950)

——. *The Neolithic Cultures of the British Isles* (Cambridge, 1954)

——. *The West Kennet Long Barrow: Excavations 1955-56* (London, HMSO, 1962)

——. *Ancient Europe* (Edinburgh, 1965)

——. *The Druids* (London, 1968)

Piggott, S. and Daniel, G. E. *A Picture Book of Ancient British Art* (Cambridge, 1951)

Piggott, S. and Powell, T. G. E. 'The Excavation of Three Neolithic Chambered Tombs in Galloway, 1949', *PSAS*, LXXXIII (1948-9), 103-61

Pitt Rivers, A. H. *Excavations in Cranborne Chase*, vol IV (printed privately, 1898)

Pobe, M. and Roubier, J. *The Art of Roman Gaul* (London, 1961)

Pool, P. A. S. 'William Borlase, the Scholar and the Man', *JRIC*, new series V (1966), 120-72

Powell, A. *John Aubrey and His Friends* (London, 1948)

Powell, T. G. E. 'A New Passage Grave Group in Southeastern Ireland', *PPS*, VII (1941), 142-3

Powell. 'The Excavation of a Megalithic Tomb at Carriglong, Co Waterford', *JCHAS*, XLVI (1941), 55–62
——. *Megalithic Enquiries in the West of Britain*, ed T. G. E. Powell (Liverpool, 1969)
Proudfoot, V. B. 'Ancient Irish Field-Systems', *Advancement of Science*, 56 (1958), 369–71
Radford, C. A. R. 'Celtic Monastery on St Helen's, Isles of Scilly', *Ant J*, XXI (1941), 344–6
——. 'Report on the Excavations at Castle Dore', *JRIC*, new series I, (1951), appendix volume
——. 'Roman Cornwall', *PWCFC*, 2 (1957–8), 55–8
Reid, C. *Submerged Forests* (Cambridge, 1913)
Rice Holmes, T. *Ancient Britain and the Invasions of Julius Caesar* (Oxford, 1936)
Ritchie, J. *The Influence of Man on Animal Life in Scotland* (Cambridge, 1920)
Roe, F. E. S. 'The Battle-Axe Series in Britain', *PPS*, XXXII (1966), 199–245
Rogers, E. H. 'The Raised Beach ... and the Submerged Stone Row of Yelland', *PDAES*, III (1946), 109–35
Ross, A. *Pagan Celtic Britain, Studies in Iconography and Tradition* (London, 1967)
Rouzic, Z. Le, *Les Cromlechs de Er Lannic* (Vannes, 1930)
Russell, V. and Pool, P. A. S. 'Excavation of a Menhir at Try, Gulval', *CA*, 3 (1964), 15–26
Saunders, A. D. 'Harry's Walls, St Mary's, Scilly: A New Interpretation', *CA*, 1 (1962), 85–91
Savory, H. N. 'The Excavation of a Neolithic Dwelling and a Bronze Age Cairn at Mount Pleasant Farm, Nottage, Glamorgan', *TCNS*, LXXXI (1953), 75–92
——. 'A Welsh Bronze Age Hillfort', *Antiquity*, XLV (1971), 251–61
——. 'Copper Age Cists and Cist-Cairns in Wales', *Prehistoric Man in Wales and the West*, essays in honour of Lily F. Chiffy (Bath, 1972) 117–39

Simpson, D. D. A. 'Beaker Houses and Settlements in Britain', *Economy and Settlement in Neolithic and Early Bronze Age Britain and Europe*, ed D. D. A. Simpson (Leicester, 1971), 131–52

Smith, A. 'Barrow at Samson, Scilly', *JRIC*, XLV (1862–3), 50–3

Smith, D. 'The Shrine of the Nymphs and the Genius Loci at Carrawburgh', *AA*, XL, 4th series (1962), 59–81

Stone, J. F. S. 'Report on Beads from Knackyboy Cairn, St Martin's, Isles of Scilly', in O'Neil, 'The Excavation of Knackyboy Cairn etc', *Ant J*, XXXII (1952), 30–4

Tebbutt, C. F. 'A Cist in the Isles of Scilly', *Ant J*, XIV (1934), 302–3

Thomas, A. C. 'Megalithic Tombs on the Island of Teän, Scilly', *PWCFC*, 2 (no 1, 1956–7), 33–6

——. 'The Palaeolithic and Mesolithic Periods in Cornwall', *PWCFC*, 2 (1957–8), 5–12

——. 'Cornwall in the Dark Ages', *PWCFC*, 2 (1957–8), 59–72

——. 'Post-Roman Rectangular House Plans in the South-West', *PWCFC*, 2 (no 4, 1959–60), 156–62

——. 'A New Cist from Trevedra Common, St Just-in-Penwith', *PWCFC*, 2 (no 5, 1960–1), 189–96

——. 'The Character and Origins of Roman Dumnonia', *Rural Settlement in Roman Britain*, ed Charles Thomas, Council for British Archaeology, Research Report 7 (1966), 74–98

——. *The Christian Antiquities of Camborne* (St Austell, 1967)

——. 'Grass-marked Pottery in Cornwall', *Studies in Ancient Europe, Essays presented to Stuart Piggott*, ed J. M. Coles and D. D. A. Simpson (Leicester, 1968), 311–31

——. *Britain and Ireland in Early Christian Times, A.D. 400–800* (London, 1971)

Thomas, A. C. and Wailes, B. 'Sperris Quoit: The Excavation of a New Penwith Chamber Tomb', *CA*, 6 (1967), 9–23

Tierney, J. J. 'The Celtic Ethnography of Posidonius', *PRIA*, LX (C) (1960), 189–275

Townsend, M. 'The Common Limpet (*Patella vulgata*) as a Source of Protein', *Folia Biologica*, XV no 3 (1967), 343–51

BIBLIOGRAPHY

Toynbee, J. M. C. 'Pagan Motifs and Practices in Christian Art and Ritual in Roman Britain', *Christianity in Britain, 300–700*, ed M. W. Barley and R. P. V. Hanson (Leicester, 1968), 177–92

Troutbeck, J. *A Survey of the Scilly Islands* (Sherborne, 1794)

Turk, F. A. 'Report on the Animal Remains from Nor-Nour', *JRIC*, new series V (pt 3, 1967), 250–66

——. 'Bones from an Early Christian Midden, Teän, Isles of Scilly', in 'Notes on Cornish Mammals in Prehistoric and Historic Times, I', *CA*, 7 (1968), 75–8

De Válera, R. and Ó Nualláin, S. *Survey of the Megalithic Tombs of Ireland*, II, County Mayo (Dublin, 1964)

Victoria County History. *Victoria County History of Cornwall*, vol I (London, 1906)

Wailes, B. 'The Bronze Age in Cornwall', *PWCFC*, 2 (1957–8), 26–35

Wainwright, G. J. 'Three Microlithic Industries from South-west England and Their Affinities', *PPS*, XXVI (1960), 193–201

Ward, E. M. *English Coastal Evolution* (London, 1922)

Wheeler, R. E. M. *Verulamium, A Belgic and Two Roman Cities*, Reports of the Research Committee of the Society of Antiquaries of London, no XI (1936)

Wheeler, Sir Mortimer, and Richardson, K. M. *Hillforts of Northern France*, Reports of the Research Committee of the Society of Antiquaries of London, no XIX (1957)

Whitfield, H. J. *Scilly and Its Legends* (London, 1852)

Whitley, N. 'Flint implements from the Drift Not Authentic', *JRIC*, I (1864–5), 19–49

Wright, L. B. *The History and Present State of Virginia, 1705*, ed L. B. Wright (Williamsburg, Virginia, 1947)

Wright, W. B. *The Quaternary Ice Age* (London, 1936)

Zeuner, F. E. *A History of Domesticated Animals* (London, 1963)

——. *The Pleistocene Period* (London, 1964)

Zimmerman, D. W. and Huxtable, J. 'Recent Applications and Developments in Thermoluminescent Dating', *Archaeometry*, II (1969), 105–8

Index of Personal Names

These names do not include pages 327–40 (Bibliography) or names given in parentheses, as sources, in text. Page numbers in italic indicate illustrations.

Ashbee, P., 295
Athelstan, 227
Atkinson, R. J. C., 113
Aubrey, John, 23, 24
Augustine, St, 228
Aurelius, Marcus, 276

Barrow, G., 42, 45, 47
Bersu, G., 271, 272
Birkenshaw, Mrs, 239
Bonsor, George, 27, 61, 73, 84, 92, 93, 98, 101, 105, 107–12, 159, 161, 219, 240, 251, 252, 264, 297, 302
Borlase, William, 13, 17–25, *18, 20,* 37, *38,* 47, *49,* 51, 52, 56, 59, 73, 94, 96–9, 100, 105, 106, 113, 118, 123, 131, 149, 151–3, 156, 211, 214, 220, 229, *241,* 257, 268, 277, 294, 305, 306, 307
Borlase, William Copeland, 26, 127, 241
Brooks, C. E. P., 61
Buckland, William, 25
Butcher, S., 15, 198, 201
Butler, J. J., 243

Caesar, Julius, 217
Camden, William, 277
Case, H. J., 273
Childe, V. G., 73
Colt Hoare, R., 23
Constantine, 222, 276
Cotton, H. C., 32
Crawford, O. G. S., 28, 29, 42, 43, 47, 52–4, 56, 58, 59, 62, 64, 66, 69, 78, 100, 131, 146, 214, 231, 235

Curwen, E. C., 272

Daniel, Glyn, 31, 42, 47, 62, 73, 87, 295, 296, 307, 310
Darwin, Charles, 26
De la Beche, H. T., 47
Dollar, A. J., 31
Dorrien Smith, Major A., 29, 32, 34, 219, 236, 251
Douch, H. L., 15
Dudley, Dorothy, 15, 35, 36, 135, 144, 145, 204
Dugdale, William, 23
Dumnonii, 291
Dunbar, J., 59
Dunning, G. C., 15, 134

Evans, J., 23

Gibson, Alexander, 14, 28, 29, 30, 52, 53, 59, 101, 130, 131, 153, 185, 187, 229, 230, 231, 235, 236, 238, 242, 249, 251, 255, 258, 300, 325
Gibson, Frank, 15
Gibson, James, 28, 30, 242, 249, 255
Gluyas, W. M., 107, 117
Goddard, Alan, 59, 180
Godolphin, Thomas, 220
Godwin, H., 43
Goodchild, R. G., 272
Goodwin, A. J. H., 55
Gratian, 276
Gray, Alec, 14, 15, 30, 31, 35, 57, 59, 60, 61, 62, 102, 159, 162, 163, 164, 170, 173, 174, 177, 178, 184, 185, 186, 187, 207, 212, 224, 234, 245,

341

INDEX OF PERSONAL NAMES

Gray, Alec—*cont.*
   248, 249, 251, 255, 256, 267, 268, 269, 270, 271, 306, 315
Grimes, W. F., 32, 97, 108, 248, 251, 252, 254, 287
Guy, Alfred, 324
Guy, George, 323

Hawkes, C. F. C., 258
Hawkes, J., 73
Heath, Robert, 39, 40, 191, 193, 238
Hencken, H. O'Neill, 15, 27, 29, 30, 42, 47, 62, 73, 78, 88, 91, 93, 99, 106–8, 149, 159, 184, 186, 211, 234, 236, 252, 255, 276, 278, 284, 287, 295, 297, 307, 308, 310
Henry, Duke of Grafton, 229
Hicks, Obadiah, 28
Higgins, L. S., 46
Honorius, 222, 276
Hopkins, John, 16
Hull, M. R., 143, 222, 243

Illtyd, St, 224
Instantius, 222

Jenkins, Frank, 261
Julian, 222, 276

Kendrick, T. D. (Sir Thomas), 27
Killigrew, John, 220

Leisner, G. and V., 285
Lewis, Rev H. A., 32, 33, 58, 113, 133, 146, 164, 168, 172, 177, 179, 180, 181
Lide (or Elidius), St, 225
Lubbock, John, 25
Lyttleton, Charles, *18*, 19, 118

Maclaren, Major R., 36
Magnus Maximus, 221
Mayhew, Rev S. M., 26
Mitchell, G. F., 41
Movius, H., 42, 43

Newton, Isaac, 25

O'Neil, B. H. StJ., 13, 14, 33, 34, 48, *49*, 57, 58, 62, 73, 89, 100, 101, 113–16, 128, 155, 164–6, 168, 172, 179, 180, 182–4, 186, 204, 205, 212, 241, 247, 249, 256, 258, 272, 287, 296, 300, 311, 316, 317, 318
O'Neil, Mrs Helen, 14, 15, 167, 168, 169, 171, 180, 181
Opie, S. A., 153

Patrick, St, 148
Pender, Jack, 324
Phillips, D. K., 324
Piggott, Stuart, 31, 32, 55, 87, 127, 216
Plenderleith, H. J., 241
Plot, Robert, 23
Powell, T. G. E., 31

Radford, C. A. Ralegh, 32, 96, 135, 147
Reid, Clement, 42, 43
Robertson, A. S., 276

Samson, St, 224
Saunders, Andrew, 15
Savory, H. N., 293
Severus, Septimus, 276
Severus, Sulpicius, 62, 69, 221
Skrimshire, E. H. N., 263
Smith, Augustus, 25, 26, 30, 32, 125, 127, 131, 214, 219, 264, 308
Smith, R. A., 27, 129, 258, 311
Smith, T., 123, 257, 312
Stone, J. F. S., 246
Stukeley, William, 24, 25, 217
Symons, R., 233, 237

Tacitus, 217
Tebbutt, C. F., 15, 30, 133, 134
Thomas, Charles (A. C.), 14, 15, 34, 41, 56, 59, 64, 65, 147, 202, 214, 227, 262, 319
Thompson, Roy, 324
Tibericus (or Tiberianus), 222
Treneary, J. H., 14, *86*, 102, 129, 130, 187, 233, 234, 239, 256, 262, 325
Troutbeck, John, 21, 57, 58, 59, 101, 133, 146, 213, 230, 268
Tryggvason, Olaf, 228

INDEX OF PERSONAL NAMES

Ussher, James, 24

Vespasian, 276

Wailes, B., 59, 147

Ward, E. M., 42
Warna, St, 229
Wheeler, Sir Mortimer, 218
Whitfield, Rev H. J., 57
Woolf, Charles, 15

Index of Place Names

Page numbers in italic indicate illustrations.

Anglesey, 217
Annet, 56, 63, 156, 222, 240, 319, 323
Antrim, 41
Apple Tree Bay, 61, 174
Argyll, 127
Arthur, 31, 33, 34, 77, 82, 90, 94, 105, 204, 214, 295–6
Arthur, Great, 57, 78, 295
Arthur, Little, 57, 76–7, 177, 179, 180, *181*, 258, 259, 296, 315, 318
Arthur, Middle, *95*, 125, 177, 295–6, 315, 318
Atlantic Hotel, Hugh Town, 218–19
Avebury, 24

Bangor, 228
Bant's Carn (place), 149, 151, 249
Bargrennan, Galloway, 275, 284
Bar Point, 40, 173, 256, 317
Beacon Down, 324
Beacon Hill, 310
Beaghmore, Co Tyrone, 66
Behy, Co Mayo, 66
Black Ledge, 52
Boat Carn, 321
Bodmin, 37
Bodmin Moor, 186
Bodrifty, 259
Bollard Point, 307
Bonfire Carn, 60, 174, 296, 315
Brean Down, 44
Bristol Channel, 46, 47
Brittany, 123, 224, 257, 273, 285, 287, 290
Bryher, 28, 31, 42–3, 53, 57, 60, 66, 76, 78, 96, 101, 155, 177, 204, 212, 213, 222, 231, 233, 236, 295, 296–7, 313, 315, 321, 323

Bryher Flats, 57
Burnt Hill, 212, 321
Buzza Hill, *20*, 21, 76, 94, 100, 106, 113, 125, 239, 306–7

Caldey Island, 47
Carn Menellis, 37
Carn Morval Down, 306
Carn Near, 61, 173, 174, 317
Carn of Works, 296
Carn Valla, 28, 298
Carriglong, Co Waterford, 284, 286
Carron Rocks, 242, 325
Cassiterides, 27, 277, 278
Castle Dore, 259
Castle Down, 41, 76, 184, 310
Chad Girt, 42
Channel Islands, 123, 209, 285, 289, 290
Chapel Brow, 229
Chapel Down, 40, 41, 48, 76, 300
Church Point, 303
Chysauster, 179, 183, 238, 261
Constantine, 101, 149
Content Farm, 86, 129–30, *130*, 234, 258, 311, 323
Cornwall, 19, 23–6, 30, 32, 41, 44–8, 51, 73, 101, 105, 118, 127, 148, 179, 208, 209, 214, 223, 224, 225, 235, 238, 239, 244, 259, 274, 277, 286–7, 290, 291
Creeb Rocks, 305, 306
Crow Bar, 58, 61
Crow Point, 40, 45
Cruther's (Crethus) Hill, 57, 58, 76, 77, 84, 90, 146, 299, 312

Dartmoor, 78, 186

INDEX OF PLACE NAMES

Devonshire, 44, 105, 209, 227
Diamond Ledges, 59
Dol, Brittany, 224
Dorchester, Oxfordshire, 286
Dorset, 288
Downderry, 31
Dozmare Pool, 281
Drum Rock, 302

Eastern Islands, 35, 43, 66, 214
East Par, 59, 61
East Porth, 174, 317, 319
English Island Carn, 33, 57, 77, 155, 156, 164–6, *165*, 170, 172, 179, 204–6, 234, 256, 287, 312, 316
English Island Point, 76, 146
Er Lannic, 44

Falmouth, 44
Finistère, 209
France, 285, 292

Garrison, Hugh Town, 41, 135, 144, 218, 219, 322
Garrison Hill, 64
Garton Slack, Yorkshire, 241
Gaul, 143, 222, 225, 275
Giant's Castle, 152, 153, 211, 222, 258, 321
Gimble Point, 310
Gimble Porth (Bay), 179, 184, 208
Glamorgan, 287
Glendorgal, 287
Goldberg, 287
Great Bay, 316–17
Great Hill (Teän), 309, 310
Gugh, 17, 19, 27–8, 42–3, 63, 66, 74, 77–8, 89, 92–4, *93*, 101, 106, 108, *109*, 113, 115, 117, 149, 151, *157*, 177, 213, 236, 240, *240*, 248, 251, *251*, 274, 297–8, 313, 325
Gun Hill, 300, 310
Gweal Hill, 76, 297
Gwithian, 238, 289

Halangy Down, 27, 31, 35, 45, 64–5, 89, 100, *121*, 140, 145, 153, 155, 159, 176, 178–9, *178*, 183–90, *188*, *190*, 194–7, 203, 205–8, 213, 234, 236–9, 243, 245–7, 258, 260–2, 265–7, 270, 272, 275, 291, 293, 305–306, 312–13, 318, 319
Halangy Point, 30, 173
Halangy Porth, 27, 31, 35, 60, 63, 65, 67, 76, 102, 129, *140*, 159, *159*, 161, 162, *163*, 170, 172–4, *175*, 186, 187, 189, 196, 203, 205–8, 234, 237, 239, 248, 251, 254–6, 258, 264, 265, 267–9, 270, 271, 282, 287, 288, 293, 311, 312, 317, 323
Hampshire, 287
Harlyn Bay, 29, 120
Harristown, Co Waterford, 74, 82, 284, 286
Harry's Walls (Battery), 19, 105, 149, 151, 220, 313
Hayle River, 46
Hebrides, 193
Helvear Down, 125, 305
High Cross, 230
High Cross Lane, 26, 229
High Lane, 233
Higher Moors, 51
Higher Town Bay, 67, *132*, *168*, *180*, *182*
Higher Trenoweth, 305
Holy Vale, 42, 51, 131
Hugh Town, 30, 36, 39, 41, 76, 125, 135, *139*, 144, 162, 191, 218, 219, 230, 233, 239, 249, 251, 255, 294, 319; *see also* Porth Cressa

Inishmurray, Ireland, 225
Inner Blue Carn, 66, 78, 303
Innisidgen, 28, 76, 77, 79, 85, 88, 89, 98, 102, 304, 306, 307
Ireland, 48, 51, 66, 74, 112, 148, 209, 223
Isle of Man, 209
Itford Hill, Sussex, 272

Kallimay Point, 321
King Edward's Tower, 307
Kittern Hill, 28, 66, 74, 78, 90, 92, 151, 297–8, 313
Klondyke Field, *86*, 129, 311

Landing Corner, 323

345

INDEX OF PLACE NAMES

Land's End, 37, 223
Lawrence's, 58
Lawrence's Brow, 33, 147, 166, 316
Little Bay, *171*, 172, 212, 317, 323
Loire Inférieure, 209
Ludgvan, 23, 25
Lyonesse, 31, 47

Madron, 101
Maypole, 324
May's Hill, 33, 147, 166, *167*, 184, 204, 208, 288, 316, 318, 325
McFarland's Down, *104*, 151, 313
Mediterranean, 225, 246, 277, 291
Mên-Perhen, 149
Middle Town, 58, 133
Millin Bay, Ireland, 66
Mincarlo, 39
Minehead, Somerset, 55
Morbihan, France, 209
Mount Batten, Devon, 120, 123
Mount Flagon, 149, 151
Mount Holles, 220
Mount Todden, 84, 96, 213, 305, 321
Mount's Bay, 44

Newfort, 123, 257, 312
New Grimsby, 41, 310
New House, St Mary's, 314
Newquay, 46
Normandy Down, 29, 74, 88, 90, 95, 100, 125, 301
Normandy Farm, 233, 236, 237, 274, 324
Nornour, 35, 60, *122*, 143, *158*, 197, *198*, 199, 200, *201*, 202, 204, 205, 207, 221, 234, 237–9, 243, 244, 246, 247, 257, 258, 261, 262, 265, 267, 268–70, 272, 275, 276, 282, 315, 318
Northern Ireland, 280, 291
Northumberland, 221
Northwethel, 76, 77, 90, 298–9

Old Blockhouse Promontory, 322, 324
Old Guard Room, Hugh Town, 41
Old Man, 30, 43, 45, 59, 61, 63, 66, 76, 77, *133*, 134, 135, 141, 246, 295, 309–10, 312

Old Rock, 302
Old Town, 78, 107, 117, 129, 211, 229, 230, 258, 294, 311, 324
Old Town Bay, 41, 42, 229
Old Town Lane, 51

Padstow, 120
Paignton, Devon, 95
Par Beach (St Martin's), 33, 57, 100, 128, 130, *132*, 146, 155, 168, *168*, 179, *180*, 181, *182*, 204, 205, 206, 208, 277, 311, 316, 318
Par Beach (St Mary's), 254, 258
Parson's Field, 144, 145
Paul, 149
Pednathise Head, 43
Pelistry, 305
Pembrokeshire, 47
Pendrathen, 155, 173, 204, 205, 206, 208, 256, 317
Peninnis Head, 27, 37, 42, 102, 152, 238, *241*, 243, 274, 325
Penwith, 101, 118, 147, 149, 206, 208
Penzance, 23, 164, 236
Periglis, 60, 177, 315
Pernagie Carn, 177, 317
Perpitch, 168, *169*, 205, 206, 207, 213, 272, 316
Perranporth, 46
Pig Rock, 303
Piper's Hole, 41, 324
Plymouth, Devon, 120, 243
Portalloch, Argyll, 127
Porth Cressa, 30, 34, 35, 60, 65, 100, *103*, 123, 135, *136*, *137*, *138*, 141, 142, 144–6, 147, 220, 234, 236, 239, 242–4, *242*, 246, 247, 260, *260*, 262, 265, 267, 269, 275, 276, 292, 312, 319, 324
Porth Hellick, 37, 51, 74, 229, 302, 303
Porth Hellick Down, 27, 29, 34, 37, 48, *50*, 51, 68, 73, 74, 76, 77, 79, *80*, *83*, 84, 88, 90, 92, 94, 95, 102, 107, 252, 284, 285, 301–3
Porth Killier (Perkillier), 60, 177, 178, 208, 249, 256, 267, 315
Porthloo, 39, 238
Porth Mellon, 42, 78, 88, *104*, 149, 191
Porth Seal, 212

346

INDEX OF PLACE NAMES

Poynter's Garden, 35, 65, 100, 135, 144–6, 220, 243, 265, 312
Pungies, 151, 313

Quelvezin, Brittany, 257

Redruth, 153
Rocky Hill, 101, 220
Round Island, 43, 77

St Agnes, 17, 28, 31, 43, 60, 63, 153, 177, 208, 222, 229, 249, 256, 267, 268, 297, 313, 315–16, 321, 323
St Austell, 37, 44
St Eval, 288
St Helen's, 32, 34, 60, *140*, 225–8, *226*, 234, 239, 240, 246, 262, 277, 292
St Helen's Porth, 319
St Ives, 23
St Just, 37, 147
St Keverne, 120
St Martin's, 31–4, 40, 41, 43, 45, 46, 48, 57, 58, 60, 63, *67*, 76, 77, 79, 84, 90, 106, 108, 113, *114*, 117, 128, 130–3, *132*, 146, 153, 155, *157*, 159, 162, 164–9, *165*, *167*, 168, *168*, *169*, *171*, 172, 174, *176*, 179, 180, *180*, *182*, 184, 204–6, 212–14, 223, 229, 231, 234, 236, 241, 242, 244–7, *245*, *248*, 249, *250*, 258, 261–3, 272, 275, 291, 292, 299–301, 311–13, 316–17, 318, 321, 323, 325
St Martin's Bay, 172, 323
St Martin's Head, 301
St Mary's, 21, 26, 27, 31, 34, 35, 37, 39–43, 46, *50*, 51, 58, 60, 63–6, *67*, *68*, 74, 76, 78, 79–88, *81*, *82*, *83*, *85*, *86*, 92, 94, 97, *98*, 99, 101–4, *103*, *104*, 106–8, 112, 117, 118, *121*, **123**, *130*, 131, 135, *136*, *139*, *140*, 149, 152, 153, *163*, 172, *175*, *176*, *178*, **188**, *190*, 191, 213, 214, 218–20, 222, 231, 233, 234, 236, 238, *241*, *242*, 243, 248, 251–2, *253*, 256–8, 260, *260*, 277, 295, 297, 301–7, 311–12, 313–14, 317, 318, 321–2, 323, 325
St Piran, 46
Salakee Down, 26, 32, 76, 87, 88, 94, 97, 107, 108, 152, 229, 248, 251, 254, 287, 303
Samson, 19, 26, 28, 30, 31, 32, 40, 42, 43, 45, 53, 56, 59, 61, 64, 66, 74, 77, 78, 79, 82, *85*, *86*, 90, *91*, 99, 100, *104*, 106, 125–7, *126*, 131, 174, 177, 204, 213, 214, 222, 224, 233, 234, 237, 255, 276, 307–9, 317, 324
Samson Flats, *50*, 52, 53, 55, 56, 65, 156, 214, 231, 235, 324
Samson, North Hill, 66, 74, 77, 78, *85*, *86*, 90, *91*, 107, 125, *126*, 307–8, 324
Samson, South Hill, 65, 74, 77, 84, 309
Samson Hill (Bryher), 76, 101, 233, 323
Sark, 289
Scotland, 74, 209
Shetland Islands, 289
Shipman Head, 212, 321
Shipman Head Down, 76, 77, 96, 295, 297
Skellig Michael, Ireland, 225
Somerset, 209
Somerset Levels, 44
South Hill (Gugh), 298
South Wales, 46
Sussex, 272

Tavistock, Devon, 227
Teän, 31, 34, 43, 56, 59, 61, 63–6, 76, 77, 84, 90, 134, 135, 141, 159, 183, 202, 214, 227, 233, 240, 246, 247, 262, 265, 269, 270, 271, 277, 295, 309–10, 319
Telegraph Hill, St Mary's, 43, *86*, 129, 130, 233, 239, 311
Tinkler's Hill, 301
Tiverton, Devon, 23
Toll's Porth, 145
Tol's Hill, 118
Top Rock, 296
Top Rock Hill, 76, 212, 299, 321
Town Lane, 29, 131, 233, 312
Townlyhall, Co Louth, 284
Tramore, Co Waterford, 283, 284
Tregarthen Hill, 76, 310
Trelan Bahow, 120, 123

347

INDEX OF PLACE NAMES

Tremelethen, 324
Tresco (Trescaw), 19, 28, 34, 41, 42, 46, 52, 53, 57, 58, 59, 61, 64, 66, 76, 173, 177, 179, 184, 208, 212, 224, 227, 228, 231, 251, 255, 277, 310, 317, 322, 324
Tresco Abbey, 59, *139*
Tresco Flats, 59
Tresvennack, 149
Trevedra Common, 147
Truro, 27, 102

Vane Hill, 310
Verulamium, 261

Wales, 51, 208, 209, 223, 225
Ward Hill, 303
Wash, The, 44

Waterford, Co, 31
Watermill, 28, 101
Wessex, 82, 214, 288, 292
West Broad Ledge, 59, 320
West Kennet, 117
West Porth, 59, 65
Western Rocks, 43
White Island, 37, 41, 43, 59, 76, 94, 301
Wiltshire, 271, 286

Yelland, Devon, 44
Yellow Rock Carn, 32, 60, 131, 174, 258, 275, 300, 312
Yorkshire, 241

Zennor, 26

Subject Index

Page numbers in italic indicate illustrations

altar, *140*, 227
altar, Roman, *139*, 218–19
Anchorites, 228
Ancient history, study of, 24
Antiquity, study of, 24
arrowheads, flint: barbed and tanged, 129, 233, 234, 288, 289; petit-tranchet derivative, 199, 233
Arthur: H3:D3, 94, *95*; Arthur 1, 82
awls: bronze, 112, 240–1, *240*, 274, 279, 288, 325; flint, 233
axes: bronze, 243, 279, 325; flint, 231, 234, 235, 288; stone, 236, 274, 283, 288

Bant's Carn, chamber tomb (H2:D3), 19, 27, 34, *68*, 73, 76, 77, 79, *81*, *82*, 92–3, 99, 105, 108, 112, 123, 252–3, *253*, 255, 304, 305, 307
barrows, 17, 21, 26, 30, 70–119, 125, 128, 286, 295–310
battle-axe, 236–7, 274, 283, 289
beads, 36; amber, 131, 275; faience, 115, *176*, 246, 274–5; glass, 115, 142, *176*, 202, 246–7, 275
Beaker people, 280
blown sand, 19, 40, 45–7, 61, 166, 204
bone points, 112, 177, 240, *240*, 288
bones: animal, 156, 166, 177, 262; fish, 144, 267; horse, 144, 161, 269; ox, 144, 269; pig, 144, 269; red-deer, 161, 268; seal, 161, 178, 208, 267; sheep, 144, 161, 267, 269
Bronze Age, 197, 199, 204, 205, 282, 286, 293
bronze: armlets (torques), 26, 102, 241–3, *241*, 274, 279, 325; bracelets, 36, 243, 325; objects, 202, 240, 243, 275, 325; pieces, 115, *133*, 134, 241; pin, 145, 243; *see also* brooches
brooches, bronze, 35, 36, 60, 123, *133*, 134, 142, *142*, 143, 197, 200, 202, 221, 222, 242–5, *242*, *245*, 275
building methods, chamber tombs, 96–101, *98*
burials, 32, 35, 57, 58, 100, 107, *109*, 111, *114*, 120, 135, 141, 146, 280, 290

cassiterite, 183, 277
Castor ware, 196, 247, 275, 291
causeways, 58, 60
caves, 41
'caves', 17
cemeteries, 58, 69, *72*, *103*, 145, 220, 222, 262, 276, 290
cereal cultivation, 270, 281
chambers, in chamber tombs, 87, 96
chamber tombs, 27, 28, 29, 31, 33, 42, 62, 66, 70–119, 147, 151, 186, 222, 248, 279, 283, 284–5, 289, 295–310
chambered tumuli, 26
chapel, 203, 229
chemical weathering, 106
chronology, 24
climate, 48
circles, stone, 151–3
circular enclosure, St Mary's, 96, 213, 321
cist, tongued and grooved, *86*, 125–8, *126*
cists, 28, 29, 30, 32, 35, 56, 57, 58, 60, 63, 66, 67, *86*, 100, *103*, 120–47, 234, 257, 311–12
cists (Porth Cressa type), 60, 220, 222, 262, 276, 292

349

SUBJECT INDEX

cist-graves, 45, 58, 65, *103*, 120–47, 197, 220, 262, 290, 292, 311–12
cliff-exposure, 35, 60, 61, 63, 66, 131, 158, 159, 173, 174, 197, 205, 248, 255
coffin, stone, 230
coins, Roman, 35, 36, 60, 200, 221, 222, 276
column bases, *139*, 219
comb-stamp ornament (on pottery), 157, 252–4, *253*, 288, 289
cover-stones: on chamber tombs, 97–9, *98*, 249; on cists, 138–9, *138*, 183
cremations, 108, 112, 115, 116, 123, 128, 129, 130, 147, 148, 279
crosses, stone, 26, 229–30, 280
Cruther's Hill, chamber tomb (H1:D2), 84, 90
cult centre, 207; sites, 216–30
cultivation terraces, 234, 270
cup-marks, 154–5, 166, 219

dagger, bronze, 242, 325
Day Mark, *104*, 149
deposits, in chamber tombs, 101–18, *109*, *114*
Deverel-Rimbury, 286–8
diameters, chamber tombs, 70, *71*, *72*, 94
discs, stone, 199
distribution, chamber tombs, 74–7, *75*
drains, stone, 35, 162, 168, 173, 185, 191, 192, 193, 207
dressing, stone, 151, 154
Druids, 217–18

enclosures, 213–14, 321–2
entrance graves, chamber tombs, 27, 73, 279

fertilisation, crops, 271
fields, 69, 184, 187, 196, 208, 213–14, 282
figurines, 36, *158*, 200, 221, 261
fish-traps, 55
flint, 40, 41, 162; blades, 129, 235; flakes, 162, 165, 172, 174, 181, 231; implements, 162, 174, 179, 186, 202, 231–5; industries, 56, 60, 61, 63, *232*, 233, 323–4
'founder's barrow', 77

Giant's graves, 22, 118
grain impressions, on pottery, *175*, 270, 273
granite, 37–8
graves, Christian, 225, *226*
Gugh, chamber tomb (H2:D2), 92

Halangy Down Lower, chamber tomb, 89, 102
hammer-stone, 199
head, geological, 39
hearths, 165, *165*, 168, *168*, *169*, 170, 192, 194, 197, 199, 200, 202, 207, 221
hedges, stone, 19, 52–3, 57, 58
hermitage, St Helen's, 32
holed stone, 101
hone, 186, 239
houses (huts), stone-built, 31, 33, 56, 58, 59, 60, 64, 67, 154, 156–208, 212, 279, 287, 315–20; courtyard, 187, *188*, 189, 192, 194, 195, 293; earlier, 156–78, 287; later, 178–203; oval, 158, *171*, 179, 183, 184, 185, 187, *190*, 191, 192, 194, 195, 196, 197, 202, 205, 206, 287; rectangular, 159, 161, 164, *171*, 179, 185, *190*, 234, 287; round, 158, 172, 174, 179, *180*, *182*, 185, 186, *198*, *201*, 205, 206, 287

inhumation, 120, 135, 141, 146, 148, 279
Innisidgen, chamber tomb (H4:D2), 28, 76, 77, 79, *81*, *85*, 89, *98*, 100
Innisidgen, Lower, chamber tomb (H17:D1), 88, 102
Irish, immigration, 223, 291, 293
Irish missionaries, 69
iron, 131, *133*, 134, 145, 174, 186, 196, 245–6; pin, 145
Iron Age, 120, 156, 158, 179, 181, 196, 199, 200, 203, 258–9, 260, 279, 282, 290, 292

350

SUBJECT INDEX

Knackyboy Cairn, chamber tomb (D8), 32, 33, 34, 60, 79, 84, 89, 99, 101, 105, 108, 113–17, *114*, 131, *157*, 165, 166, 170, *176*, 199, 204, 234, 241, 242, 246, 248, *248*, *250*, 252, 254, 258, 275, 281, 292, 300, 312, 325

Larnian type flints, 235, 281
limpet shells, 57, *133*, 134, 144, 156, 161, 162, 166, *176*, 177, 262, 264–7, 280, 281
logan stones, 24, 25, 42
Long Rock, *104*, 151
Lyonesse, 47–8

marine transgression, 64, 66, 69
material culture, 231–63
memorial stone, Tresco, 224
menhirs, 148–9
Mesolithic period, 281
middens, 27, 31, *136*, 144, 156, 158, 159, 161, *161*, 166, 173, *176*, 177, 186, 197, 203, 204, 208, 262, 264–5, 269
Middle Ages, 277, 292
mortar, 39, 99–100, 126, 183, 192
mould, for metal dish, 291
Mount Todden, chamber tomb (No 23), 84

Neolithic period, 280–1, 282–3, 285, 286
Normandy Down, chamber tombs: H6:D4, 88; H15:D6, 90; H14:D5, 95

Obadiah's Barrow, chamber tomb (H1:D5), 28, 89, 92–4, *93*, 99, 105, 108–13, 115, 117, 325
oil, trade in, 274, 291
oratories, *140*, 225, 227, 229
orientation, chamber tombs, 70–1, 73, *73*
outer settings, chamber tombs, 74
ovens, corn-drying, 170, 183, 195, 207, 271–2

partitions, Room I Nornour, 200

passage graves, *68*, 73, 74, 79, *80*, 95, 284
pivot stones, 161, 195
pollen grains, 51
Porth Hellick Down, chamber tombs: H1:D7, 92, 95; H3:D9, 88; H5:D8, 94; H12:DE, 84
post-holes, *169*, 179, 181, *181*, 197, 199, 206
post-Roman period, 203, 247, 277, 293
pottery, 'bar-lug' or 'bar-lip', 247, 262, 280, 292; base ornamentation, 250; cord-ornamentation, 166, 289; decoration, 252, *253*, 256–7, 258, 281; 'duck' ornament, 212, 258; early or 'usual type' (Gray), 60, 61, 63, 65, 100, 105, 107, 112, 117, 123, 128, 129, 144, 156, 159, 162, 165, 166, 168, 170, 172, 173, 174, 177, 199, 247; grass-marked, 144, 196, 227, 247, 262, 280; Iron Age, 181, 196, 200, 247, 279, 290; later, 143, 144, 156, 181, 247; lugs, 249–252, 251, 254, 256, 258, 259; rims, 251; Romano-British, 192, 196, 247, 261, 279; shapes, 249; wheel-turned wares, 259, 260, 262, 277
Priscillian heresy, 221–3
promontory forts, 209–15, *210*, 293, 321–2
puffins, 268
pumice, 107

quartz: implements, 196, 235–6; pendant, 199
querns, 191, 196, 219, 237–9, 270; beehive, 186; bowl, *140*, 196, 237, 238, 270, 271; rotary, 196, 238, 239, 270; saddle, *140*, 159, 166, 172, 196, 237, 238, 239, 270, 273

'rabb' (or 'ram'), 39, 141, 162, *163*, 164, 166, 170, 181, 191, 195, 197
raised beaches, 41
rings, finger, 243, 247
rock-basins, 24, 25, *50*
Romano-British period, 66, 69, 135, 143, 156, 159, 179, 181, 184, 192, 196, 203, 204, 218, 261, 279, 282

SUBJECT INDEX

roofing: stone, 192, 194, 227; thatch, 193, 208

Salakee Down, chamber tombs: excavations, 108; H9:D15, 88
Samian ware, 184, 196, 247, 275, 291
Samson, chamber tombs: H1:D5, 91, *91*, 99; H2:D12, 82, 84; H3:D11, 82; H4:D10, 82; H7:D2, *85*
sand-bars, 45
sand-dunes, 45–7, 173, 174, 222, 293
sanding, floors, 191, 193
scrapers, flint, 129, 181, 233, 234, 281
sea-birds, as food, 268
seals, 268, 281
shale mould, Porth Cressa, 239
signal station, native-built on St Mary's, 213
siting, chamber tombs, 77–8
skeletons, 145
slate, discs, 192, 239
spindle whorls, 192, 239
standing stones, 28, *104*, 105, 148–55, *150*, 218, 313–14
stones: circular, rubbing, 177; dished, *104*, 193, 207, 224; perforated, 193

storage pots, *163*
submerged walls, 21, 28, *50*, 52–3, 59, 65
submergence, 44–5, 52–69, *54*, *67*

Teän, chamber tombs: No 2, 90; No 3, 84
territories, of settlements, 282
timber coffins, 120
tin ore, 183, 277–8
trig-stones, 97

urns, 33, 111, 112, 116, 117, 123, 131, 149, *157*, 162, 173, 247, *248*, 249, *250*, 279, 288

votive artifacts, 202, 221; offerings, 221, 244; pots, 221, 261, 288

walls, connecting chamber tombs, 74, 78
windmill, on cairn above Hugh Town, 76
winkles, as food, 280
workshop, for votive offerings, 202, 207, 244